BRITISH FICTION 1750-1770

BRITISH FICTION 1750-1770

A Chronological Check-List of Prose Fiction Printed in Britain and Ireland

JAMES RAVEN

DELAWARE

Newark: University of Delaware Press
London and Toronto: Associated University Presses

Associated University Presses
440 Forsgate Drive
Cranbury, NJ 08512

Associated University Presses
25 Sicilian Avenue
London WC1A 2QH, England

Associated University Presses
2133 Royal Windsor Drive
Unit 1
Mississauga, Ontario
Canada   L5J 1K5

The paper used in this publication meets the requirements
of the American National Standard for Permanence of Paper
for Printed Library Materials Z39.48-1984.

Library of Congress Cataloging-in-Publication Data

Raven, James, 1959–
British fiction, 1750–1770.

Includes index.
1. English fiction—18th century—Bibliography.
2. English fiction—18th century—Chronology.
3. Bibliography—Early printed books—18th century.
4. Bibliography—Early printed books—18th century—
Chronology.   5. Great Britain—Imprints—Chronology.
6. Ireland—Imprints—Chronology.   I. Title.
Z2014.F4R34   1987   [PR851]   016.823'6'08   87-6041
ISBN 0–87413–324–6 (alk. paper)

For Eileen and Leonard Raven

Contents

Illustrations

Tables

Figures

BRITISH FICTION 1750-1770

Introduction

The catalogue which follows aims to ease some of the difficulties in researching the wider history of fiction printed in mid-eighteenth-century Britain. The fundamental problem for the student of this literature is ignorance about the actual dimensions of published output. Even if works survive, the number of reprintings they enjoyed has not always been clear. It is an obvious and frustrating obstacle to attempts to chart the development of the early novel - of authorship, literary influences, readership tastes and bookselling practices. Evaluating the contemporary popularity of the most celebrated of authors has also been problematic given the difficulty in placing assessments of their reprinting (and that of their imitators) in the context of the sale of rival fiction. The location of surviving minor works has always been an arduous task. Unique copies of eighteenth-century novels and imaginative miscellanies are scattered in university and research libraries on both sides of the Atlantic. In addition, as this catalogue reveals, a surprisingly large amount of the fiction published is not preserved in any of the university and research collections of Great Britain and North America. Where copies of such works do not survive, however, contemporary reviews and other descriptive references often do, adding much to an appreciation of the output of certain writers and booksellers and to the history of public taste and public criticism.

Between 1750 and 1770 a number of now famous works were promoted as the fashionable novels of the age, making celebrities of their authors and inspiring dozens of imitators. Amidst great controversy over pirated copies, *Sir Charles Grandison* was published in the winter of 1753-4 and went through a further four editions within the year. In 1751, in a sensationalism of a quite different kind, Smollett's *Peregrine Pickle* was issued and then quickly re-issued. Both books, together with the earlier *Joseph Andrews*, *Tom Jones*, *Clarissa*, *Pamela* and *Roderick Random* enjoyed frequent reprinting during the 1750s and 1760s. In December 1759 Laurence Sterne found a York printer for *Tristram Shandy*. In 1764 Horace Walpole produced the first copies of *The Castle of Otranto* from his own press and in 1766 Newbery finally published Goldsmith's *Vicar of Wakefield*. Critical acclaim and imitation, reprinting and abridgment, and part-issue in library sets and collected works, enhanced the dominance of these writers to the end of the century.[1] Concentration on such literary lions, however, inevitably introduces distortion into the history of the early period of the "rise of the novel." From the perspective of many contemporary readers, the fiction industry extended well beyond the lives and works of the fêted few.

"The manufacturers of novels," wrote a periodical reviewer in the 1760s, "resemble the bakers of gingerbread; for their ingredients are the same and the chief difference lies in the manner of

---

[1]   In the longer term, reputations fluctuated. See in particular, Fred W. Boege, *Smollett's Reputation as a Novelist* (Princeton, 1947).

disposing the decorations."[2] In the production of commercial fiction in the mid-eighteenth century, quality of writing was certainly not always of first consideration; sales success could also be achieved by presenting books as attractive and fashionable consumer products. Many of the new novels published in the twenty years after 1750, were associated more with their bookseller-publishers than with their authors - even where authorship was announced. Many works from these commercial printing-houses offered well-tried formulas of plot and characterization. Hurriedly-written tales abound with distressed heroes and heroines, assorted orphans, cripples, dowagers and step-mothers. There are several examples of writers unwittingly changing the occupation, nationality and even name of a character during the course of the narrative. The consequences of lechery and deceit are depicted in spectacularly implausible denouements. Some novels are little more than disjointed epistolary exchanges in the modish Sentimental manner. A contemporary reviewer regarded one of their number as "a puny, miserable reptile that has here crawl'd into existence, happily formed to elude all attack by its utter insignificance."[3] Similar views were expressed in perhaps two-thirds of all reviews of fiction of the period.

Even more disturbing to eighteenth-century critics were what were considered to be the immoral effects of this deluge of fiction issuing from the bookshops and new circulating libraries. Mass production of a hitherto smaller and more regulated form of publication was ridiculed and condemned by those applying critical standards quite foreign to the modest origins and intentions of the new works. In a memorable outburst - and one inviting censure of the more inflated critical outrage - Sheridan's Sir Anthony Absolute condemned the novel-touting circulating-library as "an evergreen tree of diabolical knowledge."[4]

The targets for such charges, however, whether producers, distributors or consumers, are frustratingly elusive. Knowledge of the operations of many of the firms producing best-selling imaginative literature during this period is very imperfect.[5] Given the patchiness and often highly localized nature of the evidence, advances are slow in researching the means for the circulation of the books and of the relationship between the changing commercial base of the trade and changing audiences, authorship and literary style.[6] What did sell best in the eighteenth century? Could sales of works by second-rank writers be sustained by the author's name alone? Did

2   *Critical Review*, 34 (November 1767): 350.

3   *Critical Review*, 4 (July 1757): 95, notice of *The Fair Citizen*.

4   *The Rivals*, Act I.

5   Some of the consequences of this ignorance are considered in Josephine Grieder, *Translations of French Sentimental Prose Fiction in Late Eighteenth-Century England : The History of a Vogue* (Durham, NC, 1975).

6   Modern discussion dates from A. S. Collins, *Authorship in the Days of Johnson* (New York, 1927) and his *Profession of Letters* (New York, 1929). Of many recent contributions, Pat Rogers, *Grub Street* (London, 1972); Graham Pollard, "The English Market for Printed Books," *Publishing History* 4 (1978): 7-48; John Feather, "British Publishing in the Eighteenth Century," *The Library* , 6th ser., 8, no. 1 (March 1986): 32-46; Isabel Rivers, ed., *Books and their Readers in Eighteenth-century England* (Leicester, 1982); and Robin Myers and Michael Harris, eds., *Sale and Distribution of Books from 1700* (Oxford, 1982), with annual volumes thereafter.

particular firms market particular types of fiction?

When first published many now-forgotten works gave fame to a dozen or more authors and booksellers. Novels by Eliza Haywood matched the contemporary popularity of Fielding and Richardson. Few London seasons were without a new or reprinted work by Edward Kimber, Charlotte Lennox, Frances Brooke or Sarah Fielding. John Hill issued his *Inspector* and a succession of best-selling miscellanies. Robert Goadby's *Life of Carew* was perhaps the most famous of a number of greatly-reprinted Adventures or Memoirs originating in the provinces. Samuel Derrick headed an energetic band of literary hacks and translators of foreign fiction. New translations from the French were heavily advertised, led by the works of Madame Riccoboni, Voltaire and Marmontel. Supporting these ranks was a further army of scribblers from Grub Street hacks to provincial gentlefolk, from Carr and Cleland to Lady Pennington and Madame Le Prince de Beaumont.

As Paternoster Row came to rival and then eclipse Fleet Street and St. Paul's Church Yard as the centre of the British book trade, novel-selling developed as a high-profile, competitive and often lucrative business. In 1700 a handful of works, recognizable as novels, were published by a very small number of London booksellers. By 1759 over fifty works of fiction, some part-issues, some belonging more to the world of chapbooks than to the 6s. two-volume novel, were published or reprinted in the year. In 1769 nearly one hundred self-proclaimed "novels" were issued. The number of fiction publishers in London, Edinburgh and Dublin had tripled. Readership of imaginative literature probably increased by an even greater magnitude, stimulated by the development of circulating libraries and of provincial retailing and distribution.[7] Baldwin, Millar, Cooper, the Dodsleys and other London booksellers made great efforts to exploit the market for the novel. In the 1750s, before the well-known commercial operations of Lane and Hogg, the Noble brothers established themselves as the most notorious fiction sellers in the country. In the 1760s the firm of Becket and De Hondt became a brand name for new fiction. Across the Irish Channel, Dublin boasted a flourishing trade in pirated and cheaply-produced fiction. Alderman Faulkner, Robert Main, the Hoeys, and the many collaborative ventures of the Irish congers strove to undercut original London publishers by the export of quickly-copied and half-priced versions of the season's new works.[8]

---

[7]   Summarized in Roy McKeen Wiles, "The Relish for Reading," in *The Widening Circle. Essays on the Circulation of Literature in Eighteenth-century Europe*, ed. Paul J. Korshin (Philadelphia, 1976), 87-115. Also, his "Middle-class Literacy in Eighteenth-century England : Fresh Evidence," in *Studies in the Eighteenth Century*, ed. R. F. Brissenden (Canberra, 1968), 49-65; Ian Watt, *The Rise of the Novel* (Berkeley, 1957); and John Feather, *The Provincial Book-trade in Eighteenth-century England* (Cambridge, 1985).

[8]   Dublin was not subject to the 1710 Copyright Act or the 1711 Stamp Act. Concise legal details are given in John Feather, "The English Book Trade and the Law, 1695-1799," *Publishing History* 12 (1982): 51-75. Irish bookselling is considered in Robert E. Ward, *Prince of Dublin Printers. The Letters of George Faulkner* (Lexington, Ky, 1972); Catherine Coogan Ward and Robert E. Ward, "Literary Piracy in the Eighteenth-century Book Trade," *Factotum* 17 (November 1983): 25-35; and Richard Cargill Cole, *Irish Booksellers and English Writers 1740-1800* (Atlantic Highlands, NJ, 1986).

The listings provided here aim to clarify some of these developments by offering new information about authorship, bookselling, pricing and re-publication. The catalogue continues the work of McBurney and Beasley, providing a chronological checklist of surviving and lost fiction published in the twenty years after 1750.[9] New edition numbering and cross-referencing enables new authorship attribution and the correction of dating, and should encourage further study of particular ranges of works and bookselling firms.

In addition to the specific details of coverage given below, one point needs to be stressed. The *Eighteenth-century Short Title Catalogue* project continues to extend our knowledge of eighteenth-century publications. Some 200,000 items are currently catalogued (January, 1987). Clearly, the listings which follow should not be taken in isolation from the full *E.S.T.C.* database. Care has been taken to include references from the first microfiche edition of *E.S.T.C.* There are, however, two obvious problems in using *E.S.T.C.* to locate the full range of fiction of this period. The first is that *E.S.T.C.* catalogues only surviving works. The second is that without category notation there is no means to access fiction by type. Even on-line searches, calling up works with "novel" or "letters" or "history" in their titles obviously fail to isolate the many works with no such labels in their title-pages, while incidentally generating an overwhelming quantity of superfluous material.

The following listings therefore offer the easiest approach to locating fiction of the period, but one where, for specific titles, accompanying use might also be made of *E.S.T.C.*[10] Only by re-checking the continuing project in future years can the reader be certain of an up-to-date appraisal of all the locations of works, of variations within an edition, and of the possibility of newly-discovered additional pirated editions, especially from Dublin. The listings here provide currently available locations for rare titles and editions, and selected locations for popularly-held works. Where, in summary, the following catalogue does aim to be as comprehensive as possible is in its listing of London-printed editions, including non-surviving works and advertised Irish and Scottish reprintings, and in the provision of references to contemporary reviews in the *Monthly* and the *Critical*, the two periodicals offering the fullest critical appraisal of the period.

---

9   William Harlin McBurney, comp., *A Check List of English Prose Fiction 1700-1739* (Harvard, 1960) and Jerry C. Beasley, comp., *A Check List of Prose Fiction Printed in England 1740-1749* (Charlottesville, 1972). Also, the much earlier A. Esdaile, comp., *A List of English Tales and Prose Romances Printed Before 1740* (New York, 1912). These are preceded by Charles C. Mish, comp., *English Prose Fiction, 1600-1700. A Chronological Checklist* (Charlottesville, 1967); Sterg O'Dell, comp., *A Chronological List of Prose Fiction in English 1475-1640* (Cambridge MA, 1954); and Paul A. Scanlon, comp., "A Checklist of Prose Romances in English 1474-1603," *The Library*, 5th ser., 23, no.2 (June 1978): 143-152.

10   For *E.S.T.C.* coverage see introduction to the microfiche edition, ed. R. C. Alston (British Library, October 1983).

Catalogue Coverage

The catalogue comprises works still surviving in library collections and works that have perished. It remains impossible to be certain of the total publication of fiction in the 1750s and 1760s. The output was vast; certain material is now lost and survival rates can be estimated only from consideration of periodical review notices, end-page advertisement lists and booksellers' announcements in newspapers. These last must be treated with particular care given the extravagances of eighteenth-century commercial puffing.[11] In addition, any cataloguer of imaginative publications from this period faces the problem of how to categorize the diverse forms of fictional work. No survey, however thorough its use of surviving contemporary sources, can provide a full listing of novels when it is impossible to follow a wholly satisfactory definition of what a novel was. Both McBurney and Beasley included appendices of material of doubtful provenance, and were forced to rely on personal judgment in placing works in the main sections of their checklists. Can early novels really be differentiated from imaginative biographies and romances, prose epics, imaginary voyages and educational tales? How are non-surviving but advertised editions to be enumerated when booksellers frequently mis-numbered them in order to promote sales? Can editions always be distinguished from re-issues? When was a part-issue really a part-issue? Should the listings be restricted to London publications or should they include the often more problematic provincial work? For many of these questions the criteria for inclusion rests ultimately on the purpose of the catalogue. Is it designed to provide a list of works which claim with varying accuracy in the title or introduction to be a "novel"? Is it intended to be a catalogue of all those works which by form and style influenced the production of the novel proper and the acclaimed novels in particular? Or is the list to be a source for all those interested in the production of all forms of fiction as a major aspect of the history of bookselling of the period?

With such questions in mind it is clear that for some the following catalogue will adhere to too narrow a definition of the novel. Nevertheless, the full listings do follow a wider interpretation of fiction than that generally adopted by checklists of early fiction. Reprints of novels first published before 1750 are listed, as are all works advertised as "novels" even if containing few pages and with printing only slightly superior to chapbooks.[12] Equally, the catalogue includes works adopting a form recognizable as that of a novel, irrespective of the title-page description. Also listed are collected tales and those bawdy publications issued as "novels" but clearly not designed for the public of Charlotte Lennox or Fanny Burney. Where possible, subsequent eighteenth-century editions of the works are noted. Where evidence from printers' ledgers is

---

[11] A few circulating library catalogues also exist for these decades - notably Lownds, Hookham and Noble - but the problems in identifying many generally-listed titles are often insuperable.

[12] "Novels" such as the 1751 *Clarinda* were under thirty pages in length. Format information within the entries will indicate such works.

available, the number of copies printed in the edition is also indicated. Such detail is rare, however, and where appearing can often be supplemented by further information from specialist bibliographies listed in secondary references within the entry. Documented variations within editions are noted, but are not given separate entries unless a further issue of an edition clearly occurred some years after orginal publication.

Some attempt has also been made to include representative additional works ranging from fictional biographies to the colourful narratives of imaginary voyages.[13] For the literary historian this additional material is even more elusive than the hundreds of two- or three-volume novels also consigned to obscurity. More elegant and substantial than the penny or sixpenny chapbook and designed for a different audience, most of these tales still fall short of the sophisticated and expensive novel proper. Such works are included in the cataloguing, although in separate "miscellany" listings within each year. Some works of fiction categorized as miscellanies are inevitably borderline cases.[14] Listings in the miscellany sections, it must be emphasised, are designed to be representative only.

There are, however, other limitations to the catalogue for those following the very widest interpretation of imaginative literature available during the period. The catalogue does not include works printed in English but published outside the British Isles and Ireland.[15] A case could also be made against restricting the catalogue to prose fiction. Several verse-tales were produced during the period and their issue obviously affects analyses of the output of individual booksellers. Nevertheless, the total number of such works is extremely small in comparison to both the prose novels and the individually published poems. The catalogue also omits jest books, chapbooks,[16] children's books,[17] and serialized and magazine fiction.[18] Primers and grammars incorporating illustrative fables have been excluded where they were apparently designed only

[13]   Travel tales are considered in Philip B. Gove, *The Imaginary Voyage in Prose Fiction* (New York, 1941) and Percy G. Adams, *Travellers and Travel-liars* (Los Angeles, 1962).

[14]   Amory's *Ladies of Great Britain* of 1755, for example, is included in the miscellanies. Genard's *School of Woman* is included in the main listings for 1753, while the very different *School of Man*, a manual of politesse, is omitted even from the miscellanies. Certain works, seemingly outside even the miscellanies, such as the 1759 *Memoirs of Madame de Stahl* were regarded by contemporary reviewers as novels proper, and are included in the secondary listings. Other notable omissions include Bunyan's *Pilgrim's Progress*.

[15]   English fiction published during this period in Paris, Rotterdam, Utrecht and the Hague would together be well under 1% of the total books listed in this catalogue. Works with a foreign imprint but which were actually printed in Britain and Ireland are included.

[16]   The chapbook exclusions result in some distinguished casualties including the Deloney reprints and cheap versions of *Robinson Crusoe*. This leads to obvious under-representation of Aldermary Church Yard and St Paul's Church Yard as publishing centres during this period. The best guides to the chapbook (although not focusing on this period) are Victor Neuburg, *Popular Literature. A History and Guide* (London, 1977) and Margaret Spufford, *Small Books and Pleasant Histories : Popular Fiction and its Readership in Seventeenth-century England* (London, 1981).

[17]   The leading mid-century publisher of children's books has been catalogued by S. Roscoe in *John Newbery and his Successors* (Hertford, 1973). Of the educational works omitted from the following listings, the most famous are the translations of Rousseau's *Emile*.

[18]   The great majority of serialized works has been catalogued by Robert Mayo in *The English Novel in the Magazines 1740-1815* (London, 1962) and Edward Pitcher, "New Facts," *The Library*, 5th ser., 31, no. 1 (March 1976): 20-30, & 6th ser., 2, no. 3 (September 1980): 326-332.

for the schoolroom and where the primary object was direct rather than informal instruction.[19] Other notable exclusions include all specifically political propaganda including works about the Duke of Newcastle and John Wilkes, and the journalistic publications reporting the Canning case.[20] Also omitted are tales relating lesser trials and crimes, a popular genre and one usually derived from incidents reported by newspapers.[21]

The catalogue cannot, of course, claim to have discovered every edition of prose fiction printed in the period, but the work is based on discriminating use of all former checklisting, new library searches and a much greater range of eighteenth-century sources than ever before.[22] Some updating of this survey will be necessary : in particular, contemporary Irish booksellers' advertisements listed numerous additional editions of London novels, not all of which can have been fictive puffs. In particular, much use has been made of Irish advertisements to locate reprinted works. It is amongst these works that non-survival rates are highest, possibly because some of the Irish editions were very limited issues, designed only to test the initial market for a piracy. The discovery of further advertisements in copies of Hoey or Chamberlaine or Saunders publications, may well extend the number of piracies listed.

The Literature

Table 1 gives a breakdown of the location and annual output of new titles and editions from the total production of novels as recorded in the main listings.[23] Overall, the totals for the printing of fiction in the two decades suggest a period of marked if sometimes halting growth. In 1769 both the number of new titles and the number of reprints was double that of 1750. The total output of all literature increased by a similar rate. Two years (1758 and 1763) do show sudden (and largely inexplicable) falls from the general trend. Too much should not be read into this, however. Fluctuation between individual annual totals in part reflects bunching caused by the division of a publishing season between two calendar years, with booksellers in some seasons

---

[19] Many of those omitted are listed in Robin Alston, ed., *A Bibliography of the English Language from the Invention of Printing to the Year 1800* (Ilkeley, 1974).

[20] Thus tales of Tom Dunderhead (the Duke of Newcastle) and the *Memoirs of the Bedford Coffee House* have been omitted, as well as some of the political satires adapted from the Betty Ireland story. Of the Wilksite literature, only the novels proper are included. The Elizabeth Canning episode is represented by a small fraction of the dozens of works published. One of the main contributors and beneficiaries of this and other causes célèbres, John Hill, would have complained bitterly about the under-representation of his many pamphlets and miscellanies. Walpole's *Chinese Letters* of 1757-8 are also excluded.

[21] Of the most famous highwaymen tales omitted are the much reprinted *Memoirs of the Life and Remarkable Exploits of the Noted Dennis Neale* (1750-) and *The Life of Nicholas Mooney* (c.1751 -). Other examples of reprinted newspaper-based works omitted include the 1751 *Vindication of an Innocent Lady*, the 1757 *Damien the Assassin* and the large number of "Authentick Memoirs" of hanged men.

[22] Although detail would be inappropriate, it should be noted that quite appart from the additional works listed, there are many corrections to previous checklists, and especially to the most recent for this period by Leonard Orr, comp., *A Catalogue Checklist of English Prose Fiction 1750-1800* (Troy, NY, 1979). Cf. J. C. Beasley, *Literary Research Newsletter*, 5, no. 3 (Summer 1980): 140-147.

[23] That is not including the works in the "miscellany" sections. As noted, more Dublin and non-London reprintings may well be discovered.

releasing more new works before Christmas than in the new year. Reprinting by English booksellers outside London increases steadily over the period, with many country booksellers for the first time sponsoring their own reprintings. Even more marked is the increase in Dublin reprinting, with especial activity in the mid-1760s. Significantly, the overall ratio between new publications and reprintings does not change greatly between 1750 and 1770, with the slight fall-off in the rate of reprinting in London compensated by the output from Dublin. What the table does not take into account, however, are variations in the size of the editions. Many London reprintings, particularly by the end of the period, could be up to three times the size of provincial editions. Overall, the new levels of production anticipate the dramatic increase in the

Table 1: **Printing of novels 1750-1769 by place of publication**

Year	London New[*]	London Reprint	Dublin New	Dublin Reprint	Other New	Other Reprint	Total New	Total All edns
1750	22	10		6	2		24	40
1751	24	10		8			24	42
1752	18	7		7	1		19	33
1753	19	6	1	7			20	33
1754	30	10	1	9	1		32	51
1755	21	17	1	7		2	22	48
1756	25	6		5			25	36
1757	27	2		2		1	27	32
1758	17	5		1			17	23
1759	27	23		7	1	2	28	60
1760	33	23	2	10	1	2	36	71
1761	22	19		12		2	22	55
1762	19	11	2	11		3	21	46
1763	15	12	2	14	1		18	44
1764	26	19	3	19		1	29	68
1765	19	19		21		8	19	67
1766	28	27		15	1	3	29	74
1767	34	24	1	27	1	6	36	93
1768	37	19		13	1	3	38	73
1769	44	23		18	1	2	45	88
Total	507	292	13	219	11	35	531	1077

* All "new" titles include 1st English edns of translated works

publication of fiction in the 1770s and 1780s. The later expansion followed from the success of the mid-century booksellers and authors who created and sustained the fashion for reading novels.

This pattern of growth, but also the caution required in describing it, is clearly seen when considered in relation to publishing trends of the first half of the century. The output of each decade, 238 new titles between 1750 and 1759 and 292 new titles between 1760 and 1769, compares with an estimated 45 titles, 1700-9; 60, 1710-19; 135, 1720-9; 95, 1730-9; and 210, 1740-9. Production trends of new titles and editions 1700-69 are shown in figure 1, although it must be noted that the pre-1750 data is based on slightly different coverage criteria to that used in this catalogue.[24] The most obvious feature is the support given to those highlighting the 1740s

Figure 1

— new titles

.... all edns

Publication of novels 1700-1769

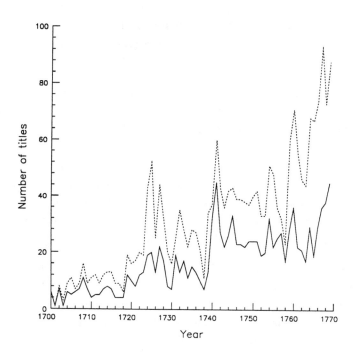

---

[24] Estimates 1700-49 from McBurney and Beasley, disregarding works falling into the equivalent of miscellany listings and adding new discoveries.

as a period of especial interest in the new novel form.[25] The increased production of new titles
between 1750 and 1770, including the quickening growth of the late 1760s, does not achieve the
rate of increase apparent from the mid-1730s to the mid-1740s. In the twenty years after 1750,
the most dramatic surge in output derived from reprinting. Not only were the booksellers of the
1760s reprinting more than double the number of titles reissued in the 1740s, but the ratio
between new title publication and reprinting also increased. This might suggest several features
of the market for the novel in the later period. That the demand for tried works so significantly
outstripped the demand for new titles, seems to confirm the development of a market of readers
for whom the reputation of a known bestseller was paramount. The supply of new works
submitted to the press might also have reached a temporary plateau. The interest shown by
writers in subscription schemes - often for first and only works - certainly fluctuates markedly
during this period. It is more likely, however, that new titles were not issued at the peak rates of
the early 1740s exactly because of the commercial considerations of London booksellers who
were reprinting established works for the expanding market of new readers, rather than taking
the unnecessary risk of extending their number of new titles. Against this, there was also an
increase in the market for ephemeral works, usually restricted to one edition. This was especially
so in the two decades before the 1774 judgment against perpetual copyright, and there were
famous exceptions of individual firms whose business success was built on the publication of at
least allegedly new titles. Nonetheless, the aggregate response was clearly determined by
commercial reprinting.

Although it would shed more light on such issues, it is difficult to estimate the number of novel
titles as a proportion of all books printed in each year during the two decades.[26] The proportion
of all fiction (new titles and reprints) to total book and pamphlet production for the 1750s and
1760s (about 4%) compares to 1.0% for 1700-09, 1.1% for 1720-29, 2.2% for 1730-39, and
4.0% for 1740-49.[27] If reprinting rates are taken into account, it does seem that fiction as a
proportion of all literature increases slowly during the 1750s but then accelerates towards the end
of the 1760s. Such calculations are difficult to make, however, when many of the titles in the
other categories of publication - notably political pamphlets and locally printed sermons or
proposals - were of various and often small length and edition size.

The content of mid-eighteenth-century fiction was extremely wide-ranging, and this introduction
can only indicate very briefly the variety of the lesser-known imaginative literature listed in the
catalogue. Clara Reeve's classic definition from the 1780s of the distinction between the fantasy
of the romance and the authenticity of the novel, would have been quite familiar thirty years

---

[25]   Adding in particular to the emphasis given in Jerry C. Beasley, *Novels of the 1740s* (Athens, Ga, 1982).

[26]   Annual book totals are given in Ian Maxted, *The London Book Trades* (London, 1977), xxxi, table 11; and
       category totals in Feather, "British Publishing."

[27]   Book production figures, 1710-19, are not available.

earlier.[28] It was then that the traditional romance was eclipsed in production by fictional histories with contemporary and topical settings, many entailing complex engagements with the 'reality' of narratives.[29] Novels were peppered with ***** and —— s in elaborate attempts to persuade readers of the authenticity of the tale. Realism was pursued in both satirical and sentimental writing. Titles boasted of "authentic memoirs," "genuine recollections" and novels "founded on fact."

The subject of these works was by no means always domestic, however. Each season contains its serious homespun moralities and its full-blooded adventure yarns. Some are very lively tales indeed with rollicking histories of marauding huns, West and East Indians and pirates on the high seas. Some of the most animated works were derived from successful plays, a form of narrative work selling well in the earlier decades of the century. Settings are rich in variation, from the Indies in such publications as Hill's *George Edwards* to desert islands and the moon in Goodall's *Captain Greenland* and Morris's *John Daniel*. Novels which never venture beyond aristocratic salons or the leafy sanctuaries of country estates contrast with the detailed scenes of London low-life in Dodd's *Sisters* or Fielding's *Amelia*. The picaresque novel also continued to attract, with contrasting scenes juxtaposed within the narrative journey. Edward Kimber's *Joe Thompson* of 1750 heads fifty or more ramble novels including *Jasper Banks*, the *Memoirs of an Oxford Scholar*, Wollaston's *Pilgrim*, Toldervy's *Two Orphans* and Lewis's *Rake*. Skits such as Kimber's *David Ranger* (a portrayal of Garrick), Kidgell's *Card* (a burlesque of the letter-writing style) or Shebbeare's satires on the state of England accompanied far cruder works of comedy in the booksellers' stocks. The 1759 *Juvenile Adventures of Miss Kitty F-r* and the 1768 *Memoirs of the Seraglio... by a Discarded Sultana* vie with many other spicy stories during two decades which produced a succession of reprints and imitations of Cleland's *Woman of Pleasure*, an equally large number of reissues of Mrs Rowe's moralizing works and a constant stream of didactic and sedate novels of manners.

Narrative techniques were equally diverse, with three types of work which can be set aside from the tale offered as an objective history : fiction written from the perspective of the privileged observer or spy, the novel written in letters, and the personal memoir.

The "spy" novel, in particular, flourished during the 1750s and early 1760s. "Adventures" included everything from those of a flea to those of a corkscrew. Improbable spy narrators ranged from the title-character of the 1757 *Sedan* to Eliza Haywood's Exploralibus in her 1755 *Invisible Spy*. In Mrs Haywood's work the narrator, girded with a belt of invisibility, salaciously

---

[28]   *The Progress of Romance* (Colchester, 1785). There are similar comments on the state of the novel during the 1750s - as in Coventry's *Pompey the Little* and the 1751 *Constantia* with its "Short Discourse on Novel-writing."

[29]   Beasley, *Novels of the 1740*, esp. ch.3; and Michael Crump, "Stranger than Fiction : the Eighteenth-century True Story," in *Searching the Eighteenth Century*, ed. M. Crump and M. Harris (London, 1983), 59-73.

records the less attractive habits of society. More discreet but equally popular was Francis Coventry's *Pompey the Little; or, The Adventures of a Lap-dog*, first published in 1751 and setting the pattern for dozens of imitators.[30] By far the most famous and reprinted of the spy novels, however, was one of the last of its type, Charles Johnston's *Chrysal; or, The Adventures of a Guinea*. It was published early in 1760 by Thomas Becket, then only recently established in the Strand, and looking for a popular work to sustain his business.

Although the number of new "memoirs" is variable over the decade, some of the most popular titles are from this category. Increasingly during the 1760s these memoirs are written as "adventures" and "genuine histories" in the first person. The publishing history of the most celebrated and eccentric of their number, *Tristram Shandy*, should almost be considered in a category of its own. Sterne's novel spawned an industry of imitations and anarchic and whimsical miscellanies.

The number of epistolary novels also increased steadily from a handful of new titles and reprints in the early 1750s to well over two dozen in 1769. During the 1750s this genre was still dominated by the novels of Richardson and various translations of Mesdames Grafigny, Le Prince de Beaumont and Riccoboni, with only the Griffiths and Mary Collyer supplying popular new novels in letters. During the 1760s however, translations of Rousseau's *Eloisa*, further reprintings of Richardson, and the early works of Treyssac de Vergy, were rivalled by Mrs Brooke's own work in letters, the epistolary novels of the Minifie sisters and John Langhorne, and the more modest offerings of Maria Cooper, Phoebe Gibbes and Jean Marishall. Whereas between 1750 and 1760 new letter-novels averaged no more than a tenth of the annual total of new fiction, in 1766 and 1768 nearly one quarter and in 1769 over one third of new titles were written in letters. Many of the most reprinted novels of this decade were also in letters, further stimulating the vogue for this form.[31]

Even more varied than these works are the titles listed in the miscellany sections. The importance of the sub-novel group of fiction becomes clear in any survey of the history of the sellers of imaginative literature in the eighteenth century.[32] By the 1740s pseudo-biographies,

---

[30] Both works were reprinted eight times by the end of the century.

[31] *New* titles of epistolary works are as follows :

1750	0	1755	2	1760	1	1765	4
1751	1	1756	1	1761	3	1766	7
1752	1	1757	2	1762	4	1767	12
1753	3	1758	2	1763	5	1768	10
1754	1	1759	3	1764	7	1769	16

   The early history of this genre may be found in Robert A. Day, *Told in Letters. Epistolary Fiction before Richardson* (Ann Arbor, 1966) and Frank Gees Black, *The Epistolary Novel in the late Eighteenth Century* (Eugene, 1940). Note that in the following listings a narrative "N" may contain a few episodes written in letters. Those with many such episodes are signified "N/E."

[32] The earlier period is surveyed in John H. Richetti, *Popular Fiction before Richardson* (Oxford, 1969).

travels and other rogue literature totalled over one tenth of all fiction published.[33] For the next twenty years nearly all booksellers supplemented their range of novels with a variety of lesser tales and adventure books. Recognizable patterns are repeated, not only in plot and theme, but also in volume, title arrangement and typographical 'house style'. With the increased output of domestic and sentimental novels, all contributed to the extension of the literary market. There are many examples of small-sized, well-printed works which although included in catalogues of chapmens' books, were clearly designed more for the middle-class customers of provincial bookshops than for the clients of pedlars.[34] The columns of mid-century provincial newspapers are littered with advertisements for finely-printed but slender novels and tales available by order from the London booksellers and their country agents.

Such activity was far from universally praised, however. Attacks made upon the manufacture of new literature increased. "Clean straw, a dark room, plentiful evacuations, a thin diet, and a total privation of pen, ink and paper, may perhaps make the author of this melancholy piece useful to society," wrote a periodical reviewer of one of the Nobles' productions.[35] From mid-century the opposition to the novel was to grow until by 1800 there was a vociferous lobby for the suppression of much of the fiction then circulating.[36] Protests against the immorality and unsavouriness of the novel were also accompanied by cries of foul-play over the booksellers' commercial practices. A common complaint was of short-weight and over-pricing. Broad margins and large type resulted in few words per page, even though this did relieve the reader of another source of bitter criticism - the padding inserted by authors hoping for payment *per* volume.[37] By well-advertised contrast, certain printers adopted minute print, providing very long texts and ones that were not always easy to read. Outraged periodical reviewers assumed an undiscriminating audience for fiction, but the competitive commercialism of the novel manufacturers did result in dissatisfied as well as poorly-served customers.

---

[33] Beasley, *Novels of the 1740s*, 90.

[34] The 1759 *Fortunate Imposter* is one such example. Some Dublin piracies were also very finely printed, notably the 1754 reprint of Miss Smythies's *Stage Coach*.

[35] *Critical Review*, 5 (February 1758): 170, on *Memoirs of a Young Lady of Family*, 1758.

[36] John Tinnon Taylor, *Early Opposition to the English Novel* (New York, 1943). Cf. F. W. Gallaway, "The Conservative Attitude Towards Fiction 1770-1830," *P.M.L.A.* 50 (1940): 1041-1059.

[37] Of many complaints from mid-century reviewers, see the *Monthly*, 11 (December 1754): 467, on *Sir Harry Herald*. The Nobles' range includes many of large type. The 1759 *Agenor and Ismena* by Cooke, is a further example of a work with small fine print but with such generous margins that there are very few words to the page.

The Authors

In the full listings 236 different authors have so far been identified. Table 2 lists the twenty most reprinted authors of fiction during this period. The total number of titles ascribed to these novelists amounts to a quarter of the total number of works in the catalogue. In addition to their own novels (and excluded from the publication figures of table 2), Smollett was responsible for at least thirteen editions of translated fiction 1750-69, Mrs Brooke for six, Kimber for three, and Mrs Haywood for two. The basis for the popularity of these authors also varies greatly. Sterne and Johnston were responsible for one or two best-selling works. Other writers, notably Eliza Haywood (d.1756) and Mrs Lennox, sold well because of the number of their individual titles. The reprintings of Mrs Haywood's works comprise thirteen separate titles, with only *Betsy Thoughtless* and *The Invisible Spy* achieving more than three editions in the twenty years. It must also be noted that Sterne's *Tristram Shandy* was issued in two-volume stages, swelling the number of editions listed under his name.

Table 2: **The most popular novelists by editions printed 1750-1769**

Sterne[a]	35	Richardson[d]	23	Voltaire	16	Lennox[e]	14
Fielding, H.	33	Riccoboni	17	Langhorne	15	Cervantes	13
Haywood	31	Kimber	17	Marmontel	15	Brooke, F.[f]	11
Smollett[b]	28	Fielding, S.	16	Cleland	14	Rousseau	11
Defoe[c]	28	Johnston	16	Goldsmith	14	le P. de Beaumont	11

a. includes *Political Romance*, 1759.   b. includes *Habbakkuk Hilding*, 1752, and *Adventures of an Atom*, 1769. c. includes an edn of *Captain Singleton*, 1768.   d. includes 2 derived works & 2 compilations.   e. includes 2 edns of the recently attributed *History of Eliza*, 1766.   f. excludes 1st *periodical* edn of *The Old Maid*, 1755. * Chapbook versions of the authors' works are not included.

Table 3 is in two sections. The first part lists the reprintings of the works of the most popular novelists of the period, showing the relative popularity of these works and also their long-term publication history. Some minor works are omitted (see notes to table 2) and the breakdown for Mrs Haywood gives only her two most popular works.[38] Within each group, the novels are listed in order of publication. The second part of table 3 provides comparative publication details of the remaining individual best-selling titles. These are ranked according to the number of reprintings between 1750 and 1769. In both parts, known later editions from 1770 to 1800 are also given. Crude tables of a book's popularity over twenty years must be set against publication

---

[38]   As noted, none of her other books reprinted in these years went through more than three editions.

Table 3: **Publication of novels by the most popular authors**[*]

	pre-1750	1750-59			1760-69			Total 1750-1769	1770-1800	1700-1800
		London	Dublin	Other	London	Dublin	Other			
Tristram Shandy				1	13	11		25	+17	+42
Sentimental Journey					4	3		7	31	39
Joseph Andrews	7	1	1		5	2	1	10	19	36
Tom Jones	4	2	2		3	2	1	10	21	35
Amelia		1	2		1			4	12	15
Jonathan Wild		2	2					4	3	7
Collected Works					4		1	5	8	13
Betsy Thoughtless		2	2		2	1		7	3	10
Invisible Spy		2	2		1	1		6	3	9
Roderick Random	5	3	1		3	2		9	27	41
Peregrine Pickle		2	1		2	2(?3)		7(?8)	17	+24
Count Fathom		2	1					3	12	15
Launcelot Greaves					1	2	1	4	13	17
Robinson Crusoe	+14	6			4		8	18	39	+71
Moll Flanders	+11	2			3			5	4	+20
Roxana	4	2	1		1			4	1	9
Pamela	9	1			4			5	10	24
Clarissa	2	4	1		3	1		9	8	19
Chas Grandison		3	+2		3			8	13	21
Chrysal					10	3		13	8	21
Vicar of Wakefield					3	5	3	11	52	63
Don Quixote	12	2		1	6	1	1	11	14	37[a]
Julia Mandeville					6	3		9	5	14
Gil Blas	5	1	1		4	1	2	9	+13	+26
Castle of Otranto					4	3		7	9	16

[*] not including chapbook versions.　　　+ strong likelihood of further edns (all totals 1770-1800 liable to be updated by eventual full *E.S.T.C.* database).

a. 1st English trans. 1612, with many reprints to 1700. Also, listed as miscellanies, 11 edns of *Friendship in Death* & 13(+) edns of *Æsop's Fables*.

totals for the whole of the century. Although writing some forty years later, Goldsmith is second only to Defoe as the most popular author of prose fiction of the century. *The Vicar of Wakefield* was not published until 1765 and the appearance of its author in table 2 is a striking indication of the rapidity of the sales of the book over the next four years.[39] One other qualification to these tables is the variation between the sizes of the editions listed in the full catalogue. Even so, Strahan's successive and large printings of works by Fielding and Smollett were clearly exceptional,[40] and as their authors discovered, certain large editions took years to sell out. The number of reprintings of the other best-selling novels, in what were usually 1,000 and occasionally 2,000 copy runs, does therefore give a general guide to the comparative popularity of the works. Where variation in edition size might have greater consequences for such estimates of popularity is in the authorship rankings of table 2. It is possible, for example, that some of Mrs Haywood's minor works were not issued in large editions, although her reputation as a novelist should have given her bookseller, Gardner, confidence in launching all further works in editions of 1,000.

The importance of Richardson, Fielding, Smollett and Sterne in the development of the novel during this period requires little elaboration. An enormous literature details their effect upon imaginative writing and the construction of the novel.[41] Almost 7% of all titles and editions listed in this catalogue were written by these authors.[42] As table 3 shows, however, there was much variation in the popularity of the works by each author, both when first published and in the decades immediately following. It can also be seen that in terms of reprinting, these four writers were closely challenged by Mrs Haywood and Defoe. The popularity of the latter was largely sustained by one work, *Robinson Crusoe*.[43] Provincial booksellers in particular launched their

---

[39]   Secondary criticism is fully listed in Samuel H. Woods, Jr., comp., *Oliver Goldsmith. A Reference Guide* (Boston, 1982).

[40]   Including the 1st edn of 2,000, Strahan printed 6,500 copies of Roderick Random between January 1748 and November 1749. Between 1749 and 1750 10,000 copies of *Tom Jones* were printed, Lewis Mansfield Knapp, "Smollett's Works as Printed by William Strahan, with an unpublished letter of Smollett to Strahan," *The Library*, 4th ser., 13 (1933): 282-291. The largest single printing order for a novel seems to have been the extraordinary 8,000 copies of *Amelia* printed in two stages in December 1751 and January 1752, Strahan ledgers.

[41]   Comprehensive surveys may be found in Richard Gordon Hannaford, comp., *Samuel Richardson : An Annotated Bibliography of Modern Criticism* (New York, 1980) and John Carroll, comp., *Richardson* (London, 1974); H. George Hahn, comp., *Henry Fielding : An Annotated Bibliography* (Metuchen, N.J. and London, 1979) and Martin C. Battestin, comp., *Fielding* (London, 1974); Mary Wagoner, comp., *Tobias Smollett. A Checklist of Editions of his Works and an Annotated Secondary Bibliography* (New York, 1984), Robert D. Spector, comp., *Tobias Smollett : A Reference Guide* (Boston, 1980) and Lewis M. Knapp, comp., *Smollett* (London, 1974); Lodwick Hartley, comp., *Laurence Sterne. An Annotated Bibliography 1965-1977* (Boston, 1978). Also, T. C. Duncan Eaves and Ben D. Kimpel, *Samuel Richardson : A Biography* (Oxford, 1971); Ronald Paulson, *Satire and the Novel in Eighteenth-century England* (New Haven, 1967); Coenraad B. A. Proper, *Social Elements in English Prose Fiction between 1700 and 1832 (New York, 1965); and James R. Foster, History of the Pre-Romantic Novel in England (New York, 1949).*

[42]   For some, weaned only on accounts of these four writers, such a total might seem startlingly low. It should be added, of course, that there was in addition a large group of writers who owed everything to the influence of the major novelists.

[43]   The fullest guides are M. E. Novak, comp., *Defoe* (London, 1974); J. M. Moore, comp., *Checklist of the Writings of Daniel Defoe* 2d ed. (Hamden CT, 1971) [but without reprintings]; and John A. Stoler, comp., *Daniel Defoe : An Annotated Bibliography of Modern Criticism* (New York, 1984). Also, Henry Clinton Hutchins, *Robinson Crusoe and its Printing, 1719-1731* (New York, 1925).

own editions of *Crusoe* during the 1760s. The work was greatly circulated in chapbook form, and as such might even have encouraged later investment by a reader in a more substantial version. Many of the editions listed in this catalogue, while usually over a hundred pages long, are cheaply and often crudely printed. Like his later rivals, Defoe was also important for spawning a large number of imitators, notably the voyager works of William Chetwood many of which were republished in the 1750s. The vogue for *Crusoe* also encouraged the reprinting of Longueville's *Hermit*, five editions of which have been located for 1750-69. The other leading author, Eliza Haywood was already a popular novelist and dramatist of some three decade*s*' standing by 1750. Her early works of the 1720s and 1730s sold well despite and perhaps even because of their mauling by the critics. Swift's "stupid, infamous, scribbling woman," she was immortalized as the buxom prize in the contest between Curll and Chetwood in Pope's *Dunciad*. With the exception of the 1755 *Invisible Spy*, however, Haywood's later works, including *Betsy Thoughtless* and *Jemmy and Jenny Jessamy*, were much more the respectable novels of manners with clear didactic intent. Her part-conduct books, the *Wife* of 1755 and *Husband* of 1756, even reveal debts to the earnest sermonizing of Mrs Rowe. At the time, this change in her writing was welcomed as a moral apostasy, but as a recent commentator has pointed out, it also "shows her adaptability and sensitivity to a changing literary market."[44]

Mrs Haywood was in fact one of six women listed in the best-sellers of table 2. Sarah Fielding (1710-68) enhanced a reputation established by *David Simple* (1744) with further works during the 1750s. Although her various publications were of inconsistent quality and received poor as well as excellent notices, her popularity is confirmed by the listings in dozens of contemporary library and booksellers' catalogues. The theme of all her works is sentimental, while she sought to instruct by careful characterization and recurrent episodes of social satire. Charlotte Lennox was born in New York in 1729, coming to England at the age of fifteen. Her greatest success, *The Female Quixote* was published in March 1752 with a second edition in June. Her name did not appear on the title page until 1783. New works were issued frequently between 1750 and 1766 (as well as a final work in 1790). Her reputation was supported by Fielding, Richardson and Johnson who wrote at least three and possibly five of the dedications to her works. Mrs Lennox was, however, shunned by the various genteel blue-stocking circles of the period. She lived in poverty and apparent loneliness in the final years of her life, the novels of her early and middle life quickly forgotten by an increasingly fickle reading-public. She died in 1804 to be buried, according to Nichols, "with the common Soldiery in the further burying-ground of Broad Chapel [Westminster] undistinguished even by a head-stone to say where she lies."[45]

---

[44] Jane Spencer in Todd, *Dictionary*, 160. Also, Richetti, *Popular Fiction*, ch. 4-5; and James E. Erickson, "The Novels of Eliza Haywood" (Ph.D. diss., University of Minnesota, 1961). The fullest guide remains George F. Whicher, *The Life and Romances of Mrs Eliza Haywood* (New York, 1915). In all, Haywood wrote nearly 70 separate works.

[45] John Nichols, *Literary Anecdotes of the Eighteenth Century* 9 vols. (London, 1812-15), 3: 201, 8: 435. The only full biography is Miriam Small, *Charlotte Ramsay Lennox* (New Haven, 1935).

Mrs Frances Moore Brooke (1724-89), was the third most popular woman novelist of this period. Her first novel, *The History of Lady Julia Mandeville*, enjoyed huge and immediate popularity, achieving nine editions within the decade. The novel was, like her *Emily Montague*, an epistolary tale influenced greatly by Riccoboni and Richardson but finding wide approval from the reviewers. In another example of cross-Channel exchange in mid-century novels, Mrs Brooke was translated into French and sold almost as well in Paris as in London.

The popularity of these writers might seem to have one other effect, namely to enhance the reputation of this period as one of predominantly women novelists. This may well be misleading, however. Even if the popular Mrs Rowe is added to the list of women writers in table 2, their contribution is 7% of the total imaginative literature listed in this catalogue. Of the 236 authors and translators of novels published and re-published in these twenty years 40 (17%) were definitely by women. Of the 1077 novels translated, published and re-published between 1750 and 1769, 185 (17%) can be attributed to women. An even smaller percentage of the new titles published during the period can be identified as by women writers (14% or 76 of 531). There are, of course, several unattributed works "by a Lady," but some of these, as well as some with women's names on the title-pages, were actually written by male hacks, hoping for public sympathy and critical leniency. Moreover, the number of works so labelled is not as great as has often been assumed. There are more seasons in the 1750s without a novel entitled "By a Lady" or "Young Lady" than with one. Table 4 lists the annual number of works now *known* to have been written by women. A peak is reached in 1763-64 when between a third and a quarter of all novels are by women - a total boosted by the bubble popularity of Mrs Brooke's *Julia Mandeville*. Inevitably, there remains a group of works for which no author could be traced, but even if *all* these works (listed also in table 4) are assumed to be by women and added to the titles known to be women, the case for a predominance of women writers of early fiction is far from overwhelming. Only eleven years between 1750 and 1769 have more novels written by women and unknown authors than novels written by men.[46]

There are other unexpected inclusions in the ranks of best-selling novelists.[47] Like Sterne, Charles Johnston was the author of one hugely popular work, *Chrysal*, and a successful subsidiary one, *The Reverie*. There is still no study of the writer available. Cleland's *Fanny Hill* or *Memoirs of a Woman of Pleasure* was circulating in a number of different versions.[48] Probably the most unfamiliar of the leading names is that of Edward Kimber. Although he has

---

[46]   This large group, which for some seasons such as 1757 where there is exceptional uncertainty over authorship, probably greatly exaggerates the contribution of women. Works by this combined total of women and unknown authors amounts to 55% of the output of the 1750s (219 of 298) and 51% of the output of the 1760s (345 of 679).

[47]   See above, tables 2 and 3.

[48]   The best account of its early publication history is David Foxon, *Libertine Literature in England 1660-1745* (London, 1964).

suffered from sad neglect, he was one of the most popular novelists of his day, and also one of the most prolific. Almost nothing is now known of his life.[49]

The sales of certain of the remaining 216 authors, while obviously extensive, were either too concentrated in a few years, too close to the end of this period, or too dispersed over a number of briefly fashionable works to be registered in the above tabulations. Johnson's *Prince of Abissinia (Rasselas)* was published in 1759 to be re-issued fourteen times by 1790. Apparently written to assist with the expenses of Johnson's mother's funeral, *Rasselas* combines a didactic intention with extremely humourous imaginative episodes. It inspired various imitations, including Miss Knight's sequel, and was quickly translated all over Europe. A further best-seller was Walpole's *Castle of Otranto*, published in 1764-65, reprinted six times by 1769 and heralding a passion for the Gothic.[50] Henry Brooke's *Fool of Quality*, issued in stages between 1766 and 1770, was similarly published late in this period, but gained enormous popularity in

Table 4: **Publication of novels by women writers 1750-1769**

Year	Works by Women		Unknown author	Annual output	Year	Works by Women		Unknown author	Annual output
	New*	Reprint				New*	Reprint		
1750	2	1	17	40	1760	4	5	35	71
1751	2	2	13	42	1761	2	5	13	55
1752	3	5	9	33	1762	5	5	8	46
1753	5	3	11	33	1763	2	10	14	44
1754	5	4	18	51	1764	7	15	20	68
1755	3	5	19	48	1765	3	8	17	67
1756	4	3	16	36	1766	6	8	21	74
1757	2		23	32	1767	7	11	26	93
1758	2	1	11	23	1768	1	6	32	73
1759	5	4	21	60	1769	6	8	35	88
Total	33	28	158	398	Total	43	81	221	679

* including 1st English edns

---

[49] F. G. Black, "Edward Kimber, anonymous novelist," *Harvard Studies in English* 17 (1935).

[50] Gothic fiction is checklisted in Montague Summers, comp., *A Gothic Bibliography* (London, 1941), and surveyed in Dan J. McNutt, comp., *The Eighteenth-century Gothic Novel : An Annotated Bibliography of Criticism and Selected Texts* (London, 1975). A further bibliographical guide is Peter Sabor, comp., *Horace Walpole. A Reference Guide* (Boston, 1984).

subsequent seasons.[51]

Of those responsible for a single best-selling work, the contrasting figures of Coventry and Paltock head the lists of the 1750s. Francis Coventry died in 1754 at the age of twenty-eight. A well-connected clergyman with an unsuccessful volume of poetry behind him, his one work of fiction, *Pompey the Little*, won enthusiastic notices. Even the *Monthly* opinioned that it was "not easy to do justice to the merit of it."[52] *Pompey*'s authorship, unacknowledged until the third edition, was the centre of much literary attention. The work was pirated and also translated many times by the end of the century. By 1824 it had enjoyed over a dozen English editions. Robert Paltock (1697-1767), an attorney at Clement's Inn, enjoyed considerable success with his great imaginative work, *The Life and Adventures of Peter Wilkins* published in 1751. Written during poverty, the original copyright was sold by Paltock for £20 and twelve free copies of the book. Like *Pompey*, the work gained greatest repute long after its author could profit from it. *Peter Wilkins* was admired by Coleridge, Lamb, Shelley and Southey, and was still well known in the time of Dickens.

More prolific and controversial were the lively and varied contributions of Shebbeare and Hill. John Shebbeare (1709-1788), a surgeon and political pamphleteer twice imprisoned for libel, is now best remembered for his bitter rivalry with Smollett. In 1751 Shebbeare sabotaged *Peregrine Pickle* with his own version of *The Memoirs of a Lady of Quality*.[53] During the next five years his satirical skills were exercised in more diverse projects including the novel, *The Marriage Act*, and his attacks on Newcastle and the Whig ministry in the *Letters on the English Nation*. His great satire of 1756, *Lydia*, crisply divided England into haves and have-nots. One of its more unfortunate targets was George II. Rather as Shebbeare was rediscovered early this century, there has been a recent reassessment of the career of Sir John Hill, a man vilified in his day and in almost every survey of mid-eighteenth-century literature since. Hill, it seems, should be rescued from the image created by Smart's *Hilliad* and the pamphlet war with Fielding and Smollett. His attempts to undermine Smollett's novel-writing career were, after all, surprisingly successful, and his *Inspector* series between 1751 and 1753 a massive popular hit.[54] His two novels of the early 1750s, *George Edwards* and the *Woman of Quality*, are actually satirical "anti-novels." The *Woman of Quality* was another direct response to Smollett's "Memoirs." The owner of a smart town house in Arlington Street in St James, Hill bought properties in Bayswater during the next decade, almost certainly from the profits from his many and varied writings.

---

[51] Helen Margaret Scurr, *Henry Brooke* (Minneapolis, 1927), the only full, if brief, study, with some information given in J. M. S. Tompkins, *The Popular Novel in England 1770-1800* (London, 1932).

[52] *Monthly Review* 4 (February 1751): 316.

[53] James R. Foster, "Smollett's Pamphleteering for Shebbeare," *P.M.L.A.*, 57, no. 3 (1942): 1053-1100.

[54] Hill was also responsible for major contributions to botany and medical learning, G. S. Rousseau, *Letters and Papers of Sir John Hill* (New York, 1982). Hill's works are checklisted in *The Renaissance Man in the Eighteenth Century* (Los Angeles, William Andrews Clark Memorial Library, 1978), 107-129.

A further contribution to the increased publication of novels was made by works in translation. Both foreign authors and translators feature prominently in the catalogue listings. At the same time, untranslated French fiction also went through periods of high fashion. In his 1767 Circulating Library catalogue, John Noble listed 525 titles of "Nouvelles Français" for loan together with 488 other French works.[55] Several translated authors are highly placed in table 2, notably Madame Riccoboni, Voltaire and Marmontel. Indeed, in terms of the reprinting of works between 1750 and 1769, six of the leading twenty and ten of the leading thirty writers were French (Cervantes is the prominent exception).

Table 5: **Publication of translated fiction in Britain 1750-1769**

Year	from the French		from the Spanish		Other	
	New	Reprint	New	Reprint	New	Reprint
1750	4	4				
1751	5	2				
1752	2	3				
1753	7	2				
1754	6	1			1	
1755	3	3	1		1	
1756	1	1	1	1		
1757	2			1		
1758	6	3				
1759	10	10				
1760	5	7				
1761	4	7		1	1	1
1762	3	2				
1763	1	4				
1764	4	11			2	1
1765	3	10		2		1
1766	7	9		3		1
1767	4	12			1	1
1768	3	8			2	
1769	4	6		2	1	1
Total	84	105	2	10	9	6

Table 5 indicates the annual total of newly translated titles and of reprints from foreign originals

---

[55] *Catalogue of the Large and Valuable Collection of Books (both English and French) in John Noble's Circulating Library... which are Lent to be Read... at Dryden's Head, in St Martin's Court, near Leicester-Square* (London, 1767).

already published in Britain. The eighty-four new titles in translation from the French comprise 15% of all new titles issued 1750-1769. All translations from the French, including reprints, comprise some 17% of the total output of prose fiction during the same period. Voltaire's *Candide* was translated in several different editions during 1759, Madame Riccoboni's *Lady Catesby* was popularized in English by Mrs Brooke, and numerous translations were issued of works by Crébillon, Fénelon, Mme Élie de Beaumont, Mme Grafigny, Baculard d'Arnaud, and the Marquis d'Argens.[56]

An increase in translations from the French since the beginning of the century was noted by Grieder but she also believed that during the 1750s there was a fall in demand for novels first published abroad. The new listings show that this is not the case. Instead, publication rates remained almost constant.[57] Despite the popularity of these works, translations were frequently poorly executed. *True Merit* of 1757 is a particularly fine example of the botched translation. In the same year the *Critical* provided a long demonstrative review of the failings of the translators of modern fiction.[58]

Of the English writers, most lived and wrote in London, although there were notable writers working in country towns such as Reading, Colchester, Birmingham and Ipswich, and a prolific community of novelists in Dublin. The lives of many provincial authors, however, are often poorly recorded. The Miss Minifies of Fairwater and Miss Smythies of Colchester contributed some of the liveliest imitations of Richardson during this period. Their narratives and letters counsel virtuous social behaviour, while including repeated satires against clearly identified social evils. Miss Smythies's works were reprinted several times during the century, and also found particular popularity in translation in Germany. These three women were amongst the very few committing a name to the title-page of their works. By the marriage of one sister, the Minifies were soon to exchange their Somerset retirement for embroilment in the "Gunninghiad," one of the most salacious scandals of the age. Miss Smythies, more typically for the eighteenth-century provincial novelist, has vanished without trace. She is not included in the recent and most thoroughgoing of guides to women writers of the century.[59] The life of Mrs Woodfin, who published her first work of fiction, *Northern Memoirs* in 1756, is yet another mystery. By 1765

---

56   The end of this period also saw the beginning of the popularity of the many novels of Treyssac de Vergy. A full length study of Riccoboni is Emily A. Crosby, *Une Romancière oubliée, Mme Riccoboni : sa vie, ses oeuvres, sa place dans la littérature anglaise et françise, du XVIIIe siècle* (Paris, 1924). Marmontel is considered in S. Lenel, *Un Homme de Lettres au XVIIIe siècle : Marmontel* (Paris, 1902); and Grieder, *Translations*, 55-58.

57   Translations of the 1750s do not number fewer than a third of those of the 1740s. Grieder's figures were obviously dependant upon the availability of checklisting and were as follows : 1700-1709, 18; 1710-1719, 10; 1720-1729, 31; 1730-39, 25; 1740-49, 51. There was also further two-way traffic, as described in H. W. Streeter, *The Eighteenth-Century English Novel in French Translation (New York, 1936)*.

58   *Critical Review* 3 (May 1757): 467-9.

59   For nearly all the female authors mentioned here, Janet Todd's *Dictionary of British and American Women Writers 1660-1800* (Totowa NJ, 1985) is an invaluable guide. Also, B. G. MacCarthy, *The Later Women Novelists 1744-1818* (Cork and Oxford, 1947). Smythies is considered in F. G. Black, "A Lady Novelist of Colchester," *Essex Review* 64 (1935): 180-185.

she had published at least a further four works of fiction, moved to London and opened a school off the Strand. A puzzle to contemporary reviewers, Mrs Woodfin's novels, with their extremely complex plots and discussions of a variety of social issues, are now her only legacy.

As with their fame, there was enormous variation in the financial position of the different novelists. Some, like Thomas Amory, the author of *John Buncle*, did not have to push the quill for a living and were always able to command a comfortable income from landed estates or from their commercial or legal profession (or from that of their husband). Many more were of modest means, and several dozen of the novelists publishing during this period wrote from necessity. It is true that many authors claimed some success by launching their work by subscription. The number of subscription editions, however, should not be overestimated, and the great majority of writers could expect very small reward for their efforts. In 1757 Samuel Foote, grieving over the decline in subscription publication for all types of work, believed there to be "more money laid out upon Islington turnpike in a month than upon all the learned men in seven years."[60] Indeed, the number of works of fiction from the full catalogue *known* to have been published by subscription is no more than fourteen, with five further subscription editions.[61] Some popular works were indeed initially launched by subscription, although the reasons for this were various. The Miss Minifies collected their 700 subscribers to *The Histories of Lady Frances S— and Lady Caroline S—* from necessity. Fighting off bankruptcy, Richard and Elizabeth Griffith put out four successive subscription editions of their *Letters between Henry and Frances*. On the other hand, Sterne's first two subscription schemes for *A Sentimental Journey* (like his schemes for the *Sermons of Yorick*), were modelled on the example of Pope and of other celebrated cases of vast sums raised directly from the public by an established author.[62] Two hundred and eighty-one subscribers paid 5s, but a further 135 paid half-a-guinea for copies printed on imperial paper.

For all this, most new works were sold outright to the bookseller. Copyrights to fiction were bought at extremely low prices compared even to the sums paid for more serious literature. Unfortunately, there are few specific references to payments made by booksellers to authors in the 1750s and 1760s. Only details of those commanding large sums have been easily accessible. As a young writer Fielding gained £183.11s from surrendering the copy of *Joseph Andrews*. Copy to *Tom Jones* was first sold at £700 and in 1751 Fielding was given 1,000 gns by Millar for rights to his *Amelia*. Sterne collected £1,000 from the subscription *Sentimental Journey*

---

[60]   Samuel Foote, *The Author* Act I.

[61]   These are, by catalogue entry number, 1752 [126], 1754 [223] [232], 1755 [296] [332], 1757 [412] [422], 1758 [447], 1759 [506], 1760 [573] [580], 1761 [651], 1763 [785], 1766 [1013], 1768 [1208] [1234] [1235], 1769 [1314] [1356]. Many others catalogued may also have been subscription works, however. Their lists have not survived, but research continues.

[62]   Pope supposedly made over £5,000 from the first edition of his translation of Homer, Harry Ransom, "The Rewards of Authorship in the Eighteenth Century," *University of Texas Bulletin : Studies in English* no.3826 (July 1938): 47-66, but see also Pat Rogers, "Pope and his Subscribers," *Publishing History* 3 (1978): 7-36.

before it was printed, but had probably made £3,000 in the previous seven years from the successive volumes of *Tristram Shandy*. Such colossal purses were far in excess of the usual sum paid for the copy to a manuscript of a novel or associated work. By the 1780s the leading novel publisher, William Lane, was paying his authors £10-20 for outright purchase of the manuscript. But both then, and it is safe to assume, in the earlier decades, a payment of half-a-guinea per volume was the final offer to many an untried novelist. Dodsley was regarded by many as paying over the odds when he presented Coventry with £30 for the revised third edition of *Pompey*. Richardson himself had sold two-thirds of his copyright in *Pamela* for £20. Cleland had similarly sold his copyright in the *Woman of Pleasure* to the Griffiths for £20. In all such negotiations, save for those undertaken by a very select band of established writers, contractual agreements almost never considered the future success of a work. Even where some allowance was made, the more confident booksellers could choose to ignore earlier pledges given to authors. "I never knew a bookseller who was not a scoundrel," complained Shebbeare, "I was cheated plaguily about *Lydia*, and the rascal who sold the *Marriage Act* promised to share the profits, yet though I know that there have been six editions, he always calls it the first."[63] Payment to the original author of a translated work was a matter of ethics only and therefore almost unheard of. Madame Riccoboni, who managed to extract payment in kind if not in cash, was clearly an exception.[64]

Despite pathetic prefaces pleading widowhood or a husband's bankruptcy it is therefore likely that unless an author was especially prolific, subscription or the sale of copyright to the bookseller would not have provided sufficient return to re-establish an impecunious household. Nevertheless, it seems that many turned to writing for financial support. Perhaps the sums known to have been gained by the literary lions of the day were, as now, a glittering attraction to the impoverished well-educated. We still know too little about the mechanics of subscription collection to be sure of the bounty gained by that style of publication. Some booksellers advertising as agents for collection certainly announced their benevolent intentions. Charity was good for business. There is also evidence that many subscribers made the author an advanced gift of the book, presumably to allow resale. Takings from a particularly appealing destitute author might therefore have been greater than might be suggested by a mere multiplication of the book price by the number of subscribers (minus publication charges).[65] In these first decades of periodical reviewing, even the critics were lenient to works like the 1757 *Memoirs of Harriot and Charlotte Meanwell*, apparently written to save a poor relation from bankruptcy. Of course, prefaces and advertisements varied as much in their authenticity as in their persuasiveness. Just as many "first works by a young lady" were merely the latest production of a mature male hack,

---

[63]   Foster, "Smollett's Pamphleteering," 1071. Such re-issues can also cheat the modern cataloguer.

[64]   Grieder, *Translations*, 26.

[65]   K. I. D. Maslen, letter, *T.L.S.*, 29 September 1972: 1157.

so many authors almost certainly invented or embroidered upon tales of woe to encourage sales, the acceptance of a manuscript by a bookseller, or sympathy from the reviewers. On the other hand, there were many cases of genuine distress. Charlotte Lennox's husband relied upon the small income from his wife's writing to subsidize his own paltry wage when working for Strahan the printer. Mrs Sheridan's patronage by Johnson and various peeresses was not welcomed with any false gratitude. Sarah Fielding had to continue to write to support herself to the end of her life.

The Readers

If the identity of the readership of much eighteenth-century literature is still uncertain, it has not been for want of trying. Since A. S. Collins's essays in the 1920s, there have been various reconstructions of the reading public of Johnson, Gibbon and their contemporaries. Readership, it is generally agreed, was a "widening circle," stimulating and supported by the prodigious growth in newspapers and circulating libraries, both metropolitan and provincial. There was money to be made from new literacy and the commercial products of the booksellers provide us still with the best evidence of readerships.[66]

A very crude calculation of the number of copies of works of fiction produced between 1750 and 1770 can be made by multiplying the 1,400 titles listed here by 800 - no more than a guess at the average between a common commercial size of an edition (500) and the normal upper limit of 1,000, itself exceeded in rare cases of clearly proven works or authors. Such a total of 1,120,000 printed books will include books purchased as remainders many years after their original publication date, but also works sent to circulating libraries and lent out to dozens of readers. To this can be added the well-known but sparse records of individual sales and print-runs. Five thousand copies of the first edition of Fielding's *Amelia* were sold within a week of publication. Two years later Richardson's *Grandison* was printed in a third edition of 2,500, the first edition of 4,000 copies having been sold out within the previous four months.[67] Sterne's *Tristram Shandy* was first printed in an edition of no more than 500 copies but subsequent volumes enjoyed editions of at least 4,000.[68] But of all those reading fiction, what was the average number of works purchased or borrowed and read? And what sort of person was reading fiction?

---

[66]   Collins, and Helen Sard Hughes, "The Middle-class Reader and the English Novel," *Authorship, Journal of English and Germanic Philology* 25 (1926): 362-378. ch. Cf. Wiles, "The Relish for Reading," and his "Middle-class Literacy".

[67]   Wilbur L. Cross, *The History of Henry Fielding* 3 vols. (New Haven, 1918); Alan D. McKillop, *Samuel Richardson, Printer and Novelist* (Chapel Hill, 1936). Also, above, note 40.

[68]   Kenneth Monkman, "The Bibliography of the Early Editions of Tristram Shandy," *The Library*, 5th ser., 25, no. 1 (March 1970): 11-39 (14,27,29), citing Whitefoord Papers and Strahan Ledgers. The first edition of the first two volumes may have been of only 200 copies.

Sources have been meagre and problematic. Evidence of readership has been sought in the history of the circulating libraries, book subscription lists, and of changes in the products of the press. Apparently "middle-class" forms of publication - number-books and newspapers - have been identified as keys to changing readerships. By 1750 London newspapers were circulated widely in the country and complex but efficient networks for books were established within the regions and out of the metropolis from London booksellers to their country agents. The London wholesalers were buying ever-greater lengths of column-space in provincial newspapers to advertise their publications.[69] Subscription lists have also been analysed to explore the growth in provincial and often far-flung personal support for a book. Many lists, as inserted in surviving copies of works, are detailed and provide the names and sometimes addresses and professions of subscribers.[70] Illuminating studies have been made of the social composition of those subscribing to a number of individual works.[71] The upper limit to the number of subscription works, however, is suggested as 3,500, and, as already noted, only a very small proportion of this total were works of fiction. Sponsors of a few authors may be identified, but information gained must be applied with great caution to the far wider readership of fiction, buying and borrowing predominantly commercial books and almost certainly of very different means and motivation to those paying out to support an unknown work. Indeed, some subscription lists were no more than an exercise in aristocratic name-dropping - a commercial embellishment intended to give a work respectability and social cachet.

A parade of contemporary witnesses has also attested to the general increase in those reading literature in the second third of the eighteenth-century, with greatest controversy reserved for the question of whether - as Lackington suggested - servant girls of the Pamela variety did indeed acquire books to read.[72] Much-cited testimony, such as the diary of Thomas Turner or the letters of Henry Purefoy, has been used to show that the establishment of charity schools and cut-price circulating libraries and outlets for second-hand books increased both the opportunity for those of modest means to buy or borrow books and also their ability to read them. Some Pamelas, it seems, did read simple literature.[73]

---

[69]   R. M. Wiles, *Freshest Advices. Early Provincial Newspapers in England* (Columbus, Ohio, 1965); G. A. Cranfield, *The Development of the Provincial Newspaper 1700-1760* (Oxford, 1962); Robert Munter, *The History of the Irish Newspaper 1685-1760* (Cambridge, 1967); Feather, *Provincial Booktrade.*

[70]   P. J. Wallis, "Book Subscription Lists," *The Library*, 5th ser., 29, no.3, (September 1974): 255-286. F. J. G. Robinson and P. J. Wallis, *Book Subscription Lists. A Revised Guide* (Newcastle upon Tyne, 1975); and R. C. Alston, F. J. G. Robinson, and C. Wadham, comps., *A Check-List of Eighteenth-Century Books Containing Lists of Subscribers* (Newcastle upon Tyne, 1983).

[71]   In particular, Pat Rogers, "Pope and his Subscribers," and his "Book Subscriptions Among the Augustans," *T.L.S.*, 15 December 1972: 1539-40; and E. W. Playfair, letter, *T.L.S.*, 22 December 1972: 1558. Cf. the work on library catalogues, notably Paul Kaufman, *Libraries and their Users* (London, 1969); and his "Readers and their Reading in Eighteenth-century Lichfield," *The Library*, 5th ser., 28, no.2 (June 1973): 108-115.

[72]   James Lackington, *Memoirs of the First Forty-Five Years*, 1st ed. (London, 1791), letter xxx, an exaggerated claim according to Richard D. Altick, *The English Common Reader : A Social History of the Mass Reading Public 1800-1900* (Chicago, 1957), but one defended in Wiles, "Middle-Class Literacy".

[73]   Wiles, "Middle-Class Literacy," 50; David Vaisey, ed., *The Diary of Thomas Turner* (Oxford, 1986); G. Eland, ed., *Purefoy Letters 1735-55* 2 vols. (London, 1931).

The student of eighteenth-century literary readerships will continue to be a prisoner of such sources, and the danger remains of concentrating on the *reading* and not on the *readers*. The listings which follow can make only a very modest contribution to the question of readership. Three areas in particular may be assisted. Potential readerships can be assessed from new information provided about the price of all the imaginative literature available. The leading critical reviews are listed, and together with the booksellers' follow-up responses, can also provide clues about the audience. Lastly, the catalogue offers a more definite idea of the types of work sold and reprinted in a market especially responsive to fashion and the constituency of the readership. To extend the methodology of a contemporary traveller to England, "The common people of England read their authors! You can tell it, among other things from the number of editions of their works."[74]

The price of books listed here suggests a powerful constraint to the market. Many servants who might well have boasted modest reading skills would have been prevented from reading very much - certainly very much new literature - by the limits of their purchasing-power. Even novels sold sewed and unbound by the London booksellers average at just over 2s. a volume. Many works were in two volumes, while many bound, prestige sets cost over a guinea. One of the most striking features of the novels listed in this catalogue is the consistency in London booksellers' pricing. Novels proper sold at 2s. or 2s.6d sewed and up to 3s. bound per volume. This obtained for single-volume novels as well as for sets of two or three. In 1760 one unbound volume was therefore approximately the same price as a stone of beef or the most basic pair of shoes.[75] Amongst the main rivals to books in the advertising columns of provincial newspapers in the 1750s, were patent medicines offered from between 9d and 2s. a bottle, best ale for 8d a gallon, oysters for 2s. a barrell, and luxury goods such as chocolate for 6s. a pound. It has been suggested that 150,000 households boasted an income of between £50-400 per annum in 1780, which was 15% of all households in 1750% and 25% in 1780.[76] Annual income of £50 may well be a realistic threshold at which it was possible for book-buying to be considered. Between 1750 and 1770, some 2,000 owners of great estates or leading financiers and merchants were collecting over £20,000 a year, while mercantile clerks or journeymen might be earning £1 a week and artisans in the south 8s.

The most obvious feature of wealth distribution in the eighteenth century, however, was not only the extraordinary financial gulf between the very richest and the poorest in society, but also the

---

[74] Carl Philip Moritz, *Journeys of a German in England in 1782*, trans. Reginald Nettel (London, 1965): 65.

[75] It is of course, impossible to give exact prices, with variations between seasons and regions as well as between the specific types of goods. Some ideas might be gleaned from a committee report on prices, *The Journals of the House of Commons* 30 (1765-66): 787-788 (1st May 1766); Arthur Young, *Northern Tour* 4 vols. (London, 1770), 4: 440-472; J. D. Chambers, *Nottinghamshire in the Eighteenth Century*, 2d ed. (London, 1966).

[76] D. E. C. Eversley, "The Home Market and Economic Growth in England, 1750-1780," in *Land, Labour and Population in the Industrial Revolution*, ed., E. L. Jones and G. E. Mingay (London, 1967), 206-259.

wide income variation between those of the "middling sort." If the poorest general domestic
servant was earning £5 a year, the more fortunate of agricultural labourers might be paid well
over £12 per annum.[77] This, however, was exactly the annual wage agreed for Walter Gale, the
schoolteacher.[78] Many other men regarded as educated and socially superior to manual workmen,
such as curates, were also earning between £12 and £15 a year. By contrast, some of the most
successful of the petty bourgeoisie, including Dent, the shopkeeper of Kirkby Stephen, boasted
annual turnovers approaching £1,000.[79] More typically of the successful country tradesman,
Samuel Wightman, glover of Framlingham, Suffolk, was the owner of three small farms and a
pub by the time of his death. In Petworth, Sussex, some 30% of inventoried tradesmen left
goods and property valued between £100 and £500. With such variation apparent across a
multitude of professions and occupations within the middle-classes, it is not difficult to account
for the rising temperature of the debate over who could and did read the new literature. For
many social critics, concerned by the apparent irresponsibility of new wealth, the price of fiction
could not be exclusive enough. For many poorer members of the middling-ranks, booksellers'
price-tags must have put much new fiction out of reach. In the enlarging of an audience for
fiction, therefore, other developments in the booktrades were especially important : the
establishment of circulating libraries, the availability of cheap piracies, and the printing of a new
range of works slightly superior to the chapbook but much cheaper than the novels which they
imitated.

By 1770 at least twenty commercial circulating libraries were operating in London.[80] In Dublin
the Hoey family had sponsored circulating libraries since 1737, and the rival establishments of
Watts, Armitage and Williams were opened between 1754 and 1765.[81] In many English country
towns bookshops, such as those of Binns of Halifax and Leeds, long served as surrogates for
local lending libraries. For avid readers, subscriptions to such libraries were certainly a bargain,
although some smaller commercial libraries adopted the private library practice of levying an
additional charge on each book borrowed. Despite stern warnings against clients loaning library-
books to friends and family, it is likely that many more than the borrower benefitted from library
membership. The commercial circulating libraries were particularly effective in expanding the
audience for fiction, assisting those eager to find ways of quickly and cheaply obtaining the latest
fashionable book, reading it, and then passing on to the next. Again, however, these libraries

---

[77]   Cf Arthur Young's estimates, including seasonal variations, *Northern Tour*, 4: 451-454.

[78]   R. W. Blencowe, ed., "Extracts from the Journal of Walter Gale, Schoolmaster at Mayfield, 1750," *Sussex Archaeological Collections* 9 (1857): 182-207.

[79]   T. S. Willan, *An Eighteenth-century Shopkeeper. Abraham Dent of Kirkby Stephen* (Manchester, 1970).

[80]   Hilda Hamlyn, "Eighteenth-century Circulating Libraries in England," *The Library*, 5th ser., 1 (1947): 197-218; Devendra P. Varma, *The Evergreen Tree of Diabolical Knowledge* (Washington, 1972). Also, Paul Kaufman, "The Community Library : A Chapter in English Social History," *Transactions of the American Philosophical Society*, n.s., 57, pt.7 (1967).

[81]   Richard Cargill Cole, "Community Lending Libraries in Eighteenth-century Ireland," 44, no.2 (April 1974): 111-123.

were affordable by only the more substantial members of the propertied classes. In the 1750s London circulating libraries were charging subscribers from between 15s. and one guinea annually, and although this charge was reduced in the early 1760s, it was re-imposed by the end of the decade. In the mid-1750s Francis Noble was advertising his Otway's Head library at half-a-guinea a year or 3s. quarterly. In November 1766 there appeared an advertisement issued jointly by "The Reputable Circulating Libraries" of John and Francis Noble, William Bathoe, Thomas Lownds, T. Vernor and J. Chater, Thomas Jones, and William Cooke, announcing that the cost of borrowing was to be increased by 1s. for quarterly subscribers and by 1s.6d for annual subscribers, making the full subscriptions at all these libraries 4s. per quarter or 12s. per annum.[82] In Dublin James Williams's commercial library was charging 16s.3d annually, or 6d weekly.

In addition to the pre-Lackington second-hand market - for which evidence of ordinary transactions is extremely scarce - booksellers from Ireland, Scotland and even the Low Countries were supplying cheap copies of current fiction. By far the most important of these operations were based in Dublin. Many Irish reprints were half the price of the London originals. As the following catalogue shows, a novel selling in London for 5s. could be offered by Hoey or Chamberlaine for 2s.8½d bound or 2s.2d sewed. Cheaper paper was employed, while closer printing and sometimes hidden abridgment enabled two- or three-volume works to be issued in a single volume. A great question mark remains, however, over the circulation of Irish fiction in mainland Britain. Many editions were certainly intended for an Irish audience and the complaints of London booksellers about competition in their own Irish operations should not be ignored.[83] Nevertheless, by 1739 the mounting unease of the London booksellers about cheap Irish imports was publicly registered in an Act to prohibit imports of books from abroad. Nor does the Act appear to have been successful. Twenty years later, the leading booksellers of Cambridge and Oxford were still selling Irish imprints when they, like all country booksellers, received a warning letter sent on behalf of the London publishers. The only other novels priced under 2s. a volume were the occasional publications of leading booksellers including Cooper, Lownds and Dodsley, and clearly designed to appeal to the man or woman of modest means, perhaps even of the £12-15 range. Editions of Ford's *History of Montelion* are among many examples of these cheaper books given in the listings which follow.

To the constraints of purchasing-power were added increasingly specific social associations with different forms of publication. Literacy levels, which in England in 1750 may have been about

---

[82] One copy of the advertisement is to be found bound in the BL copy of the Nobles' *History of Mrs Drayton*, 1767.

[83] This has recently been re-emphasized by Cole, *Irish Booksellers*.

50% sign-literacy for labourers and servants and 40% for all women,[84] were one clear determinant of the audience for the ½d ballad or 1d chapbook, even though a large aural audience also existed for such works. Of the publications considered here, limitations in the ability to read must certainly have affected the market for various of the works listed in the miscellany sections and a very few of those styled "novels" and written in simple language and few pages. Booksellers and customers alike were also careful to discriminate between types of fiction according to their respectability - a status derived from their content, their bookseller-publisher, their style of printing, their place in the critical reviews and library stock-lists, and their price. Here, the content of the literature can reveal much about projected readerships. The shorter, cheaper tales, imitating the polite novel may not all have been intended for the leisured classes, but unlike the chapman's twenty-four-page black-letter histories, were fashionably packaged and at least aimed at a more socially specific audience. Various of these smaller productions told of the adventures of women servants and men of humble occupation. In a similar range were short tales such as the popular abridgments of *Robinson Crusoe*, the history of *Phillip Quarll*, and the cheap "Adventures of" books. By contrast, the more finely printed and usually octavo novels include obvious appeals to a young, female, and leisured audience. Domestic heroes and heroines condemn, praise or are surrounded by the very latest fashion products. Many epistolary novels lecture on the dangers of a new age of Luxury.

Having identified increasing market specialization, however, one clear danger also emerges from the search for the readers of fiction. The readership of novels was certainly not homogenous. The very variety of the listed publications which follow demonstrates the range of interests to which writers and booksellers appealed. The tinsel works on the borders of fiction and listed in the "miscellany" sections, were offered to very diverse groups. Political satires, accounts of Society scandals, fabulous travels, and smoking-room pornography, all had their own separate but not exlusive following. Certain works were indeed designed to appeal to overlapping interest groups. Such combinations, for example, included local readerships, clearly encouraged by writers setting fiction in familiar parts of the country, and by London publishers courting provincial readerships. By the end of this period, some local writers were publishing books in their own country town. London writers, however, were frequently baffled by the composition of their audience. "I never knew the Public's place of residence before," wrote Fanny Burney upon receiving a letter from

---

[84] Determining the ability to read and write is a complex historical question which cannot be addressed here. Discussion is led by R. S. Schofield, "The Measurement of Literacy in Pre-Industrial England," in Jack Goody, ed. *Literacy in Traditional Societies* (Cambridge, 1968), 311-325; David Cressy, *Literacy and the Social Order. Reading and Writing in Tudor and Stuart England* (Cambridge, 1980); Rab Houston, "The Literacy Myth? Illiteracy in Scotland 1630-1760," *Past and Present* no.96 (August 1982): 81-102; Lawrence Stone, "Literacy and Education in England 1640-1900," *Past and Present* no.42 (February 1969): 69-139. Further implications are given in J. Goody and I. Watt, "The Consequences of Literacy," in Goody, *Literacy*, 27-68; and Brian V. Street, *Literacy in Theory and Practice* (Cambridge, 1984).

an admirer a decade or so after this period.[85]

The only obvious way of identifying further characteristics of the diverse audience for imaginative literature is to ask how it differed from other readerships. Clearly the readership of fiction was largely not a library-owning but a library-going public. These were the ladies (and some gentlemen) pursued by the Nobles, by Hookham, by Lownds, and later by Lane. In terms of purchasing power, what was of importance for the booksellers and their marketing strategies was not only the levels but also the nature of the incomes of the new fiction readership. Appeals were made to those enjoying new disposable income, often suddenly acquired and directed to more than just spending on property or traditional goods. The clientele of the Nobles' bookshops and libraries was predominantly young and female, many of whom had gained by marriage or an allowance a modest personal income, certainly exceeding £20 a year but probably not £100. The cultural consequences of an expansion in the middling groups in English society (especially provincial society) has been explored in much recent writing.[86] There is no doubting the appeal made by booksellers to the youthful members of families of new if still modest means, or that such works were by, for and about this group. Fashion was the keynote. Richardson may or may not have been citing a genuine letter when he recorded a young lady from a country town complaining that "in this foolish town we are obliged to read every foolish book that fashion renders prevalent in conversation."[87] "The booksellers, those pimps of literature," mused one contributor to the *Critical*, "take care every winter to procure a sufficient quantity of tales, memoirs and romances for the entertainment of their customers, many of whom, not capable of distinguishing between good and bad, are mighty well satisfied with whatever is provided for them : as their female readers in particular have most voracious appetites, and are not over delicate in the choice of their food, every thing that is new will go down."[88]

Beneath such hostility is a basic recognition of the type of readers visiting the bookshops and circulating libraries. Even the periodical reviews, and especially the *Critical*, increased their reviewing of fiction in proportion, it must be assumed, to public interest. The many long review references given in the listings which follow demonstrate the seriousness with which certain fiction was taken. An increasing number of women did have the leisure, wealth, ability and

---

[85] Burney to Mrs Thrale, 20 August 1781, Berg MSS, New York Public Library, cit., Edward A. Bloom, ed. *Evelina* Oxford English Novels ed. (Oxford, 1970), xiv. "The Public and Transubstantiation," remarked Bob Southey in the next century, "I hold to be the two greatest mysteries in or out of nature," cit., A. S. Collins, *Authorship*, 270.

[86] Notably Peter Borsay, "The English Urban Renaissance : The Development of a Provincial Urban Culture c.1680-c.1760," *Social History*, ii (1977): 581-603; J. H. Plumb, "The Public, Literature and the Arts in the Eighteenth Century," in *The Triumph of Culture : Eighteenth-century Perspectives*, ed. Paul Fritz and David Williams (Toronto, 1972), 27-48; J. H. Plumb, "The Commercialization of Leisure in Eighteenth-century England," in *The Birth of a Consumer Society*, ed. Neil McKendrick, John Brewer and J. H. Plumb (London, 1982), 265-285.

[87] John Carroll, ed., *Selected Letters of Samuel Richardson* (Oxford, 1964), p.341.

[88] *Critical Review* 16 (December 1763): 449.

inclination to support the Nobles and their like. The "place of residence" which Fanny Burney had discovered was said by her anonymous correspondent to be Snow Hill, home in Burney's novel of the Branghtons and the Smiths, students of fashion and exemplars of the "mushroom breed." Pastor Wendeborn, who arrived in London in 1768, concluded that, "the romances of Richardson and Fielding and others, which were formerly in high repute, begin to be laid aside, as books which make the reader sleepy; and the rather, since almost every week new romances, in two or more little pocket volumes, are published in London, which are written with so much ease, and are so entertaining, because they compare so much with the manners and the fashions of the present age."[89]

Such developments might therefore be seen as part of a more consumer-orientated society. Literature, like other fashion and leisure wares, was taken up by entrepreneurs with a sharp eye to the market. Like many of the new manufactures of household goods and consumables, customer identification, metropolitan trend-setting and the exploitation of a country market determined the success of many products. To this extent, reading of second-rank literature, its social setting and its implied appeal to new groups in society, might reveal more about the constituency of the broader readership of the early novel.

The Booksellers

As is well-known, the eighteenth-century definition of a "bookseller" was much wider than in modern usage. "Bookseller" referred to one engaged in wholesale and copy-holding and/or retail aspects of the trade.[90] Many booksellers, both wholesalers and retail specialists, were leading agents in determining the kind of literature produced during this period, although paucity of evidence, not least of the full range of literary output and identification of the traders, has prevented much detailed investigation. Certainly, the imprints of the books in the listings which follow, even though the booksellers' details and addresses are exactly reproduced, demonstrate the difficulty in using the booksellers' own product alone to determine sales and distribution patterns. Some works "Printed and sold by" a bookseller seem clear enough, as do works "Printed by Mr. Smith for Mr. Brown." Smith is the contracted printer and Brown the bookseller and publisher. But Smith might also be a bookseller in his own right and Brown might not be the only individual venturing capital in the project. Far more ambiguous are the listings of groups of booksellers. The significance of the order in which the names appear has long been a

---

[89]   Fred. Aug. Wendeborn, *A View of England. Towards the Close of the Eighteenth Century* 2 vols. (Dublin, 1791), 2: 61.

[90]   Terminology is discusssed in Terry Belanger, "Publishers and Writers in Eighteenth-century England," in Rivers, *Books and their Readers*, 5-26 (8-9).

subject of debate.[91] The formation of a 'conger' or trade association and the ownership in the copy of the shares of a work is certainly suggested by many of the multiple-bookseller imprints. Such lists were lengthening during the protectionist 1750s and 1760s, as London booksellers tried to maintain control over copyright and distribution.[92] Far less clear are the looser associations suggested by the words "Sold also by..." especially where the bookseller is from a provincial town. Some sort of wholesaling and distributional arrangements are implied, but it is not always easy to determine the exact relationship between copy-holders, other booksellers, or retail agents.[93] The provision of capital for individual publications was also not exclusive to the bookseller or printer. It remained common, in the first instance at least, for the author to provide money for private printing. The bookseller was still operating as a vanity press for various ladies and gentlemen of leisure, as well as for a few individuals who sought a subscription edition.[94]

Whatever the technicalities of publication financing, however, the influence of the booksellers should certainly not be underestimated. Again, much of what has been written about the birth of a new consumerism in eighteenth-century Britain could be applied to the book business. As the *Monthly* wearily put it, "we seem to live in an age when retailers of every kind of ware aspire to be the original manufacturers, and particularly in literature."[95]

London was easily the dominant publishing centre. Recent attention has been given to the rapid mid-century growth in the provincial booktrade, but apart from their much-increased job-printing, provincial booksellers largely conducted retail sales of works from London. Locally-printed books were still very rare.[96] The only challenge to the supremacy of the London booksellers came from Dublin (and, for certain types of publication, from Edinburgh and Glasgow). Figures 2 and 3 give the output of leading fiction publishers and of all other fiction publishers in geographical groups, each as a percentage of the total number of booksellers so employed. Of the contributing booksellers of all novels issued in the 1750s, over three-quarters gave London addresses. Nearly a fifth were Dublin booksellers, and only 3% and 1% were, respectively, English provincial and Scottish booksellers. Of the contributing booksellers of the novels of the 1760s, just under two-thirds gave London addresses. Well over a quarter were Dublin booksellers, and some 2% provincial and Scottish booksellers.

---

[91] Cyprian Blagden, "Booksellers' Trade Sales 1718-1768," *The Library*, 5th ser., 5, no.4 (March 1951): 243-257; Terry Belanger, "Booksellers' Trade Sales 1718-1768," *The Library*, 5th ser., 30, no.4 (December 1975): 281-302; Terry Belanger, "Booksellers' Sales of Copyright : Aspects of the London Book Trades 1718-1768" (Ph.D diss., Columbia University, 1970).

[92] The fight to retain *de facto* perpetual copyright is considered in Gwyn Walters, "The Booksellers in 1759 and 1774 : The Battle for Literary Property," *The Library*, 5th ser., 29, no.3 (September 1974): 287-311.

[93] Of the books listed in this catalogue there are many examples of works advertised in other works as sold by particular booksellers but which do not include such specific references in the imprint. Robinson, for example, is listed specifically as a seller of the 1752 *Life of Howell ap David* in the 1754 *Scotch Marine* but is not so listed on the original title-page of the Osborne published *Howell*.

[94] Examples of this are given in William M. Sale, Jr., *Samuel Richardson. Master Printer* (Ithica, NY, 1950), ch.6.

[95] *Monthly Review*, 34 (June 1766): 480.

[96] See above, table 1.

Figure 2

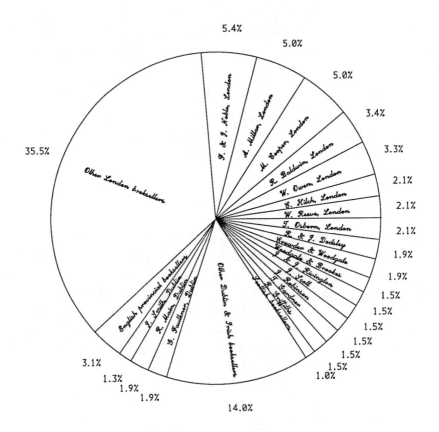

Booksellers of Novels 1750—1759

5.4%
5.0%
5.0%
3.4%
3.3%
2.1%
2.1%
2.1%
1.9%
1.9%
1.5%
1.5%
1.5%
1.5%
1.5%
1.0%

35.5%

J. & J. Nobles, London
A. Millar, London
M. Cooper, London
R. Baldwin, London
W. Owen, London
C. Hitch, London
W. Reeve, London
J. Osborn, London
R. & J. Dodsley
Crowder & Woodgate
Woodgate & Brookes
J. & J. Rivington
J. Scott
T. Lardison
R. Robinson
S. Griffiths
J. & R. Noble, London

Other London booksellers

English provincial booksellers
J. Leathley, Dublin
R. Main, Dublin
J. Faulkner, Dublin

Other Dublin & Irish booksellers

3.1%
1.3%
1.9%
1.9%
14.0%

Figure 3

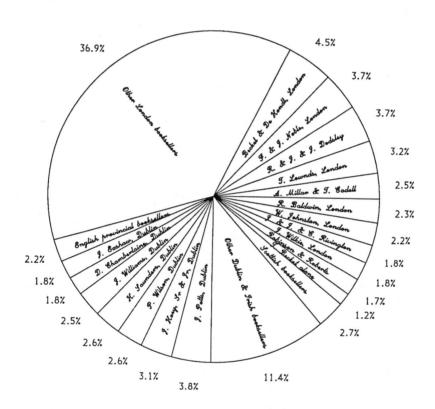

Booksellers of Novels 1760-1769

36.9% Other London booksellers

4.5% Becket & De Hondt, London
3.7% T. & J. Noble, London
3.7% R. & J. & J. Dodsley
3.2% T. Lowndes, London
2.5% A. Millar & T. Cadell
2.3% R. Baldwin, London
2.2% W. Johnston, London
1.8% J. & J. & C. Rivington
1.8% G. Wilkie, London
1.7% Robinson & Roberts
1.2% Becket alone
2.7% Scottish booksellers

11.4% Other Dublin & Irish booksellers

3.8%
3.1% J. Potter, Dublin
2.6% J. Hoey Jr & Jr, Dublin
2.6% P. Wilson, Dublin
2.5% H. Saunders, Dublin
1.8% J. Williams, Dublin
1.8% D. Chamberlaine, Dublin
2.2% J. Exshaw, Dublin
      English provincial booksellers

Three London traders each provided 5% or more of the total output of fiction during the 1750s. The Noble brothers, Francis and John, began trading in the late 1730s, establishing one of the earliest of the London circulating libraries as an adjunct to their publishing activities. Their catalogue of 1746 suggests an early interest in children's literature, while they also conducted a business in the sale of second-hand books. By 1750 however, they were notorious as the greatest "novel manufacturers" in the land. The engraving on Francis Noble's trade card is particularly illuminating, with a rare representation of the interior of a mid-century book shop. Always independent firms, the Nobles' partnership separated in 1752 with John Noble issuing a separate catalogue. It seems to have been an astute business strategy, Francis explaining his move as the result of "being greatly confined for want of room."[97] The brothers continued to collaborate with each other, Francis operating from Otway's Head, Covent Garden, Holborn, and John from Dryden's Head, St. Martin's Court, near Leicester Square. Within the decade Francis had moved again, to Middle-Row Holborn, an address which is variously described in the Nobles' imprints of the 1760s and may even reflect further changes in the location or size of the shop and library. For the devotee of fashionable novels in the mid-eighteenth century these addresses would have been the most famous in London. Much more the gentleman bookseller than the Nobles, was Andrew Millar (d. 1768). He had arrived in London from Edinburgh in 1728, opening a shop in the Strand near to that of Tonson. Millar, according to Johnson, "the Mæcenas of the Age," who had "raised the price of literature," was the publisher of Mrs Lennox and Fielding. He accumulated a fortune from reprintings of Thomson's *Seasons* and, to a lesser extent, from Fielding's novels. When he died in 1768 he was succeeded by Thomas Cadell, apprenticed in 1758 and his partner since 1765. The third major London fiction-seller of the 1750s was Mary Cooper. She was the widow of Thomas Cooper who between 1732 and his death some ten years later became one of the century's most prolific publishers of pamphlets and small miscellanies. Mary Cooper continued the business from the Globe in Ivy Lane, off Paternoster Row, until 1761. Many of her novels were produced in association with the Dodsleys, but as a woman continuing a family bookselling business, her situation was not as rare as might be imagined.

During the 1750s, Cooper, Millar and the Nobles together contributed nearly a sixth of the total fiction produced throughout the kingdoms. The contribution of the Nobles, in particular, has been underestimated, but other booksellers have also been neglected. Robert Baldwin of the Rose in Paternoster Row and William Owen of Homer's Head near Temple Bar contributed a major share of the total publications of these decades. Other major London publishers of fiction of the period are led by Hitch, trading in the Row 1733-64, Reeve of Fleet Street, trading only in the 1750s, Osborn, trading at Gray's Inn 1738-67, and the Dodsleys of Pall-Mall, 1735-64. In the 1760s the Nobles faced stiff competition from Becket and De Hondt and also from the far larger

---

[97]   *General Advertiser*, 14 June 1752.

establishments of the Dodsleys and Lownds, who both tripled their output of fiction from the previous decade, but for whom the publication of novels was only a small part of their undertakings. Thomas Becket had also been an apprentice of Millar. He opened his famous Tully's Head premises in the Strand in 1760 and within a year had taken as his partner Peter Abraham De Hondt. Their joint imprint is to be found on some of the most fashionable literature of the age. By the end of the 1760s the great majority of novels were issued by single firms, although many collaborative ventures also continued. For the entire period 1750-69, 69% of all fiction listed in this catalogue was published (according to the imprint) by one bookseller or bookselling firm. Nearly 20% of all works were published by two booksellers, although often the exact relationship is uncertain. Some 3% of all works were published by three firms, just over 2% by groups of between four and six firms, and 2% by the great congers of seven or more booksellers. The remaining 3% of all books give no bookseller in the imprint. Despite the various attempts to assess the significance of the imprint lists and changes in the order of the given booksellers, the relationships between and within the various associations put together during this period is still not clear. Whatever the shared arrangements for copyholding and printing expenses, final production of the book was often conducted independently. In many works produced by a combination of sellers the end-page advertisements were inserted by each firm.

The greatest number of works published outside London were those from the Dublin booksellers. In the 1750s, of all the Irish booksellers involved in the publication of fiction, three names are dominant, Faulkner, Main and Smith. In the 1760s, an even larger band, including Potts, the Hoeys, Wilson, Saunders, Williams, Chamberlaine and Exshaw, together comprised some 18% of all the contributing booksellers of fiction in Britain and Ireland.[98] Little is known of any of them. George Faulkner, trading at Essex Street between 1724 and 1775, was easily the most respected, becoming a land-owner and an alderman of the city. Robert Main enjoyed a brief but productive career in Dame Street in the first half of the decade, while John Smith's business on Blind Quay had been established since the late 1730s. James Hoey senior was taken into partnership by Faulkner in 1727. His son was later pre-eminent among the Dublin pirates. Here it should be added that the term 'pirate' must be used with caution. Certain of the Dublin booksellers did pay authors or London booksellers copyright fees. *Clarissa*, for example, was contracted to Faulkner for a fee of seventy guineas. Nevertheless, the opportunity to print outside legal restrictions operating in England and Wales was often too great a business temptation. "If I were a bookseller in this town," wrote Dean Swift, "I would use all safe means to reprint London books and run them into any Town in England that I could'.

---

[98] No account is taken here of either contributory but unlisted bookselling agents or of the obvious bias in such totals towards the bookselling congers. Figs. 2 & 3 should therefore be compared with table 1.

The other reprint centre for the period was Edinburgh. On a far smaller scale than in Dublin, Scottish booksellers including Donaldson, Reid, Kincaid and Martin and Wotherspoon, issued new or collected editions of recent fiction. Some operated in partnership with London firms, and Donaldson had actually moved to London by the end of this period, advertising shops in both capital cities. Richardson was one of several London booksellers who made arrangements with Kincaid or Hamilton and Balfour to try to prevent Irish piracies from being circulated in Edinburgh.[99] Of the other activities of the Scottish booksellers, however, the strategy of the London traders seems to have been to leave well alone. Although Scotland was technically subject to the book importation provisions of 1739, the only actions taken in the English courts do not appear to have been effective. North of the border, the booksellers were certainly left free to reprint and distribute their publications.[100] Although not as cheap as the Dublin reprints, certain Scottish products were much cheaper than the London originals. Some impressions were made on small type and coarse paper and aimed specifically at the lower end of the market.[101]

In all of this the economics of bookselling and of the sale of fiction in particular still requires considerable research.[102] It was from the ownership of copy that the great profits were to made and there is a major distinction to be drawn between the brash but probably fragile commercial operations of booksellers like the Nobles and Crowder and Woodgate, and the copyholding investments of wholesale-booksellers like Millar and Longman. Of the leading booksellers of 1750-69, Charles Dilly left £80,000 at his death and James Dodsley over £70,000 and a landed estate near Chislehurst.[103] James Ralph's 1758 *Case of Authors* told how booksellers aimed to buy as cheaply and sell as expensively as possible. Copyrights to books, bought outright from authors, changed hands by inheritance, by private sales (of which we know very little) and by the public auctions of the London trade sales. Before 1740 most copyrights sold for under £400, with the most valuable copyrights belonging to religious works and dictionaries. Verse, plays and fiction were at the very bottom of the rankings of copy value. A great number of the works listed in this catalogue would have been virtually worthless in the eyes of the most successful dealers in copyright, although certain novels did fetch respectable prices at auction. In 1753 half the copyright in *Roderick Random* sold for £64 (that is a total value of £128). In 1760 a sixth share in *Pamela* exchanged hands for £20. By comparison, in 1759 copy to Pope's *Works* was worth in total £3,500. The only copy of a novel to be appraised highly in this period seems to have been that of *Clarissa*, seven twenty-fourth shares in which sold in 1767 for £172 (that is, a

99   William Merritt Sale, Jr., *Samuel Richardson. A Bibliographical Record of his Literary Career with Historical Notes* (New Haven, 1936), 67.

100 Warren McDougall, "Gavin Hamilton, John Balfour and Patrick Neill : a Study of Publishing in Edinburgh in the Eighteenth Century" (Ph.D diss., Edinburgh University, 1974).

101 McDougall, "Gavin Hamilton," p.102, on Millar's *Gardener's Dictionary*.

102 A study of the economics of the eighteenth-century booktrade is in preparation.

103 Nichols, *Literary Anecdotes*, 6: 438-9; William Granger, *New Wonderful Museum* (London, 1804), 48.

total value of over £500).[104]

There are, however, some clear financial success stories even from the publication of fiction. William Taylor was alleged to have accumulated over £50,000 from the reprinting of Defoe's writings including his popular novels. Nichols claimed that Griffiths made more than £10,000 out of Cleland's *Memoirs*. Even if this is an exaggeration, half that sum would still have been a massive fortune from one work. Samuel Richardson rebuilt his printing establishment in 1755 from the profits of his trade.[105] The greatest returns clearly came from books for which the initial payment to the author was low but which sold out quickly in first printing and then achieved further best-selling editions. Here is another explanation for the promotion of translated works. For the bookseller one way out of paying the author was to borrow a work from abroad. No payment was deemed necessary - or often possible - for the original author, even if living. The translations of Chaigneau published by Johnston might well be one such success, while, as seen, many European authors enjoyed popularity in translation.

For the smaller or non-investor in valuable copy, the outlook was quite different. Even though the market and the potential for profits was expanding, there is little doubting the underlying infirmity of the trade. Hundreds of small firms, many of them part-time establishments, attempted to survive from the sale of books. Relatively few succeeded. In Dublin during Faulkner's lifetime, 264 printers and booksellers opened their shops and the majority of them failed.[106] The margin for commercial error was small and increasingly independent literary entrepreneurs had to boast varied skills in business management and production. Most could not escape burdensome overheads, with warehousing a particular problem. Heavy investment was required before acceptable returns were made and many works - even by such extrovert merchants as the Nobles - could take a decade to clear. Public subscription continued to insure against heavy losses on large, technically difficult or unusual undertakings, but in the pursuit of market-based profit, booksellers could not escape high-risk investment in fickle public taste. This last affected the production of novels more than any other single type of publication. Many publisher-booksellers had to diversify to survive. As already noted, many booksellers established their own circulating libraries. Meyer opened in May's Buildings in about 1750, Hookham was established by 1764, and Lownds had first opened a circulating library in Exchange Court in 1751, taking it with him when he moved to Fleet Street in 1756. All but the most successful London booksellers also supplemented the printed word with patent medicines, artists' materials, ticket-broking and a variety of consumer wares. Many bookshops exchanged old books for new, sold ink, vellum, paper hangings, household wares, musical instruments, lottery-tickets and served as clearing-

---

[104] Further details are given in Belanger, "Booksellers' Trade Sales 1718-1768."

[105] In 1750 Richardson had 40 employees in 3 offices, Sale, *Samuel Richardson*, 18-20.

[106] Ward, *Prince of Dublin Printers*, 8.

houses for local information and services.

One obvious consideration in the economics of publishing was the size and costing of the edition and the flexibility with which different sizes or numbers of editions could be produced for different markets. Increased output was usually the result of an increase in the number of editions rather than in their size. As discussed above, few editions of novels exceeded 1,000 copies.[107] Large editions were not only commercially dangerous but also technically difficult. Philip Gaskell has argued that at this period an edition of 1,500 was the most economical to produce.[108] Editions of 2,000 or more were contemplated only for the most feted of authors or works, and it is safe to assume that the great majority of titles in this catalogue were first issued in a conservative printing of 500-800 copies. It also has to be added that separate editions are not always easily distinguished from re-issues, with booksellers frequently mixing volumes of different editions and recovering, re-issuing or rearranging old works. The actual details of printing, and indeed even the identity of a contracted printer, are often unknown. Richardson's career has been well-documented, and the Strahan ledgers have been used extensively, but they cannot stand for all the fifty or so independent printers at work in London in 1750, many used by London booksellers and for whom all accounts are now lost. The Nobles used two printers for their novels during this period, W. Adlard of Fleet Street and W. Hoggard. They were often engaged at the same time. Little is known of either. Most of the booksellers listed here were of course their own printers. This is especially true of the Dublin publishers. Potts, Faulkner, Exshaw and Hoey all printed their own books, relying on contract printing only for special orders. In 1760 there were at least thirty-three printers at work in Dublin, and forty-six booksellers.

As noted, the price of the volumes does not vary greatly. The leading booksellers were anxious to avoid a price war, when certain cutting of costs would have been possible for the most successful of the London traders. The cost of different binding - almost always left to the customer's discretion - is noted in the catalogue entries. There was a far greater variation in the price for single volumes than for multi-volume works. This reflects both greater variation in the type of single-volume work and a greater tendency to offer single volumes unbound sewed or in various bindings. The offer of binding by the bookseller is much more common in this decade than in the 1730s or 1740s, even though in practice many booksellers still despatched customers'

---

[107] See above, page 14. 90% of the 514 books printed by Strahan 1738-1785 were in editions of less than 2,000. Strahan's full career is discussed in J. A. Cochrane, *Dr. Johnson's Printer. The Life of William Strahan* (Cambridge, MA, 1964). Also, Patricia Hernlund, "William Strahan's Ledgers : Standard Charges for Printing, 1738-1785," *Studies in Bibliography* 20 (1967): 89-111, and "William Strahan's Ledgers II : Charges for Papers, 1738-1785," *Studies in Bibliography* 22 (1969): 179-195.

[108] "It was almost impossible to get the real unit cost of a substantial book below 90% of the unit cost for an edition of 1,500 copies, however many were printed, and unless the interest charges were very small, the real unit cost began to rise again shortly after the edition quantity exceeded 2,000 copies," *New Introduction to Bibliography* (Oxford, 1974), 160-163.

orders to a separate binder or had a stock of works already bound by a contractor. This is particularly true of the multi-volume novels, where there was also a narrower price range. With production costs and pricing relatively inflexible, the key commercial consideration was the promotion of wares and the encouragement of new markets rather than competing, via cost-reduction, in existing ones.

There is one further caution to regarding this period as one of a new "commercialization" of literature. Technical originality can be claimed for very few of the developments in the promotion of fiction between 1750 and 1770. While the technology - with the notable exception of typography - remained much the same as during the first century of printing, many of the commercial techniques had also been tried before. What made the mid-eighteenth century so different was not only the devices used to create market interest, but the scale, efficiency and competitiveness of their application. It was, for example, important for the publisher of fiction to present his wares as up-to-the-minute. Many works were post-dated to seem new. The Nobles preferred not to date at all, leaving them free not only to produce works for each new season and sell them before it, but also able to provide a catalogue of "New Books" many of which had actually been available for many years. This does, of course, add considerably to the problems in dating works.[109] This provision of a back-list and an apparent stock of new books was clearly an important part of the Nobles' success. Of just one of their advertisements from the late 1760s, for example, nearly a dozen of the books listed as "lately printed for F. & J. Noble," can be found in the listings of this catalogue as printed by the firm before 1756.

The new emphasis on advertising was certainly obvious. Some novels actually carried puffs within the text. As is well known, many of the Newberys' tales included references to their benevolent publishers and other wares currently on offer. The Nobles were even earlier but just as enthusiastic in the use of this promotional device.[110] The title-page was also fair game for advertising. Many booksellers were anxious to alert the public to their opening of a circulating library or to their sale of other vital household or leisure products. *The Batchelor Keeper* of c.1750 contains a complete advertisement for the skills and products of T. Bailey in the lines following his name on the title-page. Tradesmens' bills can be printed at this address, he notes, and he also sells Maredant's Anti-scorbatic Drops, "Price Six Shillings the Bottle, which Cures the most inveterate Scurvy, Leprosy &c, &c." Addresses were usually precisely given, with full directions for the future use of the reader. According to the title-page, Lewis's 1759 *Adventures of a Rake* was printed for (amongst others) R. Withy, "at the Dunciad, the third door from the

---

[109] Reliance on Nobles' catalogues or end-page advertisements has often misled libraries. Thus the Bodleian still dates as 1760 a work (*Supposed Daughter*) actually printed in 1756. Certain works included in previous catalogues (eg *Unnatural Mother*, Orr, 15, and Margaret of Navarre's *Novels* formerly given as 1750) are omitted in this catalogue because of new dating evidence.

[110] Of many examples, the 1763 *Each Sex in Their Humour* assured readers at one point in the narrative (p.449) that "the excellency of Mr. Noble's novel-manufacture is already so well-known."

East End of the Royal Exchange in Cornhill." Numerous other examples of advertising can be found in the full catalogue. Inevitably, as gambling on the market-place replaced subscription methods, the identification and satisfaction of public taste became more important. As the periodical reviewers were quick to point out, this could easily lead to a debasement of literary values. In 1761 Oliver Goldsmith created his satirical commercial bookseller, Mr. Fudge, to consider the changes in the popular book trade. "Others may pretend to direct the vulgar," said Mr. Fudge, "but that is not my way : I always let the vulgar direct me : wherever popular clamour arises, I always echo the million."[111] Two hundred years later, the charge is not an unfamiliar one.

---

[111] *Citizen of the World*, letter li.

The listings of each year give an alphabetical arrangement of anonymous works followed by an alphabetical arrangement of works attributed to an author. Works published anonymously but with authorship later admitted or identified are classified under author (in square parenthesis). Obvious pseudonyms where no other authorship can be traced are not regarded as proper names. Where works are translations they are listed under the original author if known. An index of authors and translators and an index of titles are appended in order to identify the often more familiar English translators. Each index also allows the identification of works formerly or more familiarly attributed to alternative authors (or to no one).

Editions are given separate entries rather than placed within a sub-divided entry. This enables clear differentiation between authorized further editions and Dublin and other pirated copies. Earlier and further editions of the work are listed in the first entry of that work with cross-references to the listing in subsequent entries. Such cross-references are far more extensive than those in the indexes. Where publications survive, the names of the booksellers and their addresses are exactly reproduced, including the many variations by booksellers in the spelling of their own names. As in the original, imprint details are preceded by the town of publication, except where direct quotation is necessary, as for example, with "London, Printed : Dublin, Reprinted." Each entry is separately numbered. For ease of reference, consecutive numbering includes the miscellanies as well as the novels. Numbering alone, therefore, cannot be used as an indication of output totals.

Within the entries conflicts between reliable sources are noted. Where these provide suspicion of different editions or even works, and where supportive eighteenth-century evidence can be found, separate entry is given to each work. Where books have not been personally examined (entries without a "*" in the final line), imprint information may be incomplete and unreliable in detail.[1]

Booksellers' advertisements in both newspapers and end-page insertions have provided much evidence for the verification of editions, dating of works and general provenance. Contemporary reviews and advertisements have also been of major importance to the dating and often re-dating of works. Limitations of space restrict the inclusion of all source advertisements in the entries however. Some works have been found listed in over two dozen separately placed advertisements. Such sources are included in the catalogue only where there is conflict or the need for further verification of date, price, or even publication itself.

Date of publication is given as in the original, but roman numerals have been converted into arabic numerals. It should be noted that totals for calendar years, as given, do not correspond to

---

[1]   Where such works are noted as extant, future consultation of the full *E.S.T.C.* database may add to the imprint description.

the bookselling year or "season" which generally extended from November to June. Thus further editions issued in the next year may have been issued in the same season. Similarly, a series of works advertised by a bookseller as printed in the new season, might indeed have been so, even though separated into two calendar years by the following listings. In addition, dating on the imprint can often also be a post-dating. A book published in December (or even as early as October in some instances) may carry the date of the next calendar year. Nichols claimed that "the Rule in general observed among Printers is, that when a Book happens not to be ready for publication before November, the date of the ensuing year is used."[2] Where such an earlier publication date can be established - most notably by a review-notice (details of which will be included in the entry) but also by book and newspaper advertisements - then this catalogue deviates from the practice usually adopted and lists the book under its real year of publication rather than the imprinted one. In some cases this highlights early reviewing of a book dated for a new year some two or three months away. Equally, pre-dating was also practised by certain booksellers - most notably by some Dublin operators - to suggest that a work was a first or early edition of a work. If convincing evidence can be found, the correct rather than the earlier imprint date is given. In all cases where new dating evidence has been used, alternative dates given by earlier checklists are corrected or omitted. If this causes confusion for a reader searching for a work under the more familiar imprint date, the general index at the end of the catalogue should be consulted. Many date attributions made by libraries have been corrected and in some cases works have been moved by a dozen years or more.[3] Again, the index should locate a work apparently missing from the chronological listings.

Full bibliographical description is not given, but basic format and the number of numbered pages are listed as an indication of the size of the work. Multi-volumes bound "in one" or "in two" are regarded as separate volumes unless continuously paginated : binding alone does not provide evidence of the style of the work at issue.

All former checklists citing a work are noted in abbreviated form. Past checklists which cited source material are given with their own sources in parentheses. The abbreviation BL is used throughout, rather than retaining secondary source use of BM. Sources are listed in the alphabetical order of the abbreviations adopted. There are many unsupported card entries in the Greenough card index of fiction at Harvard for the years 1750 and 1760. The British Library and Bodleian also attribute many works to these years in order to provide a general indication of date. In a few cases, where no other evidence could be found, obviously generalized dating is retained. Many Greenough and other entries with general dating which have been proved

---

[2]   Nichols, *Literary Anecdotes*, 3: 249.

[3]   Of many examples, the more extreme include [Green] *Life of Mr. John Van*, 1757, not 1750; *The Bubbled Knights*, 1757, not 1775; *Friga Reveep*, 1770, not 1755; *Fatal Obedience*, 1769, not 1780; *Lydia Tongue-Pad and Juliana Clack-it*, 1750, not 1760, but also with 1768 reissue; *Two Young Gentlemen*, 1768, not 1780.

incorrect by other sources have been disregarded. "Unauthenticated" works - that is, non-specific titles listed in contemporary advertisements but without further supportive evidence of publication - may also appear within entries of an original or associated work. Full quotation of primary and secondary sources within each entry invites the user to judge an entry's validity for himself. The fullest contemporary reviews of the novels appeared in the *Monthly* and *Critical*, and references are given to all notices of works listed below - many in fact providing prime supportive evidence of publication. References to other periodicals, including the *Gentleman's Magazine*, the *General Magazine*, the *Scots Magazine* and the *Universal Magazine* are given where cited by secondary catalogues or where they are the only source for the existence of a work.[4]

The present location of works is given in the penultimate line to each entry, although if the exact edition is widely available, only major institutions are listed. For such works, *N.U.C.* will provide further references to libraries holding copies, as will *E.S.T.C.* when the full database extends to North American coverage. One extremely useful development of the past decade has been the commencement of the *Eighteenth-Century Microfilm* project. Some of the rarest of the works in the following listings may be consulted on film. Where this is possible (Jan. 1987) indication is given ("EC"), together with the reference number, in the listings of secondary sources within each entry. Such listings may also give a general indication of the type of work. "PBG", for example, indicates a work catalogued in Gove's list of travel tales. The abbreviations used are given below. The exact entry format is shown overleaf. In a few entries, constraints of space have forced some slight modification to this ordering.

---

[4]   The only existing guide to the review-notices of novels is for a later period, William S. Ward, *Literary Reviews in British Periodicals 1789-1797 : A Bibliography* (New York and London, 1979). For the *Monthly Review* , contributors and main articles but *not* reviews in the "Monthly Catalogues" are indexed in Benjamin Christie Nangle, *The Monthly Review First Series 1749-1789* (Oxford, 1934) and *The Monthly Review Second Series 1790-1815* (Oxford, 1955).

Entry Format

Where possible each entry is as follows :

Catalogue number

AUTHOR (and/or translator) as given in title-page [and in parenthesis if attributed].

    TITLE as given on title-page or as by the most reliable source available, with uppercase lettering for short-title [For very long titles, number of lines omitted given in parentheses].

    Indication, "+" if it is not the first edition.

    Place of publication : publisher, address and date of publication as given in title page. If by other sources, details are provided in parentheses with references.

    Number of pages or volumes. Basic format information where available, and sources where there is conflict. Price as given (usually according to advertised binding) on title-page or by contemporary advertisements or late-eighteenth-century sources. Indication, "Subn" if a subscription edition.

References to reviews of the work in the *Critical* and *Monthly.*

Secondary catalogues, checklists and other sources identifying the work (abbreviations listed below).

Additional information including origins of translations, former authorship attributions etc.

Former and/or subsequent editions and cross-references within this catalogue.

Present location of extant copies (major libraries only if widely-held work; abbreviations given below).

Indication, "*" of whether work has been examined, and general category of work (abbreviations given below).

Abbreviations

The following abbreviations are used for contemporary and secondary published and unpublished sources, contemporary reviews, collections, and locations of extant copies of work :

AAS   American Antiquarian Society, Worcester, Massachusetts

AB   Andrew Block, comp., *The English Novel 1740-1850, A Catalogue Including Prose Romances, Short Stories and Translations of Foreign Fiction* (London, 1939)
Key to selected sources (other than those listed independently in this table) used in the 2d ed. (1961) of Block and cited by kind permission of the publishers, Wlm Dawson and Sons Ltd (abbreviations given in parenthesis after AB) :

AR	Arthur Rogers (bookseller)
As	Ashley Library
B&G	Birrell and Garnet (booksellers)
BH	B. Halliday (booksellers)
BHB	Borrow Head Bookshop
Bk	Blackwell (booksellers)
BsB	Baker's Bookshop
ByB	Bailey Bros (booksellers)
CB	Court Bookshop
CHL	A. W. Ward and A. R. Walter, eds., *The Cambridge History of English Literature* 15 vols. (Cambridge, 1907-16)
CLP	Catalogus Librorum Prohibitorum
Cw	Crowe (bookseller)
Do	Dobell (bookseller)
ELG	M. B. Price and L. M. Price, *The Publication of English Literature in Germany in the Eighteenth Century* (Berkeley, 1934)
EM	Elkin Mathews (booksellers)
FE	Francis Edwards (booksellers)
G	Gratton (booksellers)
GBF	Ernest A. Baker and James Packman, comps., *A Guide to the Best Fiction* 2d ed. (London, 1913) [post-Block, a new ed., 1967]
GW	G. Worthington
HC	H. B. Copinger (bookseller)
HN	Dr. Hubert J. Norman
Ht	The Huth Collection
HW	H. B. Wheatley
IW	Iolo Williams
JH	Dr. J. C. Hardy
JM	James Miles (bookseller)
L	Lownds
LW	Lyle H. Wright (Librarian)
McL	McLeish (booksellers)
McM	MacManus (bookseller)
Mg	Maggs (booksellers)
MH	Murray Hill (bookseller)
Mk	Marks (booksellers)
MPC	Minerva Press Catalogue
My	Myers (bookseller)
pa	"Publisher's Advertisement"
Pi	Pickering (booksellers)
Pk	Parker and Sons
RI	Roger Ingpen (bookseller)
RK	Raphael King (bookseller)
Rn	Robson (booksellers)
SA	S. Austin Allibone, comp., *A Critical Dictionary of English Literature, and British and American Authors, Living and Deceased* 3 vols. (Philadelphia

	and London, 1859) and
	John Foster Kirk, comp., *A Supplement to Allibone's Critical Dictionary of English Literature* 2 vols. (Philadelphia and London, 1891)
SH	Stephen Hunt (bookseller)
So	Sotheby's Auctioneers
St	Stonehill (booksellers)
Sx	Sexton (booksellers)
T	Tregaskis (booksellers)
TW	T. D. Webster (bookseller)
Ts	*The Times*
TT	T. Thorp (booksellers)
WB	W. Brown (bookseller)
WC	William Cross
Wo	Woore
WS	William Smith (booksellers)
WTS	W. T. Spencer (booksellers)

Adv-	Advertisements appearing in other works. Host works given by catalogue entry-numbers
ATH	A. T. Hazen, comp., *A Bibliography of Horace Walpole* (New Haven, 1948)
AUC	*Eighteenth Century British Books. An Author Union Catalogue extracted from the British Museum General Catalogue of Printed Books, of the Bodleian Library and of the University Library Cambridge*, ed. F. J. G. Robinson, G. Averley, D. R. Esslemont, and P. J. Wallis (PHIBB, 1981)
BB	Robert Watt, comp., *Bibliotheca Britannica; or A General Index to British and Foreign Literature* 4 vols. (Edinburgh and London, 1824)
BCat	Bookseller's catalogue
BL	British Library
BMC	Bryn Mawr College, Pennsylvania
Bn	Boston Public Library
Bod	Bodleian Library, Oxford
BU	Brown University and John Carter Brown Library, Rhode Island
CBEL	F. W. Bateson, ed. and comp., *Cambridge Bibliography of English Literature* vol. 2, *1660-1800*, 4th ed. (Cambridge, 1969)
CG	From the card index of Chester Noyes Greenough held at the Houghton Library, Harvard University
CNY	Columbia University, New York
CR	*Critical Review; or Annals of Literature*, 1st ser., 70 vols. (London, 1756-90)
CUL	Cambridge University Library
CUNY	Cornell University, Ithica, New York
DB	Dorothy Blakey, *The Minerva Press 1790-1820* (London, 1939)
DF	David Foxon, *Libertine Literature in England 1660-1745* (London, 1964)
DHE	Dorothy Hughes Eshleman, *Elizabeth Griffith. A Biographical and Critical Study* (Philadelphia, 1949)
DU	Duke University, Durham, North Carolina
DWW	Janet Todd, ed. and comp., *A Dictionary of British and American Women Writers 1660-1800* (Totowa, NJ, 1985)
EC	*The Eighteenth Century. Microfilm Collection*, Research Publications (Woodbridge CT & Reading, 1984-)
EdM	*Edinburgh Magazine and Review* 5 vols. (Edinburgh [1773]-1776)
EK	Samuel Richardson, *Pamela*, ed. T. C. Duncan Eaves and Ben D. Kimpel (Boston, 1971)
EP	Edward W. Pitcher, "Robert Mayo's "The English Novel in the Magazines 1740-1815" : New Facts," *The Library*, 5th ser., 31, no. 1 (March 1976): 20-30, & 6th ser., 2, no.3 (September 1980): 326-332
ESTC	*The Eighteenth-Century Short-Title Catalogue*, 1st microfiche ed. (London, 1983)
FB	Frank Gees Black, *The Epistolary Novel in the Late Eighteenth Century : A Descriptive and Bibliographical Study*, (Oregon, 1940)

FL	Folger Shakespeare Library, Washington
GM	*Gentlemen's Magazine; or, Monthly Intelligencer* [2d ser.] (Jan 1736-Dec 1807)
GS	Godfrey Frank Singer, *The Epistolary Novel : Its Origin, Development, Decline and the Residuary Influence* (Philadelphia, 1933)
HCH	Henry Clinton Hutchins, *Robinson Crusoe and Its Printing, 1719-1731* (New York, 1925)
HCL	Harvard College Library (access, Houghton)
HkCat	Catalogue of Thomas Hookham's Circulating Library (1794, Bodleian copy)
H&L	Samuel Halkett and John Laing, comps., *Dictionary of Anonymous and Pseudonymous English Literature*, ed. James Kennedy, W. A. Smith and A. F. Johnson 7 vols. (Edinburgh, 1926)
HL	Huntington Library, San Marino, California
HU	Harvard University : the Widener Library and Houghton Library
IU	Indiana University, Bloomington
JB	Jerry C. Beasley, comp., *A Check List of Prose Fiction Printed in England 1740-1749* (Charlottesville, 1972)
JDR(1791)	Jeremias David Reuss, comp., *Das Gelehrte England Oder Lexikon Der Jeztlebenden Schriftsteller In Grosbritannien, Irland und Nord-Amerika Nebst Einem Verzeichnis Ihrer Schriften. Vom Jahr 1770 bis 1790* (Berlin and Stettin, 1791)
JDRsc	Jeremias David Reuss, as above, *Nachtrag und Fortsezung vom Jahr 1790 bis 1803* [Supplement and Continuation from the year 1790 to 1803] (Berlin and Stettin, 1804)
JkB	Jakob Brauchli, *Der Englische Schauerroman um 1800 unter Berücksichtigung der unbekannten Bucher. Ein Beitrag zur Volksliteratur* (1928)
JM	John Robert Moore, comp., *A Checklist of the Writings of Daniel Defoe* 2d ed. (Hamden, CT, 1971)
JS	Joseph Sabin et al, comps., *A Dictionary of Books Relating to America* 29 vols. (New York, 1868-1936)
JT	Joyce Marjorie Sanxter Tompkins, *The Popular Novel in England 1770-1800* (London, 1932)
KM	Kenneth Monkman, "The Bibliography of the Early Editions of Tristram Shandy," *The Library*, 5th ser., 25, no. 1 (March 1970): 11-39
KO	Kent State University, Ohio
LC	Library of Congress, Washington
LCP	Library Company of Philadelphia
LMK	Lewis M. Knapp, *Tobias Smollett* (New York, 1963)
LO	Leonard Orr, comp., *A Catalogue Checklist of English Prose Fiction 1750-1800* (New York, 1979)
LU	Louisiana State University, Baton Rouge
LWL	Lewis Walpole Library, Farmington, Connecticut
McB	William Harlin McBurney, comp., *English Prose Fiction 1700-1800 in the University of Illinois Library* (Urbana, Illinois, 1965)
MLN	*Modern Language Notes*
MR	*Monthly Review*, 1st ser., 81 vols. (London [1749]-1789) and 2d ser., 108 vols. (London, 1790-1825)
MW	Mary Wagoner, comp., *Tobias Smollett. A Checklist of Editions of his Works and an Annotated Secondary Bibliography* (New York, 1984)
NCBEL	G. Watson, ed. and comp., *The New Cambridge Bibliography of English Literature*, vol. 2, *1660-1800* (Cambridge, 1971)
newSG	The updated copy of the Sidney Gecker catalogue held at the Van Pelt Library, Philadelphia
NLC	Newberry Library, Chicago
NLI	National Library of Ireland, Dublin
NUC	*National Union Catalog*
NYPL	New York Public Library
NYSL	New York Society Library
NYSL(HC)	The Catalogue of the Hammond Circulating Library, New York Society Library.

OU	Ohio State University, Columbus
PBG	Philip Babcock Gove, *The Imaginary Voyage in Prose Fiction. A History of its Criticism and a Guide for its Study, with an Annotated Check List of 215 Imaginary Voyages from 1700 to 1800* (New York, 1941)
PMLA	*Papers of the Modern Language Association*
PU	Princeton University
RCC	Richard Cargill Cole, *Irish Booksellers and English Writers 1740-1800* (Atlantic Highlands, NJ, 1986)
RFP	Rosenbach Foundation, Philadelphia (Free Library of Philadelphia)
RKM	Richard K. Meeker, comp., "Bank Note, Corkscrew, Flea and Sedan : A Checklist of Eighteenth-Century Fiction," *The Library Chronicle*, 35, no. 1-2 (1969): 52-57
RL	Baron N. M. V. Rothschild, *The Rothschild Library : A Catalogue of the Collection of Eighteenth-Century Printed Books and Manuscripts formed by Lord Rothschild* 2 vols (Cambridge, 1954)
RM	Robert D. Mayo, *The English Novel in the Magazines 1740-1815 with a Catalogue of 1375 Magazine Novels and novelettes* (London, 1962)
RS	Ralph Straus, *Robert Dodsley. Poet, Publisher and Playwright* (London, 1910)
RU	Rutgers University, New Jersey
ScM	*Scots Magazine* 65 vols. (Edinburgh, 1739-1803)
SG	Sidney Gecker, comp., *English Fiction to 1820 in the University of Pennsylvania Library* (Philadelphia, 1954)
SI	Southern Illinois University, Edwardsville
SU	Syracuse University, Syracuse, New York
SW	Lewis Mansfield Knapp, "Smollett's Works as Printed by William Strahan, with an unpublished letter of Smollett to Strahan," *The Library*, 4th ser., 13 (1933): 282-291
T&C	*Town and Country Magazine; or, Universal Repository of Knowledge, Instruction and Entertainment for 1769* (-1791) 24 vols. (London, 1769-92)
TCD	Trinity College, Dublin
TCU	Texas Christian University, Fort Worth
TLS	*Times Literary Supplement*
TS	Temple Scott, *Oliver Goldsmith Bibliographically and Biographically Considered* (New York, 1928)
Tx	University of Austin, Texas
UC	University of Chicago, Chicago
UCB	University of California, Berkeley
UCLA	University of California, Los Angeles
UCo	University of Colorado, Boulder
UF	University of Florida, Gainesville
UG	University of Georgia, Athens
UI	University of Illinois, Urbana
UIC	University of Iowa, Iowa City
ULPA	Union Library Catalogue of Pennsylvania, Michigan
UM	University of Michigan, Ann Arbor, and William L. Clements Library
UMin	University of Minnesota, Minneapolis
UMo	University of Missouri, Columbia
UMR	*Universal Magazine of Knowledge and Pleasure* 113 vols (London, 1747-1803)
UNC	University of North Carolina, Chapel Hill
UNH	University of New Hampshire, Durham
UO	University of Oregon, Eugene
UP	Van Pelt Library, University of Pennsylvania. Eighteenth-century English fictional holdings are based on the collections of Godfrey F. Singer and John C. Mendenhall
UV	University of Virginia, Charlottesville
UW	University of Wisconsin, Madison
VU	Virginia State University, Richmond
WCL	William Andrews Clark Memorial Library, Los Angeles
WLC	Wilbur L. Cross, *The History of Henry Fielding* 3 vols. (New Haven, 1918)
WLCS	Wilbur L. Cross, *The Life and Times of Laurence Sterne*, 3d ed. (New Haven,

	1929)
WMcB	William Harlin McBurney, comp., *A Check List of English Prose Fiction 1700-1739* (Harvard, 1960)
WS	William Merritt Sale, Jr., *Samuel Richardson. A Bibliographical Record of his Literary Career with Historical Notes* (New Haven, 1936)
YU	Yale University : The Stirling Memorial Library and the Beinecke Rare Book and Manuscript Library

Key to Other Abbreviations and Symbols

+	not the first edition
[]	enclosing the name of author, translator or date not given on title-page (references provided)
(-)	no source cited by secondary source
edn	edition
imperf	incomplete or damaged copy
n	source notes work, but few or no details provided
nd	no date given on title-page (of any volume)
rev	review notice
sat	specific satire
Subn	work published by subscription
tp	title-page
trans	translator
trans	translation of

Examination of Work and Category

*	work has been examined personally
(*)	to verify category, work has been examined in a different edition to that cited
C	collection of tales or short novels
E	epistolary novel
M	miscellaneous work - including imaginative biographies and accounts of causes-célèbres
N	novel (narrative rather than epistolary)

Acknowledgments

Personal examination of works has been essential to this project : I am indebted to the English-Speaking Union of New Brunswick, New Jersey, to the Master and Fellows of Clare College, Cambridge, and to the Social Science Research Council for travelling scholarships which enabled three separate visits to collections in the United States. My fellowship at Pembroke College allowed the final compilation of the book. I have been helped greatly by the rare books' librarians of the universities of Yale, Harvard, Columbia and Pennsylvania, the Lewis Walpole Library, Connecticut, the New York Public Library, the New York Society Library, the British Library, the Bodleian and Cambridge University Library. Leonard Raven generously assisted in cross-referencing the editions. Mary Alcock sacrificed much of her valuable time to recheck works at Yale. Beth Durkee tracked down a particularly elusive work at Rutgers. For their encouragement and advice I am most grateful to Jerry Beasley, Delaware; Michael Harris, London; and Neil McKendrick, Cambridge. Without the Cambridge University Computing Service and patient guidance from Martin Cassell, Jinny Crum-Jones and Maggie Carr, this catalogue could not have been compiled in its present form. Graphics for the pie-charts were made especially user-friendly by Ian Jones.

1.
THE ADVENTURES OF MR. LOVEILL, Interspers'd with many Real Amours of the Modern Polite World.
London : Printed for M. Cooper, at the Globe in Pater-noster Row. 1750.
2 vols. 12mo. 6s (BB,MR).
MR III 58 (May 1750).
AB(AR,WB); BB; EC 365:4; ESTC t068056 [once attributed to Mary Lloyd]; LO 1 (UI,UP); McB 6; SG 12.
BL UI UP
* N

2.
+THE ADVENTURES OF MR. LOVEILL, Interspers'd with many Real Amours of the Modern Polite World. The Second Edition.
London : Printed for M. Cooper, at the Globe in Pater-noster Row. 1750.
2 vols. 12mo.
ESTC t067635; SG 13.
BL CUL UP
* N

3.
THE BATCHELOR KEEPER : OR, THE EFFECTS OF A FRIEND.
London : Printed by T. Bailey, at the Ship and Crown, Leadenhall-street; where Tradesmen's Bills are Printed at the Letter-press, and off Copper-plates. Also may be had Maredant's Anti-scorbatic Drops, Price Six Shillings the Bottle, which Cures the most inveterate Scurvy, Leprosy &c. &c. [1750] (BL).
32pp. 8vo.
AB(BL); ESTC t077671.
BL
* N

4.
+CYNTHIA; With the Tragical Account of the Unfortunate Loves of Almerin and Desdemona : Being a Novel. Illustrated with Variety of the Chances of Fortune; Moraliz'd with many useful Observations, drawn from thence, whereby the Reader may reap both Pleasure and Profit. Done by an English Hand. The Tenth Edition, Corrected.
London : Printed for R. Ware, at the Sun and Bible on Ludgate-Hill; C. Hitch, at the Red-Lion in Paternoster-Row, and J. Hodges, at the Looking-Glass on London Bridge [1750?] (BL).
154pp. 8vo.
ESTC t068060.
1st edn, 1687. Also, 1709, 1715, 1722, 1726, 1730(2x), 1760 [530], 1785, 1797, 1798.
BL
* N/M

5.
THE FEMALE FOUNDLING; OR, VIRTUE, TRUTH, AND SPIRIT, OPPOSING EVERY DIFFICULTY. Shewing, The happy Success of constant Love, In The true and entertaining Life of Mademoiselle D——. Translated from the French. In Two Volumes.
London : Printed for T. Waller, at the Mitre and Crown, opposite Fetter-lane, Fleet-street. 1751 [1750].
2 vols. 12mo. 5s sewed on blue paper (MR).
MR IV 156 (Dec. 1750).
AB(Bk,BL,Pi); BB; ESTC t108462; LO 22 (UI); McB 264.
BL UI
* N

6.

THE FEMALE SOLDIER; OR, THE SURPRISING LIFE AND ADVENTURES OF HANNAH SNELL, Born in the City of Worcester
[25 more lines]
London : Printed for, and Sold by R. Walker, the Corner of Elliot's Court, in the Little Old-Bailey. 1750.
42pp. 8vo. 1s (tp).
AB(BL,WB); LO 4 (UI); McB 265.
BL CUL UI
* N/M

7.

(+)THE FORTUNATE TRANSPORT; OR, THE SECRET HISTORY OF THE LIVES AND ADVENTURES OF POLLY HAYCOCK, Alias Mrs B— the Lady of the Gold Watch. By a Creole. In Two Parts.
London : Printed for T. Taylor, near the Corner of Friday-Street, Cheapside [1750?] (BL).
2 parts. 44pp & 45pp. 8vo. 1s (tp).
AB(BL); ESTC pt.1 t065359 & pt.1 variant, t065360, & pt.2 t065361.
1st part, 1st published 1748 - JB 239 (NL).
BL
* N/M

8.

THE HISTORY OF ABDALLAH AND ZORAIDE : OR FILIAL AND PATERNAL LOVE.
[29 more lines]
To which is added, The Maiden Tower, Or a Description of an Eastern Cave. Together with Contentment, a Fable.
London : Printed for J. Miller, No.74, Rosemary-Lane [1750?] (BL).
31pp. 8vo.
EC 59:4; ESTC t077763 [now given as '1780?'].
BL
* N/M

9.

THE HISTORY OF CHARLOTTE SUMMERS, THE FORTUNATE PARISH GIRL. In Two Volumes.
London : Printed for the Author; Sold by Corbett, the Publisher, at Addison's Head, opposite St. Dunstan's Church, in Fleet-Street [1750] (BL). Bod as [1749].
2 vols. 12mo. 6s bound (MR).
MR II 352 (Feb. 1750).
BB; EC 231:5; ESTC t066897.
BL Bod
* N

10.

+THE HISTORY OF TOM JONES THE FOUNDLING, IN HIS MARRIED STATE.
London : Printed for J. Robinson, at the Golden Lion in Ludgate-Street. 1750.
323pp. 12mo.
ESTC t116310.
Anon. continuation of Fielding's novel.
1st edn, Dublin, 1749. Also, 1750 [11] and 1786.
BL CUL
* N

11.
+THE HISTORY OF TOM JONES THE FOUNDLING, IN HIS MARRIED STATE. The
Second Edition Corrected, with an additional Chapter, communicated to the Author by Mr.
Allworthy &c. concerning Plays, and the French Strollers in Particular.
London : Printed for J. Robinson, at the Golden Lion in Ludgate-Street. 1750.
323pp. 12mo.
ESTC t126476; McB 461.
1st edn, 1750 [10].
BL CUL UI
* N

12.
A LOVE TALE, FOR THE USE OF THE FAIR SEX. Exemplified in the History, of
Charlotte Marton.
London : 'Bailey, Printer (No, 110,) Leadenhall Street' [1750] (BL).
31pp. 12mo.
EC 198:9; ESTC t066380.
BL
* N/M

13.
MEMOIRS OF LYDIA TONGUE-PAD, AND JULIANA CLACK-IT.
London : Printed for M. Thrush, in Salisbury-Court, Fleet-Street [1750?] (BL,UP).
272pp. 12mo. 2s6d (BB).
AB(BL); ESTC t070097 (altering BL attrib. to ?1760); LO 11 (UP); SG 723.
Cf 1768 [1188].
BL UP
* N

14.
MEMOIRS OF THE LIFE OF MRS A–A W–T.
[21 more lines]
London : Printed and Sold by W. Reeve, in Fleet-Street; and A. Dodd, opposite St. Clement's
Church, in the Strand. 1750.
51pp. 4to. 1s (tp).
ESTC t114903.
BL CUL
* N/M

15.
THE NOMINAL HUSBAND : OR, DISTRESS'D INNOCENCE. A True Secret History,
Taken From an Old Saxon Manuscript, Found among the Papers of a late Noble
Antiquarian, Modernised For the Service of the Youth of both Sexes.
London : Printed for W. Owen, at Homer's Head, near Temple-Bar; and G. Woodfall, at the
King's Arms, Charing-Cross. 1750.
120pp. 12mo.
AB(BL); ESTC t073235; newSG.
2nd edn, 1751 [74].
BL UP
* N

16.
REVIVED FUGITIVE. A Novel. Translated from the French.
Liverpool : Printed and sold by J. Sadleir. 1750.
70pp. 12mo.
Bod
* N

17.
THE TRUE HISTORY OF HENRIETTA DE BELLGRAVE, A Woman born to great
calamities, a distressed virgin, unhappy wife, and most afflicted mother
[17 more lines]
London : Printed and Sold at Bailey's Printing Office, in Leadenhall Street [1750?] (BL).
81pp. 8vo.
AB(BL); EC 206:5; ESTC t066918.
Reprinted in 1800.
BL
* N/M

18.
CAMUS Jean Pierre
[CROUCH Nathaniel *trans.*]
THE TRIUMPHS OF LOVE. Containing The Surprizing Adventures, and Accidents and
Misfortunes, that many Persons have Encountered in The Eager Pursuit of their Amorous
Inclinations. In Fifteen Pleasant Relations or Histories
[3 more lines & 15 titles]
Written Originally in French by P. Camus one of the Prime Wits of that Nation.
Translated by R. B. Gent.
Glasgow : Printed for John Hall in the middle of Salt-mercat. 1750.
134pp. 12mo.
AB(RI); McB 123.
'R. B. Gent', for Richard or Robert Burton, the pseudonym of Nathaniel Crouch.
BL has a 1784 edn.
UI
N/C

19.
[CLELAND John]
(+)MEMOIRS OF FANNY HILL.
London : Printed for R. Griffiths, in St. Paul's Church-Yard [1750] (BL).
272pp. 12mo. 2s6d (BB) 3s calf bound (MR).
MR II 431-432 (Mar. 1750).
BB; ESTC t014882.
An abridgment by Cleland of his 1749 *Memoirs of a Woman of Pleasure* (JB 246). Under title of 'F****
H***', also, 1779, 1784. As 'Memoirs of a [Woman] of [Pleasure]', 1755 [305] [306], 1766 [1000], 1784. Early
publication history of 'Fanny Hill' discussed in DF.
BL HU
* N/E

20.
[DEFOE Daniel]
+THE FORTUNES AND MISFORTUNES OF THE FAMOUS MOLL FLANDERS, &C.
[8 more lines]
Written from her own Memorandums.
London : [1750?] (YU).
Publishers included the Nobles, adv-1757 [393].
276pp. 3s (adv-1757 [393]).
1st edns 1722 (7x, JM 446, WMcB 128-128f). Also, 1722, 1737, 1741(JB 52), 176- [567], 1799, 1761 [645],
1765 [908], 1776 [as *Lætitia Atkins*], 1780, 1790, and abridgment, 1759 [481]. Also, 24pp chapbook versions.
YU
N

21.
[DEFOE Daniel]
+ROXANA; OR, THE FORTUNATE MISTRESS. Being a History of the Life and vast Variety of Fortunes of Mademoiselle de Beleau. The Second Edition, revised and corrected.
London : Printed for J. Hodges, H. Slater, F. Noble, J. Rowlands. 1750.
347pp. 12mo. 3s (adv-1757 [393]).
1st edn, 1724 (JM 456, WMcB 155). Also, 1740 (JB 18), 1742 (JB 18a), 1745 (JB 18b), 1755 [310], 1756 [370], and abridgments, 1765 [907], 1775.
Bn RFP
N

22.
[DEFOE Daniel]
(+)THE TRAVELS OF ROBINSON CRUSOE ROUND THREE PARTS OF THE GLOBE. Written by Himself.
London : Printed for M. Cooper [c.1750] (Bn).
364pp.
Edns of Crusoe listed, 1752 [129].
Bn WCL
N

23.
[FARGAN M. A.]
KANOR, A TALE. Translated from the Savage.
London : Printed for R. Griffiths, at the Dunciad in St. Paul's Church-Yard. 1750.
151pp. 12mo.
MR III 52-53 (May 1750).
AB(Bk,BL); EC 62:3; ESTC t057344; LO 8 (UP); SG 554.
BL UP
* N/M

24.
FIELDING Henry
+THE HISTORY OF TOM JONES, A FOUNDLING. In Four Volumes. By Henry Fielding, Esq.
London : Printed for A. Millar, over-against Catherine-street in the Strand. 1750.
4 vols. 12mo.
McB 293.
1st advertised, Dec. 9-12, 1749, WLC ii 123. 1,000 copies, Strahan Ledger.
1st edns, 1749 (4x, JB 272-272c). Also, 1750 [25], 1759 [486] [487], 1763-5 [774], 1765 [914], 1766 [1005], 1767 [1095] [1096], 1768 [1210], 1771, 1773, 1774, 1775(2x), 1778, 1780(3x), 1781, 1782(2x), 1783, 1787, 1789, 1791, 1792(2x), 1794, 1795, 1797.
CUL UI
* N

25.
FIELDING Henry
+THE HISTORY OF TOM JONES, A FOUNDLING. In Three Volumes. By Henry Fielding, Esq.
Dublin : Printed for John Smith, at the Philosophers Heads on the Blind-Quay. 1750.
3 vols. 12mo. 8s8d.
ESTC t133824; RCC p.239.
A reprint of Smith's '2nd' edn of 1749.
1st edn, 1749. Edns listed, 1750 [24].
BL TCD
* N

26.
GREENE Robert
THE PLEASANT AND DELIGHTFUL HISTORY OF DORESTUS PRINCE OF SICILY, AND FAWNIA, Only Daughter and Heir to Pandosto King of Bohemia
[5 more lines]
By R. Green, M.A. in Cambridge.
London : Printed for Henry Woodgate and Samuel Brookes, at the Golden Ball, in Pater-noster-Row [1750?] (BL).
116pp. 12mo.
ESTC t067323.
BL
* N

27.
[KIMBER Edward]
THE LIFE AND ADVENTURES OF JOE THOMPSON. A Narrative founded on Fact. Written by Himself. In Two Volumes.
London : Printed for J. Hinton, at the King's Arms in St. Paul's Church-yard; and W. Frederick, Bookseller in Bath. 1750.
2 vols. 12mo. 6s (BB,MR).
MR III 366-367 (Sept. 1750).
AB(AR,BL,RI); BB; EC 167:5; ESTC t064730; LO 9 (BL,UP,YU); PBG 318; SG 567.
Dublin edn, 1750 [28]. Also, 1751 [92], 1763 [776], 1775, and 1783.
BL UP YU
* N

28.
[KIMBER Edward]
+THE LIFE AND ADVENTURES OF JOE THOMPSON. A Narrative founded on Fact. Written by Himself.
Dublin : Printed by S. Powell, For Robert Main, Bookseller in Dame-street, opposite to Fownes's-street. 1750.
2 vols. 12mo.
ESTC t098310; McB 510; PBG 318.
1st edn and edns listed, 1750 [27].
BL HU NLC UI UP YU
* N

29.
[LENNOX Mrs Charlotte Ramsay]
THE LIFE OF HARRIOT STUART. Written by Herself. In Two Volumes.
London : Printed for J. Payne, and J. Bouquet, in Pater-noster Row. 1751 [1750].
2 vols. 12mo. 5s (MR).
MR IV 160 (Dec. 1750).
AB(BL,Pi,T); BB; ESTC t071313; FB; LO 10 & 25 (FB,HU,UI); McB 549.
BL Bod HU UI
* N

30.
MARIVAUX Pierre Carlet de Chamblain de
LOCKMAN John *trans.*
PHARSAMOND : OR, THE NEW KNIGHT-ERRANT. In which is introduced The Story
of the Fair Anchoret, With that of Tarmiana and her Unfortunate Daughter. Written
Originally in French by M. de Marivaux, Member of the French Academy in Paris :
Author of The Life of Marianne &c. Translated by Mr. Lockman.
London : Printed for C. Davis, opposite Gray's-Inn, Holborn; and L. Davis, at Lord Bacon's
Head, Fleet-street. 1750 [1749 - but not in JB].
2 vols. 12mo. 6s (MR).
MR II 91-92 (Dec. 1749).
AB(GBF,Pi); EC 15:2; ESTC t105237; McB 635; SG 697.
Trans. from *Pharsamon, ou les nouvelles folies romanesques*, 1737. Dublin edn, 1750 [31].
BL CUL UI UP
* N

31.
MARIVAUX Pierre Carlet de Chamblain de
LOCKMAN John *trans.*
+PHARSAMOND : OR, THE NEW KNIGHT-ERRANT. In which is introduced The Story
of the Fair Anchoret, With that of Tarmiana and her unfortunate Daughter. Written
Originally in French, By Monsieur de Marivaux, Member of the French Academy in Paris:
Author of The Life of Marianne, &c. Translated by Mr. Lockman.
Dublin : Printed by George Faulkner, in Essex-street. 1750.
2 vols. 12mo.
ESTC t084643.
1st English edn, 1750 [30].
* N

32.
[PALTOCK Robert]
MEMOIRS OF THE LIFE OF PARNESE, A SPANISH LADY OF VAST FORTUNE.
Written by Herself
[9 more lines]
Interspersed with the Story of Beaumont and Sarpeta. Translated from the Spanish
Manuscript, By R. P. Gent.
London : Printed for William Owen, at Homer's Head, near Temple-Bar; And for William
Clarke, under the Royal Exchange, Threadneedle-Street. 1751 [1750].
284pp. 12mo. 3s (BB,MR).
MR IV 156-157 (Dec. 1750).
AB(BL,Do,McL); BB; ESTC t130917; LO 29 (HU,UP); SG 788.
BL Bod HU UP
* N

33.
[PALTOCK Robert]
THE LIFE AND ADVENTURES OF PETER WILKINS, A CORNISH MAN
[21 more lines]
By R. S. a Passenger in the Hector. In Two Volumes.
London : Printed for J. Robinson, at the Golden Lion, in Ludgate-street; and R. Dodsley, at
Tully's Head, in Pall-Mall. 1751 [1750].
2 vols. 12mo. 6s (BB).
MR IV 157 (Dec. 1750).
AB(BL,Mg) as 1751; BB; CG(GM Nov. 1758); ESTC t092780; LO (BL,HU); McB 688; PBG 320-327.
Published 3 Dec 1750, RS p.340. Dublin edn, 1750 [34] and 1783, 1784, 1797, 1800.
BL CUL HU UI
* N

34.
[PALTOCK Robert]
+THE LIFE AND ADVENTURES OF PETER WILKINS. A CORNISH MAN:
[21 more lines]
By R. S. a Passenger in the Hector. In Two Volumes.
Dublin : Printed by George Faulkner in Essex-street. 1751 [1750].
2 vols. 12mo.
ESTC t066930; PBG 321.
1st edn, 1750 [33].
BL
* N

35.
[PRÉVOST D'EXILES Abbé Antoine François]
+THE LIFE AND ENTERTAINING ADVENTURES OF MR. CLEVELAND, Natural Son
of Oliver Cromwell, written by himself.
Dublin : Printed for Augustus Long and Henry Hawker. 1750.
2 vols. 12mo.
McB 718; PBG 280.
Trans of *Le Philosophe Anglais, ou Histoire de Monsieur Cleveland*, 1731.
1st edn, 1734-35 (WMcB 265 & EC 88:1). PBG p.279 also gives English 1731 edn. Also, 1735, 1736, 1741 (JB
79), 1760 [581].
UI UV
N/M

36.
[le SAGE Alain René]
[SMOLLETT Tobias *trans.*]
+THE ADVENTURES OF GIL BLAS OF SANTILLANE. A New Translation, by The
Author of Roderick Random. In Four Volumes.
London : Printed for J. Osborne, at the Golden Ball in Pater-noster-Row. 1750.
4 vols. 12mo.
AB(AR,Pi,Pk); ESTC t130653.
Published Feb. 1,000 copies, SW p.285.
1st edn, 1749 (JB 280). Also, 1759 [504], 1761 [669], 1764 [865], 1766 [1037], 1767 [1131] [1132], 1771-8,
1773, 1773-80, 1781, 1784, 1785(2x), 1789, 1792, 1793, 1794(2x), 1795-7.
Other trans, 1735 (McB 85) and 1742 (JB 105) and extract, 1745 (JB 105), 1760 [583], 1765 [938].
BL Bod CUL
* N

37.
le SAGE Alain René
[SMOLLETT Tobias *trans.*]
THE DEVIL UPON CRUTCHES : From the Diable Boiteux of Mr. Le Sage. A New
Translation.
[7 more lines]
In Two Volumes.
London : Printed for J. Osborn, in Pater-noster-Row. 1750.
2 vols. 18mo.
AB(T); LO 3 (UP).
2,000 copies, Strahan ledgers.
'That Smollett prepared this translation is all but certain', LMK pp.104-105.
Also, 1759 [505], 1770(2x), 1773, 1777, 1778, 1780, 1782, 1784, 1785. Cf derivative satirical work, with edns
listed, 1755 [285].
Bod UP
* N

38.
[SCOTT Mrs Sarah Robinson]
THE HISTORY OF CORNELIA.
London : Printed for A. Millar, opposite to Katherine-Street, in the Strand. 1750.
271pp. 12mo. 3s (BB,MR).
MR III 59-61 (May 1750).
AB(Bk,BL,McL); BB; ESTC t119494; LO 14 (HU,UI); newSG.
Dublin edn, 1750 [39].
BL CUL HU UI UP
* N

39.
[SCOTT Mrs Sarah Robinson]
+THE HISTORY OF CORNELIA.
Dublin : Printed for John Smith on the Blind-Quay. 1750.
271pp. 12mo.
ESTC t068654.
1st edn, 1750 [38]
BL
* N

40.
[SMOLLETT Tobias]
+THE ADVENTURES OF RODERICK RANDOM. In Two Volumes. The Third Edition.
London : Printed for J. Osborn, in Pater-noster-Row. 1750.
2 vols. 12mo.
ESTC t055368; MW 33.
1st edns, 1748 (3x incl. JB 253). Also, 1749(2x), 1755 [326] [327], 1756 [378], 1760 [584], 1762 [737], 1763 [794], 1766 [1040], 1768 [1232], 1770(2x), 1773, 1774, 1775(3x), 1776, 1777, 1778, 1779, 1780(2x), 1781, 1783, 1784(2x), 1789, 1791(2x), 1792, 1793(3x), 1794, 1795, 1799.
BL IU Tx YU
* N

Miscellanies

41.
Adventures Under-ground. A Letter from a Gentleman Swallowed up in the late Earthquake to a Friend on his Travels.
London : Printed for William Falstaff, near St. Paul's. 1750.
28pp. 8vo. 6d (tp).
ESTC t121400; FB; LO 2 (GS,FB).
BL Bod
* M (sat)

42.
The Cloisters laid Open, Or, Adventures of the Priests and Nuns. With Some Account of Confessions, and the lewd Use they make of them
[7 more lines]
London : Printed for Meanwell, near Dutchey-Lane [1750] (BL).
142pp. 12mo. 3s (tp).
ESTC t116629 (now suggesting ?1770).
BL
* C/M

43.
Fables and Tales for the Ladies. To which are added, Miscellanies, By Another Hand.
London : Printed for the Proprietor : And Sold by C. Hitch and L. Hawes, in Pater-noster-Row, and H. Whitridge at the Royal Exchange. 1750.
126pp. 8vo. 3s6d bound (BB,MR).
MR IV 16-17 (Nov. 1750).
BB; ESTC t078510.
Much in verse. 2nd edn, 1754 [265]. Later reissue, 1767 [1151].
BL Bod CUL
* M/C

44.
A Faithfull and full Account of the Surprising Life and Adventures of the Celebrated Doctor Sartorius Sinegradibus. As also Of the many wonderful Operations he performs in this City.
Edinburgh : Printed for the Auhtor, [sic] and sold by the Society of Running Stationers [1750?] (BL).
42pp. 8vo.
ESTC t128533.
BL suggests John Taylor as author. Cf 1761 [659].
BL
* M

45.
(+)Memoirs of the Bashaw Count Bonneval, from his Birth to his Death
[17 more lines]
Written by Himself, and collected from His Papers.
London : Printed for E. Withers, at the Seven Stars, near the Temple-Gate : G. Woodfall, the Corner of Craig's-Court, Charing-Cross; and Sold by R. Griffiths, at the Dunciad in St. Paul's Church-Yard. 1750.
2 vols. 8vo. 6s bound (MR).
MR II 428-431, III 236-240 (Mar, July 1750).
AB(RI); BB.
Cf 1736 Payne (2nd) edn, *Memoirs of the Famous Bashaw Bonneval.*
Bod CUL
* N/M

46.
(+)A New Collection of Fairy Tales, none of which were ever before printed; containing many useful lessons, moral Sentiments, surprizing Incidents and amusing Adventures. In Two Volumes.
London : Printed for Davis, Hitch, Dodsley, and Woodfall. 1750.
2 vols. 12mo. 5s bound (MR).
MR III 111 (June 1750).
MR has by Henry Brooke and 1st published in Dublin.
Published 15 Mar, RS.
M/C

47.
The Protical Son; A Welch Preachment, by the Parson of Llangtyddre. On the Return of his Protical Son. Published from an Authentic Manuscript.
London : Printed for H. Carpenter in Fleetstreet, and Sold at the Pamphlet Shops. 1750.
23pp. 8vo.
ESTC t128538; LO 13 (UI); McB 719.
Further edns, 1750 [48] [49], 1752 [152].
BL [imperf] Bod UI
* M/N (sat)

48.
+The Protical Son: A Welch Preachment. By the Parson of Llangtyddre. On the Return of his Protical
Son. Published from an Authentic Manuscript.
½tp - The Second Edition.
London : Printed for H. Carpenter in Fleetstreet, and Sold at the Pamphlet Shops. 1750.
27pp. 8vo. 6d (½tp).
1st edn, 1750 [48].
CUL
* M/N (sat)

49.
+The Protical Son: A Welch Preachment. By the Parson of Llangtyddre. On the Return of his Protical
Son. Published from an Authentic Manuscript.
½tp - The Fourth Edition.
London : Printed for H. Carpenter in Fleetstreet, and Sold at the Pamphlet Shops. 1750.
27pp. 8vo. 6d (½tp).
ESTC t063066.
1st edn, 1750 [48].
BL CUL
* M/N (sat)

50.
The Secret History of Betty Ireland
[15 more lines]
London : Published by S. Lee, 70, Fetter Lane. Burton, Printer, Fetter Lane, London [1750?] (BL).
37pp. 12mo.
AB(BL).
1st edn, [1741?]. Also, 1755 [333], 1760 [609], 1765 [954], 1766 [1047], [1770?]. Cf 1753 [203] [204].
BL
* M

51.
The Story on which the New Tragedy, Call'd, The Roman Father, Is Founded. With some Account of
The author, and His Writings.
London : Printed and Sold by W. Reeve, in Fleet-Street; and A. Dodd, opposite St. Clement's Church, in the
Strand. 1750.
8vo. 6d (tp).
The play was written by W. Whitehead.
CUL ·
* M

52.
[Coyer Gabriel François]
A Discovery of the Island Frivola; or, the Frivolous Island. Translated from the French, now privately
handed about at Paris, and said to be agreeable to the English Manuscripts concerning that Island, and
its Inhabitants. Wrote by order of A-l A-n.
London : Printed for T. Payne in Bishopgate-street; and sold by M. Cooper in Paternoster-Row. 1750.
40pp. 8vo. 6d (tp).
AB(St); PBG 316-318.
2nd edn, 1750 [53]. Cf 1752 [155].
CUL
* M

53.

[Coyer Gabriel François]

+A Discovery of the Island Frivola : Or, The Frivolous Island. Translated from the French, now privately handed about at Paris, and said to be agreeable to the English Manuscripts concerning that Island, and its Inhabitants. Wrote by order of A-l A-n. The Second Edition.

London : Printed for T. Payne in Bishopgate-street; and sold by M. Cooper in Paternoster-Row. 1750.

40pp. 8vo. 6d (tp).

ESTC t006318; PBG 316.

1st edn, 1750 [52].

BL

* M/N

54.

[Goadby Robert]

+An Apology for the Life of Mr. Bampfylde-Moore Carew, Commonly call'd the King of beggars; Being an impartial Account of his life, from his leaving Tiverton school, at the age of fifteen, and entering into a society of gypsies, to the present time with his travels twice through great part of America. A particular account of the original government, language, laws, and customs of the gypsies. And a parallel dream after the manner of Plutarch, between Mr. B-M C and Mr. Thomas Jones.

London : Printed for R. Goadby [Sherborne] and W. Owen at Temple-Bar [1750?] (BL).

344pp. 12mo.

ESTC t144517.

1st London edn 1749 as version of an edn of 1745. Also, 1750 [55] [56], 1760 [617] [618], 1763 [801], 1765 [961], 1768 [1251], 1771, 1775, 1779, 1780, 1785, 1788, 1793, 1798.

BL

* M

55.

[Goadby Robert]

+An Apology for the Life of Mr. Bampfylde-Moore Carew, Commonly call'd the King of Beggars; Being an impartial Account of his life, from his leaving Tiverton school [&c. as above] The Second Edition.

London : Printed for R. Goadby [Sherborne] and W. Owen at Temple-Bar [1750?] (YU).

240pp. 12mo.

1st London edn, 1749. Edns listed, 1750 [54].

HU UV YU

* M

56.

[Goadby Robert]

+An Apology for the Life of Mr. Bampfylde-Moore Carew, Commonly call'd the King of beggars; Being an impartial Account of his life, from his leaving Tiverton school [&c. as above] The Third Edition.

London : Printed for R. Goadby [Sherborne] and W. Owen at Temple-Bar [1750?] (YU).

240pp. 12mo.

1st London edn, 1749. Edns listed, 1750 [54].

YU

* M

57.

[Haywood Mrs Eliza]

+The Female Spectator. The Third Edition.

London : Printed and published by T. Gardner, at Cowley's-Head, opposite St. Clement's-Church in the Strand. 1750.

4 vols. 12mo.

1st edn, 1744. Also, 1745, 1745-6, 1755 [337], 1766 [1053], 1771.

CUL

* C/M

58.
[Haywood Mrs Eliza ?]
A Letter from H— G—G, Esq; One of the Gentlemen of the Bed-Chamber to the Young Chevalier, And the Only Person of his own Retinue that attended him from Avignon, in his late Journey through Germany, and elsewhere : Containing Many remarkable and affecting Occurences, which happened to the P—¬ during the Course of his mysterious Progress. To a Particular Friend.
London : Printed, and Sold at the Royal Exchange, Temple-Bar, Charing-Cross, and all the Pamphlet-shops of London and Westminster. 1750.
63pp. 8vo. 1s (tp).
MR II 167 (Jan. 1750).
ESTC t037884; FB; LO 6 (BL,FB,MR).
H— G—g is Henry Goring.
Further edn, 1750 [59].
BL CUL
* M/N

59.
[Haywood Mrs Eliza ?]
+A Letter from H— G—G, Esq; One of the Gentlemen of the Bed-Chamber to the Young Chevalier, And the Only Person of his own Retinue that attended him from Avignon [&c. as above].
London : Printed, and Sold at the Royal Exchange, Temple-Bar, Charing-Cross, and all the Pamphlet-shops of London and Westminster. 1750.
48pp. 8vo. 1s (tp).
ESTC t037885.
H— G—g is Henry Goring.
An abridged edn. of 1750 [58].
BL
* M/N

60.
Rowe Mrs Elizabeth Singer
+Friendship in Death; in Twenty Letters from the Dead to the Living. To which are added, Letters Moral and Entertaining, in Prose and verse : In Three Parts. By Mrs Elizabeth Rowe.
London : Printed for Henry Lintot. 1750.
472pp. 8vo.
ESTC t134892; SG 921.
1st edn, 1728(McB 234). Also, 1733, 1733-4, 1734, 1736, 1738, 1740, 1741(JB 65), 1743, 1745, 1746, 1750 [61], 1752 [164], 1753 [210], 1755 [344], 1756 [384], 1760 [624] [625], 1762 [753], 1764 [879], 1768 [1256], 1774, 1775, 1776, 1777, 1784, 1786, 1790.
BL UP
* M

61.
Rowe Mrs Elizabeth Singer
+Friendship in Death; in Twenty Letters from the Dead to the Living. To which are added, Letters Moral and Entertaining, in Prose and verse : In Three Parts. By Mrs Elizabeth Rowe.
[Glasgow] Printed in the Year 1750.
292pp. 8vo.
ESTC t071309.
1st edn, 1728. Edns listed, 1750 [60].
BL CUL [as ?London]
* M

62.
THE ADVENTURES OF SHELIM O'BLUNDER, ESQ; THE IRISH BEAU. Who, Within
a very few Years has passed through many surprizing Vicissitudes, and remarkable scence
of Life [7 more lines]
London : Printed for H. Carpenter, in Fleet-Street [1751]. BL has [1750?].
48pp. 8vo. 1s (tp,MR).
MR V 158 (July 1751).
BB; ESTC t116632.
BL
* N/M

63
THE ADVENTURES OF THE RD. MR. JUDAS HAWKE, THE RD. MR. NATHAN
BRIGGS, MISS LUCRETIA BRIGGS, &c. Late Inhabitants of the Island Querumania.
After the Manner of Joseph Andrews.
London : Printed for T. Waller, opposite Fetter-Lane, Fleet-Street. 1751.
126pp. 12mo. 1s6d (BB,MR).
MR V 73-74 (June 1751).
BB; ESTC t146306.
BL
* N

64.
AMELIA, OR, THE DISTRESS'D WIFE : A History Founded on Real Circumstances. By
a Private Gentlewoman.
London : Printed for the Authoress. 1751. 'To be had of J. Swan and other booksellers' (MR).
251pp. 8vo. 5s sewed (BB,MR).
MR V 72-73 (June 1751).
AB(BL); BB; EC 175:5; ESTC t057343 [Elizabeth Justice as subject]; LO 16 (YU).
BL YU
* N

65.
CLARINDA; OR A GENUINE NARRATIVE OF ALL THAT BEFEL A LADY Whose
distinguishing Characteristic was Chastity. Her Escapes from her many Lovers, and the
Method used by a Jesuit Priest to obtain her good Graces, are fully narrated, with the
Manner of his putting her to Death.
London : Printed for the Author, and sold by J. Robinson, in Ludgate Street; and by A.
Henderson, in Westminster-Hall; by E. Withers, in Fleet-Street and at the Royal-Exchange. 1751.
26pp. 8vo. 6d (tp).
AB(Do); ESTC t068031.
BL
* N/M

66.
CONSTANTIA; OR, A TRUE PICTURE OF HUMAN LIFE; Represented in Fifteen
Evening Conversations after the manner of Boccace. In Two Volumes.
London : Printed for A. Millar. 1751.
2 vols. 12mo. 6s bound (MR).
MR V 8-23 (June 1751).
AB(WB); LO 19 (HU,UP); SG 193.
Dublin edn, 1751 [67].
HU UP
N/C

67.
+CONSTANTIA: OR, A TRUE PICTURE OF HUMAN LIFE, Represented in Fifteen
Evening Conversations After the Manner of Boccace. In Two Volumes. To which is
prefixed, A Short Discourse on Novel Writing.
Dublin : Printed for J. Smith, on the Blind-Quay; and M. Williamson in Dame-Street,
Booksellers. 1751.
2 vols. 12mo.
ESTC t107852.
1st edn, 1751 [66].
BL
* N/C

68.
THE DOUBLE INTRIGUE; OR, THE ADVENTURES OF ISMAEL AND SELIMA. A
Novel.
London : Corbet. 1751.
8vo. 1s (MR).
MR V 75 (June 1751).
N

69.
ELEANORA; OR A TRAGICAL BUT TRUE CASE OF INCEST IN GREAT BRITAIN.
London : Printed for M. Cooper, at the Globe in Pater-noster-Row. 1751.
62pp. 8vo. 1s (MR,tp).
MR V 317 (Sept. 1751).
ESTC t137696.
Dublin edn, 1751 [70].
BL Bod
* N/M

70.
+ELEANORA; OR, A TRAGICAL BUT TRUE CASE OF INCEST IN GREAT-BRITAIN.
Dublin : Printed for G. Faulkner in Essex-street, J. Exshaw on Cork-hill, and R. James in Dame-
street, Booksellers. 1751.
48pp. 8vo.
1st edn, 1751 [69].
CUL
* N/M

71.
THE FAIR WANDERER : OR, THE ADVENTURES OF ETHELINDA, NIECE TO THE
LATE CARDINAL B—-
London : Printed for F. Stamper, and E. Downham, in Pope's-Head-Alley, Cornhill. 1751.
60pp. 8vo. 1s (MR,tp).
MR V 458 (Nov. 1751).
AB(BL); EC 169:7; ESTC t066892; LO 21 (UI); McB 257.
BL UI
* N

72.
MEMOIRS AND INTERESTING ADVENTURES OF AN EMBROIDERED WAISTCOAT.
London : Printed for and sold by J. Brooke, at the Golden Head, under St. Dunstan's Church, Fleet-street. 1751.
54pp. 8vo. 6d (BB,MR).
MR V 69 (June 1751).
BB; RKM(YU).
YU
* M/N

73.
MEMOIRS OF THE LIFE AND ACTIONS OF CHARLES OSBORN, ESQ; Natural Son to the E–l of A–e. Written by himself in the Decline of Life.
London : Printed for M. Cooper. 1752 [1751].
321pp. 12mo. 3s (MR).
MR V 460 (Nov. 1751).
LO 41 (UP); SG 728.
UP
N

74.
+THE NOMINAL HUSBAND : OR, DISTRESS'D INNOCENCE. A True Secret History, Taken From an Old Saxon Manuscript. Found among the Papers of a late Noble Antiquarian : For the Service of the Youth of both Sexes. The Second Edition.
London : Printed for W. Owen, at Homer's Head, near Temple-Bar; and G. Woodfall, at the King's-Arms, Charing-Cross. 1751.
120pp. 8vo.
1st edn, 1750 [15].
Bod
* N

75.
[CLELAND John]
MEMOIRS OF A COXCOMB.
London : Printed for R. Griffiths, at the Dunciad in Paul's Church-Yard [sic] 1751.
386pp. 12mo. 3s sewed (BB,MR).
MR V 385-387 (Oct. 1751).
AB(B&G,CLP,LC); BB; ESTC t057321; LO 18 (HU,RL,UI); McB 146.
Dublin edn, 1751 [76].
BL HU PU UI WCL YU
* N

76.
[CLELAND John]
+MEMOIRS OF A COXCOMB.
Dublin : Printed for G. Faulkner, in Essex-street. 1751.
251pp. 12mo.
McB 147.
1st edn, 1751 [75].
NLC UI UP
N

77.
[COVENTRY Francis]
THE HISTORY OF POMPEY THE LITTLE, OR, THE LIFE AND ADVENTURES OF A
LAP-DOG.
London : Printed for M. Cooper, at the Globe in Paternoster-Row. 1751.
272pp. 8vo. 3s bound (MR).
MR IV 316-317, 329-337, 457-465 (Feb,Mar,Apr. 1751).
AB(BL,RI); BB; ESTC t108586; LO 20 (HU,UI,UP); SG 210; McB 162.
Dublin edn, 1751 [78]. Also, 1751 [79], 1752 [127], 1753 [181], 1761 [644], 1773, 1785, 1799.
BL Bod CUL HU UI UP
* N

78.
[COVENTRY Francis]
+THE HISTORY OF POMPEY THE LITTLE, OR, THE LIFE AND ADVENTURES OF
A LAP-DOG.
Dublin : Printed by George Faulkner, in Essex-street. 1751.
176pp. 12mo.
ESTC t120586; SG 211.
1st edn and edns listed, 1751 [77].
BL UP
* N

79.
[COVENTRY Francis]
+THE HISTORY OF POMPEY THE LITTLE : OR, THE LIFE AND ADVENTURES OF
A LAP-DOG. The Second Edition.
London : Printed for M. Cooper, at the Globe in Paternoster-Row. 1751.
272pp. 8vo.
ESTC t119390.
1st edn and edns listed, 1751 [77].
BL Bod CUL
* N

80.
CRÉBILLON Claude Prosper Jolyot de
THE WANDERINGS OF THE HEART AND MIND : OR MEMOIRS OF MR. DE
MEILCOUR. Translated from the French of Mr. de Crebillon the Son. By Michael Clancy,
M. D.
London : Printed for John Nourse, at the Lamb over against Katherine-street in the Strand. 1751.
267pp. 12mo.
EC 15:4; ESTC t116307.
A trans. of L'Égaramens du coeur et de l'esprit.
Dublin edn, 1751 [81].
BL UNC YU
* N

81.
CRÉBILLON Claude Prosper Jolyot de
+THE WANDERINGS OF THE HEART AND MIND : OR MEMOIRS OF MR. DE
MEILCOUR. Translated from the French of Mr. de Crebillon the Son.
Dublin : Printed for Geo. and Alex. Ewing, at the Angel and Bible, in Dame-street. 1751.
267pp. 12mo.
SG 218.
1st edn, 1751 [80].
CUL UP
* N

82.
[FABIOT AUNILLON Pierre Charles]
THE FORCE OF EDUCATION. Illustrated in the Memoirs of Mademoiselle de St. Eugene, and the Baron de Cromstad. Translated from the French of Monsieur de V–.
London : Printed for R. Griffiths, at the Dunciad, in St. Paul's Church-yard. 1751.
174pp. 12mo. 1s6d (BB).
BB; EC 60:9; ESTC t132302; SG 340.
Also, 1773 edn.
BL UP
* N/M

83.
FIELDING Henry
AMELIA. By Henry Fielding Esq; In Four Volumes.
London : Printed for A. Millar, in the Strand. 1752 [1751].
4 vols. 12mo. 12s bound (MR,WLC).
MR V 510-517 (Dec. 1751).
AB(AR,Mk,RK); BB; EC 189:2; ESTC t089846; LO 34 (HU,RL,UI,UP); McB 277; WLC iii 321-322.
2 impressions of this edition, the 1st published 18 Dec. 1751, the 2nd in Jan. 1752, with a total of 8,000 copies, Strahan ledgers, & WLC ii 304, iii 321-322.
Dublin edns 1752 [131] [132]. Also, 1771, 1775, 1777, 1780, 1781, 1782, 1785, 1790, 1793, 1795, 1797, 1798-9, and abridgment [1760?] [570].
The 2nd (revised) edn appeared in Murphy's 1762 edn of *The Works* [714].
BL Bod CUL HU PU UI UP YU
* N

84.
FIELDING Henry
+THE HISTORY OF THE ADVENTURES OF JOSEPH ANDREWS, AND HIS FRIEND MR. ABRAHAM ADAMS. Written in Imitation of The Manner of Cervantes Author of Don Quixote. By Henry Fielding, Esquire. The Fifth Edition, revised and corrected. In Two Volumes.
London : Printed for A. Millar, opposite to Katherine Street, in the Strand. 1751.
2 vols. 12mo.
EC 189:1; ESTC t089885; McB 286.
2,000 copies, Strahan ledgers.
1st edns, 1742 (3x, JB 90-90b). Also, 1743, 1745, 1747 (JB 90d), 1749 (JB 90e), 1754 [233a], 1762 [713], 1764 [834], 1767 [1093] [1093a] [1094], 1768 [1209], 1769 [1310] [1311], 1770, 1773, 1775, 1778, 1780(2x), 1781(2x), 1783, 1784, 1785, 1788, 1790, 1791, 1792(3x), 1793, 1794.
BL CUL HU UI
* N

85.
[HAYWOOD Mrs Eliza]
THE HISTORY OF MISS BETSY THOUGHTLESS. In Four Volumes.
London : Printed for T. Gardner, and sold at his Printing-Office at Cowley's-Head, facing St. Clement's Church, in the Strand; and by all Booksellers in Town and Country. 1751.
4 vols. 12mo. 12s (MR).
MR V 393-394 (Oct. 1751).
AB(GBF,Pk,So); BB; ESTC t073274; FB; LO 23 (FB,HU,UI,UP); McB 420; SG 436.
2nd edn, 1751 [86], Dublin edn, 1751 [87]. Also, 1752 [136], 1762 [720], 1765 [921], 1768 [1214], 1772, 1783, 1784.
BL Bod CUL HU UI UP YU
* N

86.
[HAYWOOD Mrs Eliza]
+THE HISTORY OF MISS BETSY THOUGHTLESS. In Four Volumes. The Second
Edition.
London : Printed for T. Gardner, and sold at his Printing-Office at Cowley's-Head, facing St.
Clement's Church, in the Strand; and by all Booksellers in Town and Country. 1751.
4 vols. 12mo.
1st edn and edns listed, 1751 [85].
TCU
N

87.
[HAYWOOD Mrs Eliza]
+THE HISTORY OF MISS BETSY THOUGHTLESS, In Four Volumes.
Dublin : Printed for Oliver Nelson, at Milton's-Head in Skinner-Row. 1751.
4 vols. 12mo.
1st edn and edns listed, 1751 [85].
CUL
* N

88.
[HILL John]
THE ADVENTURES OF MR. GEORGE EDWARDS, A CREOLE.
London : Printed for T. Osborne, in Gray's-Inn. 1751.
269pp. 12mo. 3s (MR).
MR V 237-239 (Aug. 1751).
AB(BL,FE,Pi); BB; ESTC t010613; LO 24 (HU,UI).
MR suggests by the author of 1750 [1].
2nd edn, 1751 [89], Dublin edn, 1751 [90], and 1788.
BL HU UI
* N

89.
[HILL John]
+THE ADVENTURES OF MR. GEORGE EDWARDS, A CREOLE. The Second Edition.
London : Printed for T. Osborne, in Gray's-Inn. 1751.
269pp. 12mo.
ESTC t127180; SG 468.
1st edn and edns listed, 1751 [88].
BL CUL UP
* N

90.
[HILL John]
+THE ADVENTURES OF MR. GEORGE EDWARDS, A CREOLE.
Dublin : Printed for P. Wilson. 1751.
202pp. 12mo.
McB 448.
1st edn and edns listed, 1751 [88].
UI
N

91.
[HILL John]
THE HISTORY OF A WOMAN OF QUALITY : OR, THE ADVENTURES OF LADY
FRAIL. By an Impartial Hand.
London : Printed for M. Cooper, at the Globe in Pater-noster Row, and G. Woodfall, at the
King's Arms, the Corner of Craig's-Court, Charing Cross. 1751.
227pp. 12mo. 3s (MR).
MR IV 307-308 (Feb. 1751).
AB(BL,Pi); BB; EC 136:5; ESTC t012622.
BL Bod
* N

92.
[KIMBER Edward]
+THE LIFE AND ADVENTURES OF JOE THOMPSON. A Narrative founded on Fact.
Written by Himself. The Second Edition.
London : Printed for John Hinton, at the King's-Arms in St. Paul's Church-yard; And W.
Frederick, Bookseller in Bath. 1751.
2 vols. 12mo.
ESTC t066922; SG 568; PBG 319.
1st edns and edns listed, 1750 [27].
BL FL UP
* N

93.
[LONGUEVILLE Peter]
+THE HERMIT : OR, THE UNPARALLEL'D SUFFERINGS AND SURPRISING
ADVENTURES OF MR. PHILIP QUARLL, an Englishman : who was lately discovered by
Mr. Dorrington, a Bristol Merchant, upon an uninhabited Island in the South-Sea [&c.]
London : Printed for J. Wren, J. Jefferies, and J. Fuller. 1751.
263pp. 12mo.
1st edn, 1727. Also, 1746, a 52-part issue [1750?], 1755 [321] (abridgment), 1759 [499], 1763 [782], 1768
[1220], 1770, 178¬ 1780, 1781, 1786(2x), 1788, 1790, 1792, 1794, 1795(2x), 1797.
Bod OU
N/M

94.
[MAINVILLERS Genu Soalhat de]
THE BEAU-PHILOSOPHER; OR, THE HISTORY OF THE CHAVALIER DE
MAINVILLERS. Translated from the French Original.
London : Printed for R. Freeman, near St. Paul's. 1751.
269pp. 12mo. 3s (BB,MR).
MR V '385'-403 (Nov. 1751).
AB(GW,RI); BB; EC 96:5; ESTC t099625; LO 17 (UI); McB 616; newSG.
BL Bod UI UP
* N/E

95.
MORRIS Ralph (pseud?)
A NARRATIVE OF THE LIFE AND ASTONISHING ADVENTURES OF JOHN
DANIEL, A Smith at Royston in Hertfortshire [sic; 19 more lines] By Mr. Ralph Morris.
London : Printed for M. Cooper, at the Globe in Pater-noster-Row. 1751.
319pp. 12mo. 3s (MR).
MR V 518 (Dec. 1751).
ESTC t067638; LO 26 (BL); PBG 328-330 [as published, Nov. 1751].
BL
* N

96.
[RICHARDSON Samuel]
+CLARISSA. OR, THE HISTORY OF A YOUNG LADY : Comprehending The most
Important Concerns of Private Life. In Eight Volumes. To Each of which is added A Table
of Contents. The Third Edition
[7 more lines]
London : Printed for S. Richardson : And Sold by John Osborn, in Pater-noster Row; By
Andrew Millar, over-against Catharine-street in the Strand; By J. and J. Rivington, in St. Paul's
Church-yard; And by J. Leake, at Bath. 1751.
8 vols. 12mo. £1.4s bound (WS).
Only vol I dated 1751. Vols II-VIII dated 1750, but all published in 1751.
ESTC t058989; WS 34.
Published 20 Apr.
1st edn, 1747-48. Also, 1747-49 (JB 229), 1751 [97], 1759 [503], 1764 [860], 1765 [936], 1768 [1229], 1774,
1780, 1783, 1784, 1785, 1792(2x), 1795. Abridgments, 1756 [376a], 1769 [1327a]. Cf 1751 [98].
BL CUL YU
* E

97.
[RICHARDSON Samuel]
+CLARISSA. OR, THE HISTORY OF A YOUNG LADY : Comprehending The most
Important Concerns of Private Life. In Seven Volumes. To Each of which is added A Table
of Contents. The Fourth Edition.
[7 more lines]
London : Printed for S. Richardson : And Sold by John Osborn, in Pater-noster Row; By
Andrew Millar, over-against Catharine-street in the Strand; By J. and J. Rivington, in St. Paul's
Church-yard; And by J. Leake, at Bath. 1751.
7 vols. 8vo. £1.15s bound (WS).
ESTC t058988; WS 35.
Published 20 Apr. with 1751 [96].
1st edn, 1747-48. Edns listed, 1751 [96].
BL CUL HU YU
* E

98.
[RICHARDSON Samuel]
LETTERS AND PASSAGES RESTORED FROM THE ORIGINAL MANUSCRIPTS OF
THE HISTORY OF CLARISSA
[7 more lines]
Published for the Sake of doing Justice to the Purchasers of the Two First Editions of that
Work.
London : Printed for S. Richardson : And Sold by John Osborn, in Pater-noster Row; By
Andrew Millar, over-against Catharine-street in the Strand; By J. and J. Rivington, in St. Paul's
Church-yard; And by J. Leake, at Bath. 1751.
304pp. 8vo.
EC418:5; ESTC t058993; LO 30 (HU,RL,UI); McB 758; WS 37.
Published 20 Apr. with 3rd and 4th edns [96] [97], intended for the purchasers of the 1st 2 edns by providing
omitted material in one vol. In July Richardson also published *Meditations of Clarissa* for private circulation.
Cf 1751 [96], with edns of full work listed.
BL Bod HU UI
* E

99.
[SMOLLETT Tobias]
THE ADVENTURES OF PEREGRINE PICKLE. In Which are Included, Memoirs of a Lady of Quality. In Four Volumes.
London : Printed for the Author, and sold by D. Wilson, at Plato's Head, near Round-Court, in the Strand. 1751.
4 vols. 12mo. 12s bound (MR). MR IV 355-365 (Mar. 1751).
AB(BL,RI,Mg); BB; ESTC t055344; LO 31 (HU,RL,UI,UP,YU); McB 843; MW 136; SG 997.
Dublin edn, 1751 [100], and 1758 [446], 1762 [Nov. '2nd' edn advertised by Saunders, Potts and Dyton, but re-issue?], 1763 [794], 1765 [939], 1768 [1231], 1769 [1333], 1773, 1775, 1776, 1778, 1779, 1781, 1784, 1785, 1786, 1787, 1788, 1791, 1793, 1794, 1795, 1799. Abridgment, 1788.
BL Bod CUL HU NYPL UI UP YU
* N

100.
[SMOLLETT Tobias]
+THE ADVENTURES OF PEREGRINE PICKLE. In Which are Included, Memoirs of a Lady of Quality. By the Author of Roderick Random. In Three Volumes.
Dublin : Printed for Robert Main, Bookseller in Dame-Street, opposite to Fownes's-Street. 1751.
3 vols. 12mo. 7s6d.
ESTC t055345; MW 137.
1st edn and edns listed, 1751 [99].
BL HU NLI YU
* N

101.
[la SOLLE Henri François de]
[HILL John *trans.*]
MEMOIRS OF A MAN OF PLEASURE; OR, THE ADVENTURES OF VERSORAND. Translated from the French.
London : Printed for T. Osborne, in Gray's Inn. 1751.
2 vols. 16mo. 6s (BB,MR).
MR V 43-44 (June 1751).
AB(BL); BB; ESTC t138028; SG 599.
A trans. of la Solle, *Mémoires de Versorand.*
A '3rd edn', 1751 [102].
BL UP
* N

102.
[la SOLLE Henri François de]
[HILL John *trans.*]
+MEMOIRS OF A MAN OF PLEASURE, OR THE ADVENTURES OF VERSORAND. Translated from the French. The Third Edition.
London : Printed for T. Osborne, in Gray's Inn. 1751.
2 vols. 12mo.
CUL copy, vol.II tp has 'Fifth Edition'.
SG 600.
1st edn, 1751 [101].
CUL UP
* N

103.
[TENCIN Madame Claudine Alexandrine Guérin de]
(+)THE SIEGE OF CALAIS, AN HISTORICAL NOVEL. Translated from the French.
London : Printed by Charles Say Junior, for R. Wilson Bookseller to His Royal Highness the
Duke, in Pall-Mall. 1751.
2 vols in 1. 8vo. 3s sewed (BB,MR).
MR IV 476 (Apr. 1751).
BB [BL has a 1740 *Siege of Calais* [by de Tencin].
YU
* N

Miscellanies

104.
The Artful Lover, or the French Count Turned Doctor. Translated from the Latin Original.
London : Cooper. 1751.
8vo. 1s (BB,MR).
MR V 70-71 (June 1751).
BB.
Later edn/reissue as *The Female Apothecary*, 1753 [200].
N

105.
The Genuine Memoirs and most Surprising Adventures of a very Unfortunate Goosequill.
London : Printed for M. Cooper, and G. Woodfall. 1751.
26pp. 8vo. 6d (BB,MR).
MR V 69 (June 1751).
BB; RKM(HU).
HU
M (sat)

106.
Truth Triumphant; or, Fluxions for the Ladies. By X, Y, Z.
London : Printed for W. Owen, and sold by the booksellers in town and country. 1752 [1751].
40pp. 8vo. 1s (BB).
BB; ESTC t078180.
BL has by R. Heath.
BL CUL
M

107.
[d'Argens Jean Baptiste de Boyer, Marquis]
**The Chinese Spy, Being a Series of Letters between a Chinese Traveller at Paris and his Countrymen in
China, Muscovy, Persia and Japan.**
London : J. Whiston and B. White. 1751.
12mo. 3s (MR).
MR V 460 (Nov. 1751).
Also, 1752 [154]. Cf the 6 vol work trans. from Ange de Goudar, 1764 [874].
M

108.

[Crébillon Claude Prosper Jolyot de]

Letters of Ninon de Lenclos, to the Marquis de Sevigne. Translated from the French.

London : Printed for D. Wilson, at Plato's Head in the Strand. 1751.

273pp. 12mo. 3s (MR).

MR IV 537-543, V 32-40 (May, June 1751).

BB; ESTC t139824.

French edn published, Amsterdam, 1750. Also attributed to Louis Damours.

Cf 1761 [694].

BL CUL DU NLC

* M/E

109.

[de Curli]

The Life and Amours of Owen Tideric Prince of Wales, otherwise Owen Tudor

[13 more lines]

London : Printed for William Owen, at Homer's Head, near Temple-bar. 1751.

147pp. 12mo.

ESTC t136081.

BL CUL

* M

110.

[Fielding Sarah]

+The Governess; Or, The Little Female Academy. Calculated for the Entertainment and Instruction of Young Ladies in their Education. By the Author of David Simple. The Third Edition. Revised and Corrected.

London : Printed for A. Millar, over-against Catharine Street, in the Strand. 1751.

242pp. 12mo.

ESTC t000472.

1st edns, 1749. Also, 1752 [161], 1758 [454], 1765 [960], 1768 [1250], 1781; and adaptations 1770, 1786.

BL NLC

* M/C

111.

[Hill John]

A New Tale of an Old Tub; Or, The Way to Fame. An Odd Sort of a Story.

London : Printed for M. Cooper in Pater-noster-Row. 1752 [1751].

94pp. 8vo. 1s6d (BB,MR,tp).

MR V 524 (Dec. 1751).

BB (as 'of an Old Tub'); ESTC t073662.

BL suggests John Pinkerton as author.

BL Bod

* M

112.

[Hughes John *trans.*]

+Letters of the celebrated Abelard and Heloise. With the History of their Lives Prefix'd. In both of which are described their various Misfortunes, and the fatal consequences of their Amours. Translated by Mr. John Hughes. To which is added, Eloisa to Abelard; A Poem, By Alexander Pope Esq;

Glasgow : Printed and sold by Robert and Andrew Foulis. 1751.

200pp. 8vo.

1st Hughes edn, 1718. Also, 1722, 1729, 1731, 1735, 1736, 1743, 1755 [338], 1760 [621], 1764 [875], 1765 [963], 1769 [1357], 1773, 1775, 1776, 1779, 1780, 1781, 1782, 1783, 1785, 1787(2x), 1788, 1794, 1798(2x).

CUL LC

* M/E

113.
[Montesquieu Charles Louis de Secondat, Baron de]
+Letters from a Persian in England to his Friend at Isaphan.
Glasgow : Printed in the Year 1751.
12mo.
1st English edn, 1722. Also, 1730, 1731, 1736, 1755 [339], 1760 [623], 1761 [696], 1762 [752], 1767 [1164], 1773, 1775, 1777.
Bod
M/E

114.
[Painter J.]
An Oxford Dream. Most Dutifully and Pathetically Address'd to His Royal Highness The Duke. In Two Parts.
London : Printed for the Author. 1751.
39pp (the 2 pts, continuously paginated). 8vo.
ESTC t091249; LO 27 (UI); McB 686.
BL UI
* M

1752

115.
THE ADVENTURES OF A VALET. Written by Himself. In Two Volumes.
London : Printed for J. Robinson, at the Golden Lion, Ludgate-street. 1752.
2 vols. 12mo. 6s bound (BB,MR).
MR VI 110-123 (Feb. 1752).
AB(CB); BB; ESTC t138243.
BL
* N

116.
CLEORA; OR, THE FAIR INCONSTANT. A Recent and Authentic History of the Life and Adventures of a celebrated Lady of Distinction, lately very eminent in High Life
[4 more lines]
London : Printed by J. Everingham and T. Reynolds; and Sold by J. Hodges, on London-Bridge; A. Strahan, in Cornhill; G. Keith, in Cheapside; M. Cooper, and R. Baldwin, in Pater-noster-Row; A. Millar, and W. Bathoe, in the Strand; and M. Piers, and J. Wren, in Holborn. 1752.
316pp. 12mo. 3s (BB,MR).
MR VI 311 (Apr. 1752).
BB; EC 64:6; ESTC t057430.
BL
* N

117.
CLIO; OR, A SECRET HISTORY OF THE LIFE AND AMOURS OF THE LATE CELEBRATED MRS. S— N—M. Written by Herself, in a Letter to Hillarius.
London : Printed for M. Cooper, in Pater-noster-Row. 1752.
207pp. 12mo. 2s6d (BB,MR).
MR VI 148-149 (Feb. 1752).
AB(BL,CLP,T); BB; FB; LO 33 (UP,YU); SG 180.
BL [unlocated] UP YU
* E

118.
THE EUNUCH : OR, THE NORTHUMBERLAND SHEPHERD. In Four Chapters,
Whereon hangs a Tale. Apply it who may.
London : Printed for M. Cooper, at the Globe in Pater-noster Row. 1752.
81pp. 8vo. 1s (MR,tp).
MR VI 147 (Feb. 1752).
BB.
Bod
* N/M

119.
THE IMPORTANCE OF DRESS; OR, FEMALE RIVALRY: Being a Real History with
the Proper Names of the Parties, In a Letter from a Gentleman who lives at the Scene of
the Transaction.
London : Printed for M. Sheepy, under the Royal-Exchange; M. Cooper, at the Globe, in Pater-
noster-row; and J. Swan, over-against Northumberland-house in the Strand. 1752.
44pp. 8vo. 6d (MR,tp).
MR VI 395 (May 1752).
ESTC t094378; FB; LO 38 (BL,FB).
BL
* N/E

120.
THE LIFE OF PATTY SAUNDERS. Written by Herself.
London : Printed for W. Owen, at Homer's Head, Temple-Bar. 1752.
307pp. 12mo. 3s (BB,MR).
MR VI 77 (Jan. 1752).
AB(EM); BB.
CUL
* N

121.
THE MEMOIRS OF FIDELIO AND HARRIOT : Wherein the Contrast between Virtue
and Vice is fully exhibited from a real fact, transacted in the year 1720. Preserved in the
Original Manuscript of Mrs Hervey.
London : R. Manby. 1752.
12mo. 3s (MR).
MR VII 470 (Dec. 1752).
AB; newSG.
Dublin edn, 1753 [172].
UP
N

122.
A NARRATIVE OF THE LIFE AND DISTRESSES OF SIMON MASON,
APOTHECARY. Containing A Series of Transactions and Events, both Interesting and
Diverting.
Birmingham : Printed for the Author; And Sold by F. Noble, at his Circulating Library, in King-
Street, Covent-Garden; And J. Noble, at his Circulating Library, in St. Martin's-Court, near
Leicester-Square [1752] (BL).
117pp. 8vo. 2s6d bound (tp).
BB; ESTC t075680.
'Simon Mason' almost certainly a pseudonym.
CUL has [?1754]. ESTC notes 'printed not before 1752 on internal evidence'.
Also, 1754 [225]. Cf 1756 [357].
BL Bod CUL
* N/M

123.
VIRTUE TRIUMPHANT, AND PRIDE ABASED; In the Humorous History of Dicky Gotham, and Doll Clod; Digested from antient Tractates, and the Records of those memorable Families, now extant at Addle Hall, in Nottinghamshire. By R. P. Biographer.
London : Printed for M. Cooper, at the Globe, in Pater-noster Row. 1753 [1752].
2 vols. 12mo. 6s (BB,MR).
MR VII 470 (Dec. 1752).
BB; ESTC t092756.
BL UP
* N

124.
[CHAIGNEAU William]
THE HISTORY OF JACK CONNOR.
London : Printed for W. Johnston, at the Golden Ball, in St. Paul's-Church-Yard. 1752.
2 vols. 12mo. 6s (MR).
MR VI 447-449 (June 1752).
Vol. II entitled 'The History of Jack Connor, Now Conyers'.
AB(BL,RI,WTS); EC 11:1; ESTC t108074; LO 32 (HU,UI,UP); McB 139 (as Peter Chaigneau); SG 170.
Dublin edn, 1752 [125], and 1753 [179] [180], 1766 [997].
BL HU UI UP
* N

125.
[CHAIGNEAU William]
+THE HISTORY OF JACK CONNOR. In Two Volumes.
Dublin : Printed for Abraham Bradley, at the King's Arms and Two Bibles in Dame-street. 1752.
2 vols in 1. 362pp. 12mo.
ESTC t101674.
1st edn and edns listed, 1752 [124].
BL CUL LC
* N

126.
[CHETWOOD William Rufus]
+THE VOYAGES, DANGEROUS ADVENTURES, AND MIRACULOUS ESCAPES OF CAPT. RICHARD FALCONER
[11 more lines]
Dublin : Printed for, and Sold by the Editor W. R. Chetwood, in the Four-court-marshalsea; G. Risk, Messrs G. and A. Ewing, P. Wilson, R. James, R. Maine, S. Price, and M. Williamson, in Dame-street; G. Faulkner, and A. Long, in Essex-street, J. Esdal, on Cork hill, and S. Cotter, in Skinner-row, Booksellers. 1752.
232pp. 12mo. Subn.
1st edn, 1719-20 (WMcB 110). Also, 1724, 1734, 1744, 1764 [826], 1765 [903], 1769 [1303].
CUL
* N

127.
[COVENTRY Francis]
+THE HISTORY OF POMPEY THE LITTLE; OR, THE ADVENTURES OF A LAP-DOG. The Third Edition.
London : Printed for M. Cooper, at the Globe in Paternoster-Row. 1752.
291pp. 12mo.
ESTC t066931; SG 212.
1st edn and edns listed, 1751 [77].
BL CUL UP
* N

128.
[DAVYS Mrs Mary]
+THE REFORMED COQUET; OR, MEMOIRS OF AMORANDA The Sixth Edition.
London : Printed for A. Stephens. 1752.
154pp. 12mo.
SG 245.
1st edn, 1724. Also, 1735, 1736, 1744, 1760 [565] [566].
UP
N

129.
[DEFOE Daniel]
+THE WONDERFUL LIFE AND MOST SURPRIZING ADVENTURES OF ROBINSON
CRUSOE OF YORK, MARINER. Epitomized in Three Parts [&c].
London : Printed for C. Hitch, R. Ware, and J. Hodges. 1752.
2 vols. 12mo.
McB 204 (vol.I).
Pt I, *Life and Strange Surprizing Adventures*, 1st edn, 1719. Pt II, *The Farther Adventures*, 1st edn, 1719. Pt III,
Serious Reflections, 1st edn, 1720. The major abridgment, *Life and Most Surprizing Adventures*, 1st edn, 1722.
Details in HCH.
Edns of all parts include, 1719-20 (JM 412,417,436), 1721, 1722, 1726, 1730, 1734, 1736(2x), 1739, 1744,
1747, 1748, 1753 [182], 1755 [311], 1759 [482] [483], 1760 [568] [569], 1761 [646] [647], 1762 [710] [711],
1765 [909] [910], 1766 [1002], 1767 [1092], 1768 [1205], 1769 [1307], 1770, 1772, 1773, 1775, 1777,
1778(2x), 1779, 1780, 1781, 1782, 1783, 1784(2x), 1785(2x), 1786, 1789(3x), 1790(4x), 1791(3x), 1792(3x),
1793, 1794, 1795(2x), 1797, 1798(2x), 1799(2x). Cf 1750 [22].
Also, many 24pp chapbook versions.
LC UI
N/M

130.
DINSDALE Joshua *trans.*
PARMENIDES PRINCE OF MACEDONIA : Or, Fidelity Crowned, &c. An Heroic Novel.
Translated from the French, By Mr. Joshua Dinsdale.
London : Printed for J. Wren, at the Bible and Crown, near Great Turnstile, Holborn. 1752.
227pp. 12mo.
AB(RI,WB); EC 85:11; ESTC t131180.
Trans. from *Le Coq Madeleine*.
BL Bod
* N

131.
FIELDING Henry
+AMELIA. By Henry Fielding Esq.
Dublin : Printed for J. Smith, at the Philosophers-Heads on the Blind-Quay. 1752.
4 vols in 2. 12mo. 4s4d sewed or 5s5d bound.
ESTC t089848; RCC pp.71,239.
Published, 7 Jan. 1752, RCC, p.71.
1st edn and edns listed, 1751 [83].
BL Bod CUL HU YU
* N

132.
FIELDING Henry
+AMELIA. By Henry Fielding Esq; In Four Volumes.
Dublin : Printed for G. Risk, C. Wynne, O. Nelson, P. Wilson, J. Exshaw, J. Esdall, S. Price, M. Williamson, and H. Saunders, Booksellers. 1752.
4 vols. 12mo. 4s4d (adv-1752 [143]).
ESTC t089847; RCC pp.71,239-240.
Published, 7 Jan. 1752, RCC, p.71.
1st edn and edns listed, 1751 [83].
BL HU TCD YU
* N

133.
[FIELDING Sarah]
+FAMILIAR LETTERS BETWEEN THE PRINCIPAL CHARACTERS IN DAVID SIMPLE, And Some Others. Being a Sequel to his Adventures. To which is added, A Vision. By the Author of David Simple. The Second Edition.
London : Printed for A. Millar, opposite Katharine-Street in the Strand. 1752.
2 vols. 12mo.
BB(nd); ESTC t108078; SG 329.
Intended as a sequel and vols numbered III and IV.
1st edn, 1747 (JB 223). Edns of *David Simple* listed, 1753 [183].
BL UP
* E

134.
[FIELDING Sarah]
THE HISTORY OF BETTY BARNES. In Two Volumes.
London : Printed for D. Wilson and T. Durham, at Plato's Head, in the Strand. 1753 [1752].
2 vols. 12mo. 6s (BB,MR).
MR VII 470 (Dec. 1752).
AB(BL,EM,Pi); BB; EC 136:3; ESTC t066896; LO 53 (UI,UP); McB 314; SG 331.
BL Bod UI UP
* N

135.
[GOODALL William]
THE ADVENTURES OF CAPTAIN GREENLAND. Written in Imitation all those wise, learned, witty and humourous authors, who either already have, or hereafter may write in the same stile and manner.
London : Printed for R. Baldwin. 1752.
4 vols. 12mo. 12s (BB,MR).
MR VI 311-312 (Apr. 1752).
AB(ByB,T); BB; LO 35 (BL,HU,UP); PBG 331-2; SG 375.
BL HU UP
N

136.
[HAYWOOD Mrs Eliza]
+THE HISTORY OF BETSY THOUGHTLESS.
Dublin : R. Main. 1752.
2 vols. 12mo.
1st edn and edns listed, 1751 [85].
NLC
N

137.
[LEAF Jeremy (pseud?)]
WORLDLY COMPLIANCES. Dedicated to the Lady Frances Shirley.
London : Printed for D. Job, at the Spread-Eagle in King-street, Covent-Garden; R. Baldwin, at
the Rose, in Pater-noster-row; and P. Stevens, facing Stationers-Hall. 1752.
58pp. 4to. 1s6d (BB,MR,tp).
MR VI 146-147 (Feb. 1752).
BB; ESTC t140141; LO 39 (UP); SG 603.
2nd edn, 1753 [189].
BL UP
* N/M

138.
[LENNOX Mrs Charlotte Ramsay]
**ENTERTAINING HISTORY OF THE FEMALE QUIXOTE, OR THE ADVENTURES OF
ARABELLA. Containing A Remarkable Account of her Reading Romances,**
[4 more lines]
Second Edition.
London : Printed for R. Snagg, No. 29. Pater-noster-row. [1752?] (BL).
93pp. 12mo.
ESTC t067325.
An abridgment. Full edns listed, 1752 [139].
BL
* N

139.
[LENNOX Mrs Charlotte Ramsay]
THE FEMALE QUIXOTE; OR, THE ADVENTURES OF ARABELLA. In Two Volumes.
London : Printed for A. Millar, over-against Catherine-street in the Strand. 1752.
2 vols. 12mo. 6s (MR).
MR VI 249-262 (Apr. 1752).
AB(BL,Mg,RI); BB; EC 57:7; ESTC t071886; LO 40 (RL,UI); McB 544; SG 617.
Also, 1752 [140] [141], 1763 [781], 1783, 1799; and abridgment, 1752 [138].
BL Bod CUL UI
* N

140.
[LENNOX Mrs Charlotte Ramsay]
**+THE FEMALE QUIXOTE; OR, THE ADVENTURES OF ARABELLA. In Two Volumes.
The Second Edition : Revised and Corrected.**
London : Printed for A. Millar, over-against Catherine-street in the Strand. 1752.
2 vols. 12mo.
ESTC t088671; McB 545.
1st edn and edns listed, 1752 [139].
BL Bod CUL UI
* N

141.
[LENNOX Mrs Charlotte Ramsay]
+THE FEMALE QUIXOTE; OR, THE ADVENTURES OF ARABELLA. In Two Volumes.
Dublin : Printed for J. Smith, at the Philosophers-Heads on the Blind-Quay. 1752.
2 vols. 12mo.
1st edn and edns listed, 1752 [139].
CUL
* N

142.
[MOZEEN Thomas]
YOUNG SCARRON.
London : Printed and Sold by T. Trye, near Gray's-Inn-Gate, Holborn; and W. Reeve, in Fleet-Street. 1752.
182pp. 12mo.
AB(BL,RI,T); EC 228: 3; ESTC t077687.
Dublin edn, 1752 [143].
BL CUL
* N/M

143.
[MOZEEN Thomas]
+YOUNG SCARRON.
Dublin : Printed for Sam. Price, opposite Crane-lane in Dame-street, and Richard Wilson, in Eustace-street. 1752.
147pp. 8vo.
NewSG.
1st edn, 1752 [142].
CUL UP
* N/M

144.
[PRÉVOST D'EXILES Abbé Antoine François]
+THE DEAN OF COLERAINE. A Moral History, Founded on the Memoirs of an Illustrious Family in Ireland. Translated from the French. In Three Volumes.
London : Printed for C. Davis against Gray's Inn Gate in Holbourn; C. Hitch and L. Hawes, in Pater-noster Row. 1752.
3 vols. 12mo.
AB(AR,BL,GBF); ESTC t131036; McB 715.
A trans. by William Erskine of *Le Doyen de Killerine*, 1735-40. 1st edns, 1742. Also, 1780 version.
BL Bod UI
* N

145.
[PRICE Howell ap David]
A GENUINE ACCOUNT OF THE LIFE AND TRANSACTIONS OF HOWELL ap DAVID PRICE, GENTLEMAN OF WALES [8 more lines] **Written by Himself.**
London : Printed for T. Osborne, in Gray's Inn. 1752.
302pp. 12mo. Adv-1754 [226] as sold by Jacob Robinson, 3s.
LO 37 (HU); PBG 332.
BL CUL HU
* N

146.
RAMSAY Andrew Michael
+THE TRAVELS OF CYRUS. To which is annexed, A Discourse upon the Theology and Mythology Of the Pagans. By the Chevalier Ramsay. The Eighth Edition.
London : Printed by James Bettenham : And sold by C. Hitch and L. Hawes, at the Red Lion in Pater-noster-Row. 1752.
358pp. 12mo.
ESTC t129760.
1st English edn, 1727 (from Paris edn of 1727). Also, 1728(2x), 1730(3x), 1736, 1739, 1745, 1755 [323], 1763 [787] [788], 1765 [934], 1775, 1778, 1793.
BL
* M/N

147.
S., H.
MEMOIRS OF THE LIFE, SUFFERINGS, AND SURPRISING ADVENTURES OF A NOBLE FOREIGNER AT *******. To which are added Some Instructive Remarks on the Vicissitudes of Fortune. Written by Himself.
London : Printed for C. Corbett, at Addison's Head, in Fleet-street. 1752.
71pp. 12mo. 1s (BB,MR).
Preface signed 'H.S.'
MR VI 77 (Jan. 1752).
AB(BL); BB; EC 218:4; ESTC t072462.
BL Bod
* N/M

Miscellanies

148.
The Female Parricide : or, the History of Mary-Margaret d'Aubray, Marchioness of Brinvillier
[13 more lines]
Reading : Printed by C. Micklewright, And Sold by J. Newbery at the Bible and Sun in St. Paul's Church-Yard, and by all the Booksellers and Pamphlet sellers in Town and Country. 1752.
52pp. 8vo. 1s (tp).
ESTC t078281.
BL CUL
* M

149.
Honesty the Best Policy; or, the History of Roger.
London : Printed for R. Griffiths, in St. Paul's Church-Yard. 1752.
24pp. 8vo. 6d (BB,MR).
MR VII 74-75 (July 1752).
BB; ESTC t036627.
Roger is Henry Boyle, 1st earl of Shannon.
Also, 1752 [150] [151].
BL Bod
* M (sat)

150.
+Honesty the Best Policy; or, the History of Roger.
London : Printed for T. Freeman. 1752.
24pp. 8vo.
ESTC t075754.
1st edn, 1752 [149].
BL CUL
* M (sat)

151.
+Honesty the Best Policy; or, the History of Roger. The Seventh Edition.
London Printed : Dublin; Reprinted in the Year 1752.
32pp. 8vo.
ESTC t058877.
1st edn, 1752 [149].
BL CUL
* M (sat)

152.
+The Protical Son : A Second Welch Preachment, by the Parson of Llangtyddre. On the Return of the
Protical Son.
London : Printed for J. Dorrison, near the Royal Exchange, and sold at the Pamphlet Shops. 1752.
26pp. 8vo.
ESTC t131323.
1st edns and edns listed, 1750 [47].
CUL
* M

153.
The Secret History of Miss Blandy from her First Appearance at Bath, to her Execution at Oxford.
London : Printed for Henry Williams, and sold by the Booksellers at the Exchange, in Ludgate-Street, at
Charing-Cross, and St. James's [1752].
100pp. 8vo. 1s6d (BB,MR)
MR VII 74 (July 1752).
Adv in 1754 [226] as sold by Jacob Robinson, 1s6d.
AB(ELG); BB; ESTC t047392.
There were dozens of miscellaneous pieces relating to the Blandy affair 1752-3. Cf 1752 [160] [162] [163].
BL
* M

154.
[d'Argens Jean Baptiste de Boyer, Marquis]
+The Chinese Spy, Being a Series of Letters between a Chinese Traveller at Paris and his Countrymen in
China, Muscovy, Persia and Japan. The Second Edition.
London : J. Whiston and B. White. 1752.
12mo.
1st edn and edns listed, 1751 [107].
NLC NYPL YU
M

155.
Coyer Gabriel François
A Supplement to Lord Anson's Voyage Round the World. Containing A Discovery and Description of the
Island of Frivola. By the Abbé Coyer. To which is prefix'd An introductory Preface by the Translator.
London : Printed for A. Millar in the Strand, and J. Whiston and B. White, in Fleet-street. 1752.
63pp. 8vo.
AB(BB;SA); BB; ESTC t048934; PBG 317.
Cf 1st version, 1750 [52]. Also, 1752 [156] [157] [158].
BL Bod CUL
* M

156.
Coyer Gabriel François
+A Supplement to Lord Anson's Voyage Round the World. Containing A Discovery and Description of
the Island of Frivola. By the Abbé Coyer. To which is prefix'd An introductory Preface by the
Translator. The Second Edition.
London : Printed for A. Millar in the Strand, and J. Whiston and B. White, in Fleet-street. 1752.
63pp. 8vo. 1s (tp).
ESTC t087967.
1st edn, 1752 [155].
BL Bod
* M

157.
Coyer Gabriel François
+A Supplement to Lord Anson's Voyage Round the World. Containing A Discovery and Description of the Island of Frivola. By the Abbé Coyer. To which is prefix'd An introductory Preface by the Translator. The Second Edition.
Dublin : 1752.
PBG 317, cit. JS v p.53.
1st edn, 1752 [155].
M

158.
Coyer Gabriel François
+A Supplement to Lord Anson's Voyage Round the World. Containing A Discovery and Description of the Island of Frivola. By the Abbé Coyer. To which is prefix'd An introductory Preface by the Translator.
Dublin : Printed for P. Wilson and M. Williamson. 1752.
PBG 317.
1st edn, 1752 [155].
Hispanic Society, NY, as separate from 1752 [157]
M

159.
[Cranstoun Hon. William Henry]
The Memoirs of Miss M– P-¬ a Celebrated Bristol Toast.
1752.
8vo. 1s (MR).
MR VI 140 (Feb. 1752).
M

160.
[Cranstoun Hon. William Henry]
Original Letters to and from Miss Blandy and C– C–
[10 more lines]
London : Printed for S. Johnson near the Hay-market, Charing-cross. 1752.
37pp. 8vo. 1s (tp).
ESTC t043435; LO 42 (BL).
Cf 1752 [153].
BL Bod
* E/M

161.
[Fielding Sarah]
+The Governess; or The Little Female Academy. Being the History of Mrs. Teachum, and her nine girls. With their nine days amusements. By the Author of David Simple. The Fourth Edition.
Dublin : Printed for A. Bradley, and R. James. 1752.
1st edn, 1749. Edns listed, 1751 [110].
FL
M

162.
[Hill John]
Letters from the Inspector to a Lady, With the Genuine Answers. Both printed verbatim from the Originals.
London : Printed for M. Cooper, at the Globe in Pater-noster-Row. 1752.
48pp. 8vo. 1s (BB,MR).
MR VI 145 (Feb. 1752).
AB(AR,BL); BB; ESTC t038491; FB; LO 36 (BL,FB).
Cf 1752 [153].
BL CUL
* M/E

163.
[Hill John]
(+)Letters to a Lady, with Her Genuine Answers. Both printed verbatim from the Originals.
Dublin : Reprinted for P. Wilson, and R. James, Booksellers, in Dame-Street. 1752.
48pp. 8vo.
ESTC t110290.
Cf 1752 [153].
BL CUL
* M/E

164.
Rowe Mrs Elizabeth Singer
+Friendship in Death; In Twenty Letters from the Dead to the Living. To which are added, Letters Moral and Entertaining. In Prose and Verse. In Three Parts. By Mrs Elizabeth Rowe. With the Author's Life prefixt; And other Additions.
Dublin : Printed for John Exshaw, at the Bible on Cork-hill. 1752.
328pp. 8vo.
1st edn, 1728. Edns listed, 1750 [60].
CUL
* M

165.
[Smollett Tobias?]
A Faithful Narrative of the Base and inhuman Arts That were lately practised upon the Brain of Habbakkuk Hilding, Justice, Dealer, and Chapman. Who now lies at his House in Covent-Garden, in a deplorable State of Lunacy; a dreadful Monument of false Friendship and Delusion. By Drawcansir Alexander, Fencing-Master, and Philomath.
London : Printed for J. Sharp, near Temple-Bar. 1752.
24pp. 8vo. 6d (tp).
AB(As,BL); ESTC t033246.
An attack on Fielding.
BL
* M (sat)

166.
ANGELINA. Interspersed with the Histories of Dona Vittorina, Dom. Matheo, and the Chevalier de Riva Franca. Translated from the French.
London : Printed for J. Hinton, at the King's-Arms, in Newgate-Street. 1753.
370pp. 12mo. 3s (BB,MR).
MR VIII 394 (May 1753).
AB(BL); BB; ESTC t088377; NYSL(HC).
H&L suggest trans by Callou from an Italian text.
BL
* N

167.
+ARABIAN NIGHTS' ENTERTAINMENTS. Consisting of one thousand and one Stories, told by the Sultaness of the Indies. Containing a familiar account of the Customs, Manners, and Religion of the Eastern Nations. The Tenth Edition.
London : Longman. 1753.
6 vols.
1st English edn of this version, 1706. Also, 1712, 1715, 1728, 1728-30, 1767 [1061], 1778, 1781, 1785, 1789, 1792(3x), 1793, 1794(2x), 1796(2x), 1798.
DU
C

168.
THE FEMALE RAMBLER, BEING THE ADVENTURES OF MADAM JANETON DE *****. Taken from the French.
London : Reeve. 1753.
12mo. 2s (BB,MR).
MR IX 315-316 (Oct. 1753).
BB.
N

169.
THE HISTORY OF FANNY SEYMOUR.
London : Printed for William Bathoe, at his Circulating-Library in Exeter-Exchange in the Strand. 1753.
319pp. 12mo. 3s (MR).
MR VIII 314 (Apr. 1753).
AB(BL,Pi); BB; ESTC t138868; LO 48 (UP).
Dublin edn, 1752 [170].
BL
* N

170.
+THE HISTORY OF FANNY SEYMOUR.
Dublin : Printed for A. M'Culloch, for John Exshaw, Sarah Cotter, and Richard Watts. 1753.
301pp. 12mo.
SG 484.
1st edn, 1752 [169].
UP
N

171.
THE HISTORY OF SOPHIA SHAKESPEAR.
London : Printed and sold by W. Reeve, in Fleet-Street; H. Slater, in Drury-Lane; and at the
Printing-Office, in Hind-Court, Fleet-Street. 1753.
200pp. 8vo. 3s bound (BB,MR) 2s6d sew'd (½tp).
MR VIII 230 (Mar. 1753).
AB(JH); BB; EC 231:2; ESTC t066906.
BL Bod
* N

172.
+THE MEMOIRS OF FIDELIO AND HARRIOT : Wherein the Contrast between Virtue
and Vice is fully Exhibited from a Real Fact. Translated in the Year 1720. Preserved in the
Original Manuscript of Mrs Harvey.
Dublin : 1753.
AB(TDW).
1st edn, 1752 [121].
N

173.
MEMOIRS OF SIR CHARLES GOODVILLE AND HIS FAMILY : In a Series of Letters
to a Friend. In Two Volumes.
London : Printed for Daniel Browne, without Temple-Bar, and J. Whiston, and B. White, in
Fleet-Street. 1753.
2 vols. 12mo. 6s (BB,MR).
MR VIII 187-189 (Mar. 1753).
AB(T,TDW); BB; ESTC t140100; LO 51 (HU,UP); SG 727.
Cf WS, p.65.
BL HU UP
* E

174.
THE TRAVELS AND ADVENTURES OF WILLIAM BINGFIELD, ESQ; Containing; As
surprizing a Fluctuation of Circumstances, both by Sea and Land, as ever befel one Man.
With an accurate Account of the Shape, Nature, and Properties of that most furious and
amazing Animal, the Dog-Bird.
London : Printed for E. Withers, at the Seven Stars, in Fleet-street; and R. Baldwin, at the Rose
in Pater-noster-Row. 1753.
2 vols. 12mo. 5s (MR).
MR VIII 77 (Jan. 1753).
BB; EC 126:4; ESTC t070722; LO 43 (BL,UI); McB 91; PBG 335.
Also, 1799.
BL Bod UI YU
* N

175.
THE TRAVELS OF MONS. LE POST-CHAISE. Written by Himself.
London : Printed for J. Swan, near Northumberland-House in the Strand. 1753.
63pp. 8vo. 1s (BB,MR,tp).
MR VIII 311 (Apr. 1753).
AB(BH); BB; ESTC t059719.
BL
* N

176.
THE TRAVELS OF ZOROASTER, KING OF THE BACTRIANS, Composed chiefly for the Instruction of a Young Prince.
London : Printed, and sold by J. Fuller, at the Bible and Dove in Ave-Maria Lane; J. Fuller, in Butcher-hall Lane; J. Heath, at Nottingham; A. Bently, at Hull; J. Fleming, at New-Castle on Tyne; Mr. Neal, at Chatham, and Mr. Matthews, at Bath. 1753.
3 vols. 12mo. 9s (BB,MR).
MR IX 229-230 (Sept. 1753).
AB(GW); BB; ESTC t107737; LO 173 (as 1763).
BL CUL UP
* N/M

177.
BARRY Melinda
[and MARCHANT John]
THE AMOROUS MERCHANT : OR, INTRIGUING HUSBAND. Being a Curious and Uncommon Process of Love and Law. [8 more lines]
Written by Mrs Graham, now Mrs Barry, in the Manner of Constantia Phillips.
London : Printed for and Sold by Mrs Barry, in Prujean-court, in the old-baily; where may be seen at full length the original Pictures, together with the love-letters, Bonds &c. 1753.
64pp. 8vo. BL copy MS note as never published, the victim having bought up all the copies.
AB(BL); ESTC t099934.
BL
* N/M

178.
du BOSCQ Jacques
THE ACCOMPLISH'D WOMAN. Written in French by M. Du Boscq, a Franciscan, Counsellor and Preacher in ordinary to the King in the Year MDCXXX. In Two Volumes. Translated by a Gentleman of Cambridge.
London : Printed by and for J. Watts; and Sold by him at the Printing-Office in Wild-Court near Lincoln's-Inn Fields, And by B. Dod at the Bible and Key in Ave-Mary-Lane near Stationers-hall. 1753.
2 vols. 12mo.
AB(BL); ESTC t127505.
BL CUL
* N

179.
[CHAIGNEAU William]
+THE HISTORY OF JACK CONNOR. The Second Edition, Corrected.
London : Printed for W. Johnston, at the Golden Ball, in St. Paul's Church-Yard. 1753.
2 vols. 12mo.
ESTC t066943.
1st edn and edns listed, 1752 [124].
BL CUL HU YU
* N

180.
[CHAIGNEAU William]
+THE HISTORY OF JACK CONNOR. The Third Edition.
Dublin : Printed for Abraham Bradley, at the King's Arms and Two Bibles in Dame-street. 1753.
2 vols in 1.
ESTC t066942.
1st edn and edns listed, 1752 [124].
IU
N

181.
[COVENTRY Francis]
+THE HISTORY OF POMPEY THE LITTLE; OR, THE LIFE AND ADVENTURES OF
A LAP-DOG. The Fourth Edition.
Dublin : Printed by George Faulkner, in Essex-street. 1753.
182pp. 12mo.
SG 213.
1st edn and edns listed, 1751 [77].
CUL UP
* N

182.
[DEFOE Daniel]
+THE LIFE AND STRANGE SURPRISING ADVENTURES OF ROBINSON CRUSOE;
OF YORK, MARINER
[7 more lines]
Written by Himself. The Tenth Edition, Adorn'd with Cuts. In Two Volumes.
London : Printed for T. and T. Longman, C. Hitch and L. Hawes, J. Hodges, B. Dod, J. and J.
Rivington, T. Trye, R. Baldwin, W. Johnston, and M. Cooper. 1753.
2 vols. 12mo.
EC 53:3; ESTC t072280; McB 221.
Vol II, 'The Farther Adventures of Robinson Crusoe; Being the Second and Last Part of his Life [4 more lines]
The Eighth Edition'. Both vols issued together.
1st edn, 1719. Edns listed, 1752 [129].
BL Bn NYPL UI YU
* N/M

183.
[FIELDING Sarah]
(+)THE ADVENTURES OF DAVID SIMPLE. Volume The Last, In which His History is
concluded.
London : Printed for A. Millar, in the Strand. 1753.
240pp. 12mo. 3s (MR).
MR VIII 143 (Feb. 1753).
AB(Bk); BB; ESTC t108079.
1st 2 vols published 1744 (2x, JB 149-149a). Full edns, 1761 [648], 1772, 1782, 1788, 1792, and abridgment,
1775. Cf 1752 [133].
BL Bod NYPL UP YU
* N

184.
[GÉNARD François]
THE SCHOOL OF WOMAN; OR, MEMOIRS OF CONSTANTIA. Address'd to the
Dutchess of ***. By the Author of the School of Man, a Moral Work: Suppress'd at Paris,
by Order of the King of France. Translated from the French.
London : Printed for J. Robinson, in Ludgate-Street. 1753.
210pp. 12mo. 3s (BB,MR).
MR IX 396 (Nov. 1753).
AB(EM,Pi); BB; EC 60:4; ESTC t130915.
Sometimes attributed to Dupuis.
BL CUL
* N/M

185.
[GRAFIGNY Françoise d'Issembourg d'Happoncourt de]
+LETTERS WRITTEN BY A PERUVIAN PRINCESS. Translated from the French.
London : Printed in the Year. 1753.
176pp. 12mo.
ESTC t127973.
Trans. from *Lettres d'une Peruvienne*, 1747. 1st English edn, 1748. Also, edns and further versions, 1748, 1749,
1755 [315], 1759 [490], 1768 [1212], 1771, 1774, 1782, 1787, 1792, 1795.
BL
* E

186.
[HAYWOOD Mrs Eliza]
**THE HISTORY OF JEMMY AND JENNY JESSAMY. In Three Volumes. By the Author
of The History of Betsy Thoughtless.**
London : Printed for T. Gardner, at Cowley's Head, facing St. Clement's Church, in the Strand;
and sold by all Booksellers in Town and Country. 1753.
3 vols. 12mo. 9s (MR).
MR VIII 77 (Jan. 1753).
AB(AR,BL); BB; ESTC t075382; FB; LO 46 (FB,HU,UI,UP); McB 419; SG 434.
Dublin edn, 1753 [187], and 1769 [1316], 1785.
BL [imperf] Bod CUL HU Tx UI UP
* N

187.
[HAYWOOD Mrs Eliza]
**+THE HISTORY OF JEMMY AND JENNY JESSAMY. By the Author of The History of
Betsy Thoughtless.**
Dublin : Printed for R. Main. 1753.
3 vols. 12mo.
ESTC t075383.
1st edn and edns listed, 1753 [186].
BL DU
N

188.
[HAYWOOD Mrs Eliza?]
**MODERN CHARACTERS : Illustrated by Histories in Real Life, and Address'd to the
Polite World.**
London : Printed for T. Gardner, at Cowley's Head in the Strand; and sold by all Booksellers in
Town and Country. 1753.
2 vols. 12mo. 6s (MR).
MR IX 144 (Aug. 1753).
AB(Do,Pi); BB; ESTC t067806; LO 47 (HU,UP); SG 447. Cf 1767 [1163].
BL Bod HU UP
* N/C

189.
[LEAF Jeremy?]
+WORLDLY COMPLIANCES. The Second Edition, with Additions.
London : Printed for D. Job, at the Spread-Eagle, in King-street, Covent-Garden; R. Baldwin, at
the Rose, in Pater-noster-Row; and P. Stevens, facing Stationers-Hall. 1753.
92pp. 4to.
ESTC t140142.
1st edn, 1752 [137].
BL
* N/M

190.
[LEZAY-MARNESIA Charlotte-Antoinette de Bressey, Marquise de]
LETTERS FROM JULIA, THE DAUGHTER OF AUGUSTUS, TO OVID. A Manuscript
Discovered at Herculaneum. Translated from a Copy of the Original. To which is annexed,
The Lady and the Sylph. A Visionary Tale.
London : Printed for Lockyer Davis, near Salisbury-Court, Fleet-street. 1753.
216pp. 12mo. 2s (BB,MR).
MR IX 145 (Aug. 1753).
BB; FB; LO 44 (BL,FB,MR,UP); SG 639.
BL CUL UP
* E/M

191.
[RICHARDSON Samuel]
THE HISTORY OF SIR CHARLES GRANDISON. In a Series of Letters. Published from
the Originals, By the Editor of Pamela and Clarissa. In Seven Volumes.
London, Printed by S. Richardson, and Dublin, Re-printed and sold by the Booksellers. 1753.
Vols I-VI dated 1753. Vol VII 'and Last' dated 1754. Vol VII is 'Re-printed, by and for H.
Saunders, at the Corner of Christ-Church Lane'.
7 vols. 12mo.
Published in Dublin, Nov. 1753. Vol. VII published Apr. 1754. A very complicated and controversial
publication history. Details given, WS, pp.65-70; RCC pp.11-12,72; & T. C. Duncan Eaves and Ben D. Kimpel,
Samuel Richardson. A Biography (Oxford, 1971), pp.377-84.
Also, 1754 [246] [247] [248] [249], ['4th' edn prepared but not published, 7 vols, 1756], 1762 [735], 1766
[1034], 1767 [1128], 1770, 1776(2x), 1780, 1781, 1783, 1785, 1786, 1796, and abridgments, [1770 with earlier
adv. Dec. 1768 but not published? SR J317], 1780, 1789, 1792. Cf 1760 [537].
Bod NLI YU
* E

192.
[SMOLLETT Tobias]
THE ADVENTURES OF FERDINAND COUNT FATHOM. By the Author of Roderick
Random. In Two Volumes.
London : Printed for W. Johnston, at the Golden Ball in St. Paul's Church-yard. 1753.
2 vols. 12mo. 6s (MR).
MR VIII 203-214 (Mar. 1753).
AB(BL,K,Mg); BB; ESTC t055294; LO 52 (RL,UI,UP); McB 840; MW 205; SG 996.
Also, 1753 [193] [194], and 1771, 1772, 1777, 1780, 1782, 1784, 1786, 1789, 1792, 1795, 1796, 1797.
A '2nd edn' was advertised in the London Chronicle in 1760 but no evidence that it appeared.
BL Bod HU PU UI UP YU
* N

193.
[SMOLLETT Tobias]
+THE ADVENTURES OF FERDINAND COUNT FATHOM. By the Author of Roderick
Random. In Two Volumes.
London : Printed for T. Johnson, at the Golden Ball in St. Paul's Church-yard. 1753.
2 vols. 12mo.
EC 198:10; ESTC t055295 (with 2 variants at BL).
This edn not listed in MW.
1st edn and edns listed, 1753 [192].
BL CUL
* N

194.
[SMOLLETT Tobias]
+THE ADVENTURES OF FERDINAND COUNT FATHOM. By the Author of Roderick
Random.
Dublin : Printed for R. Main, Bookseller, in Dame-street. 1753.
2 vols.
MW 206; RCC pp.72,240.
Published Mar. 1753. 1st edn and edns listed, 1753 [192].
NLI UC YU
N

195.
[SMYTHIES Miss]
THE STAGE-COACH : Containing the Character of Mr. Manly and the History of his
Fellow-Travellers.
London : Printed for T. Osborne in Gray's-Inn. 1753.
2 vols. 12mo. 6s (BB,MR).
MR IX 394 (Nov. 1753).
AB; BB; LO 53 (UI,UP); McB 865; SG 1010.
Dublin edn, 1754 [258] and 1789, 1791.
CUL UI UP
* N

196.
[TIPHAIGNE DE LA ROCHE Charles François]
AMILEC, OR THE SEEDS OF MANKIND. Translated from the French.
London : Printed for W. Needham over-against Gray's-Inn Gate in Holbourn; and sold by M.
Cooper at the Globe in Pater-noster-row. 1753.
111pp. 12mo. 1s (MR) 1s6d (tp, with '6d' erased in BL copy).
MR IX 228 (Sept. 1753).
AB(BL); BB; EC 15:7; ESTC t096270.
BL
* N

197.
[WOLLASTON George]
THE LIFE AND HISTORY OF A PILGRIM. By G— W—.
Dublin : Printed and Sold by Oli. Nelson, at Milton's Head in Skinner-Row. 1753.
540pp. 8vo.
EC 233:3; ESTC t070274; McB 963; SG 1104.
Dublin edn, 1753 [198].
BL Bod CUL UP
* N

198.
WOLLASTON George
+THE LIFE AND HISTORY OF A PILGRIM : A NARRATIVE FOUNDED ON FACT.
By George Wollaston Esq.
Dublin Printed : London Reprinted : For J. Whiston and B. White in Fleet-street, J. Payne in
Pater-noster-row, and M. Sheepey near the Royal Exchange. 1753.
327pp. 12mo. 3s (BB,MR).
MR IX 226 (Sept. 1753).
AB(AR,Do,HN); BB; EC 166:2; ESTC t057813; McB 964; SG 1105.
1st edn, 1753 [197].
BL Bod CUL UP
* N

Miscellanies

199.
Æsops Fables. With Instructive Morals and Reflections
[11 more lines]
London : Printed by S. Richardson for T. & T. Longman, C. Hitch & L. Hawes, I. Hodges, I. & I. Rivington, G. Keith & R. Dodsley [1753] (BL,CUL).
192pp. 12mo.
McB 10.
English versions since 1480s. From 1700, 1704, 1708, 1711, 1712, 1720, 1722, 1737, 174¬ 1743 (not a full list, with many chapbooks & verse edns). Also, 1754 [264], 1760 [595] [616], 1765 [948], 1770. Cf Croxall's edn, 1747, & incl. edns, 1760 [601], 1766 [1044], 1767 [1150]; & Dodsley's *Select Fables*, 1761 [690] & edns, 1761 [691], 1763 [798], 1764 [873], 1765 [955], 1767 [1159], 1781, 1798. From 1770 edns almost annually.
CUL UI
* M/C

200.
(+)**The Female Apothecary deprived of her Office, or a dose of French physic to de [sic] ladies. Translated from the French.**
London : Wakelin. 1753.
12mo. 6d (MR)
MR VIII 143 (Feb. 1753), as a reissue of 1751 [104], *The Artful Lover*.
M

201.
The Gamester, a True Story, on which the Tragedy of that name Now acting at the Theatre Royal in Drury-Lane, Is Founded. Translated from the Italian.
London : Printed and sold by W. Reeve, in Fleet-Street. 1753.
20pp. 8vo. 6d (MR,tp).
MR VIII 146 (Feb. 1753).
AB(BL); BB; ESTC t064277.
The play is by Edward Moore.
BL Bod
* M

202.
The Story on Which the New Tragedy, call'd, The Brothers, Now acting at the Theatre Royal in Drury Lane, Is Founded. Dedicated to the Author of the Play.
London : Printed and sold by W. Reeve, in Fleet-Street. 1753.
22pp. 8vo. 6d (tp).
ESTC t100511.
Dedication signed 'M. O.' The play was by Edward Young.
BL
* M/N

203.
The True Life of Betty Ireland. With Her Birth, Education, and Adventures. Together with Some account of her elder Sister, Blanch of Britain. Containing Sundry very curious Particulars.
London : Printed for J. Robinson, at the Golden Lion in Ludgate-street. 1753.
30pp. 8vo. 6d (BB,MR).
MR VIII 79 (Jan. 1753).
BB; ESTC t115245.
Included in the 1756 *Patriotic Miscellany*. Also, 1753 [204]. Cf 1750 [50].
BL
* M

204.
+The True Life of Betty Ireland. With Her Birth, Education, and Adventures. Together with Some Account of her elder Sister, Blanch of Britain. Containing, Sundry very curious Particulars.
London, Printed : Dublin, Reprinted for Peter Wilson, in Dame-street. 1753.
36pp. 8vo.
ESTC t1051886.
Earlier edn, 1753 [203].
BL CUL
* M

205.
d'Argens Jean Baptiste de Boyer, Marquis
+The Jewish Spy : Being a Philosophical, Historical and Critical Account Correspondence By Letters Which lately passed between certain Jews in Turkey, Italy, France &c. Translated from the Originals into French, By the Marquis D'Argens; And now done into English. In Four Volumes.
Dublin : Printed for Oli. Nelson, at Milton's-Head, in Skinner-Row; and H. Saunders, at the Corner of Christ-Church-Lane. 1753.
4 vols. 12mo.
ESTC t110242.
1st edns, 1739-40. Also, 1744, 1765 [957], 1766 [1048].
BL Bod CUL
* M

206.
Cyrano de Bergerac Savinien
Derrick [Samuel] *trans.*
A Voyage to the Moon : With Some Account of the Solar World. A Comical Romance. Done from the French of M. Cyrano de Bergerac. By Mr. Derrick.
London : Printed for P. Vaillant, in the Strand; R. Griffiths, in St. Paul's Church-Yard, and G. Woodfall, at Charing-Cross. 1754 [1753].
162pp. 12mo. 1s6d (MR).
MR IX 314-315 (Oct. 1753).
BB; EC 10:1; ESTC t131210.
Trans. of *Voyage dans la lune*. Dublin edn, 1754 [276].
BL
* M

207.
[Hamilton Count Anthony]
(+)Memoirs of the Life of the Count de Grammont. Containing the Amorous Intrigues of the Court of England; in the Reign of King Charles II. Translated from the French.
London : Vaillant. 1753.
12mo. 3s (MR).
MR IX 395 (Nov. 1753).
1st English edn, 1714, trans. of *La vie du Grammont*, 1713. Also, 1760 [619]. Cf Goldsmith trans. 1760 [620].
M

208.
[Hill John]
The Conduct of a Married Life. Laid down in a Series of Letters, written by the Honourable Juliana-Susannah Seymour, to a Young Lady, her Relation, Lately Married.
London : Printed for R. Baldwin, in Pater-noster Row. 1753.
257pp. 12mo.
AB(ELG,St,TDW); BB; ESTC t119297; McB 449.
Also 1754 edns [277] [278].
BL Bod CUL UI
* M

209.
[Moore Edward]
The Story of Mr and Mrs Wilson.
London : 1753.
AB(ELG).
M

210.
Rowe Mrs Elizabeth Singer
+Friendship in Death; In Twenty Letters From the Dead to the Living. To which are added, Letters Moral and Entertaining, In Prose and Verse : In Three Parts. In Two Volumes. By Mrs Elizabeth Rowe.
London : Printed for Henry Lintot. 1753.
2 vols. 12mo.
ESTC t070702.
1st edn, 1728. Edns listed, 1750 [60].
BL
* M

211.
Voltaire François Marie Arouet de
Micromegas : A Comic Romance. Being a Severe Satire upon the Philosophy, Ignorance, and Self-Conceit of Mankind. Together with a Detail of the Crusades : And a new Plan for the History of the Human Mind. Translated from the French of M. de Voltaire.
London : Printed for D. Wilson, and T. Durham, at Plato's Head, near Round-Court, in the Strand. 1753.
252pp. 12mo.
AB(AR,B&G,RI); BB; ESTC t137640.
BL Bod CUL
* M

1754

212.
THE ADVENTURES OF DICK HAZARD.
London : Printed and sold by W. Reeve, at Shakespear's-Head, in Fleet-Street, 1755 [1754].
247pp. 12mo. 3s (BB,MR).
MR XI 470 (Dec. 1754).
AB(BL,Pi); BB; ESTC t071393; LO 74 (UI); McB 4.
2nd edn, 1759 [463] (retitled 'Fortunate Imposter').
BL Bod UI
* N

213.
THE ADVENTURES OF MISS POLLY B–CH–RD AND SAMUEL TYRREL ESQ. Written by the Lady Herself. Wherein are introduced, the amours of Los Cardos and Zaphsharrak.
London : Woodyer. 1754.
12mo. 3s (BB,MR).
MR X 147-148 (Feb. 1754).
BB.
N

214.
THE ADVENTURES OF WILLIAM B–DS–W, COMMONLY STILED DEVIL DICK, THE SON AND BROTHER TO TWO PIOUS MINISTERS
[long title]
Drawn up for the Benefit of Mankind, by Mr. B–ds–w's own hand, and published from his papers.
London : Robinson etc. 1754.
2 vols. 12mo. 6s (MR).
MR XI 470 (Dec. 1754).
N

215.
THE HISTORY AND ADVENTURES OF A LADY'S SLIPPERS AND SHOES. Written by Themselves.
London : Printed : And Sold by M. Cooper in Pater-noster Row. 1754.
58pp. 8vo. 1s (tp).
ESTC t060655; RKM.
Reissued, 1755 [289].
BL IU NLC UP
* N

216.
THE HISTORY AND ADVENTURES OF FRANK HAMMOND.
London : Printed for R. Griffiths, at the Dunciad in Pater-noster-Row. 1754.
267pp. 12mo. 3s (BB).
MR X 391-392 (May 1754).
AB(WB) as 'Adventures of'; BB; ESTC t106456; LO 64 (UP).
2nd edn, 1755 [288].
BL UP
* N

217.
THE HISTORY OF HONORIA, BEING THE ADVENTURES OF A YOUNG LADY. Interspersed with the Histories of Emilia, Julia, and Others. By a Young Gentleman.
London : Printed for the Author, and Sold by W. Bizet, at the Golden Ball, in St. Clement's Church-Yard. 1754.
234pp. 12mo. 3s (BB,MR).
MR X 480 (June 1754).
AB(McL); BB.
CUL
* N

218.
THE HISTORY OF JASPER BANKS, COMMONLY CALL'D, THE HANDSOME MAN. In Two Volumes.
London : Reeve. 1754.
12mo. 2s6d sewed (adv-1757 [398]) 6s (BB,MR).
MR X 479-480 (June 1754).
BB.
Dublin edn, 1754 [219].
N

219.
+THE HISTORY OF JASPER BANKS, COMMONLY CALL'D, THE HANDSOME MAN.
In Two Volumes.
Dublin : Printed for G. Faulkner in Essex-street. 1754.
2 vols in 1. 316pp. 12mo.
1st edn, 1754 [218].
Bod
* N

220.
THE HISTORY OF JOSHUA TRUEMAN, ESQ; AND MISS PEGGY WILLIAMS. In Two
Volumes.
London : Printed for D. Wilson and T. Durham, at Plato's head in the Strand. 1754.
2 vols. 12mo. 6s (BB,MR).
MR XI 466 (Dec. 1754).
AB(BL,ELG); BB; EC 242:2; ESTC t066372; LO 65 (UI); McB 454.
Dublin edn, 1755 [291].
BL UI
* N

221.
THE HISTORY OF SIR HARRY HERALD AND SIR EDWARD HAUNCH. In Three
Volumes.
London : Printed for, and Sold by, F. Noble, at his Circulating Library in King-street, Covent-
Garden, and J. Noble, at his Circulating Library in St. Martin's-Court, near Leicester-Square,
1755 [1754].
3 vols. 12mo. 9s (BB,MR).
MR XI 467 (Dec. 1754).
AB(ELG,Pi,WC) as by Henry Fielding; BB; EC 232:4; ESTC t066905; WLC iii 348.
Dublin edn, 1755 [295].
BL
* N

222.
THE HISTORY OF WILL RAMBLE, A LIBERTINE. Compiled from Genuine Materials,
And The Several Incidents taken from Real Life. In Two Volumes.
London : Printed for the Author : And Sold by G. Woodfall, at the King's Arms, Charing-Cross,
1755 [1754].
2 vols. 8vo. 6s (BB,MR).
MR XI 466-467 (Dec. 1754).
AB(TT); BB; ESTC t082661.
BL
* N

223.
THE LIFE AND ADVENTURES OF JAMES FRENEY, COMMONLY CALLED
CAPTAIN FRENEY. From the Time of his first entering on the Highway, in Ireland, to the
Time of his Surrender, being a Series of Five Years remarkable Adventures. Written by
Himself.
Dublin : Printed and Sold by S. Powell for the Author. 1754.
146pp. 12mo. Subn.
ESTC t069293.
BL CUL
* N

224.
THE MOCK-MONARCHS : OR, THE BENEFITS OF HIGH BLOOD.
London : Printed for Stanley Crowder, and Henry Woodgate, at the Golden Ball, in Pater-noster Row [1754?] (BL,CUL).
2 vols. 12mo. 6s (BB,MR).
MR XI 471 (Dec. 1754).
EC 223:4; ESTC t068751.
BL CUL
* N

225.
+A NARRATIVE OF THE LIFE AND DISTRESSES OF SIMON MASON, APOTHECARY. Setting forth the injurious Treatment he hath met with; with many other translations
[5 more lines]
Birmingham : Printed for the Author by T. Warren Jun. near the New Chappel. [1754] (BL).
117pp. 8vo.
ESTC t075679.
A reissue of the 1752 [122] edn. Cf 1756 [357].
BL
* N/M

226.
THE SCOTCH MARINE : OR, MEMOIRS OF THE LIFE OF CELESTINA; A Young Lady, who secretly deserting her Family, spent two Years in strict Amity, as a Man, with her beloved Castor.
[11 more lines]
London : Printed for J. Robinson, in Ludgate Street [1754].
2 vols. 12mo. 6s (BB,MR).
MR X 148 (Feb. 1754).
BB.
Dublin edn, 1761 [638].
Bod [as 1755] HU [as ?1752]
* N

227.
THE TEMPLE BEAU; OR THE TOWN COQUETS. A Novel.
London : Printed for W. Owen, at Homer's Head, near Temple-Bar and E. Baker, at Tunbridge-Wells. 1754.
208pp. 12mo. 2s6d (MR).
MR X 148 (Feb. 1754).
AB(BL); EC228:2; ESTC t070921; LO 72 (UI,UP); McB 904; SG 1028.
2nd edn, 1754 [228].
BL UI UP
N

228.
+THE TEMPLE BEAU; OR THE TOWN COQUETS. A Novel. The Second Edition.
London : Printed for W. Owen, at Homer's Head, near Temple-Bar and E. Baker, at Tunbridge-Wells. 1754.
208pp. 12mo.
1st edn, 1754 [227].
CUL
* N

229.
THE TRAVELS OF MR. DRAKE MORRIS, MERCHANT IN LONDON. Containing his
Sufferings and Distresses in Several Voyages at Sea. Written by Himself.
London : Printed for the Author : And Sold by R. Baldwin, at the Rose in Pater-noster Row,
1755 [1754].
328pp. 12mo. 3s (MR).
MR XI 395 (Nov. 1754).
ESTC t099702; LO 73 (BL,HU,LC); PBG 338-9.
2nd edn, 1755 [299]. Also, 1797.
BL Bn Bod HU LC
* N

230.
BUTTON Edward
A NEW TRANSLATION OF THE PERSIAN TALES; From an Original Version of the
Indian Comedies of Mocles; Wherein Care has been taken to expunge all those useless
Repetitions, and trifling Circumstances, with which the Oriental Writings are encumbered :
so that The Stories are rendered less tedious, and more instructive, the Whole being
reduced into one small Volume. Designed for the Service and Amusement of the British
Ladies. By Edward Button, Gent.
London : Printed for W. Owen, at Homer's-Head in Fleet Street. 1754.
324pp. 12mo. 3s (MR).
MR XI 395 (Nov. 1754).
BB.
Also, 1761 [642].
Bod
* C

231.
[le CAMUS Antoine]
ABDEKER; OR, THE ART OF PRESERVING BEAUTY. Translated from an Arabian
Manuscript.
London : Printed for A. Millar, in the Strand. 1754.
220pp. 12mo. 3s (BB,MR).
MR XI 393 (Nov. 1754).
AB(AR,BL,RI); BB; ESTC t086863; LO 67 (UI); McB 532.
A trans. of le Camus, Abdeker, ou l'art de conserver la beauté.
Dublin edn, 1756 [366].
BL CUL UI
* N/M

232.
[CHETWOOD William Rufus]
+THE VOYAGES, TRAVELS AND ADVENTURES, OF WILLIAM OWEN GWIN
VAUGHAN, ESQ; With the History of his Brother Jonathan Vaughan, Six Years a Slave
in Tunis. Intermix'd with the Histories of Maria, Clerimont, Eleanora, and Others. Full of
various Turns of Fortune.
Dublin : Printed, and Sold by the Editor, W. R. Chetwood, in the Four-Court-Marshalsea; Messrs
G. Risk, G. and A. Ewing, P. Wilson, R. James, R. Main, S. Price, M. Williamson, W.
Whetstone, and B. Edmond, in Dover-street; G. Faulkner, in Essex-street; J. Esdall, on Cork-hill;
S. Coker, and R. Watts, in Skinner-row; T. Watson, in Caple-street; Booksellers in Dublin; and
J. Hay, Bookseller in Belfast. 1754.
328pp. 12mo. Subn.
ESTC t138251.
1st edn, 1736. Also, 1760 [564].
BL
* N

233.
[DODD William?]
**THE SISTERS; OR, THE HISTORY OF LUCY AND CAROLINE SANSON, Entrusted to
a false Friend. In Two Volumes.**
London : Printed for T. Waller, opposite Fetter-Lane in Fleet-street. 1754.
2 vols. 12mo. 6s (MR).
MR X 308 (Apr. 1754).
AB(AR,BL,ELG); BB as 1759(edn?); EC 234:1; ESTC t064735; LO 54 (UP).
Also, 1781, 1782.
BL Bod UP
* N

233a.
FIELDING Henry
**+THE HISTORY OF THE ADVENTURES OF JOSEPH ANDREWS AND HIS FRIEND
MR. ABRAHAM ADAMS. The Third Edition.**
Dublin : Printed for G. and A. Ewing, and W. Smith in Dame-street, and G. Faulkner in Essex-
street. 1754.
2 vols. 12mo.
1st edn, 1742. Edns listed, 1751 [84].
TCD
N

234.
FIELDING Henry
**(+)THE LIFE OF MR. JONATHAN WILD THE GREAT. A New Edition. With
considerable Corrections and Additions. By Henry Fielding Esq.**
London : Printed for A. Millar, in the Strand. 1754.
263pp. 12mo. 3s (MR).
MR X 238 (Mar. 1754).
BB; LO 58 (RL); McB 299.
From 1743 'Miscellanies'. Also, 1754 [235], 1755 [313], 1758 [439], 1775, 1782, 1785. Cf 1758 [449].
Bod CUL PU Tx UI YU
* N

235.
FIELDING Henry
**+THE LIFE OF MR. JONATHAN WILD THE GREAT. A New Edition, with considerable
corrections and additions. By Henry Fielding Esq.**
Dublin : Printed by S. Powell, for John Smith. 1754.
396pp. 12mo.
ESTC t089910.
1st separate edn, with edns listed, 1754 [234].
BL
* N

236.
[FIELDING Sarah and
COLLIER Jane]
THE CRY : A NEW DRAMATIC FABLE. In Three Volumes.
London : Printed for R. & J. Dodsley in Pall-mall. 1754.
3 vols. 12mo. 9s (BB,MR).
MR X 280-282 (Apr. 1754).
AB(AR,BL,RI); BB; ESTC t141110; LO 59 (UI,UP); McB 309; SG 327.
Dublin edn, 1754 [237].
BL Bod CUL UI UP
* N

237.
[FIELDING Sarah and
COLLIER Jane]
+THE CRY : A NEW DRAMATIC FABLE. In Two Volumes.
Dublin : Printed by George Faulkner in Essex-street. 1754.
2 vols. 12mo.
ESTC t134575; McB 310.
1st edn, 1754 [236].
Bod CUL UI
* N

238.
[GARDINER Richard]
THE HISTORY OF PUDICA, A LADY OF N-RF-LK. With an Account of Her Five
Lovers; [12 more lines]
By William Honeycomb.
London : Printed for M. Cooper, in Pater-Noster Row. 1754.
99pp. 8vo. 1s6d (MR).
MR X 160 (Feb. 1754).
ESTC t063048; LO 61 (UP); SG 349.
BL Bod UP
* N/M

239.
[GOMEZ Madeleine Angélique Poisson de]
[HAYWOOD Mrs Eliza trans.]
+LA BELLE ASSEMBLÉE; Being a Curious Collection of some very remarkable incidents
which happen'd to persons of the first Quality in France. Written in French. The Seventh
Edition.
London : Printed for D. Browne. 1754.
4 vols. 12mo.
1st English edn, 1724. Also, 1725, 1727, 1728, 1731, 1731-4, 1732, 1735, 1736-8, 1743, 1749, 1765 [917].
AAS HU NYPL UF WCL YU
N/M

240.
[GUTHRIE William]
THE FRIENDS : A SENTIMENTAL HISTORY : Describing Love as a Virtue as well as a
Passion. In Two Volumes.
London : Printed for T. Waller, opposite Fetter-Lane in Fleet-street. 1754.
2 vols. 12mo. 6s (MR).
MR X 144 (Feb. 1754).
AB(BL,Mg,St); BB; ESTC t072177; LO 63 (RL,UI); McB 401.
BL Bod CUL UI
* N

241.
[KIMBER Edward]
THE HISTORY OF THE LIFE AND ADVENTURES OF MR. ANDERSON. Containing
His strange Varieties of Fortune in Europe and America. Compiled from his Own Papers.
London : Printed for W. Owen, at Homer's-Head, near Temple-Bar. 1754.
288pp. 12mo. 3s (BB,MR).
MR X 147 (Feb. 1754).
AB(BL,MH); BB.
Also 1754 [242] [243], and 1780, 1782.
BL PU UP VU YU
* N

242.
[KIMBER Edward]
+THE HISTORY OF THE LIFE AND ADVENTURES OF MR. ANDERSON. Containing
His strange Varieties of Fortune in Europe and America. Compiled from his Own Papers.
The Second Edition.
London : Printed for W. Owen, at Homer's-Head, near Temple-Bar. 1754.
288pp. 12mo.
1st edn and edns listed, 1754 [241].
UCLA
N

243.
[KIMBER Edward]
+THE HISTORY OF THE LIFE AND ADVENTURES OF MR. ANDERSON. Containing
His strange Varieties of Fortune in Europe and America. Compiled from his own Papers.
Dublin : Printed by Richard James, at Newton's Head in Dame-street. 1754.
154pp. 12mo.
EC 92:7; ESTC t057345.
1st edn and edns listed, 1754 [241].
BL UM
* N

244.
[la PLACE Pierre Antoine de]
[SCOTT Mrs Sarah Robinson *trans.*]
AGREEABLE UGLINESS: OR, THE TRIUMPH OF THE GRACES. Exemplified in the
real Life and Fortunes of a young Lady of some Distinction.
London : Printed for R. & J. Dodsley, in Pall-mall. 1754.
259pp. 12mo. 3s (MR).
MR X 144-145 (Feb. 1754).
AB(Ht,Mg,St); BB; ESTC t070708; LO 69 (UP); SG 933.
Trans. of *La Laideur Amiable, et les dangers de la Beauté*, Onderwyzer, *MLN*, LXX (Dec. 1755), pp.578-580.
BL CUL UP
* N

245.
[le PRINCE DE BEAUMONT Jeanne Marie]
THE HISTORY OF A YOUNG LADY OF DISTINCTION. In a Series of Letters. In Two
Volumes.
London : Printed for F. Noble, at his Circulating Library, in King-Street, Covent-Garden; and J.
Noble, at his Circulating Library, in St. Martin's-Court, near Leicester Square. 1754.
2 vols. 12mo. 6s (BB,MR).
MR X 307-308 (Apr. 1754).
AB(BL,St,T); BB; EC 165:7; ESTC t061267; FB; SG 623.
BL gives authorship as Anne Louise Élie de Beaumont, citing MR XXXV 328, rev. of 1766 edn, although this
rev. cites only tp as 'from the French of Madame de Beaumont'. The Nobles' 1758 edn [445], however, clearly
states Madame le Prince de Beaumont. Further edns, 1754 [245a], 1758 [445], 1766 [1029], 1767 [1125].
BL Bod DU UP
* E

245a.
[le PRINCE DE BEAUMONT Jeanne Marie]
+THE HISTORY OF A YOUNG LADY OF DISTINCTION. In a Series of Letters.
Dublin : Printed and sold by James Hoey [1754?] (adv-1755 [295]).
2s2d stitched 2s8d ½bound. Adv-1755 [295].
1st edn and edns listed, 1754 [245].
E

246.
[RICHARDSON Samuel]
(+)THE HISTORY OF SIR CHARLES GRANDISON. In a Series of Letters. Published
from the Originals, By the Editor of Pamela and Clarissa. In Seven Volumes.
London : Printed for S. Richardson; and sold by C. Hitch and L. Hawes, in Pater-noster Row;
By J. and J. Rivington, in St. Paul's Church-Yard; By Andrew Millar, in the Strand; By R. and
J. Dodsley, in Pall-Mall; And by J. Leake, at Bath. 1754.
Vol.VII adds 'And by R. Main, in Dublin'.
7 vols. 12mo. 18s (MR).
MR X 70-71 (Jan. 1754).
AB; BB; ESTC t058995; FB; LO 68 (UI,UP); McB 754; SG 894; WS 39.
Simultaneously issued with 8vo edn, 1754 [247]. Vols I-IV published 13 Nov 1753; vols V-VI, 11 Dec. 1753;
vol VII, 14 Mar. 1754. 3,000 copies printed. 750 sent to Ireland.
1st official edn, but also 1753, with edns listed, and further refs [191].
BL CUL CUNY HL HU PU UI UP YU
* E

247.
[RICHARDSON Samuel]
(+)THE HISTORY OF SIR CHARLES GRANDISON. In a Series of Letters. Published
from the Originals, By the Editor of Pamela and Clarissa. In Six Volumes.
London : Printed for S. Richardson; and sold by C. Hitch and L. Hawes, in Pater-noster Row;
By J. and J. Rivington, in St. Paul's Church-Yard; By Andrew Millar, in the Strand; By R. and
J. Dodsley, in Pall-Mall; And by J. Leake, at Bath. 1754.
Vol.VI adds 'And by R. Main, in Dublin'.
6 vols. 8vo. £1.10s bound or 4s each vol. sewed (WS).
McB 755; WS 40.
Published with 12mo edn, vols I-IV, 13 Nov. 1753; vol. V, 11 Dec. 1753; vol. VI, 14 Mar. 1754; and in 2
issues. This edn, 1,000 copies. Further issue, 1754 [248]. 1st edn and edns listed, 1753 [191].
CUL UI UP
* E

248.
[RICHARDSON Samuel]
+THE HISTORY OF SIR CHARLES GRANDISON. In a Series of Letters. The Second
Edition.
London : Printed for S. Richardson; and sold by C. Hitch and L. Hawes, J. & J. Rivington.
1754.
6 vols. 8vo.
Vols II-V omit 'R. Main' from imprint.
EC 245:1; ESTC t058981; WS 40.
2nd issue of 1st 8vo London edn, with vol.I announcing '2nd edn'. 1st edn and edns listed, 1753 [191].
BL Bod CUL
* E

249.
[RICHARDSON Samuel]
+THE HISTORY OF SIR CHARLES GRANDISON. In a Series of Letters. The Third
Edition.
London : Printed for S. Richardson; and sold by C. Hitch and L. Hawes, J. & J. Rivington.
1754.
7 vols. 12mo. 1gn bound (WS).
ESTC t058977; WS 41.
Published 19 Mar. 'R. Main, Dublin' included in vols I,III,V-VII. 1st edn and edns listed, 1753 [191].
BL Bod HU NYPL YU
* E

250.
[RICHARDSON Samuel]
+PAMELA; OR, VIRTUE REWARDED. In a Series of Familiar Letters from a beautiful young Damsel, to her Parents.
London : Printed for J. Hodges; and J. and J. Rivington. 1754.
4 vols. 12mo.
WS 13 & 19.
Published 16 Apr. Vols I-II, the 7th edn. Vols III-IV, 3rd issue of 2nd edn, the Continuation.
1st edn, 1740. Also, 1741(5x) and Continuation, 1742(2x) and Continuation (3x), 1746, 1761 [664], 1767
[1129], 1771, 1772, 1775, 1776, 1785(2x), 1792(2x). Abridgments, 1769 [1328], 1779, 1780. Cf 1768 [1230].
UCB UP
E

251.
[SAURIN Bernard Joseph]
MIRZA AND FATIMA. An Indian Tale. Translated from the French.
London : Printed for T. Osborne, in Gray's-Inn. 1754.
12mo. 3s (BB,MR).
MR XI 237-238 (Sept. 1754).
AB(Do,pa,WB); BB.
Bod CUL
* N

252.
[SCOTT Mrs Sarah Robinson]
A JOURNEY THROUGH EVERY STAGE OF LIFE, Described in a Variety of Interesting Scenes Drawn from Real Characters. By a Person of Quality. In Two Volumes.
London : Printed for A. Millar in the Strand. 1754.
2 vols. 12mo. 6s (MR).
MR X 237 (Mar. 1754).
AB(BL,ELG,RI); BB; ESTC t070734.
BL
* N/C

253.
[SHEBBEARE John]
THE MARRIAGE ACT. A Novel. Containing a Series of Interesting Adventures.
London : Printed for J. Hodges, at the Looking-Glass, facing St. Margaret Church London-Bridge; and B. Collins at Salisbury. 1754.
2 vols. 12mo. 6s (MR).
MR XI 395 (Nov. 1754).
AB(AR,BL,Mg); BB; LO 70 (UI); newSG.
Also, 1755 [325], and 1766 *Matrimony* edn [1039].
BL [missing] Bod UP
* N

254.
SLADE John
THE ADVENTURES OF JERRY BUCK. By Mr. John Slade.
London : Printed for T. Osborne, in Gray's-Inn. 1754.
198pp. 12mo. 3s (BB,MR).
MR X 238 (Mar. 1754).
BB; ESTC t073499; LO 71 (-); SG 973.
2nd & 3rd edns, 1754 [255] [256].
BL UP
* N

255.
SLADE John
+THE ADVENTURES OF JERRY BUCK. By Mr. John Slade. The Second Edition.
London : Printed for T. Osborne, in Gray's-Inn. 1754.
198pp. 12mo.
McB 823; SG 974
1st edn, 1754 [254].
CUL UI UP
* N

256.
SLADE John
+THE ADVENTURES OF JERRY BUCK. By Mr. John Slade. The Third Edition.
London : Printed for T. Osborne, in Grays-Inn. 1754.
198pp. 12mo.
SG 975.
1st edn, 1754 [254].
Bod UP
* N

257.
[SMYTHIES Miss]
THE HISTORY OF LUCY WELLERS. Written by a Lady. In Two Volumes.
London : Printed for R. Baldwin, at the Rose in Pater-noster-Row. 1754 [possibly 1753].
2 vols. 12mo. 6s (BB).
MR X 75 (Jan. 1754).
AB(BL,ELG); BB; EC 230:2; ESTC t080600; LO 50 (UP); SG 488.
Adv announcing publication, Nov. 1753, SR J342.
Reissued as a 'new edition' in 1755.
BL UP
* N

258.
[SMYTHIES Miss]
+THE STAGE-COACH : Containing the Character of Mr. Manly, and the History of his
Fellow-Travellers.
Dublin : Printed for J. Esdall, on Cork-hill; and S. Price, in Dame-street. 1754.
2 vols. 12mo.
1st edn, 1753 [195].
Possibly reissued by H. Saunders and others, c.1764-7 (adv-1767 [1084]).
Bod
* N

259.
VOLTAIRE François Marie Arouet de
BABOUC; OR, THE WORLD AS IT GOES. By Monsieur de Voltaire. To which are
added, Letters concerning his Disgrace at the Prussian Court : With his letter to his Niece
on that Occasion. Also, The Force of Friendship, or, Innocence Distress'd. A Novel.
London : Printed for, and sold by W. Owen. 1754.
168pp. 8vo. 2s6d (BB).
AB(BL,T,WTS); BB.
Dublin edn, 1754 [260].
BL Bod
* N/M

260.
VOLTAIRE François Marie Arouet de
+BABOUC; OR, THE WORLD AS IT GOES. By Monsieur de Voltaire. To which are
added, Letters Concerning his Disgrace at the Prussian Court : With his Letter to his Niece
on that Occasion. Also, The Force of Friendship, or, Innocence Distress'd. A Novel.
Dublin : Printed by and for H. Saunders, at the Corner of Christ-Church-Lane. 1754.
88pp. 12mo.
1st English edn, 1754 [259].
BL
* N/M

Miscellanies

261.
An Account of Barbarossa, The Usurper of Algiers. Being the Story On which the New Tragedy, Now in
Rehearsal at the Theatre Royal in Drury-Lane, Is Founded.
London : Printed and sold by W. Reeve, in Fleet-Street, 1755 [1754].
19pp. 8vo. 6d (BB,MR).
MR XI 467 (Dec. 1754).
AB(BL); BB; ESTC t126029.
The play was by John Brown. Cf 1755 [290].
BL
* M

262.
Admonitions from the Dead, in Epistles to the Living; Addressed by Certain Spirits of both Sexes to their
Friends or Enemies on Earth, With a View either to condemn or justify their Conduct while alive; and to
promote the Cause of Religion and Moral Virtue.
London : Printed for R. Baldwin, in Pater-noster-Row. 1754.
316pp. 12mo. 3s (BB).
BB; ESTC t086010; FB; LO 54 (FB,HU).
2nd edn, 1754 [263].
BL Bod HU
* M

263.
Admonitions from the Dead, in Epistles to the Living; Addressed by Certain Spirits of both Sexes to their
Friends or Enemies on Earth, With a View either to condemn or justify their Conduct while alive; and to
promote the Cause of Religion and Moral Virtue. The Second Edition.
London : Printed for R. Baldwin, in Pater-noster-Row. 1754.
316pp. 12mo.
SG 4.
1st edn, 1754 [262].
Bod CUL UP
* M

264.
+Æsop's Fables : With his Life, And Morals and Remarks. Fitted for the meanest Capacities. The
Eleventh Edition, with large Additions.
London : Printed for R. Ware, at the Bible and Sun, on Ludgate-Hill; C. Hitch, at the Red Lion, in Pater-noster-
Row; and J. Hodges, at the Looking-Glass, over-against St. Magnus Church, London-Bridge. 1754.
156pp. 12mo.
ESTC t084708.
Edns listed, 1753 [199].
BL
* C/M

265.
+Fables and Tales for the Ladies. Written by a Country Book-seller. The Second Edition, with Additions.
To which are added, Miscellanies. By Another Hand.
London : Printed for the Proprietor : And Sold by C. Hitch and L. Hawes, in Pater-noster-Row, and H.
Whitridge at the Royal Exchange. 1754.
199pp. 8vo. 1s (tp).
ESTC t078509.
1st edn, 1750 [43].
BL
* M/C

266.
The Gentleman and Lady of Pleasure's Amusement In Eighty-Eight Questions, with their Answers on
Love and Gallantry. To which are added, the Adventures of Sophia; with the History of Frederick and
Caroline.
London : Thrush. 1754.
12mo. 3s (BB).
BB; LO 61 (UP).
UP
N/C

267.
Genuine and Impartial Memoirs of Elizabeth Canning
[12 more lines]
Also Free and Candid Remarks on Sir Crisp Gascoyne's Address.
London : Printed for G. Woodfall at Charing-Cross. 1754.
293pp. 12mo. 3s bound (MR).
MR XI 237 (Sept. 1754).
BB; ESTC t144508; LO 62 (UP) SG 356.
Dozens of Elizabeth Canning publications continue, 1754-5.
BL Bod UP
* M/E

268.
Memoirs of Madam de Montespan and Lewis the Fourteenth. Translated from the Original French.
London : Printed for M. Cooper in Pater-noster-Row. 1754.
94pp. 12mo. 1s (tp).
ESTC t119329.
BL
* M

269.
The Midnight Ramble; or, Adventures of Two Noble Females : Being a true and impartial Account of
their late Excursion through the Streets of London and Westminster
[11 more lines]
London : Printed for B. Dickinson, on Ludgate-Hill. 1754.
26pp. 8vo. 6d (BB,MR,tp).
MR X 309 (Apr. 1754).
AB(BL); BB; ESTC t039350.
BL
* N/M

270.
[d'Argens Jean Baptiste de Boyer, Marquis]
Derrick Samuel *trans.*
Memoirs of the Count de Beauval, including some Curious Particulars relating to the Dukes of Wharton and Ormond, during their Exiles. Translated by Samuel Derrick.
London : Printed for M. Cooper. 1754.
224pp. 12mo.
AB(St); BB; ESTC t106572.
A trans. from *la Mentor Cavalier*, 1736. Dublin edn, 1754 [271]. Also, 1756 [383].
BL Bod
M

271.
[d'Argens Jean Baptiste de Boyer, Marquis]
Derrick Samuel *trans.*
+Memoirs of the Count de Beauval, including some Curious Particulars relating to the Dukes of Wharton and Ormond, during their Exiles. Translated by Samuel Derrick.
Dublin : Printed for W. Whitestone and B. Edmond. 1754.
224pp. 12mo.
McB 39.
1st edn and edns listed, 1754 [271].
UI
M

272.
Breues John
The Fortunate Lovers; or, the most successful arts used in honourable courtship; set forth in the history of persons of different characters and stations. By J. Breues, late of Perth, Merchant.
London : Robinson. 1754.
8vo. 1s6d (MR).
MR X 312 (Apr. 1754), as by author of *The Fortune-Hunters* (MR IX 315), and reprinted as *The Servant's Sure Guide* [ESTC t107913].
AB(BB); BB.
M/N

273.
[Campbell Dr. John]
+The Rational Amusement: Comprehending a Collection of Letters on a Great Variety of Subjects, Serious, Entertaining, Moral, Diverting, and Instructive
[10 more lines]
London : Printed for J. Hodges, facing St. Magnus-Church, London-Bridge. 1754.
432pp. 8vo. 5s (MR)
MR X 297-300 (Apr. 1754).
BB; ESTC t097138; FB; LO 55 (FB,MR).
1st edn, [1741?].
BL Bod CUL
* C/M

274.
[Crisp Samuel]
The Story on which the New Tragedy, call'd Virginia, Now in Rehearsal at the Theatre Royal in Drury Lane, Is Founded.
London : Printed and sold by W. Reeve, in Fleet-Street. 1754.
26pp. 12mo. 6d (tp).
AB(BL); ESTC t110642.
BL
* M/N

275.
[Cruden Alexander]
The Adventures of Alexander the Corrector.
[18 more lines]
London : Printed for the Author : And sold by Richard Baldwin at the Rose in Pater-Noster-Row. 1754.
3 parts - 44pp, 40pp, 67pp. 8vo. Pt I, 6d. Pt II, 6d. Pt III, 1s (tp).
Pt II, 'Sold by M. Cooper'. Pt III, 'Sold by A. Dodd; and by J. Lewis, 1755' [1754].
MR X 72 (Jan. 1754).
BB; EC 417:26; ESTC t068585 (pt.I) t068583 (pt.II) t068584 (pt.III).
BL Bod CUL
* M

276.
Cyrano de Bergerac Savinien
Derrick Samuel *trans*.
+A Voyage to the Moon : with some account of the Solar World. A Comical Romance. Done from the
French of M. Cyrano de Bergerac. By Mr. Derrick.
Dublin : 1754.
AB(Dublin edn).
1st edn, 1753 [206].
M

277.
[Hill John]
**+The Conduct of a Married Life : Laid down in a Series of Letters, written by the Honourable Juliana-
Susannah Seymour, To a Young Lady, her Relation, Lately Married.**
London : Printed for R. Baldwin, in Pater-noster-Row. 1754.
2 vols. 12mo.
ESTC t070299.
1st edn, 1753 [208].
BL
* M

278.
[Hill John]
**+The Conduct of a Married Life : Laid down in a Series of Letters, written by the Honourable Juliana-
Susannah Seymour, To a Young Lady, her Relation, Lately Married. The Second Edition.**
London : Printed for R. Baldwin, in Pater-noster-Row. 1754.
279pp. 12mo.
ESTC t109323.
1st edn, 1753 [208].
BL
* M

279.
[King Dr. William]
The Dreamer.
London : Printed for W. Owen, at Homer's Head, in Fleet-street. 1754.
240pp. 8vo. 4s6d (MR).
MR X 71 (Jan. 1754).
BB; ESTC t136704; LO 66 (UP); SG 572.
BL CUL UP
* M (sat)

280.
[Whitehead Paul]
The History of an Old Lady and her Family.
London : Printed for M. Cooper in Paternoster-Row. 1754.
21pp. 8vo. 6d (BB,tp).
AB; BB; ESTC t060867.
Further edns, 1754 [281] [282].
BL
* M

281.
[Whitehead Paul]
+The History of an Old Lady and her Family. The Second Edition.
London : Printed for M. Cooper in Paternoster-Row. 1754.
21pp. 8vo. 6d (tp).
1st edn, 1754 [280].
CUL
* M

282.
[Whitehead Paul]
+The History of an Old Lady and her Family. The Third Edition.
London : Printed for M. Cooper in Paternoster-Row. 1754.
21pp. 8vo. 6d (tp).
ESTC t060645.
1st edn, 1754 [280].
BL
* M

1755

283.
AUTHENTIC MEMOIRS OF THE REMARKABLE LIFE AND SURPRISING EXPLOITS OF MANDRIN, Captain-General of the French Smugglers
[14 more lines]
London : Printed for M. Cooper, Pater-noster-row, H. Owen, White-Fryars, Fleet-street; and C. Sympson, in Chancery-lane. 1755.
56pp. 8vo. 1s (MR,tp).
MR XII 478 (June 1755).
BB as 1775; ESTC t100642.
Dublin edn, 1755 [284].
BL
* N/M

284.
+AUTHENTIC MEMOIRS OF THE REMARKABLE LIFE AND SURPRISING EXPLOITS OF MANDRIN, Captain-General of the French Smugglers
[11 more lines]
Dublin : Printed for John Murphy, at Mrs Owen's in Skinner-Row. 1755.
72pp. 12mo.
ESTC t069912.
1st edn, 1755 [283].
BL CUL
* N/M

285.
THE DEVIL UPON CRUTCHES IN ENGLAND, OR NIGHT SCENES IN LONDON. A
Satirical Work. Written upon the Plan of the celebrated Diable Boiteux of Monsieur Le
Sage. By a Gentleman of Oxford.
London : Printed for Philip Hodges, at the Globe in Great Turnstile, Holbourn. 1755.
73pp. 8vo. 1s6d (MR).
MR XIII 468 (Dec. 1755).
ESTC t063648; LO 78 (UI); McB 240.
Also, 1756 [348], 1759 [460] [461], 1760 [531], 1762 [700], 1764 [808]. Original work by le Sage with edns
listed, 1750 [37]; and later, *Devil Upon Two Sticks*, 1790, 1791.
BL LC UI YU
* N/M

286.
FANNY; OR, THE AMOURS OF A WEST COUNTRY YOUNG LADY, Contained in a
Series of Genuine Letters. Interspersed with some Entertaining particulars during her
travels abroad.
London : Printed for R. Manby. 1755.
2 vols. 12mo. 6s (MR).
MR XII 237 (Mar. 1755).
AB(-); BB; FB; LO 79 (FB,HU); SG 304.
HU UP
E

287.
THE HEROIC PRINCES; OR, THE CONSCIOUS LOVERS.
London : M. Cooper. 1755.
AB(JH).
N

288.
+THE HISTORY AND ADVENTURES OF FRANK HAMMOND. The Second Edition.
London : Printed for R. Griffiths, at the Dunciad in Pater-noster-Row. 1755.
267pp. 12mo.
AB(HW); SG 472.
1st edn, 1754 [216].
UP
N

289.
(+)THE HISTORY OF A LADY'S SLIPPER AND SHOES. Written by Themselves.
London : Cooper. 1755.
8vo. 1s (MR).
MR XII 237 (Mar. 1755).
FB; LO 81 (FB,GM); RKM.
1st version, 1754 [215].
N

290.
THE HISTORY OF BARBAROSSA AND POLYANNA.
London : Crowder. 1755.
12mo. 3s (adv-1756 [359], MR).
MR XIII (App. 1755ii).
AB(WB); BB.
Cf 1754 [261].
N

291.
+THE HISTORY OF JOSHUA TRUEMAN, ESQ; AND MISS PEGGY WILLIAMS.
Dublin : Printed by A. Reilly, for the Booksellers. 1755.
334pp. 12mo.
ESTC t066898.
1st edn, 1754 [220].
BL
* N

292.
THE HISTORY OF LAVINIA RAWLINS. A Work Very Proper to be Perused by all young Ladies, as a cautionary direction for avoiding those miseries, for the most part attendant on such of the female world, as place too implicit a confidence in the professions of men. Published from the genuine papers themselves, under the inspection of the aforesaid lady, by the rev. Mr. G. D. rector of F—m, in Lancashire.
London : Owen. 1755.
2 vols. 12mo. 6s (BB,MR).
MR XIII 398-399 (Nov. 1755).
BB; FB; LO 82 (FB,HU).
2nd edn, 1770.
HU
N

293.
THE HISTORY OF MY OWN LIFE. Being an Account Of many of the Severest Trials Imposed by an Implacable Father, upon the most Affectionate Pair That ever entered the Marriage State. In Two Volumes.
London : Printed for F. Noble, at his Circulating Library in King-street, Covent-Garden; and J. Noble, at his Circulating Library in St. Martin's-Court, near Leicester-Square. 1756 [1755].
2 vols. 12mo. 6s (BB,MR).
MR XIII 398 (Nov. 1755).
BB; ESTC t126595; LO 98 (UP); SG 499.
Sometimes ascribed to Adolphus Bannac. New edn in 1760 as *The History of Biddy Farmer* [536].
BL UP
* N

294.
THE HISTORY OF POLLY WILLIS. AN ORPHAN.
London : Printed and Sold by W. Reeve. 1755.
243pp. 12mo. 2s6d sewed (adv-1767 [398]) 3s bound (BB,MR).
MR XII 236-237 (Mar. 1755).
AB(ELG); BB; LO 83 (UP); SG 501.
UP
N

295.
+THE HISTORY OF SIR HARRY HERALD AND SIR EDWARD HAUNCH. By Henry Fielding Esq.
Dublin : Printed by James Hoey, at the Mercury in Skinner-Row. 1755.
274pp. 12mo. 2s2d stitched 2s8d calf bound and lettered (adv-1763 [757]).
ESTC t067337.
Adv-1763 [757] adds to title, 'Interspersed with the Adventures of Mr. Charles Herald and Miss Felicia Blanchman'.
1st edn, 1754 [221]. Not by Fielding.
BL Bod
* N

296.
THE LIFE AND UNCOMMON ADVENTURES OF CAPT. DUDLEY BRADSTREET.
Being The most Genuine and Extraordinary, perhaps, ever published
[31 half-lines and 2 lines more]
Dublin : Printed and Sold by S. Powell, in Crane-Lane, for the Author. 1755.
358pp. 8vo. Subn.
ESTC t074215.
It includes 'Bradstreet's' play *The Magician*, pp.[249]-333.
BL CUL
* N

297.
MEMOIRS OF THE LIFE AND ADVENTURES OF SOBRINA.
London : Printed for J. Woodyer, at Caesar's Head, in Fleet-street. 1755.
2 vols. 12mo. 6s (BB,MR).
MR XII 383 (Apr. 1755).
AB(TDW); BB; ESTC t125462.
BL
* N

298.
(+)THE RIVAL MOTHER : OR, THE HISTORY OF THE COUNTESS DE SALENS,
AND HER TWO DAUGHTERS. In Two Volumes.
London : Printed for F. Noble, at his Circulating Library in King-street, Covent-Garden; and J.
Noble, at his Circulating Library in St. Martin's-Court, near Leicester-Square. 1755.
2 vols. 12mo. 6s (BB,MR).
MR XII 237 (Mar. 1755).
AB(ELG); BB; ESTC t072465.
To be published Feb. 1755, adv-1754 [221].
There is a 1692-4 novel of this title.
BL
* N

299.
+THE TRAVELS OF MR. DRAKE MORRIS, MERCHANT IN LONDON. Containing his
Sufferings and Distresses in Several Voyages at Sea. Written by Himself. The Second
Edition.
London : Printed for the Author : And Sold by R. Baldwin, at the Rose in Pater-noster Row.
1755.
328pp. 12mo.
ESTC t099703; PBG 339.
1st edn, 1754 [229].
BL
* N

300.
THE UNFORTUNATE OFFICER; OR, THE HISTORY OF MONSIEUR BERTIN,
Marquis de Fratteux, Knight of the Military Order of St. Louis, and Captain of Horse
[13 more lines]
London : Printed for G. Woodfall, at the King's-Arms, Charing-Cross. [1755?] (BL).
214pp. 12mo. 3s (tp).
AB(BL); ESTC t110215.
A trans. of *L'Histoire de M. Bertin, par M. le Comte d'H****.
BL
* N

301.
A VOYAGE TO THE WORLD IN THE CENTRE OF THE EARTH. Giving An Account of the Manners, Customs, Laws, Government and Religion of the Inhabitants, Their Persons and Habits described : With several other Particulars. In which is Introduced, The History Of An Inhabitant of the Air, Written by Himself. With some Account of the Planetary Worlds.
London : Printed for S. Crowder and H. Woodgate. 1755.
12mo. 3s (adv-1756 [359], MR).
MR XII 394-395 (Apr. 1755).
AB(AR); LO 92 (BL,LC); PBG 341-342.
BL [missing] LC
N

302.
CERVANTES SAAVEDRA Miguel de
SMOLLETT Tobias *trans.*
THE HISTORY AND ADVENTURES OF THE RENOWNED DON QUIXOTE. Translated from the Spanish of Miguel de Cervantes Saavedra. To which is prefixed, Some Account of the Author's Life. By T. Smollet, M.D. In Two Volumes.
London : Printed for A. Millar, over-against Catherine-Street, in the Strand; T. Osborn, T. and T. Longman, C. Hitch and L. Hawes, J. Hodges, and J. and J. Rivington. 1755.
2 vols. 4to. £2.2s (BB,MR).
MR XIII 196-202 (Sept. 1755).
BB; EC 94:1; ESTC t059887; McB 133; MW 602.
1st English trans, 1612 and numerous versions 1612-1700. The Smollett trans. reprinted, 1761 [643], 1765 [900] [901], 1766 [996], 1770, 1782, 1783, 1784, 1786, 1792(3x), 1793, 1794, 1795, 1796. Cf Jarvis trans. with edns listed, 1756 [367]; Ozell trans, 1757 [409], 1766 [995]; Kelly trans, 1769 [1301]; and Wilmot trans, 1769 [1302].
BL Bod UI
* N

303.
CHARKE Mrs Charlotte Cibber
THE HISTORY OF HENRY DUMONT, ESQ; AND MISS CHARLOTTE EVELYN. Consisting of Variety of Entertaining Characters, and very Interesting Subjects; With some Critical Remarks on Comick Actors. By Mrs Charke.
London : Printed for H. Slater, at the Circulating-Library, the Corner of Clare-Court, Drury-Lane; and H. Slater jun. and S. Whyte, at Holborn-Bars. 1755.
257pp. 12mo. 3s (CR,MR).
CR I 136-138 (Mar. 1756); MR XIV 444-445 (May 1756).
FB; LO 76 (HU,UP).
Also, 1755 [304], 1756 [368].
HU UP
N

304.
CHARKE Mrs Charlotte Cibber
+THE HISTORY OF HENRY DUMONT, ESQ; AND MISS CHARLOTTE EVELYN. Consisting of Variety of Entertaining Characters, and very Interesting Subjects; With some Critical Remarks on Comick Actors. By Mrs Charke. The Second Edition.
London : Printed for H. Slater, at the Circulating-Library, the Corner of Clare-Court, Drury-Lane; and H. Slater jun. and S. Whyte, at Holborn-Bars. 1755.
257pp. 12mo.
1st edn, 1756 [303].
BL
* N

305.
[CLELAND John]
(+)MEMOIRS OF A ***** OF ********.
London : Printed by E. Mullins, in Hill Street [1755] (BL).
2 vols in 1. 301pp. 12mo.
AB(CLP).
1st edn, *A Woman of Pleasure*, 1749. Edns and versions listed, 1750 [19].
BL
* N

306.
[CLELAND John]
+MEMOIRS OF *********** ** ************.
London : Printed for G. Fenton [Fenton Griffiths] in the Strand [1755?] (BL).
2 vols. 12mo.
ESTC t084804.
An abridgment of *Memoirs of a Woman of Pleasure*, 1st edn, 1749. Edns and versions listed, 1750 [19].
BL
* N

307.
[COLLET John]
CHIT-CHAT; OR, NATURAL CHARACTERS; AND THE MANNERS OF REAL LIFE,
Represented in a Series of interesting Adventures. In Two Volumes.
London : Printed for R. and J. Dodsley, at Tully's Head, in Pall-mall. 1755.
2 vols. 12mo. 4s (RS) 5s (BB,MR).
MR XII 388 (Apr. 1755).
AB(BL); BB; EC 286:1; ESTC t070728; LO 77 (UP); SG 183; RS [as published 16 Mar].
BL CUL UP
* N

308.
[COLLYER Mrs Mary]
+LETTERS FROM FELICIA TO CHARLOTTE : Containing A Series of the most
interesting Events, interspersed with Moral Reflections; chiefly tending to prove, that the
Seeds of Virtue are implanted in the Mind of Every Reasonable Being. The Third Edition.
In Two Volumes.
London : Printed for R. Baldwin at the Rose in Pater-Noster-Row. 1755.
2 vols. 12mo.
ESTC t063919.
1st edn, 1744. Also, 1749-50, 1765 [905], 1780-88.
BL
* E

309.
[DAVYS Mrs Mary]
+THE ACCOMPLISH'D RAKE : OR, THE MODERN FINE GENTLEMAN. Being the
Genuine Memoirs Of a certain Person of Distinction.
London : Printed for A. Stephens, in the Butcher-Row, near Temple-Bar; F. Noble, in Kingstreet,
Covent-Garden; W. Bathoe, in Exeter-Exchange, Strand; and J. Noble, in St. Martin's-Court, near
Leicester-Square. 1756 [1755].
255pp. 12mo. 3s bound (tp).
MR XIII 510 (App. 1755ii).
BB; ESTC t008476.
1st edn, 1727. Also, 1756 [369].
BL
* N

310.
[DEFOE Daniel]
+THE LIFE AND ADVENTURES OF ROXANA, THE FORTUNATE MISTRESS; Or, Most Unhappy Wife.
London : Printed for W. Owen; and C. Sympson. 1755.
463pp.
1st edn, 1724. Edns listed, 1750 [21].
Bn HL
N

311.
[DEFOE Daniel]
+THE LIFE AND STRANGE SURPRISING ADVENTURES OF ROBINSON CRUSOE. The Eleventh Edition.
London : Printed for M. Cooper. 1755. Vol II, also 'for the Proprietors and sold by R. Baldwin'.
2 vols. 8vo.
1st edn, 1719-20. Edns listed, 1752 [129].
UI [McB 205 & 222] UM
N/M

312.
[FÉNELON François de Salignac de La Mothe]
[DES MAIZEAUX P. *trans.*]
+THE ADVENTURES OF TELEMACHUS, THE SON OF ULYSSES, Written by the Archbishop of Cambray, a new translation. In Two Volumes.
Glasgow : Printed by Robert Urie. 1755.
2 vols. 12mo.
ESTC t107750.
Trans. of *Les Aventures de Télémaque*, 1699. 1st English edn, 1699. Also, 1699(3x), 1700(2x), 1701, 1703, 1707, 1712, 1713, 1715, 1720, 1725, 1726, 1728, 1729, 1735, 1738, 1742, 1743, 1749, 1758 [438], 1759 [485], 1764 [833], 1765 [913], 1766 [1004], 1768 [1208], 1769 [1308], 1770, 1772, 1773(2x), 1774, 1775, 1776(3x), 1777, 1778, 1779, 1781, 1782, 1784(3x), 1785, 1786, 1787, 1788, 1790, 1791, 1792(5x), 1793(4x), 1794, 1798.
BL
* N/M

313.
[FIELDING Henry]
+THE HISTORY OF THE LIFE OF MR. JONATHAN WILD THE GREAT. To which is added A Journey from this World to the next.
London : Printed for John Bell, No 132 Strand. 1755.
331pp.
1st separate edn with edns listed, 1754 [234].
YU
* N

314.
[GIOVANNI Fiorentino]
THE NOVEL FROM WHICH THE PLAY OF THE MERCHANT OF VENICE, WRITTEN BY SHAKESPEAR, IS TAKEN. Translated from the Italian. To which is Added, A Translation of a Novel from the Decamerone of Bocaccio.
London : Printed for M. Cooper, at the Globe in Pater-noster-Row. 1755.
32pp. 8vo. 6d (MR).
MR XII 389 (Apr. 1755).
AB(SA); BB; ESTC t099010.
From *Il Pecorone* of Fiorentino Giovanni. The preface gives author as Giovanni Fiorentino.
BL
* N/M

315.
[GRAFIGNY Françoise d'Issembourg d'Happoncourt de]
SEGUIN James *trans.*
(+)LETTERS OF PRINCESS ZILIA, TO PRINCE AZA OF PERU, Newly translated from
the French Original. By James Seguin, Teacher of the French Tongue in Hereford.
London : Printed for the Author; and Sold by James Wilde, Bookseller, in Hereford. 1755.
322pp. 12mo.
AB(BL,Wo); ESTC t131031; LO 87 (UP); McB 374; SG 378.
Trans from *Lettres d'une Peruvienne*, 1747. 1st English trans, 1748. Other edns listed, 1753 [185].
BL Bod UI UP
* E

316.
[HAYWOOD Mrs Eliza]
THE INVISIBLE SPY; BY EXPLORALIBUS. In Four Volumes.
London : Printed for T. Gardner, at Cowley's Head, near St. Clement's Church in the Strand.
1755.
4 vols. 12mo. 12s (MR).
MR XI 498-502 (App. 1754ii).
AB(AR,BL,WB); BB; ESTC t142450; LO 80 (HU,UI,UP); McB 422.
Dublin edn, 1755 [317]. Also, 1756 [372], 1759 [494], 1767 [1104], 1768 [1215], 1773, 1777, 1788.
BL HU UI UP
* N/M

317.
[HAYWOOD Mrs Eliza]
+THE INVISIBLE SPY. BY EXPLORALIBUS.
Dublin : Printed for Robert Main, Bookseller, at Homer's-Head in Dame-Street. 1755.
2 vols. 12mo.
ESTC t135554; McB 423.
1st edn and edns listed, 1755 [316].
CUL UI
* N/M

318.
[KIDGELL John]
THE CARD.
London : Printed for the Maker, and Sold by J. Newbery, at the Bible and Sun, in St. Paul's
Church-Yard. 1755.
2 vols. 12mo. 6s (BB,MR).
MR XII 117-121 (Feb. 1755).
AB(BL,RI,St); BB; ESTC t068566; FB; LO 84 (HU,UI,UP); McB 507; SG 563.
Dublin edn, 1755 [319].
BL Bod CUL HU UI UP
* N

319.
[KIDGELL John]
+THE CARD.
Dublin : Reprinted for the Maker, and Sold by Sam. Price and Matthew Williamson. 1755.
2 vols. 12mo.
SG 564.
1st edn, 1755 [318].
UP
N

320.

[KIMBER Edward]
THE LIFE AND ADVENTURES OF JAMES RAMBLE, ESQ; Interspersed, With the various Fortunes of certain noble Personages Deeply concerned in the Northern Commotions in the Year 1715. From his own Manuscript.
London : Printed for R. Baldwin, in Pater-noster-Row. 1755.
2 vols. 12mo. 6s (BB,MR).
MR XII 144-145 (Feb. 1755).
BB; LO 85 (UI); McB 585.
Also, 1770 edn.
Bod CUL UI YU
* N

321.

[LONGUEVILLE Peter]
+[THE HERMIT : OR THE UNPARALLEL'D SUFFERINGS AND SURPRISING ADVENTURES OF MR. PHILIP QUARLL]
[London] [1755] (CUL).
88pp. 12mo.
An abridgment of the work first published, 1727. Edns listed, 1751 [93].
CUL [imperf - tp missing]
* N/M

322.

[MARIVAUX Pierre Carlet de Chamblain de]
+**THE LIFE, MISFORTUNES AND ADVENTURES OF INDIANA, THE VIRTUOUS ORPHAN. The Third Edition.**
London : Printed by M. Read. 1755.
364pp. 12mo.
SG 496, 'An adaptation of his *Vie de Marianne*, probably by Mary Collyer'.
Life of Marianne published in England, 1736-42; and this title, 1746. Also, 1765 [930], 1784.
UP
N

323.

RAMSAY Andrew Michael
+**THE TRAVELS OF CYRUS : To which is annexed, A Discourse upon the Theology and Mythology of the Pagans. By the Chevalier Ramsay.**
Glasgow : Printed and sold by R. and A. Foulis. 1755.
2 vols in 1. 381pp & 118pp. 12mo.
ESTC t118202.
1st English edn, 1727. Edns listed, 1752 [146].
BL
M/N

324.

[SHEBBEARE John]
LYDIA, OR FILIAL PIETY. A NOVEL. By the Author of The Marriage-Act, A Novel. And Letters on the English Nation.
London : Printed for J. Scott, at the Black Swan in Pater-noster-Row. 1755.
4 vols. 12mo. 6s (MR).
MR XII 478 (June 1755).
AB(BL,Mg,WTS); BB as 1786; EC 205:2; ESTC t064734; LO 89 (-); SG 955.
Also, 1763 [792], 1769 [1332], 1786, 1787.
BL Bod UI UP
* N

325.
[SHEBBEARE John]
+MATRIMONY. A Novel. Containing a Series of Interesting Adventures. The Second
Edition.
London : Printed for J. Hodges, at the Looking-Glass, facing St. Magnus-Church London-Bridge;
and B. Collins at Salisbury. 1755.
2 vols. 12mo.
EC 207:3; ESTC t066933.
1st edn and edns listed, 1754 [253] *The Marriage Act.*
BL
* N

326.
[SMOLLETT Tobias]
+THE ADVENTURES OF RODERICK RANDOM. The Fourth Edition.
London : Printed for A. Millar, J. Hodges, J. and J. Rivington, and R. Baldwin and M. Cooper.
1755.
2 vols (MW). 144pp (KU).
MW 34.
1st edn, 1748. Edns listed, 1750 [40].
KU
N

327.
[SMOLLETT Tobias]
+THE ADVENTURES OF RODERICK RANDOM. In Two Volumes. The Fourth Edition.
Dublin : Printed and Sold by Richard James, at Newton's Head, in Dame-Street. 1755.
2 vols. 12mo.
ESTC t055369; MW 35; RCC pp.67,240.
1st edn, 1748. Edns listed, 1750 [40].
BL NLI
* N

328.
[VICTOR Benjamin]
THE WIDOW OF THE WOOD.
London : Printed for C. Corbett, opposite St. Dunstan's Church in Fleet-Street. 1755.
208pp. 12mo. 3s (BB,MR).
MR XII 392 (Apr. 1755).
BB; ESTC t074392; LO 91 (UI,UP); McB 928 (2nd issue); SG 1065.
There are at least three variants or issues of this edn. 2nd edn or issue, ESTC t074393. A '3rd' issue was also
derived from this edition, ESTC t074394.
Also, 1755 [329], and Glasgow version of 1769 [1346].
BL Bod CUL UI UP
* N

329.
[VICTOR Benjamin]
+THE WIDOW OF THE WOOD. Being an Authentic Narrative of a late Remarkable
Transaction in Staffordshire.
Dublin : Printed and Sold by S. Powell, in Crane-Lane. 1755.
108pp. 8vo. 'One English Shilling' (tp).
ESTC t052487.
1st edn and edns listed, 1755 [328].
BL Bod CUL
* N

330.
[VILLANDON Marie Jeanne l'Héritier de]
[SAMBER Robert *trans.*]
THE DISCREET PRINCESS; OR, THE ADVENTURES OF FINETTA. A Novel.
London : Printed in the Year. 1755.
56pp. 12mo.
AB(BL); EC 15:8; ESTC t096269.
Trans. from *L'adroite Princesse* by Villandon.
BL
* N

Miscellanies

331.
+The Lives and Adventures of the German Princess, Mary Read, Anne Bonny, Joan Philips, Madam Churchill, Betty Ireland, and Ann Hereford.
London : Printed for M. Cooper, Pater-noster-row; W. Reeve, Fleet-street; and C. Sympson, at the Bible-warehouse, Chancery-lane. 1755.
108pp. 12mo. 1s (tp).
ESTC t118670.
BL
* M

332.
The Memoirs of Capt. Peter Drake. Containing, An Account of many Strange and Surprising Events, which happened to Him through a Series of Sixty Years, and upwards; and several material Anecdotes, regarding King William and Queen Anne's Wars with Lewis XIV of France.
Dublin : Printed and Sold by S. Powell in Crane-Lane, for the Author. 1755.
281pp. 8vo. Subn.
ESTC t145643.
BL CUL
* M/N

333.
+The Secret History of Betty Ireland
[29 more lines]
The Fourth Edition.
London : Printed and Sold by T. Sabine, No.81, Shoe-Lane [1755?] (BL).
39pp. 12mo.
1st edn and edns listed, 1750 [50].
BL
* M

334.
A Select Collection Of the Original Love Letters of Several Eminent Persons, of Distinguish'd Rank and Station, Now Living. Printed from Genuine Manuscripts.
[3 more lines and 18 names of authors of poems included]
London : Printed for the Proprietors. 1755.
152pp [69pp of prose]. 8vo. 2s sewed (tp).
ESTC t082903; LO 88 (-).
Preface signed, 'G. Gaylove, the Editor'.
BL UI
* M/C

335.

Windsor Tales : or, the Amours of a Gentleman and a Lady; with some Court-Intrigues : a Genuine History.
London : Printed for S. C. and Sold by H. Cooke, E. Lynn [1755?].
AB(BL although this now given as ?1730).
1st published as *The Amours of Philario and Olinda*, 1730.
WCL
C/M

336.

[Amory Thomas]
Memoirs Containing the Lives of Several Ladies of Great Britain.
[13 more lines]
In Several Letters.
London : Printed for John Noon, at the White-Hart, near Mercer's Chapel, in Cheapside. 1755.
527pp. 8vo.
MR XIII 128-138, 202-225 (Aug,Sept. 1755).
AB(TDW); BB; ESTC t074615; FB; LO 75 (FB,HU,UP).
Vol I only published.
Also 1769 edn [1355].
BL Bod CUL HU UP
* M

337.

[Haywood Mrs Eliza]
+**The Female Spectator. The Fifth Edition.**
London : Printed for T. Gardner, at Cowley's-Head, near St. Clement's-Church in the Strand. 1755.
4 vols. 8vo.
1st edn, 1744. Edns listed, 1750 [57].
Bod
* C/M

338.

[Hughes John *trans.*]
+**Letters of the Celebrated Abelard and Heloise. With the History of their Lives Prefixed. In both of which are described their various misfortunes, and the fatal consequences of their amours.**
Edinburgh : Printed by Wal. Ruddiman jun. and Comp. and sold by the booksellers in the town. 1755.
228pp. 12mo.
ESTC t075341.
1st English edn, 1718. Edns listed, 1751 [112].
BL
* M/E

339.

Montesquieu Charles Louis de Secondat Baron de
Flloyd Thomas *trans.*
+**Persian Letters. By M. de Montesquieu. Translated from the French, By Mr. Flloyd. The Fifth Edition.**
London : Printed for M. Cooper. 1755.
1 vol.
1st English edn, 1722. Edns listed, 1751 [113].
YU
M/E

340.

Nugent Robert jun.

The Unnatural Father, or the Persecuted Son. Being A Candid Narrative of the most unparalleled Sufferings of Robert Nugent, Junr. by the Means and Procurement of his own Father. Written by Himself [4 more lines]

London : Printed for the Author and Sufferer, now a Prisoner in the Fleet; and sold by him, and all the Booksellers in Town and Country. 1755.

64pp. 8vo. 1s6d (BB,tp).

BB; ESTC t050504.

2nd edn, 1755 [341], and *Supplement* [342].

BL Bod

* M

341.

Nugent Robert jun.

+The Unnatural Father, or the Persecuted Son : Being A Candid Narrative of the most unparalleled Sufferings of Robert Nugent, Junr. [6 more lines] **The Second Edition.**

London : Printed for the Author and Sufferer, now a Prisoner in the Fleet; and sold by him, and all the Booksellers in Town and Country. 1755.

64pp. 8vo. 1s6d (BB,tp).

1st edn, 1755 [340].

Bod

* M

342.

[Nugent Robert jun.]

A Supplement to the Unnatural Father, or, the Persecuted Son [14 more lines]

London : Printed for the Author and Sufferer, now a Prisoner in the Fleet; and sold by him, and all the Booksellers in Town and Country. 1755.

36pp. 8vo. 1s (tp).

Cf 1755 [340].

Bod

* M

343.

[Richardson Samuel derived]

A Collection Of the Moral and Instructive Sentiments, Maxims, Cautions, and Reflexions, Contained in the Histories of Pamela, Clarissa, and Sir Charles Grandison [10 more lines]

London : Printed for S. Richardson; and sold by C. Hitch and L. Hawes, in Pater-noster Row; J. and J. Rivington, in St. Paul's Church-Yard; Andrew Millar, in the Strand; R. and J. Dodsley, in Pall-Mall; And J. Leake, at Bath. 1755.

410pp. 12mo.

ESTC t058996; SG 893.

Cf full works with edns listed, 1751 [96], 1753 [191], 1754 [250]; also 1756 [377].

BL Bod CUL UP

* M

344.

Rowe Mrs Elizabeth Singer

+Friendship in Death : In Twenty Letters from the Dead to the Living. To which are added, Letters Moral and Entertaining, in prose and verse : in three parts. By Mrs Elizabeth Rowe.

Edinburgh : Printed for William Gray, and sold by him and other Booksellers. 1755.

222pp. 12mo.

ESTC t084019.

Edns listed, 1750 [60].

BL

* M

345.
[Shebbeare John]
Letters on the English Nation : By Batista Angeloni, A Jesuit, Who Resided many years in London. Translated from the Original Italian, by the Author of The Marriage-Act a Novel.
London : Printed in the Year. 1755. [Printed by Scot] (MR).
2 vols. 8vo. 10s (MR).
MR XII 387-388 (Apr. 1755).
AB; BB; ESTC t088373; FB; LO 89 (HU); SG 954.
2nd edn, 1756 [385]. Also abridged version, 1763 [802].
Bn Bod CUNY DU HL HU IU LC Tx UM UNC UP
* E/M

1756

346.
THE ADVENTURES OF JACK SMART.
London : Printed for S. Crowder, and H. Woodgate. 1756.
231pp. 12mo. 3s (BB,CR,MR).
CR I 125-129 (Mar. 1756); MR XIV 360-361 (Apr. 1756).
AB(Pi); BB.
PU
N

347.
THE AFFECTING STORY OF LIONEL AND ARABELLA, Who, By a most unhappy Accident, first discover'd the Island of Madiera, and perish'd there [11 more lines]
London : Printed for R. Griffiths, in Pater-noster Row. 1756.
88pp. 8vo. 1s6d (BB,CR,MR).
CR I 253-255 (Apr. 1756); MR XIV 453 (May 1756).
BB; EC 35:10; ESTC t091062 [as 'History of'].
From Francisco Manoel de Mello's edn of F. Alcaforado's *Relacio de descrobimento da ilha da Madeira*.
BL
* N/M

348.
+THE DEVIL UPON CRUTCHES IN ENGLAND, OR NIGHT SCENES IN LONDON. A Satirical Work. Written upon the Plan of the celebrated Diable Boiteux of Monsieur le Sage. In Two Parts. By a Gentleman of Oxford. The Second Edition.
London : Printed for Philip Hodges, at the Globe in Great Turnstile, Holborn. 1756.
66pp. 8vo. ½tp : Part II. 1s6d (MR,tp) & adv p.[67] as (both parts) 3s sewed.
MR XIV 269 (Mar. 1756).
AB(AR,MH,WB).
1st edn and edns listed, 1755 [285]. Original work by le Sage, with edns listed, 1750 [37].
CUL FL NLC UM YU
* N/M

349.
EMILY; OR THE HISTORY OF A NATURAL DAUGHTER. In Two Volumes.
London : Printed for F. & J. Noble. 1756.
2 vols. 12mo. 6s (BB,CR,MR).
CR I 122-125 (Mar. 1756); MR XIV 289-292 (Apr. 1756).
AB(ELG); BB; LO 95 (UP); SG 296.
BU UP
N

350.
THE FORTUNE-TELLER; OR FOOTMAN ENNOBLED. Being the History of the Right
Honourable Earl of R**** and Miss Lucy M-n-y. In Two Volumes.
London : Printed for the Author and sold by F. Noble, and J. Noble. 1756.
2 vols. 12mo. 6s (BB,CR,MR).
CR I 53-56 (Jan-Feb. 1756); MR XIV 268-269 (Mar. 1756).
BB.
2nd edn, 1774.
HL OU
N

351.
THE HISTORY OF CHARLOTTE VILLARS : A NARRATIVE FOUNDED ON TRUTH,
Interspersed with Variety of Incidents Instructive and Entertaining.
London : Printed for S. Crowder and H. Woodgate, at the Golden Ball in Pater-noster-Row.
1756.
261pp. 12mo. 3s (BB,MR).
MR XIII 510 (App. 1755ii).
BB; EC 171:2; ESTC t070077.
Dublin edn, 1756 [352].
BL CUL
* N

352.
+THE HISTORY OF CHARLOTTE VILLARS : A NARRATIVE FOUNDED ON TRUTH.
Dublin : Printed by Henry Saunders. 1756.
172pp. 12mo.
SG 477.
1st edn, 1756 [351].
UP
* N

353.
THE JILTS : OR, FEMALE FORTUNE-HUNTERS.
London : Printed for Francis Noble, at Otway's Head, in King-street, Covent-Garden; And John
Noble, at Dryden's Head, in St. Martin's Court, near Leicester-Square [1756].
3 vols. 12mo. 9s bound (BB,CR,MR,tp).
CR II 276 (Oct. 1756); MR XV 535-536 (Nov. 1756).
BB; ESTC t140110 [as 1755?]; newSG.
BL UP
* N

354.
THE LIFE AND MEMOIRS OF MR. EPHRAIM TRISTRAM BATES, COMMONLY
CALLED CORPORAL BATES; A broken-hearted Soldier
[19 more lines]
London : Printed by Malachi ****, for Edith Bates, Relict of the aforesaid Mr. Bates and sold
by W. Owen, at Homer's Head, Temple-bar, Anno. 1756.
238pp. 12mo. 2s (BB) 3s (CR,MR).
CR II 138-143 (Sept. 1756); MR XV 426-427 (Oct. 1756).
AB(BL); BB; ESTC t077673; LO 99 (UI,UP); McB 589; SG 641.
Also, 1759 [472].
BL CUL UI UP
* N

355.
THE MEMOIRS OF A YOUNG LADY OF QUALITY, A PLATONIST. In Three
Volumes.
London : Printed for R. Baldwin, in Pater-noster Row. 1756.
3 vols. 12mo. 9s (CR) 10s6d (BB,MR).
CR III 252-258 (Mar. 1757); MR XVI 178 (Feb. 1757).
AB(BL,Do,Pi); BB; EC 209:4; ESTC t066911; FB; LO 101 (FB,UP); SG 720.
BL NLC UP YU
* N

356.
MEMOIRS OF AN OXFORD SCHOLAR. Containing, His Amour with the beautiful Miss
L———, of Essex; And interspers'd with Several Entertaining Incidents. Written by Himself.
London : Printed and Sold by W. Reeve, in Fleet-Street; and by the Booksellers in Town and
Country. 1756.
264pp. 12mo. 3s (BB,MR).
MR XIII 510 (App. 1755ii).
AB(BL,Do,WB); BB; EC 282:6; ESTC t124820; FB; LO 100 (FB,HU,UP); SG 718.
BL HU UP
* N

357.
(+)MEMOIRS OF THE LIFE AND DISTRESSES OF SIMON MASON, APOTHECARY;
Containing a Series of Transactions and Events, both Interesting and Diverting.
London : Printed for the Author, and sold by Noble etc. 1756.
8vo. 2s6d (BB,MR).
MR XV 194 (Aug. 1756).
BB.
Cf 1752 [122] and 1754 [225].
N/M

358.
THE MODERN LOVERS : OR, THE ADVENTURES OF CUPID, THE GOD OF LOVE :
A Novel.
London : Printed for J. Cooke, at the King's-Arms, in Great-Turnstile, Holbourn. 1756.
223pp. 12mo. 3s (BB,MR).
MR XV 536 (Nov. 1756).
AB(WB); BB; EC 198:5; ESTC t066385.
BL
* N

359.
POLYDORE AND JULIA : OR, THE LIBERTINE RECLAIM'D. A NOVEL.
London : Printed for S. Crowder and H. Woodgate, at the Golden-Ball in Paternoster-Row. 1756.
218pp. 12mo. 3s (BB,CR,MR).
CR II 283-284 (Oct. 1756); MR XV 536 (Nov. 1756).
AB(BL); BB; ESTC t108184.
BL
* N

360.
THE SUPPOSED DAUGHTER; OR, INNOCENT IMPOSTER. In which is comprised the entertaining memoirs of Two North-Country Families of Distinction, in a Series of Letters of Thirty Years. Many of the Adventures, although remarkably uncommon, are attested by manuscripts now in the hands of the compiler. In Three Volumes.
London : Noble. 1756.
3 vols. 12mo. 9s (BB,CR,MR).
CR I 260-262 (Apr. 1756); MR XIV 453 (May 1756).
BB. Also, 1773.
Bod
E

361.
THE UNFORTUNATE SISTERS, OR THE DISTRESS'D LADIES, Being a History Founded upon real Truths.
London : Printed and Sold by J. How, in Long-Acre. 1756.
26pp. 12mo.
AB(BL); EC 239:8; ESTC t067649.
BL
* N/M

362.
[AMORY Thomas]
THE LIFE OF JOHN BUNCLE, ESQ; Containing Various Observations and Reflections, Made in several Parts of the World; and Many extraordinary Relations.
London : Printed for J. Noon, at the White Hart in Cheapside, near the Poultry. 1756.
511pp. 8vo. 6s (CR,MR).
CR II 219-227 (Oct. 1756); MR XV 497-512, 585-604 (Nov,Dec. 1756).
AB(AR,BL,RI); BB; ESTC t108506; LO 93 (UI,UP); McB 20; SG 26.
Part I only, with reissue/new edn, 1763 [768]. Part II, 1766 [990]. New edn, 1770.
BL Bod CUL UI UP
* N

363.
[ANSTEY Christopher]
MEMOIRS OF THE NOTED BUCKHORSE. In which, Besides a Minute Account of his past Memorable Exploits, That celebrated Hero is carried into higher Life; Containing some very Extraordinary Events. Interspersed with Remarkable Anecdotes of some Bloods of Fortune and Eminence, Companions of Mr. Buckhorse. In Two Volumes.
London : Printed for S. Crowder and H. Woodgate, at the Golden-Ball, in Pater-noster Row. 1756.
2 vols. 12mo. 6s (CR).
CR II 275-276 (Oct. 1756).
ESTC t143947.
BL Bod CUL
* N

364.
BANNAC Adolphus [pseud?]
THE APPARITION; OR, FEMALE CAVALIER. A Story Founded on Facts. By Adolphus Bannac Esq. In Three Volumes.
London : Printed for F. Noble at his Circulating Library in King Street, and for J. Noble at his Circulating Library at St. Martin's Court, near Leicester-Square. 1756.
3 vols. 12mo. 9s bound (CR,MR).
CR III 31-34 (Jan. 1757); MR XV 536 (Nov. 1756).
LC YU
N

365.
[BANNAC Adolphus?]
THE LIFE AND SURPRIZING ADVENTURES OF CRUSOE RICHARD DAVIS. In Two
Volumes.
London : Printed for F. Noble, at his Circulating Library, in King-Street, Covent-Garden; And J.
Noble, at his Circulating Library, in St. Martin's-Court, near Leicester-Square [1756].
2 vols. 12mo. 6s (BB,CR,MR).
CR II 351-357 (Nov. 1756); MR XV 656 (Dec. 1756).
BB; LO 94 (YU); PBG 342-3.
UM YU
* N

366.
[le CAMUS Antoine]
+ABDEKER: OR, THE ART OF PRESERVING BEAUTY. Translated from an Arabic
Manuscript.
Dublin : Printed for John Murphy, Bookseller in Skinner-Row. 1756.
155pp. 8vo.
ESTC t086864.
1st edn, 1754 [231].
BL
* N/M

367.
CERVANTES SAAVEDRA Miguel de
JARVIS Charles *trans*.
+THE LIFE AND EXPLOITS OF THE INGENIOUS GENTLEMAN DON QUIXOTE DE
LA MANCHA. Translated from the Original Spanish of Miguel Cervantes de Saavedra. By
Charles Jarvis, Esq; The Third Edition. In Two Volumes.
London : Printed for J. and R. Tonson and S. Draper in the Strand, and R. and J. Dodsley in
Pall-Mall. 1756.
2 vols. 4to.
ESTC t059885.
Published 26 Jan, RS.
1st edn of Jarvis trans, 1742. Also, 1743, 1747, 1749, 1766 [994]. Cf Smollett trans. with edns listed, 1755
[302], and Ozell trans. with edns listed, 1757 [409].
BL HU LC NLC
* N

368.
CHARKE Mrs Charlotte Cibber
+THE HISTORY OF HENRY DUMONT, ESQ; AND MISS CHARLOTTE EVELYN.
Consisting of Variety of Entertaining Characters, and very Interesting Subjects; With some
Critical Remarks on Comick Actors. By Mrs Charke. The Third Edition.
London : Printed for H. Slater, at the Circulating-Library, the Corner of Clare-Court, Drury
Lane; and H. Slater jun. and S. Whyte, at Holborn-Bars. 1756.
257pp. 12mo.
EC 240:4; ESTC t069299; SG 173.
1st edn, 1755 [303].
BL CUL UP
* N

369.
[DAVYS Mrs Mary]
+THE ACCOMPLISH'D RAKE : OR, THE MODERN FINE GENTLEMAN. Being the
Genuine Memoirs Of a certain Person of Distinction. The Second Edition.
London : Printed for A. Stephens, in the Butcher-Row, near Temple-Bar; F. Noble, in Kingstreet,
Covent-Garden; W. Bathoe, in Exeter-Exchange, Strand; and J. Noble, in St. Martin's-Court, near
Leicester-Square. 1756.
255pp. 12mo. 3s bound (tp).
ESTC t119331.
1st edn, 1727. Edns listed, 1755 [309].
BL
* N

370.
[DEFOE Daniel]
+THE LIFE AND ADVENTURES OF ROXANA, THE FORTUNATE MISTRESS; Or,
Most Unhappy Wife
[26 more lines]
Dublin : Printed by Alexander M'Culloh, in Skinner Row. 1756.
153pp. 8vo.
Edns listed, 1750 [21].
PU UI YU
N

371.
[HAYWOOD Mrs Eliza]
THE HUSBAND. In Answer to the Wife.
London : Printed for T. Gardner, at Cowley's Head, facing St. Clement's Church in the Strand.
1756.
279pp. 12mo. 3s (CR,MR).
CR I 133-135 (Mar. 1756); MR XIV 360 (Apr. 1756).
AB(BL,MH); BB; ESTC t118517; LO 96 (UP); SG 438.
BL Bn Bod CUL HU PU UI UP YU
* N/M

372.
[HAYWOOD Mrs Eliza]
+THE INVISIBLE SPY. By Exploralibus.
Dublin : Printed for S. Price. 1756.
2 vols.
1st edn and edns listed, 1755 [316].
NLC PU
N/M

373.
[HAYWOOD Mrs Eliza]
THE WIFE. By Mira, One of the Authors of The Female Spectator, and Epistles for
Ladies.
London : Printed for T. Gardner, at Cowley's Head, facing St. Clement's Church in the Strand.
1756.
282pp. 12mo. 3s (CR,MR).
CR I 129-133 (Mar. 1756); MR XIII 509 (App. 1755ii).
AB(BL,T); BB; ESTC t075406; LO 97 (UP); SG 453.
Also, 1762 [721], 1773.
BL Bn Bod CUL HU PU UI UP YU
* N/M

374.
[KELLEY John?]
THE MEMOIRS OF THE LIFE OF JOHN MEDLEY, ESQ; Or, Fortune Reconcil'd to Merit. By the Author of Pamela's Conduct in High Life.
London : Printed for J. Fuller, at the Bible and Dove in Ave Maria Lane. 1756.
2 vols. 12mo.
ESTC t132695; SG 559.
Vol I, first printed, London, 1748.
BL [imperf] UP
* N

375.
[KIMBER Edward]
THE JUVENILE ADVENTURES OF DAVID RANGER, ESQ. From an Original Manuscript found in the Collections of a late Noble Lord.
London : Printed for P. Stevens, at the Bible and Crown in Stationer's Court. 1757 [1756].
2 vols. 12mo. 6s (BB,CR,MR).
CR II 379 (Nov. 1756); MR XV 655-656 (Dec. 1756).
AB(My,SA,St); BB; LO 109 (UI); McB 502; newSG.
2nd edn, 1757 [413].
NCL UI UM UP
* N

376.
[LENNOX Mrs Charlotte Ramsay]
THE MEMOIRS OF THE COUNTESS OF BERCI. Taken from the French By the Author of the Female Quixote. In Two Volumes.
London : Printed for A. Millar, in the Strand. 1756.
2 vols. 12mo.
AB(BL); EC 56:1; ESTC t130916.
Adapted from *L'Histoire trage-comique de nostre temps* of Vital d'Audiguieur.
BL
* N

376a.
[RICHARDSON Samuel]
+CLARISSA. Or, The History of a Young Lady. An Abridgment.
Dublin : Printed for W. Sleater. 1756.
2 vols. 12mo. 6s6d (RCC).
Editor, 'W.M.'
1st edn of full work with edns listed, 1751 [96].
NLC NLI
E

377.
[RICHARDSON Samuel]
THE PATHS OF VIRTUE DELINEATED; OR THE HISTORY IN MINIATURE OF THE CELEBRATED PAMELA, CLARISSA HARLOWE, AND SIR CHARLES GRANDISON, Familiarised and Adapted To the Capacaties of Youth.
London : Printed for R. Baldwin, in Paternoster-Row. 1756.
232pp. 12mo. 2s6d (CR,MR).
CR I 315-316 (May 1756); MR XIV 581-582 (App. 1756i).
BB; ESTC t071401; LO 102 (HU,UI); McB 761; WS 89.
Published, 4 May. BL notes past attribution of the abridgment to Goldsmith.
Also, 1764 [861], 1773, 1777, 1784(2x). Cf 1755 [343].
BL CUL HU UI
* N/C

378.
[SMOLLETT Tobias]
+THE ADVENTURES OF RODERICK RANDOM. The Fifth Edition.
London : Printed for A. Millar, W. Strahan, J. Rivington, R. Baldwin, W. Johnston, T. Caslon, B. Law, T. Becket and P. A. DeHondt, T. Lowndes, J. Knox, W. Nicholl, T. Durham and M. Richardson. 1756
2 vols.
MW 36.
1st edn, 1748. Edns listed, 1750 [40].
N

379.
TOLDERVY William
THE HISTORY OF TWO ORPHANS. In Four Volumes. By William Toldervy.
London : Printed for William Owen, at Temple-Bar. 1756.
4 vols. 12mo. 12s (BB,CR,MR).
CR II 340-343 (Nov. 1756); MR XV 535 (Nov. 1756).
AB(adv); BB; ESTC t124619.
BL Bod
* N

380.
[WOODFIN Mrs A.]
NORTHERN MEMOIRS; OR, THE HISTORY OF A SCOTCH FAMILY. Written by a Lady.
London : Nobles [1756].
2 vols. 12mo. 6s (CR,MR).
CR II 448-451 (Dec. 1756); MR XV 656 (Dec. 1756).
AB(RI); BB.
HU NLC
N

Miscellanies

381.
A Genuine History of the Family of The Great Negroes of G—— Taken from an African Manuscript, in St. Sepulchre's Library, Dublin.
London : Printed in the Year. 1756.
17pp. 8vo.
ESTC t123842.
Negroes of G are the Agars of Gourran.
BL CUL
* M (sat)

382.
The History of Reynard the Fox, Bruin the Bear, &c.
London : Printed for G. Smith, in Fleet-Street. 1756.
160pp. 12mo. 3s (MR).
MR XV 655 (Dec. 1756).
ESTC t060047.
BL Bod
* M/C

383.
[d'Argens Jean Baptiste de Boyer, Marquis]
Derrick Samuel *trans*.
+The Memoirs of the Count Du Beauval. Including Some Curious Particulars Relating to the Dukes of Wharton and Ormond During their Exiles
[5 more lines]
Translated By Mr. Derrick.
Dublin : Printed for William Williamson, Bookseller, at Macænas's [sic] Head in Bride-street. 1756.
224pp. 12mo.
1st edn, 1754 [270].
Bod CUL
* M

384.
Rowe Mrs Elizabeth Singer
+Friendship in Death : In Twenty Letters from the Dead to the Living. To which are added, Letters Moral and Entertaining, In Prose and Verse : In Three Parts. By Mrs Elizabeth Rowe.
London : Printed for A. Todd in Fleet-street. 1756.
292pp. 12mo.
ESTC t072187.
1st edn, 1728. Edns listed, 1750 [60].
BL
* M

385.
[Shebbeare John]
+Letters on the English Nation : By Batista Angeloni, A Jesuit, Who resided many years in London. Translated from the Original Italian, By the Author of the Marriage Act a Novel. In Two Volumes. The Second Edition with Corrections.
London : Printed in the Year 1756. And Sold by S. Crowder and H. Woodgate at the Golden-Ball, and J. Scott at the Black Swan, in Pater-noster Row.
2 vols. 8vo.
ESTC t088354.
1st edn and edns listed, 1755 [345].
BL Bod CUL CUNY FL HU UC UV UW YU
* M

1757

386.
BATH EPISTLES, That Have Pass'd Between Miss Hazard, Lady Motherly, Lady Bountiful, Lady Wronghead, Miss Thoughtless, Mrs Planet, Sir Fr. Manley, Lawyer Gripe, Beau Clincher, &c. Highly proper to be read by Those who frequent Bath, Tunbridge Wells, &c.
London : Printed for J. Smyth, near Charing-Cross. 1757.
37pp. 8vo. 1s (CR,MR).
CR III 187-188 (Feb. 1757); MR XVI 179 (Feb. 1757).
FB; LO 103 (FB,YU).
YU
* E/M

387.
THE BUBBLED KNIGHTS; OR, SUCCESSFUL CONTRIVANCES. Plainly evincing in two familiar Instances lately transacted in this Metropolis, the Folly and Unreasonableness of Parents laying a Restraint upon their Childrens Inclinations, in the Affairs of Love and Marriage. In Two Volumes.
London : Printed for F. Noble, at his Circulating-Library in King-street Covent-garden; and J. Noble, at his Circulating-Library in St. Martin's-court, near Leicester-square [1757].
2 vols. 12mo. 6s (Adv-[393],CR,MR).
CR III 187 (Feb. 1757); MR XVI 178 (Feb. 1757).
YU
* N

388.
DU PLESSIS'S MEMOIRS; OR, VARIETY OF ADVENTURES With a Description of some Strolling Players, amongst whom the Memorialist travell'd awhile, before his last Departure from England. In Two Volumes.
London : Printed and sold by W. Reeve; and by the booksellers in town and country. 1757.
2 vols. 12mo. 6s bound (adv-1757 [398], CR,MR).
CR III 113-118 (Feb. 1757); MR XVI 179 (Feb. 1757).
BB; ESTC t139119.
Dublin edn, 1757 [389].
BL Bod
* N

389.
+DU PLESSIS'S MEMOIRS; OR, VARIETY OF ADVENTURES. With a Description of some Strolling Players, amongst whom the Memorialist travell'd awhile, before his last Departure from England. In Two Volumes.
Dublin : Printed for George Faulkner. 1757.
2 vols. 12mo.
AB(AR,BL, Dublin edn); ESTC t064715; NYSL(HC).
1st edn, 1757 [388].
BL
N

390.
THE FAIR CITIZEN: OR THE REAL ADVENTURES OF MISS CHARLOTTE BELLMOUR. Written by Herself.
London: Printed for T. Lownds at his Circulating Library, near Salisbury-Court, Fleet-street. 1757.
114pp. 12mo. 2s (BB,CR,MR).
CR IV 95 (July 1757); MR XVII 82 (July 1757).
BB; LO 104 (YU).
NLC YU
N

391.
THE HISTORY OF CLEANTHES, AN ENGLISHMAN OF THE HIGHEST QUALITY, AND CELEMENE, THE ILLUSTRIOUS AMAZONIAN PRINCESS : Interspersed With a Variety of most entertaining Incidents and surprizing Turns of Fortune; and a particular Account of that famous Island, so much talk'd of, but hitherto so little known. Written by a Person well acquainted with all the Principal Characters from their Original.
London : Printed for J. Scott at the Black Swan in Pater-noster-Row. 1757.
2 vols. 12mo. 6s (BB,MR).
CR IV 461 (Nov. 1757); MR XVI 567-568 (June 1757).
AB(BL); BB; ESTC t057442.
BL
* N

392.
THE HISTORY OF MADEMOISELLE CRONEL. Translated from the French.
London : Dawe. 1757.
12mo. 1s6d (BB,MR).
MR XVII 563 (Dec. 1757).
BB.
1st French edn, La Haye, 1741-3.
N

393.
THE HISTORY OF MISS KATTY N——. Containing a faithful and particular Relation of her Amours, Adventures, and various Turns of Fortune, in Scotland, Ireland, Jamaica, and England. Written by Herself.
London : Printed for F. Noble, at his Circulating-Library in King-street Covent-garden; And J. Noble, at his Circulating-Library in St. Martin's-court, near Leicester-square [1757].
225pp. 12mo. 3s bound (CR,MR,tp).
CR III 177 (Feb. 1757); MR XVI 178-179 (Feb. 1757).
AB(BL); LO 108 (UI,UP); McB 456; SG 493.
BL NLC UI UP
* N

394.
THE HISTORY OF SIR ROGER AND HIS SON JOE.
London : Printed for J. Scott, at the Black-Swan, in Pater-noster-Row [1757].
2 vols. 12mo. 6s (BB,CR,MR).
CR IV 552 (Dec. 1757); MR XVII 563 (Dec. 1757).
BB; LO 7 (UP) as 1750.
2nd edn, 1757 [395].
NLC YU
* N/E

395.
+THE HISTORY OF SIR ROGER AND HIS SON JOE. In Two Volumes. The Second Edition.
London : Printed for Francis Noble, at Otway's Head, in King-Street, Covent-Garden; and John Noble, at Dryden's Head, in St. Martin's Court, near Leicester-Square. 1757 (date on vol.II only).
2 vols. 12mo. 6s bound (tp).
1st edn, 1757 [394].
CUL
* N/E

396.
THE HISTORY OF TWO MODERN ADVENTURERS. In Two Volumes.
London : Printed for John Staples, at the Bible and Star, fronting Stationers Hall. 1757.
2 vols. 12mo. 5s (CR) 6s (BB,MR).
CR IV 464 (Nov. 1757); MR XVII 477-478 (Nov. 1757).
AB(BL); BB; EC 219:5; ESTC t083352.
BL
* N

397.
THE HISTORY OF TWO PERSONS OF QUALITY, Taken from Memoirs Written in the Reign of Edward IV, by William St. Pierre Esq; who was educated with the Earl of ***, and afterwards governor to the son of that Nobleman.
London : Noble. 1757.
12mo. 3s (MR).
MR XVI 452 (May 1757).
N

398.
LOVE AND FRIENDSHIP : OR, THE FAIR FUGITIVE. Exemplified In the Histories of two Families of Distinction, in the West of England; and interspers'd with a Variety of Characters, and several pleasing and interesting Incidents.
London : Printed and sold by W. Reeve, in Fleet-Street; and by the Booksellers in Town and Country. 1757.
252pp. 12mo. 3s (CR,MR).
CR III 476-477 (May 1757); MR XVI 285 (Mar. 1757).
EC 286:2; ESTC t070915.
Dublin edn, 1757 [399].
BL BU
* N

399.
+LOVE AND FRIENDSHIP; OR, THE FAIR FUGITIVE. Exemplified in the Histories of Two Families of Distinction in the West of England; and interspersed with a variety of Characters, and several pleasing and interesting incidents.
Dublin : 1757.
AB(TW,as Dublin edn).
1st edn, 1757 [398].
N

400.
(+)MEMOIRS OF B— TRACEY.
London : Printed for J. King, in Great Turnstile, Holborn [1757].
214pp. 12mo. 3s (BB,MR).
Drophead title reads 'The Notorious Libertine; or, The Adventures of B– Tracey'.
MR XVII 478 (Nov. 1757).
BB; ESTC t118902.
MR notes as taken from *The History of the Human Heart* (1750).
BL as [1760?] UMin as [1757]
* N/M

401.
MEMOIRS OF HARRIOT AND CHARLOTTE MEANWELL, Who from a State of Affluence are reduced to the greatest Distress. Written by Themselves.
London : Owen. 1757.
12mo. 3s (BB,CR,MR).
CR IV 95 (July 1757); MR XVI 578 (June 1757).
AB(Pi); BB.
CR as published by Scott.
N

402.

MEMOIRS OF SIR THOMAS HUGHSON AND MR. JOSEPH WILLIAMS, With the Remarkable History, Travels, and Distresses, of Telemachus Lovet. The whole calculated for the Improvement of the Mind and Manners, and a becoming and useful Entertainment for the Youth of both Sexes. In Four Volumes.
London : Printed for the Author. And sold by L. Davis, and T. Waller, Booksellers in Fleet-street; T. Osborn and J. Shipton in Gray's Inn; W. Strahan, in Cornhill; R. Griffiths, and W. Fenner, in Pater-noster-Row; J. Millan, Charing-Cross; and Mess. Wilsom and Durham, in the Strand. 1757.
4 vols. 12mo. 12s (BB,MR).
CR IV 460-461 (Nov. 1757); MR XVI 452 (May 1757).
BB.
YU
* N/C

403.

THE MOTHER-IN-LAW: OR, THE INNOCENT SUFFERER. Interspersed with the Uncommon and Entertaining Adventures of Mr. Hervey Faulconer. In Two Volumes.
London : Printed for F. Noble, at his Circulating-Library in King-street, Covent-Garden; and J. Noble, at his Circulating-Library in St. Martin's-court, near Leicester-Square. 1757.
2 vols. 12mo. 6s (BB,CR,MR).
CR IV 95 (July 1757); MR XVII 81 (July 1757).
AB(RI); BB; LO 111 (HU); NYSL(HC); PBG 346-7.
HU (noting sometime attribution to 'A. G.', author of *The Impetuous Lover* 1757 [410]).
N

404.

THE PROSTITUTES OF QUALITY; OR, ADULTERY Â-LA-MODE. Being Authentic and genuine Memoirs of several Persons of the highest Quality.
London : Printed for J. Cooke, and J. Coote, opposite Devereux-Court, in the Strand. 1757.
222pp. 12mo. 3s (BB,MR).
MR XVII 478 (Nov. 1757).
BB; EC 93:3; ESTC t046030.
BL
* M/C

405.

THE SEDAN. A NOVEL. In which Many New and Entertaining Characters are introduced. In Two Volumes.
London : Printed for R. Baldwin, in Pater-noster-Row. 1757.
2 vols. 12mo. 6s (BB,MR).
MR XVII 477 (Nov. 1757).
AB(AR,BL); BB; EC 219:1; ESTC t107718; RKM(BL).
BL NLC
* N

406.

TRUE MERIT, TRUE HAPPINESS, Exemplified in the Entertaining and Instructive Memoirs of Mr. S–. In Two Volumes.
London : Printed for Francis Noble, at Otway's Head, in King's-Street, Covent-Garden; and John Noble, at Dryden's Head, in St. Martin's Court, near Leicester-Square [1757].
2 vols. 12mo. 6s bound (BB,CR,MR,tp).
CR III 467-469 (May 1757); MR XVI 453 (May 1757).
BB; EC 124:4; ESTC t064742.
A translation of *Mémoires et aventures d'un bourgeois* by Jean Digard de Kerguette.
BL
* N

407.
THE UNFORTUNATE BEAUTY; OR, MEMOIRS OF MISS ANNA MARIA SOAMES, AND SEVERAL OTHERS. A Narrative Founded on Known Facts, Interspersed with several Uncommon Characters, and Exemplified in many Instances that befel them during the course of many years' courtship and unsuccessful love.
London : Printed for J. Scott, at the Black Swan in Paternoster-row. 1757.
248pp. 12mo. 3s (BB,CR,MR).
CR IV 461 (Nov. 1757); MR XVI 452 (May 1757).
AB(RI); BB.
HU OU
N

408.
THE VOYAGES, TRAVELS, AND WONDERFUL DISCOVERIES OF CAPT. JOHN HOLMESBY, Containing A Series of the most Surprising and Uncommon Events, which befel the Author in his Voyage to the Southern Ocean, in the Year, 1739.
London : Printed for F. Noble, at his Circulating-Library in King-street, Covent-garden; And J. Noble, at his Circulating-Library in St. Martin's-court, near Leicester-square [1757].
216pp. 12mo. 3s bound (CR,MR,tp).
CR IV 395-402 (Nov. 1757); MR XVII 563 (Dec. 1757).
ESTC t128483; LO 113 (BL,NYPL); PBG 346.
BL Bod NYPL
* N

409.
CERVANTES SAAVEDRA Miguel de
OZELL John *trans.*
+THE HISTORY OF THE RENOWNED DON QUIXOTE DE LA MANCHA. Written in Spanish by Miguel de Cervantes Saavedra. Translated by Several Hands : And Published by the Late Mr. Motteux. Revis'd a-new from the best Spanish Edition, By Mr. Ozell : Who has added Explanatory Notes from Jarvis, Oudin, Sobrino, Gregario, and the Royal Academy Dictionary of Madrid.
Glasgow : Printed and sold by R. and A. Foulis. 1757.
4 vols. 8vo.
ESTC t059496.
Motteux's trans, 1st published 1700. Also, 1706, 1712, and 4th edn, revised Ozell, 1719. Further Ozell edns, 1725, 1733, 1743, 1749, 1766 [995], 1771(2x). Cf Smollett trans. with edns listed, 1755 [302], and Jarvis trans. with edns listed, 1756 [367].
BL
* N

410.
G., A.
THE IMPETUOUS LOVER, OR THE GUILTLESS PARRICIDE, Shewing, To what Lengths Love may run, and the extream Folly of forming Schemes for Futurity. Written under the Instructions, and at the Request of one of the Interested Partys. By A. G. Esqire.
London : Printed for E. Ross, at his circulating Library, in Duke's Court, facing St. Martin's Church, Charing-Cross. 1757.
2 vols. 12mo. 6s (CR,MR).
CR IV 461 (Nov. 1757); MR XVI 451-452 (May 1757).
AB(BL); EC 62:4; ESTC t057443.
BL
* N

411.
[GREEN George Smith]
THE LIFE OF MR. JOHN VAN, A CLERGYMAN'S SON OF WOODY, IN HAMPSHIRE. Being a Series of many Extraordinary Events, and Surprising Vicissitudes... Written by his Friend and Acquaintance, G. S. Green.
London : Printed for Francis Noble & John Noble. 1757.
2 vols. 12mo. 6s (CR,MR).
CR III 476 (May 1757); MR XVI 284 (Mar. 1757).
AB(BL); EC 233:1; ESTC t037440 (as 1750?); SG 386 (as ?1750).
BL Bn Bod UP
N

412.
[GRIFFITH Richard and Elizabeth]
A SERIES OF GENUINE LETTERS BETWEEN HENRY AND FRANCES.
London : Printed for W. Johnston, in St. Paul's Church-Yard. 1757.
2 vols. 12mo. 6s (CR,MR). Subn.
CR III 428-432 (May 1757); MR XVII 416-423 (Nov. 1757).
AB(BL); BB; ESTC t117316; FB; LO 106 & 107 (FB,HU,UP).
Dublin edn, 1760 [573]. Also, 1761 [651]. Vols III-IV, 1766 [1013].
Further edns 1767 [1102], 1770(2x), 1786.
BL HU NLC PU UP
* E

413.
[KIMBER Edward]
+THE JUVENILE ADVENTURES OF DAVID RANGER ESQ; From an Original Manuscript found in the Collections of a late Noble Lord. In Two Volumes. The Second Edition.
London : Printed for P. Stevens, at the Bible and Crown in Stationer's Court. 1757.
2 vols. 12mo. 6s (tp).
CG(as 1767); ESTC t107720.
1st edn, 1756 [375].
BL Bn HU YU
* N

414.
[LONG Edward]
THE ANTI-GALLICAN; OR, THE HISTORY AND ADVENTURES OF HARRY COBHAM ESQUIRE. Inscribed to Louis the XVth, by the Author.
London : Printed for T. Lownds, at his Circulating Library in Fleet-Street. 1757.
240pp. 12mo. 3s (CR).
CR III 477 (May 1757).
AB(AR,BL,WB); BB; ESTC t117750; LO 110 (UP); SG 649.
2nd edn, 1758 [442].
BL Bod CUL HL LC UP YU
* N

415.
[MARIVAUX Pierre Carlet de Chamblain de]
(+)THE FORTUNATE VILLAGER; OR, MEMOIRS OF SIR ANDREW THOMPSON. In Two Volumes.
London : Printed for F. Noble at his Circulating Library in King Street, Covent Garden; and J. Noble, at his Circulating Library, in St. Martin's Court, Leicester Square [1757].
2 vols. 12mo. 6s (BB;CR,MR).
CR III 187 (Feb. 1757); MR XVI 284 (Mar. 1757).
BB. Adolphus Bannac [pseud?] often given as author.
Abridged from Marivaux, *Le paysan parvenu*. 1st English version, 1735. Also, Dublin edn, 1765 [929].
UP
N

416.
[NUGENT Robert]
THE OPPRESSED CAPTIVE. Being An Historical Novel, deduced from the Distresses of real Life, in an impartial and candid Account of the unparallel'd Sufferings of Caius Silius Nugenius, now under Confinement in the Fleet Prison, at the Suit of an implacable and relentless Parent.
'London : Wrote by the Author and Sufferer in the Fleet Prison, 1757'.
211pp. 8vo. 3s (BB).
AB(Do); BB; ESTC t092960.
BL HU NLC UI
* N/M

417.
[WOODFIN Mrs A.]
THE HISTORY OF MISS SALLY SABLE. By the Author of the Memoirs of a Scotch Family. In Two Volumes.
London : Printed for F. Noble, at his Circulating-Library in King-street Covent-Garden. And J. Noble, at his Circulating-Library in St. Martin's-Court, near Leicester-Square [1757].
2 vols. 12mo. 6s bound (tp).
CR V 28-32 (Jan. 1758); MR XVII 563 (Dec. 1757).
AB(as ?1770); BB; EC 163:3; ESTC t066945 (as 1770?).
Dublin edn, 1765 [947].
BL YU [as 1770?]
* N

Miscellanies

418.
The Revolutions of Modesty. To which is added, The Reign of Pleasure.
[London : Printed for M. Cooper, at the Globe in Pater-Noster-Row. 1757]
164pp. 12mo.
ESTC t109735.
2nd edn, 1757 [419].
BL [imperf]
* M

419.
+The Revolutions of Modesty. To which is added, The Reign of Pleasure. The Second Edition.
London : Printed for M. Cooper, at the Globe in Pater-Noster-Row. 1757.
164pp. 12mo. 2s (tp).
ESTC t061501.
1st edn, 1757 [418].
BL
* M

420.
The Tryal of the Lady Allurea Luxury, Before the Lord Chief-Justice Upright, On an information for a Conspiracy.
London : Printed for F. Noble, at his Circulating-Library in King-Street, Covent-Garden; and J. Noble, at his Circulating-Library, in St. Martin's Court, near Leicester-Square. 1757.
92pp. 8vo. 1s6d (tp).
CR III 478 (May 1757); MR XVI 459 (May 1757).
ESTC t070943
BL
* M (sat)

421.
[d'Auborn A.]
+**The French Convert : Being a True Relation of the Happy Conversion of a Noble French Lady, From The Errors and Superstitions of Popery, to the Reformed Religion by Means of a Protestant Gardener, her Servant.** [14 more lines] **The Eleventh Edition.**
London : Printed for C. Hitch and L. Hawes, at the Red Lion, in Pater-Noster Row; and J. Hodges, at the Looking Glass, at London-Bridge; and R. Ware, at the Bible and Sun, on Ludgate-Hill. 1757.
108pp. 12mo.
ESTC t089798.
1st edn, [17-]. Also, 1719, 1725(2x), 1737, 1746, 1762 [749], 1780, 1784, 1785, 1786, 1795.
BL
* M/N

422.
[Fielding Sarah]
The Lives of Cleopatra and Octavia. By The Author of David Simple.
London : Printed for the Author, And Sold by A. Millar in the Strand; R. and J. Dodsley, in Pall-Mall; and J. Leake, at Bath. 1757.
219pp. 4to. Subn.
AB(AR,Pi,RI); BB; ESTC t140917; LO 105 (UI,UP); McB 317; RS; SG 326.
Published 19 May. 2nd edn, 1758 [455].
BL Bod CUL UI UP
* M/N

423.
[Hellen Robert]
Letters from an Armenian in Ireland to his Friends at Trebisond &c. Translated in the Year, 1756.
London : Printed in the Year 1757.
[Printed by Owen, CR]
123pp. 8vo. 3s (CR).
CR IV 183-184 (Aug. 1757).
EC 175:6; ESTC t057333; LO 113 (BL,NYPL).
BL NYPL
* E/M

424.
W., M.
The History of Israel Jobson, the Wandering Jew
[13 more lines]
Translated from the Original Chinese by M. W.
London : J. Nickolson, Bookseller, in Cambridge. 1757.
95pp. 12mo.
ESTC t097936.
BL CUL
* M

425.

THE ADVENTURES OF A TURK. Translated from the French.
London : J. Coote. 1758.
2 vols. 12mo. 6s (CR,MR).
CR VII 287 (Mar. 1759); MR XIX 580 (Dec. 1759).
AB(JH).
Dublin edn, 1760 [525].
N

426.

ALMIRA : OR, THE HISTORY OF A FRENCH LADY OF DISTINCTION. Interspersed with the Histories of the Marquis de Montalvan; and Isabella : Lindamira, or, the Belle Espagnol, &c. &c. In Four Books.
London : Printed for, and sold by Ann and Charles Corbett, at their Correct State Lottery-Office, directly opposite to St. Dunstan's Church, Fleet-Street. 1758.
252pp. 12mo. 3s (BB,MR).
MR XVIII 492 (May 1758).
AB(BL); BB; EC 63:4; ESTC t055909.
Cf 1761 [629].
BL
* N/E

427.

THE AMOROUS FRIARS : OR, THE INTRIGUES OF A CONVENT.
London : Printed for J. Fleming, opposite Norfolk-Street in the Strand. 1759 [1758].
220pp. 12mo. 3s (BB,CR,MR).
CR VII 288 (Mar. 1759); MR XIX 581 (Dec. 1758).
BB; EC 234:3; ESTC t068058.
It includes, pp.104-138 'Jealousy Out-witted : An Italian Novel', pp.139-197 'Basil and Clara, An Italian Novel', and pp.198-220 'The Enterprising Friars. A French Novel'.
BL YU
* N

428.

THE CLOISTER, OR THE AMOURS OF SAINFROID, A JESUIT AND EULALIA, A NUN. Translated from the French.
London : Printed for J. Fleming. 1758.
259pp. 12mo. 3s (BB,CR,MR).
CR VII 288 (Mar. 1759); MR XIX 581 (Dec. 1758).
BB; CG(as 1764); SG 181.
UP (HU has an entry for 1729)
N

429.

A COLLECTION OF NOVELS, NEVER BEFORE PRINTED, FOUNDED ON FACTS, SERIOUS AND WHIMSICAL.
[5 titles follow]
London : Trye (BB,CR,MR). 1758.
12mo. 2s6d (MR) 3s (BB,CR).
CR V 349 (Apr. 1758), MR XVIII 498 (May 1758).
BB.
Cf *Theatre of Love* 1758 [435].
C

430.
THE HISTORY OF AMANDA. Written by a young Lady.
London : Printed for E. Ross, at his Circulating-Library, in Duke's Court, facing St. Martin's Church, Charing-Cross. 1758.
282pp. 12mo. 3s (BB,CR,MR).
CR V 172-173 (Feb. 1758); MR XVIII 182 (Feb. 1758).
AB(ELG); BB; FB; LO 115 (FB,MR).
RU UCLA
E

431.
THE HISTORY OF MIRA, DAUGHTER OF MARCIA. Interspersed with a Variety of Entertaining Subjects relative thereto.
London : Wilkie. 1758.
2 vols. 12mo. 6s (BB,MR).
MR XVIII 93 (Jan. 1758).
BB.
N

432.
MEMOIRS OF THE CELEBRATED MISS FANNY M–.
London : Printed for M. Thrush, at the King's-Arms in Salisbury-court, Fleet-street. 1759 [1758].
2 vols. 12mo. 3s each vol (CR,MR).
Rev of vol I : CR VII 87 (Jan. 1759); MR XIX 580 (Dec. 1758).
Rev of vol II : CR VII 288 (Mar. 1759).
2nd edn, 1759 [474].
HU [vol II only]
N/M (sat)

433.
MEMOIRS OF A YOUNG LADY OF FAMILY. Being a succinct account of the capriciousness of fortune, and an accurate survey of the heart of that incomprehensible animal, called Man.
London : Printed for J. Scott, at the Black-Swan, in Pater-Noster-Row. 1758.
235pp. 12mo. 2s6d (CR) 2s8d (BB) 3s (MR).
CR V 170 (Feb. 1758); MR XVIII 182-183 (Feb. 1758).
AB(BL); BB; EC 129:1; ESTC t124829.
BL
* N

434.
THE SOUTH-SEA FORTUNE; OR, THE CHAPLAIN ADVANCED TO THE SADDLE. Containing the Genuine Private Memoirs of a Worthy Family in Gloucestershire, from the fatal year 1720, to the year 1748. Written by Mrs Richwould, one of the interested parties.
London : Printed for J. Wren. 1758.
2 vols. 12mo. 6s (MR).
MR XIX 581 (Dec. 1758).
AB(Pi).
HU(Baker) NLC NYPL
N

435.
THE THEATRE OF LOVE. A Collection of Novels, (None of which were ever printed
before) [12 titles follow]
London : Printed and Sold by W. Reeve, at Shakespear's-Head, opposite Crane-Court, Fleet-
Street. 1759 [1758].
248pp. 12mo. 3s bound (BB,MR,tp).
MR XIX 498 (Nov. 1758).
AB(BL); BB; EC 206:6; ESTC t066917; LO 129 (UI,UP); McB 906; SG 1030.
Dublin edn, 1760 [554]. Cf 1758 [429].
BL NLC UI UP
* C

436.
[CRÉBILLON Claude Prosper Jolyot de]
[KIMBER Edward *trans.*]
THE HAPPY ORPHANS : An Authentic History of Persons in High Life. With a Variety
of uncommon Events, and surprizing Turns of Fortune. Translated and improved from the
French Original. In Two Volumes.
London:Printed for H. Woodgate and S. Brooks,at the Golden Ball,in PaterNoster-Row.1759[58]
2 vols. 12mo. 6s (CR,MR).
CR VII 174-175 (Feb. 1759); MR XIX 580 (Dec. 1758).
AB(RI). Trans. of Crébillon's 1754 *Les Heureux Orphelins*, itself based on Eliza Haywood's *Fortunate
Foundlings*, 1744(2x) and edns, 1748, 1761 [656], 1770. Further edns of this version, 1759 [479] [480].
BL
* N

437.
CRÉBILLON [Claude Prosper Jolyot de]
[HUMPHREYS Samuel *trans.*]
(+)LETTERS OF THE MACHIONESS DE M***. Translated from the Original French, of
the Celebrated Mr. Crebillon.
London : Printed for L. Davis and C. Reymers, opposite Gray's Inn, Holborn. 1758.
304pp. 12mo. 3s bound (tp).
ESTC t116317.
Trans. of *Lettres de la marquise de M*** au comte de R****, 1732. Versions, 1735, 1737; and 1766 edn [1001].
BL CUL NLC
* E/M

438.
FÉNELON François de Salignac de La Mothe
+THE ADVENTURES OF TELEMACHUS.
London : Strahan. 1758.
462pp. 12mo.
1st English edn, 1699. Edns listed, 1755 [312].
Free Library of Philadelphia
N/M

439.
FIELDING Henry
+THE LIFE OF MR. JONATHAN WILD THE GREAT. To which is Added, A Journey
From this World to the next. By Henry Fielding, Esq;
Dublin : Printed for W. Williamson, at Mecænas's-Head in Bride-street. 1758.
396pp. 12mo.
ESTC t089911.
1st separate edn, with other edns listed, 1754 [234].
BL
* N

440.
[KIMBER Edward]
THE LIFE, EXTRAORDINARY ADVENTURES, VOYAGES, AND SURPRIZING ESCAPES OF CAPT. NEVILLE FROWDE, OF CORK. In Four Parts. Written by himself, and now first published from his own Manuscript.
London : Printed for J. Wren, in the Strand, 1708 [1758].
220pp. 12mo. 3s (MR).
CR VI 261-262 (Sept. 1758); MR XVIII 311 (Sept. 1758).
BB; ESTC t107401; LO 116 (BL,LC); PBG 347.
Also, 1767 [1112], 1773, 1792, 1793.
BL YU
* N/M

441.
[LENNOX Mrs Charlotte Ramsay]
HENRIETTA. By the Author of The Female Quixote. In Two Volumes.
London : Printed for A. Millar, in the Strand. 1758.
2 vols. 12mo. 6s (MR).
CR V 122-130 (Feb. 1758); MR XVIII 273 (Mar. 1758).
AB(AR,BL,Mg); BB; ESTC t072179; LO 117 (UI,YU); McB 547; SG 619.
Also, 1761 [662], 1787.
BL CUL UI UP
* N

442.
[LONG Edward]
+THE ANTI-GALLICAN; OR, THE HISTORY AND ADVENTURES OF HARRY COBHAM ESQUIRE. Inscribed to Louis the XVth, by the Author. The Second Edition.
London : Printed for T. Lownds, at his Circulating Library in Fleet-Street. 1758.
240pp. 12mo.
SG 650.
1st edn, 1757 [414].
UP
N

443.
[MARTEILHÉ Jean]
[GOLDSMITH Oliver *trans.*]
THE MEMOIRS OF A PROTESTANT, CONDEMNED TO THE GALLEYS OF FRANCE FOR HIS RELIGION. Written by Himself
[11 more lines]
Translated from the Original, just published at the Hague. By James Willington.
London : Printed for R. Griffiths, at the Dunciad, in Pater-noster-row; and E. Dilly, at the Rose and Crown, in the Poultry. 1758.
2 vols. 12mo. 6s (BB).
AB(BL,IW); BB as Willington; ESTC t119693; McB 641; TS p32-33.
Dublin edn, 1765 [932].
BL UI
* N/M

444.
MOUHY Charles de Fieux, Chevalier de
+THE FORTUNATE COUNTRY MAID. Being the Entertaining Memoirs Of the Present
Celebrated Marchioness of L— V—
[10 more lines]
From the French of the Chevalier De Mouhy. In Two Volumes. The Fifth Edition
Corrected.
London : Printed for C. Hitch, B. Dod, R. Ware, W. Needham, R. Baldwin, S. Crowder, P.
Davey and B. Law, H. Woodgate and S. Brooks, T. Lownds, and A. and C. Corbett. 1758.
2 vols. 12mo.
McB 674.
1st English edn, 1740. Also, 1741, 1767 [1122], 1789.
CUL UI
* N/M

445.
le PRINCE DE BEAUMONT Jeanne Marie
+THE HISTORY OF A YOUNG LADY OF DISTINCTION. In a Series of Letters which
passed between Madam du Montier, and the Marchioness De ***, her Daughter.
Translated from the French of Madame le Prince de Beaumont, by Stamper Richardson.
London : Printed for F. Noble and J. Noble. 1758.
2 vols.
1st edn and edns listed, 1754 [245], with especial note on authorship.
DU PU
E

446.
[SMOLLETT Tobias]
+THE ADVENTURES OF PEREGRINE PICKLE. In which are included, Memoirs of a
Lady of Quality. In Four Volumes. The Second Edition, Revised, Corrected, and Altered by
the Author.
London : Printed for R. Baldwin, and J. Richardson, in Pater-noster-Row; and D. Wilson and T.
Durham in the Strand. 1758.
4 vols. 12mo.
McB 844; MW 138.
1,000 copies, Strahan ledgers.
1st edn and edns listed, 1751 [99].
Bod HU UI YU
* N

447.
[SMYTHIES Miss]
THE BROTHERS. In Two Volumes. By the Author of The Stage-Coach and Lucy Wellers.
London : Printed for R. and J. Dodsley, at Tully's Head, in Pall-mall. 1758.
2 vols. 12mo. 6s (BB,CR,MR). Subn.
CR VII 79 (Jan. 1759); MR XX 81 (Jan. 1759).
AB(AR,BL,RI); BB; ESTC t071306; FB; LO 119 (FB,HU); McB 111.
2nd edn, 1759 [506].
BL HU UI
* N

Miscellanies

448.

The Gentleman and Lady of Pleasure's Amusement : in eighty-eight questions, with their answers, on love and gallantry. To which is added, The Adventures of Sophia; with The History of Frederick and Caroline.
London : Printed for M. Thrush. 1759 [1758].
235pp. 12mo. 3s (CR,MR).
CR VI 526 (Dec. 1758); MR XIX 500-501 (Nov. 1758).
SG 355.
UP
M/C

449.

Jonathan Wild's Advice to his Successor.
London : Scott. 1758.
43pp. 8vo. 1s (CR,MR).
CR VI 174 (Aug. 1758); MR XIX 201-202 (Aug. 1758).
Cf 1754 [234].
NLC UI YU
M

450.

The Scourge of Pleasure. Dedicated to Fanny Murray.
London : Printed for J. Fleming. 1758.
30pp. 8vo. 1s (BB,MR).
MR XX 275 (Mar. 1759).
BB.
LC
M

451.

The Unfortunate Shipwright : Or, Cruel Captain. Being A faithful Narrative of the unparallel'd Sufferings of Robert Barker, late Carpenter on board the Thetis Snow of Bristol, in a Voyage to the Coast of Guinea and Antigua.
London : Printed for, and sold by the Author, and may be had at Mr. Samuel Collins's, the Sign of the Cardmaker's Arms on Garlick Hill, London, and no where else. 1758.
39pp. 12mo.
CUL
* M

452.

[d'Aulnoy Marie Catherine La Mothe (Jumelle de Berneville), Countess]
+The History of the Tales of the Fairies
[19 more split lines and 2 full lines]
London : Printed for C. Hitch, and L. Hawes, at the Red-Lyon, in Pater-noster-Row; S. Crowder, and Comp. at the Looking-Glass, on London-Bridge; H. Woodgate, and S. Brookes, in Pater-noster-Row; And C. Ware, on Ludgate-Hill. 1758.
143pp. 12mo. 1s (tp).
ESTC t060639.
1st edn, 1734. Also, 1749, 1766 [1049], 1781.
BL
* C/M

453.
[Caraccioli Charles]
Chiron : or, the Mental Optician.
London : Printed for J. Robinson, at the Golden Lion, in Ludgate-Street. 1758.
2 vols. 12mo. 5s (BB,MR).
MR XVIII 276 (Mar. 1758).
AB(B&G,Pi,TW); BB; ESTC t107655; RKM(UP).
BL Bod CUL HU NLC UC UCLA UP YU
* M

454.
[Fielding Sarah]
+The Governess; or the Little Female Academy. Calculated for the entertainment and instruction of Young Ladies in their Education. By the Author of David Simple. The Fourth Edition. Revised and Corrected.
London : Printed for A. Millar. 1758.
146pp. 12mo.
1st edns, 1749. Edns listed, 1751 [110].
UC UM
M

455.
[Fielding Sarah]
+The Lives of Cleopatra and Octavia. By The Author of David Simple. Second Edition Corrected.
London : Printed for the Author, And Sold by A. Millar, in the Strand; R. and J. Dodsley, in Pall-Mall; and J. Leake, at Bath. 1758.
267pp. 12mo.
ESTC t131354.
1st edn, 1757 [422].
BL HU NYPL UP YU
* M/N

1759

456.
AGENOR AND ISMENA; OR, THE WAR OF THE TENDER PASSIONS. A Novel. In Two Volumes. Translated from the French.
London : Printed for J. Cooke, at Shakespear's-Head, behind the Chapter-House, in St. Paul's Church-yard. 1759.
2 vols. 12mo. 6s (CR,MR).
CR VIII 408 (Nov. 1759); MR XXI 451 (Nov. 1759).
ESTC t118884.
BL YU [as ?1747]
* N

457.
THE CAMPAIGN; A TRUE STORY.
London : Printed for T. Harrison, near Charing-Cross. 1759.
2 vols. 12mo. 6s (CR,MR).
CR VII 78-79 (Jan. 1759); MR XX 189-190 (Feb. 1759).
EC 172:8; ESTC t068059.
From a work by de Puisieux. Dublin edn, 1759 [458].
BL UCLA YU
* N

458.
+THE CAMPAIGN A TRUE STORY. In Two Volumes.
Dublin : Printed for P. Wilson, and J. Exshaw, in Dame-Street. 1759.
2 vols. 12mo.
1st English edn, 1759 [457].
BL NYSL(HC).
* N

459.
COURT INTRIGUES. OR THE SECRET HISTORY OF ARDELISA, A Story founded on
Facts, and illustrated with Anecdotes of Persons in real Life.
London : Printed for E. Cabe, at the Circulating Library, in Ave-Maria-Lane. 1759.
251pp. 12mo. 3s (BB,MR).
MR XX 565 (June 1759).
AB(BL); BB; ESTC t075782.
BL NCL UCLA UP YU
* N

460.
+THE DEVIL UPON CRUTCHES IN ENGLAND. OR, NIGHT SCENES IN LONDON. A
Satirical Work. Written Upon the Plan of the celebrated Diable Boiteux of Monsieur Le
Sage. In Two Parts. By a Gentleman of Oxford. The Third Edition.
London : Printed for I. Pottinger, in Great Turnstile; and J. Ross, at Shakespeare's Head, Middle-
Row, Holborn. 1759.
190pp. 12mo.
ESTC t119840; SG 262.
1st edn and edns listed, 1755 [285]. Original work by le Sage with edns listed, 1750 [37].
BL Tx UP
* N/M

461.
+THE DEVIL UPON CRUTCHES IN ENGLAND. OR, NIGHT SCENES IN LONDON. A
Satirical Work Written upon the Plan the Celebrated Diable Boiteux of M. Le Sage. In
Two Parts. By a Gentleman of Oxford. The Fourth Edition.
London : Printed for I. Pottinger. 1759.
1st edn and edns listed, 1755 [285]. Original work by Le Sage with edns listed, 1750 [37].
HU
N/M

462.
EMIMA AND LOUISA. In which is contain'd, Several Remarkable Incidents relating to
Two Ladies of Distinguish'd Families and Fortunes. In a Series of Letters. By a Lady.
London : Printed for the Author, And sold by Owen, at Homer's-Head, near Temple-Bar. 1759.
239pp. 8vo.
Bod
* E

463.
+THE FORTUNATE IMPOSTER : Or, the Very Entertaining Adventures of Dick Hazard.
A True Story.
London : Printed for Henry Woodgate and Samuel Brooks, at the Golden-Ball, in Pater-noster-
row. 1759.
119pp. 12mo. 1s (tp).
EC 129:3; ESTC t064739.
1st edn, 'The Adventures of', 1754 [212].
BL
* N/M

464.
HEROICK VIRTUE : OR, THE NOBLE SUFFERERS. Exemplified in the Illustrious
Lives, and Surprizing Adventures of several Noblemen and Ladies
[17 more lines]
London : Printed. 1759.
239pp. 8vo. 2s6d bound (tp).
EC 92:3; ESTC t119928.
BL CUNY FL
* N

465.
THE HISTORY OF BENJAMIN ST. MARTIN, A FORTUNATE FOUNDLING,
Interspersed with Curious Anecdotes and Narratives of Love-affairs of some Persons in
High Life. In Two Volumes.
London : J. Coote. 1759.
2 vols. 12mo. 6s (CR,MR).
CR VII 285 (Mar. 1759); MR XX 188 (Feb. 1759).
AB(Pi).
An imitation of Tom Jones.
DU NLC
N

466.
THE HISTORY OF PORTIA. Written by a Lady.
London : Printed for R. Withy, at the Dunciad in Cornhill; J. Pottinger, in Great Turnstile,
Holborn; J. Wilkie, in St. Paul's Church-Yard; and J. Cooke, in Queen-Street, May-Fair. 1759.
2 vols. 12mo. 6s (BB,CR,MR).
CR VII 382 (Apr. 1759); MR XX 276 (Mar. 1759).
BB; ESTC t130934.
BL Bod NLC [as 1749] UC
* N

467.
THE HISTORY OF WILHELMINA SUSANNAH DORMER. Containing A Wonderful
Series of Events.
London : Printed for M. Cooper, at the Globe in Pater-noster-row. 1759.
56pp. 8vo. 1s6d (BB,CR,MR,tp).
CR VII 65-68 (Jan. 1759); MR XX 80 (Jan. 1759).
BB as 1758; EC 230:5; ESTC t072448.
BL
* N

468.
INJURED INNOCENCE, A NARRATIVE BASED ON FACT.
London : Printed for Henry Woodgate and Samuel Brooks, at the Golden-Ball in Pater-noster-
row. 1759.
120pp. 12mo.
LO 121 (UP); SG 528.
UP
N

469.
THE INTRIGUING COXCOMB : OR THE SECRET HISTORY OF SIR EDMUND GODFREY. Illustrated with a Variety of Incidents which happened to himself, and the celebrated Miss L**** C*****, in the Course of their several Years Acquaintance; the Whole calculated to amuse and instruct the attentive Reader.
London : Printed for J. Scott, at the Black-Swan, in Paternoster-Row. 1759.
2 vols. 12mo. 6s (BB,CR,MR).
CR VII 184 (Feb. 1759); MR XX 188 (Feb. 1759).
BB; EC 189:3; ESTC t070924.
CR believed this to be a further translation of a work which began publication several years before as *Memoirs of a Coxcomb*, presumably the Cleland work, 1751 [75] [76].
BL
* N

470.
JEMIMA AND LOUISA. In which is Contained, Several Remarkable Incidents Relating to Two Ladies of Distinguished Families and Fortunes. In a Series of Letters. By a Lady.
London : Printed for the Author and Sold by W. Owen. 1759.
239pp. 12mo. 3s (BB,CR,MR).
CR VIII 165-166 (Aug. 1759); MR XXI 82 (July 1759).
BB; FB; LO 122 (CR,FB,UP); SG 534.
UP
E

471.
THE JUVENILE ADVENTURES OF MISS KITTY F——R. In Two Volumes.
London : Stephen Smith. 1759.
2 vols. 12mo. 3s sewed each vol (CR,MR).
CR VIII 176 (Aug. 1759); MR XX 276, 379 (Mar,Apr. 1759).
AB(CLP); BB; LO 124 (-); McB 503.
BL [unlocated] UI
N

472.
+THE LIEE [sic] AND MEMOIRS OF MR. EPHRAIM TRISTRAM BATES, COMMONLY CALLED CORPORAL BATES, A broken-hearted Soldier
[19 more lines]
London : Printed by J. Warcus, at the Bible, the Corner of Rackett-Court, Fleet-Street. 1759.
238pp 12mo.
ESTC t077672.
1st edn, 1756 [354].
BL Bod
* N

473.
THE LIFE AND REAL ADVENTURES OF HAMILTON MURRAY. Written by Himself. In Three Volumes.
London : Printed for the Author; And Sold by J. Burd, Printer, in New-Street, Shoe-Lane. 1759.
3 vols. 12mo. 9s (BB,CR,MR).
CR VII 282-283 (Mar. 1759); MR XX 188 (Feb. 1759).
AB(BL); BB; EC 125:14; ESTC t108642.
BL Bod
* N

474.
+THE MEMOIRS OF THE CELEBRATED MISS FANNY M–. The Second Edition.
London : Printed for J. Scott, in Pater-noster-row; and M. Thrush, at the King's-Arms, in Salisbury-court, Fleet-street. 1759.
2 vols. 12mo. 3s bound [each vol] (tp of vol I).
ESTC t106196.
1st edn, 1758 [432].
HU [vol II only and doubt must remain about issue sequence]
* N/M (sat)

475.
THE NOVICIATE OF THE MARQUIS DE ***; OR, THE APPRENTICE TURN'D MASTER. Translated from the French.
London : Pottinger and Cooke. 1759.
12mo. 3s (BB,CR,MR).
CR VII 278-279 (Mar. 1759); MR XX 188 (Feb. 1759).
BB.
Trans. of *Le Noviciat du Marquis de ***, ou l'apprentif devenu mâitre*, 1747.
N

476.
THE VIRTUOUS CRIMINAL; OR, THE HISTORY OF LORD STANLEY. Translated from the French. In Two Volumes.
London : Printed for F. Noble, in King's street, Covent-Garden; and J. Noble, in St. Martin's-court, Leicester-Fields. 1759.
2 vols. 12mo. 6s (BB,MR).
MR XX 81 (Jan. 1759).
BB.
HU
N

477.
[BEHN Mrs Aphra]
+LOVE-LETTERS BETWEEN A NOBLEMAN AND HIS SISTER, With the History of their Adventures. In Three Parts. The Seventh Edition.
London : Printed for D. Brown. 1759.
2 vols. 12mo.
1st edn, 1684. Also, 1693(2x), 1708, 1712, 1718, 1734, 1735, 1765 [898].
HU UM
E

478.
[CHETWOOD William Rufus]
[or (BL) VICTOR Benjamin]
+THE VOYAGES AND ADVENTURES OF CAPTAIN ROBERT BOYLE, In Several Parts of the World
[9 more lines]
The Fifth Edition.
London : Printed (by Assignment from Mr. Watts) for T. Lownds, at his Circulating Library in Fleet-Street. 1759.
295pp. 12mo.
ESTC t078252. Not in PBG.
Sometimes attributed to Defoe.
1st edn, 1726. Also, 1727, 1728, 1735(2x), 1741, 1744, 1748, 1760 [563], 1762 [707], 1765 [902], 1771, 1773, 1778, 1787, 1788, 1792(2x), 1797.
BL UNC
* N

479.
[CRÉBILLON Claude Prosper Jolyot de]
[KIMBER Edward *trans.*]
+THE HAPPY ORPHANS : An Authentic History of Persons in High Life. With a Variety
of uncommon Events, and surprizing Turns of Fortune. Translated and improved from the
French Original. In Two Volumes. The Second Edition.
London : Printed for H. Woodgate and S. Brooks, at the Golden Ball, in Pater-Noster-Row
[1759].
2 vols. 16mo.
1st edn and earlier versions listed, 1758 [436].
HU NLC
* N

480.
[CRÉBILLON Claude Prosper Jolyot de]
[KIMBER Edward *trans.*]
+THE HAPPY ORPHANS : An Authentic History of Persons in High Life. With A Variety
of uncommon Events and surprizing Turns of Fortune. Translated from the French of
Monsieur Crebillon, the Son.
Dublin : Printed for P. Wilson, J. Exshaw, and H. Saunders. 1759.
329pp. 12mo.
ESTC t118920.
1st edn and earlier versions listed, 1758 [436].
BL
* N

481.
[DEFOE Daniel]
(+)FORTUNE'S FICKLE DISTRIBUTION; In Three Parts. Containing first, The Life and
Death of Moll Flanders. Part II The Life of Jane Hackaway her governess. Part III The
Life of James MacFaul, Moll Flanders' Lancashire husband.
London : H. Woodgate and S. Brooks. 1759.
116pp.
Edns of Moll Flanders listed, 1750 [20].
Bn
C/M

482.
[DEFOE Daniel]
+THE WONDERFUL LIFE, AND MOST SURPRIZING ADVENTURES OF ROBINSON
CRUSOE OF YORK, MARINER
[11 more lines]
London : Printed for C. Hitch, and L. Hawes, at the Red-Lion, in Pater-noster-Row; S. Crowder,
and Comp. at the Looking-Glass on London-Bridge; H. Woodgate, and S. Brookes, at the
Golden-Ball, in Pater-noster-Row; And C. Ware, at the Bible and Sun, on Ludgate-Hill. 1759.
154pp. 12mo.
ESTC t072305.
1st edn, 1719-20. Edns listed, 1752 [129].
BL HU YU
* N/M

483.
[DEFOE Daniel]
+THE WONDERFUL LIFE AND MOST SURPRIZING ADVENTURES OF ROBINSON
CRUSOE OF YORK, MARINER [&c.]
Faithfully Epitomized in Three Volumes.
London : Printed and sold by all the booksellers. 1759.
112pp. 12mo.
1st edn, 1719-20. Edns listed, 1752 [129].
UM
N/M

484.
[FAUQUES Marianne Agnés Pillement, Dame de]
ABASSAI. AN EASTERN NOVEL. In Two Volumes. Translated from the French.
London : Printed for J. Coote. 1759.
2 vols. 12mo. 6s (MR) 6s6d (CR).
CR VII 460 (May 1759); MR XX 380 (Apr. 1759).
Translation of *Abbassai, histoire orientale*, 1733.
Dublin edn, 1764 [830].
YU
N

485.
FÉNELON François de Salignac de La Mothe
+THE ADVENTURES OF TELEMACHUS, THE SON OF ULYSSES. In Twenty-Four
**Books. Written by the Archbishop of Cambray. To which is added The Adventures of
Aristonous Done into English by Mr. Littlebury and Mr. Boyer. The Sixteenth Edition,
carefully revised and corrected.**
London : Printed for W. Meadows. 1759.
1st English edn, 1699. Edns listed, 1755 [312].
BU HU LC
N/M

486.
[FIELDING Henry]
+THE HISTORY OF TOM JONES, A FOUNDLING. In Three Volumes.
Dublin : Printed for W. Smith, P. Wilson, J. Exshaw, and H. Bradley. 1759.
3 vols. 8vo.
RCC p.239.
1st edn, 1749. Edns listed, 1750 [24].
HU NLI YU
* N

487.
[FIELDING Henry]
+THE HISTORY OF TOM JONES, A FOUNDLING, In Six Volumes.
London : Printed for A. Millar. 1759.
6 vols.
1st edn, 1749. Edns listed, 1750 [24].
KO
N

488.
[FIELDING Sarah]
THE HISTORY OF THE COUNTESS OF DELLWYN. In Two Volumes. By the Author of
David Simple.
London : Printed for A. Millar, in the Strand. 1759.
2 vols. 12mo. 6s (CR,MR).
CR VII 377-378 (Apr. 1759); MR XX 380-381 (Apr. 1759).
AB(AR,Bk,BL); BB; EC 207:4; ESTC t066941; LO 120 (UI,UP,RL); McB 315; SG 335.
Dublin edn, 1759 [488a].
BL Bod HU PU UCLA UI UP YU
* N

488a.
[FIELDING Sarah]
+THE HISTORY OF THE COUNTESS OF DELLWYN.
Dublin : Printed by and for James Hoey Junior. [1759?] (adv-1764 [851]).
1s7½d sewed 2s2d bound. Adv-1764 [851].
1st edn, 1759 [488].
N

489.
[FORD Emanuel]
+THE FAMOUS HISTORY OF MONTELION, KNIGHT OF THE ORACLE
[8 more lines]
London : Printed for H. Woodgate and S. Brooks, at the Golden Ball, Pater-noster-row [1759?].
125pp. 18mo.
EC 14:3; ESTC t128481.
1st edn, 1637. Also, 1709, 1720, 1761 [649] [650].
BL Bod
* N/M

490.
[GRAFIGNY Françoise d'Issembourg d'Happoncourt de]
+LETTERS WRITTEN BY A PERUVIAN PRINCESS. Translated from the French. The
Third Edition. Revised and carefully corrected by the Translator. To which is now first
added, The Sequel Of the Peruvian Letters.
London : Printed for J. Robson, Bookseller, at the Plume of Feathers, in New Bond-Street,
Successor to Mr. Brindley. 1759.
307pp. 8vo.
ESTC t132338.
1st English edn, 1748. Edns listed, 1753 [185].
BL NLC
* E

491.
GUEULETTE Thomas Simon
FLLOYD Thomas *trans.*
TARTARIAN TALES : OR, A THOUSAND AND ONE QUARTERS OF HOURS. Written
in French by the Celebrated Mr. Guelletee [sic] Author of the Chinese, Mogul, and other
Tales. The Whole now for the first Time translated into English. By Thomas Flloyd.
London : Printed for J. and R. Tonson in the Strand. 1759.
369pp. 12mo. 3s (BB,CR,MR).
CR VII 184 (Feb. 1759); MR XX 79-80 (Jan. 1759).
AB(B&G,G,RI); BB; ESTC t065513; McB 390; NYSL(HC).
Also, 1764 [844], 1785.
BL Bod CUL HU NLC UI YU
* N/C

492.
[GUICHARD Eleonore]
THE BRACELET : OR, THE FORTUNATE DISCOVERY. Being the History of Miss Polly *****. Translated, with some Alterations, from a French Work, entituled, Memoirs de Cecile. In Two Volumes.
London : Printed for F. Noble in King-street, Covent-Garden; And J. Noble in St. Martin's Court, Leicester-Square [1759] (BL).
2 vols. 12mo. 6s bound (BB,CR,MR,tp).
CR VII 382 (Apr. 1759); MR XX 275-276 (Mar. 1759).
AB(BL); BB; EC 169:2; ESTC t054965.
BL UC YU
* N

493.
[GUTHRIE William]
THE MOTHER; OR, THE HAPPY DISTRESS. A Novel. By the Author of the Friends.
London : Printed for the Author : and sold by R. Baldwrn [sic], at the Rose, in Pater-noster-row. 1759.
2 vols. 12mo. 6s (BB,CR,MR).
CR VII 409-413 (May 1759); MR XX 380 (Apr. 1759).
AB(BsB); BB.
Also, 1761 [652].
CUL HU PU
N

494.
[HAYWOOD Mrs Eliza]
+THE INVISIBLE SPY. By Explorabilis. In Two Volumes. The Second Edition.
London : Printed for T. Gardner, at Cowley's Head, facing St. Clement's Church in the Strand. 1759.
2 vols. 12mo.
ESTC t134310.
1st edn (as 'Exploralibus') and edns listed, 1755 [316].
Bod Bn YU
* N/M

495.
[JOHNSON Samuel]
THE PRINCE OF ABISSINIA. A TALE. In Two Volumes.
London : Printed for R. and J. Dodsley, in Pall-Mall; and W. Johnston, in Ludgate-Street. 1759.
2 vols. 8vo. 4s (RS) 5s (CR,MR).
CR VII 372-375 (Apr. 1759); MR XX 428-437 (May 1759).
AB(BL,McL,RK); BB; ESTC t139510; LO 123 (UI,UP,RL,YU); McB 484; SG 543.
Published 19 Apr, RS.
Also 1759 [496] [497], and 1760 [576], 1766 [1015], 1775, 1777, 1783(2x), 1786, 1787(2x), 1788, 1789, 1790.
BL Bn Bod HU PU Tx UI UP YU
* N

496.
[JOHNSON Samuel]
+THE PRINCE OF ABISSINIA. A TALE. In Two Volumes. The Second Edition.
London : Printed for R. and J. Dodsley, in Pall-Mall; and W. Johnston, in Ludgate-Street. 1759.
2 vols. 8vo. 5s (RS).
EC 92:8; ESTC t057339; McB 487; RS.
Published 26 June. 1st edn and edns listed, 1759 [495].
BL Bn Bod CUL Tx UI YU
* N

497.
[JOHNSON Samuel]
+THE PRINCE OF ABISSINIA. A TALE. In Two Volumes.
Dublin : Printed for G. and A. Ewing, and H. Bradley, Booksellers in Dame-street. 1759.
2 vols in 1. 262pp. 12mo. 2s8½d.
EC 237:5; ESTC t057362; McB 488; RCC p.93.
Published 12 May. 1st edn and edns listed, 1759 [495].
NLI OU TCD UI YU
* N

498.
LEWIS R[obert]
THE ADVENTURES OF A RAKE. In the Character of a Public Orator. Interspersed with
several Serious and Comic Pieces, pronounced before some polite Audiences with great
Applause, and published at their Request. In Two Volumes. By R. Lewis.
London : Printed for R. Withy, at the Dunciad, the third door from the East End of the Royal
exchange in Cornhill; T. Hope, at the Bible and Anchor, the Corner of Batholomew-lane,
Thread-needle-street; and J. Pridden, at the Feathers in Fleet-street, near Fleet-Bridge. 1759.
2 vols. 12mo. 6s (BB,CR,MR).
CR VIII 408-409 (Nov. 1759); MR XXI 451 (Nov. 1759).
AB(SA); BB; LO 125 (UP); SG 638.
Bod UP
* N

499.
[LONGUEVILLE Peter]
+THE HERMIT : OR, THE UNPARALLEL'D SUFFERINGS AND SURPRISING
ADVENTURES OF MR. PHILIP QUARLL, an Englishman : who was lately discovered by
Mr. Dorrington, a Bristol Merchant, upon an uninhabited Island in the South-Sea, where
he had lived above fifty years [&c.] The Third Edition.
London : Printed for J. Wren, S. Crowder, H. Woodgate, J. Fuller, and J. Warcus. 1759.
263pp. 12mo.
ESTC t0573226. 1st edn, 1727. Edns listed, 1751 [93].
BL Bn NYPL UM YU
N/M

500.
[MOUHY Charles de Fieux, Chevalier de]
FEMALE BANISHMENT : OR, THE WOMAN HATER. Originally wrote by the
Chevalier de Mouhy, Author of the Fortunate Country Maid. In Two Volumes.
London : Printed for T. Lownds, at his Circulating Library, in Fleet-Street. 1759.
2 vols. 12mo. 6s (BB,CR,MR).
CR VIII 302-307 (Oct. 1759); MR XXI 366 (Oct. 1759).
AB(BL,Pi,RI); BB; EC 5:7; ESTC t131197.
BL OU PU YU
* N

501.
[RICCOBONI Marie Jeanne]
HISTORY OF THE MARQUIS DE CRESSY. Translated from the French.
London : Pottinger. 1759.
12mo. 3s (BB,MR).
MR XX 467 (May 1759).
BB, FB; LO 127 (BL,FB).
Trans. of L'Histoire de M. Le Marquis de Cressy, 1758. Re-issued(?) by Becket and De Hondt, 1765 [935].
UC UI
N

502.
[RICCOBONI Marie Jeanne]
[BROOKE Mrs Frances Moore *trans.*]
LETTERS FROM LADY JULIET CATESBY, TO HER FRIEND LADY HENRIETTA CAMPLEY. Translated from the French.
London : Printed for R. and J. Dodsley, in Pall-Mall. 1759.
252pp. 12mo. 3s (CR).
CR IX 420 (May 1760); MR XXII 521 (June 1760).
Trans. of *Lettres de Milady Juliette Catesby à Milady Henriette Campley, son amie*, 1759.
Also, 1760 [582], 1763 [789] [790], 1764 [859], 1769 [1327], 1780.
E

503.
[RICHARDSON Samuel]
+CLARISSA. OR, THE HISTORY OF A YOUNG LADY : Comprehending The most Important Concerns of Private Life. In Eight Volumes. The Fourth Edition.
London : Printed for S. Richardson : And Sold by [bracketed together] C. Hitch and L. Hawes in Pater-noster Row; A. Millar, over-against Catherine-street in the Strand; John Rivington, in St. Paul's Church-yard; J. Rivington and J. Fletcher, in Pater-noster Row; And by J. Leake, at Bath. 1759.
8 vols. 12mo.
tp of vols II-VIII omit 'In Eight Vols' and add 'And particularly shewing, The Distresses that may attend the Misconduct Both of Parents and Children, In Relation to Marriage'.
ESTC t058979; McB 753.
1st edn, 1747-48. Edns listed, 1750 [96].
BL HU UI YU
* E

504.
[le SAGE Alain René]
[SMOLLETT Tobias *trans*]
+THE ADVENTURES OF GIL BLAS OF SANTILLANE.
Dublin : Published for the improvement and entertainment of the British youth of both sexes. By W. H. Dilworth, London : W. Anderson. 1759.
12mo.
RCC p.79.
1st edn, 1749. Edns listed, 1750 [36].
Bod YU
N

505.
[le SAGE Alain René]
+THE DEVIL UPON CRUTCHES : From the Diable Boiteux of Mr. le Sage. A New Translation
[9 more lines]
The Second Edition.
London : Printed for T. Osborn, A. Millar, R. Baldwin, S. Crowder, J. Rivington and J. Fletcher and I. Pottinger. 1759.
2 vols. 12mo.
1st edn and edns listed, 1750 [37].
CUL PU WCL YU
* N

506.
[SMYTHIES Miss]
+THE BROTHERS. In Two Volumes. The Second Edition. By the Author of The Stage-Coach, and Lucy Wellers.
London : Printed for R. and J. Dodsley, at Tully's Head, in Pall-mall; and by W. Reymer, in Colchester. 1759.
2 vols. 12mo. Subn.
ESTC t055913.
1st edn, 1758 [447].
BL HU
* N

507.
[STERNE Laurence]
THE LIFE AND OPINIONS OF TRISTRAM SHANDY, GENTLEMAN.
[York : Printed by Ann Ward] 1760 [1759].
2 vols. 8vo. 1760.
CR IX 73-74 (Jan. 1760); MR XXIV 101-116 (Feb. 1761).
BB; ESTC t014780; LO 143(UI,UP,YU).
Printed by Ann Ward at York in Dec. 1759, KM.
Many official and pirated edns including volumes within re-issued collected edns of this work 1760-67; 1760 [585] [586] [587] [588] [589] [590], 1763 [796], 1767 [1144a]. Vols III-IV, 1761 [673] [674] [676], 1769 [1339]. Vols I-IV, 1761 [675], 1765 [941], 1768 [1233]. Vols V-VI, 1761 [677], 1762 [741], 1767 [1144]. Vols VII-VIII, 1765 [940]. Vols I-VIII, 1767 [1143]. Vols V-VIII, 1765 [942]. Vol IX, 1767 [1140] [1141] [1142]. Vols I-IX, 1769 [1338]. Also, 1772, 1772/3, 1774, 1775, 1777(2x), 1779(3x), 1781, 1782, 1791, 1792, 1793, 1794, 1796, 1798.
Cf. Carr, 1760 [562] and spurious vol.IX, 1766 [984] [985]. Cf also 'Shandiana', 1760 [544] [596] [598] [600] [607] [610] [611] [612] [614] [615] [627], 1761 [684] [688], 1762 [712] [740], 1765 [953], 1768 [1245], 1769 [1281]. The Sermons of Mr. Yorick were 1st published in 1760.
BL UV
* N

508.
[STERNE Laurence]
A POLITICAL ROMANCE ADRESSED TO — —- ESQ. OF YORK.
London : Printed, and sold by J. Murdoch, bookseller, opposite the New Exchange coffe-house [sic] in the Strand. 1759.
47pp. 12mo. 1s (BB).
BB as 1769; ESTC t014710; FB; LO 128 (FB,HU,UO).
Also known as 'The History of a Good Warm Watch-Coat'.
York edn, 1759 [509], and 1774.
BL HU IU PU UO YU
* N/M

509.
[STERNE Laurence]
+A POLITICAL ROMANCE ADDRESSED TO — —- ESQ. OF YORK.
York : Printed in the Year 1759.
60pp. 12mo. 1s (tp).
Printed in 'about 500 copies', WLCS.
1st edn, 1759 [508].
IU YU
N/M

510.
VOLTAIRE François Marie Arouet de
CANDID : OR, ALL FOR THE BEST. By M. de Voltaire.
London : Printed for J. Nourse at the Lamb opposite Katherine-Street in the Strand. 1759.
132pp. 12mo. 1s6d (BB,MR).
MR XXI 83-85 (July 1759).
AB(BL,GBF,WB); BB; EC 92:2; ESTC t083448.
Further edns, 1759 [510a] [511] [512] [513], and 1760 [592], 1761 [680] [681], 1771, 1778, 1779.
BL Bod CUL NYPL YU
* N/M

510a.
[VOLTAIRE François Marie Arouet de]
+CANDID : OR, ALL FOR THE BEST.
Dublin : Printed by and sold for James Hoey. [1759?] (adv-1764 [851]).
1s1d (adv-1764 [851]).
Adv-1764 [851].
1st English edn and edns listed, 1759 [510].
N/M

511.
VOLTAIRE François Marie Arouet de
+CANDID, OR ALL FOR THE BEST. Translated from the French of M. de Voltaire. The Second Edition.
London : Printed for J. Nourse at the Lamb opposite Katherine-Street in the Strand. 1759.
132pp. 12mo.
ESTC t137685.
1st English edn and edns listed, 1759 [510].
BL Bod HU NLC
* N/M

512.
[VOLTAIRE François Marie Arouet de]
RIDER W. *trans.*
+CANDIDUS : OR, THE OPTIMIST. By Mr. De Voltaire. Translated into English. By W. Rider, M.A. Late Scholar of Jesus College, Oxford.
London : Printed for J. Scott, at the Black Swan, in Pater-noster-Row, and J. Gratton, in Old Bond-Street. 1759.
135pp. 8vo. 1s6d (tp).
ESTC t019892.
1st English edn and edns listed, 1759 [510].
BL HU PU YU
* N/M

513.
VOLTAIRE François Marie Arouet de
+CANDIDUS; OR, ALL FOR THE BEST. By M. De Voltaire. A new Translation.
Edinburgh : Printed by Sands, Donaldson, Murray, and Cochran. For A. Donaldson, at Pope's head. 1759.
Vol I, 58pp. 12mo. 1s (tp).
A vol II, dated 1761.
ESTC t137620.
1st English edn and edns listed, 1759 [510].
BL HU PU
* N/M

Miscellanies

514.
The Castle-Builders; Or, The History of William Stephens, of the Isle of Wight, Esq; lately deceased. A Political Novel, Never before published in any Language.
London : Cabe. 1759.
320pp. 8vo. 2s6d (BB,CR,MR).
CR VII 558 (June 1759); MR XXI 81 (July 1759).
AB(Pk); BB.
As CR notes, it is far more factual than fictional.
2nd edn, 1759 [515].
M

515.
+The Castle-Builders; Or, The History of William Stephens, of the Isle of Wight, Esq; lately deceased. A Political Novel, Never before published in any Language. The Second Edition, with large Additions.
London : Printed for E. Cabe, in Avemary-Lane; R. Withy, at the Dunciad in Cornhill; and J. Cook, in Queen's-Street, May-Fair. 1759.
320pp. 8vo.
EC 201:2; ESTC t068570.
1st edn, 1759 [514].
BL
* M

516.
The Histories Of Some of the Penitents in the Magdalen-House, As Supposed to be related by Themselves. In Two Volumes.
London : Printed for John Rivington in St. Paul's Church-yard, and J. Dodsley in Pall-mall. 1760 [1759].
2 vols. 12mo. 6s (BB,CR,MR).
CR VIII 373-379 (Nov. 1759); MR XXI 449-450 (Nov. 1759).
BB; CG [as by Sarah Fielding]; EC 127:1; ESTC t092540; LO 135 (UP).
Dublin edn, 1760 [605].
BL UP
* M

517.
The Memoirs of Madame de Stahl. Translated from the French.
London : Reeve. 1759.
12mo. 3s (CR,MR).
CR VII 286-287 (Mar. 1759); MR XX 188-189 (Feb. 1759).
N/M

518.
Rosalind; or, an Apology for the History of a Theatrical Lady.
Dublin : Printed and sold by the Booksellers. 1759.
12mo.
AB(BL); ESTC t072051.
BL [now mislaid] FL HU
N

519.
Venus unmasked : Or, an Inquiry into the Nature and Origin of the Passion of Love, Interspersed with Curious and Entertaining Accounts of several Modern Amours. In Two Volumes.
London : Printed for the Author. And Sold by M. Thrush, at the King's-Arms in Salisbury-Court, Fleet-Street. 1759.
2 vols. 12mo. 3s6d (BB).
BB; ESTC t075141; newSg.
Also, 1765 [956].
BL Bod FL UP
* M

520.
[Almon John]
London Courtship; Or, a New Road to Matrimony, Consisting of Original Letters Which passed between a celebrated Young Lady of the City of London and several of her Suitors.
London : Printed for M. Thrush, in Salisbury-Court Fleet Street [1759?] (BL & tp MS addition).
48pp. 8vo. 1s (BB,MR).
MR XXII 157 (Feb. 1760).
AB(BL); BB as 1760; ESTC t119978; FB; LO 126 (BL,FB).
BL UP
* M/E

521.
Latter Mrs Mary
The Miscellaneous Works, in Verse and Prose, of Mrs Mary Latter, Of Reading, Berks. In Three Parts.
Reading : Printed and sold by C. Pocock. 1759. Sold also by J. Wilkie in St. Paul's Church-yard, London; J. Wimpey in Newbury, and R. Aillen in Basingstoke. 1759.
212pp. 8vo. 3s sewed (BB,CR,MR).
CR VIII 171 (Aug. 1759); MR XXI 82 (July 1759).
BB; ESTC t078295.
Much verse.
2nd edn, 1759 [522].
BL NLC PU
* M/C

522.
Latter Mrs Mary
+The Miscellaneous Works, in Verse and Prose, of Mrs Mary Latter, Of Reading, Berks. In Three Parts. The Second Edition.
Reading : Printed and sold by C. Pocock. 1759. Sold also by J. Wilkie in St. Paul's Church-yard, London; J. Wimpey in Newbury, and R. Aillen in Basingstoke. 1759.
212pp. 8vo.
1st edn, 1759 [521].
PU
M/C

523.
[Richer Adrien]
The Life of Belisarius, Translated from the French; With some Explanatory Notes and Observations.
London : Printed for J. Hinton, at the King's-Arms in Newgate-street. 1759.
82pp. 8vo. 1s (BB,CR,MR,tp).
CR VII 469 (May 1759); MR XX 565 (June 1759).
BB; ESTC t104591.
Cf 1767 [1115].
BL [imperfect]
* M/N

524.
THE ADVENTURES OF A BLACK COAT. Containing a Series of Remarkable Occurrences and Entertaining Incidents, That it was a Witness to in its Peregrinations thro' the Cities of London and Westminster, in Company with Variety of Characters. As related by Itself.
London : Printed for J. Williams under St. Dunstan's-Church, and J. Burd, at the Temple Exchange, Fleet-street. 1760.
166pp. 12mo. 2s6d (CR) 3s (MR).
CR IX 499 (June 1760); MR XXII 548 (App. 1760i).
AB(MH,Pi,WB); CG; EC 804:9; ESTC t128642; LO 130 (UP).
Also, 1762 [697] and [1780?] (formerly given as 1750 by BL & HU).
BL IU NLC UI UP YU
* N

525.
+THE ADVENTURES OF A TURK. To which is Annexed, Letters to and from a Turkish Bashaw, a beautiful French Slave, and several other Personages. Translated from the French.
Dublin : Printed by Dillon Chamberlaine, in Dame-street. 1760.
2 vols in 1. 2s2d bound 1s7½d sewed (adv-1766 [1022]).
Adv-1766 [1022].
1st edn, 1758 [425].
PU
N

526.
THE ADVENTURES OF GEORGE STANLEY; OR, THE CAMPAIGN. A True History In Two Volumes.
London : Wilkie [1760] (UnM).
2 vols. 6s (UnM).
UnM XXXVII 334 (Dec. 1760).
CG(UnM).
N

527.
THE ADVENTURES OF MISS SOPHIA BERKLEY. Written by a young Lady.
Dublin : Printed by James Hoey, at the Mercury in Skinner-Row. 1760.
173pp. 12mo.
ESTC t074440.
No other edn located.
BL
* N

528.
THE ADVENTURES OF SYLVIA HUGHES. Written by Herself.
London : Printed for J. Williams, near the Mitre Tavern, in Fleet-Street. 1761 [1760] (CR).
230pp. 12mo. 3s (CR,MR).
CR X 486 (Dec. 1760); MR XXIII 523 (App. 1760ii).
AB; CG(MR); EC 207:1; ESTC t066886; LO 146 (UP).
BL NLC UP
* N

529.
BELINDA; OR, HAPPINESS THE REWARD OF CONSTANCY. Mannifested in a Series
of the most interesting and Surprizing Events ever yet made publick.
London : Printed for T. Bailey at his Printing Office, the Ship and Crown in Leadedhall-street
[sic]; where tradesmen's bills are printed off copper plates, and letter press neat and reasonable
is executed [c.1760] (HU).
153pp. 12mo.
CG(HU).
HU
* N

530.
+CYNTHIA; With the Tragical Account of the Unfortunate Loves of Almerin and
Desdemona : Being a Novel. Illustrated with Variety of the Chances of Fortune; Moraliz'd
with many useful Observations, drawn from thence, whereby the Reader may reap both
Pleasure and Profit. Done by an English Hand. The Eleventh Edition, Corrected.
London : Printed for R. Ware, at the Sun and Bible on Ludgate-Hill; C. Hitch, at the Red-Lion
in Paternoster-Row, and J. Hodges, at the Looking-Glass on London Bridge [1760?] (BL).
155pp. 8vo.
ESTC t114951.
1st edn, 1687. Edns listed, 1750 [4].
BL
* N/M

531.
+THE DEVIL UPON CRUTCHES IN ENGLAND, Or Nights Scenes in London; a Satirical
Work. Written upon the plan of the Diable Boiteux of Monsieur le Sage. By a Gentleman
of Oxford. The Sixth Edition with additions.
London : Printed for F. Noble, 1760 (CG,BL).
170pp. 8vo.
CG(BL).
1st edn and edns listed, 1755 [285]. Original work by Le Sage and edns listed, 1750 [37].
BL [copy missing since 1979] LC
N/M

532.
DID YOU EVER SEE SUCH DAMNED STUFF? OR, SO MUCH THE BETTER. A Story
without Head or Tail, Wit or Humor.
London : Printed for C. G. Seyffert in Pall-Mall. 1760.
168pp. 12mo. 3s (CR) 2s6d (MR).
CR X 357 (Aug. 1760); MR XXIII 84 (July 1760).
AB(CLP); CG(BL,MR); EC 284:3; ESTC t077689; newSG.
BL UP
* N/M

533.
THE GENUINE LETTERS OF BARON FABRICIUS.
London : Beckett [1760] (UnM).
4s in boards (UnM).
UnM XXVII 334 (May 1760).
M/E

534.
THE HISTORY OF A NOBLEMAN AND HIS FAMILY.
Dublin : Richard Watts [1760] (adv-1760 [536]).
Adv-1760 [536].
N

535.

THE HISTORY OF FREDERICK THE FORSAKEN. Interspersed with Anecdotes relative
to several Personages of Rank and Fashion in this Metropolis. In Two Volumes.
London : Printed for F. Noble, at his Circulating Library, opposite Gray's-Inn-Gate, Holborn;
and J. Noble at his Circulating Library in St. Martin's Court, near Leicester Square. 1761 [1760].
2 vols. 12mo. 6s (CR,MR).
CR X 280-290 (Oct. 1760); MR XXIII 408 (Nov. 1760).
CG(MR); LO 150 (UP).
Dublin edn, 1761 [632].
NLC UP YU
* N

536.

+THE HISTORY OF MISS BIDDY FARMER, Or, Memoirs of My Own Life. Interspersed
with A Variety of Characters, both in High and Low Life.
Dublin : Printed for Richard Watts, Bookseller, at the Bible in Skinner-Row. 1760.
268pp. 12mo.
1st published, 1755 [293] as History of my own Life. Ascribed in CBEL to Adolphus Bannac.
HU YU
* N

537.

THE HISTORY OF SIR CHARLES GRANDISON SPIRITUALIZED In Part A Vision.
With Reflections thereon. By Theophila.
London : Printed for George Keith, at the Bible and Crown in Grace-Church-street. 1760.
12mo. 1s6d sewed 2s neatly bound (CR,MR,WS).
CR X 79 (July 1760); MR XXIII 255-256 (Sept. 1760).
WS 90.
Published 19 June. Edns of Richardson's Grandison, listed 1753 [191].
BL copy destroyed by WWII bombing, but details fortunately recorded in WS 90.
N

538.

THE ILLUSTRIOUS UNFORTUNATE; Or, The Adventures of Ulysses, the Father of
Telemachus. With the History of several of the greatest Heroes of Antiquity. Translated
from the French.
London : Noble [1760] (MR).
2 vols. 8vo. 5s (MR).
MR XXII 157 (Feb. 1760).
CG(MR).
N

539.

THE IMPOSTORS DETECTED: Or, The Life of a Portuguese. In which The Artifices and
Intrigues of Romish Priests are humorously displayed. The Whole Interspersed with several
curious and entertaining Anecdotes, relating to some of the principal Personages of the
Kingdom of Portugal. In Two Volumes.
London : Printed for W. Bristow, in St Paul's Church-Yard; and C. Etherington, at York. 1760.
2 vols. 12mo. 6s (CR).
CR X 405 (Nov. 1760).
EC 227:4; ESTC t066907; LO 137.
BL CUL LC UI
* N

540.
THE LIFE AND ADVENTURES OF A CAT. By the late Mr. Fielding.
London : Printed for Willoughby Mynors, in Middle-Row, Holborn. 1760.
190pp. 12mo. 2s6d bound (CR,MR).
CR X 420 (May 1760); MR XXII 435-436 (May 1760).
AB(Mg,RI); ESTC t130534.
Published Apr. 1760, WLC iii 348. HU (2nd edn) notes doubtful attribution to William Guthrie, 1708-1770.
2nd edn, 1760 [541].
BL
* N

541.
+THE LIFE AND ADVENTURES OF A CAT. By the late Mr. Fielding. The Second
Edition.
London : Printed for Willoughby Mynors, in Middle-row, Holborn. 1760.
CG(HU).
1st edn, 1760 [540].
HU HL IU Tx UM
* N

542.
THE LIFE AND ADVENTURES OF AN AMOROUS ANIMAL.
London : Trueman [1760] (UnM).
3s (UnM).
UnM XXVII 334 (Dec. 1760).
CG(UnM)
N/M

543.
THE LIFE AND IMAGINATIONS OF SALLY PAUL.
London : Hooper [1760] (MR).
12mo. 2s sewed (MR).
MR XXIII 524 (App. 1760ii).
CG(MR).
N

544.
THE LIFE AND OPINIONS OF MISS SUKEY SHANDY, Of Bow-Street, Gentlewoman.
In a Series of Letters to her Dear Brother, Tristram Shandy, Gent.
London : Printed for R. Stevens, at Pope's Head in Pater-noster-Row. 1760.
163pp. 8vo. 2s (CR,MR).
CR X 72 (July 1760); MR XXIII 83 (July 1760).
BB; LO 139 (HU).
Cf 1759 [507].
HU YU
* E

545.
LOUISA : OR, VIRTUE IN DISTRESS. Being the History of a natural Daughter of Lady
****
London : Printed for A. and C. Corbett at their State-Lottery-Office, Opposite St. Dunstan's
Church, Fleet-Street; and W. Flexney, under Gray's Inn Gate, Holbourn. 1760.
212pp. 12mo. 3s (MR).
CR IX 318-319 (Apr. 1760); MR XXII 329 (Apr. 1760).
BB; CG(BL); EC 98:6; ESTC t057447; FB; LO 140 (FB,YU).
BL YU
* N

546.
MEMOIRS OF THE CHEVALIER DE ***** A Novel. Translated from the French.
London : Cooke [1760] (CR,MR).
12mo. 3s (CR,MR).
CR IX 77 (Jan. 1760); MR XXII 156-157 (Feb. 1760).
CG.
N

547.
MEMOIRS OF THE LIFE OF A MODERN SAINT. Containing his Adventures in England, Scotland, and America.
London : Printed for H. Ranger, near the Temple-Gate, Fleet-Street. 1761 [1760] (CR,MR).
118pp. 8vo. 2s (BB,MR).
CR X 486 (Dec. 1760); MR XXIII 524 (Dec. 1760).
BB; CG(MR).
RU UG YU
* N

548.
THE NARRATIVE COMPANION : Or, Entertaining Moralist : Containing Choice of the most elegant, interesting, and improving Novels and Allegories, from the Best English Writers, viz. The Spectator, Rambler, World, Adventurer, Connoisseur, etc etc. In Two Volumes.
London : Printed for T. Becket, at Tully's Head, nr Surry-Street, in the Strand. 1760.
2 vols. 12mo. 6s (CR,MR).
CR IX 243 (Mar. 1760); MR XXII 330 (Apr. 1760).
CG(HU); ESTC t077507.
BL Bod HU
* C

549.
THE RAKE OF TASTE, Or The Elegant Debauchee : A True Story.
London : Printed for P. Wicks, in Pater-Noster-Row. 1760.
108pp. 8vo. 2s sewed (CR,MR).
CR XXIII 327 (Oct. 1760); MR X 237 (Oct. 1760).
BB; CG(BL,MR); EC 284:2; ESTC t057454.
BL YU
* N

550.
THE ROMANCE OF A DAY; Or, An Adventure in Greenwich-Park, last Easter.
London : Printed for I. Pottinger, in Pater-Noster-Row. 1760.
81pp. 8vo. 1s (tp).
MR XXIII 327 (Oct. 1760); CR X 241-242 (Sept. 1760).
BB; CG(BL).
BL
* N

551.
THE SOLDIER'S AMUSEMENT; A NOVEL. By the Author of the Memoirs of ****.
London [1760] (BB).
78pp. 8vo.
BB; CG(BB); [McB unlisted].
UI
N

552.

THE STOLEN MARRIAGES; OR, TRIPS TO SCOTLAND. Containing the History of Mr. Smith and Miss S. Green, Mr. James and Miss Lamb, and of Mr. King and Miss Henrietts. To which is Added, A Practical Essay on Old Maids.

[London] : Printed and sold by A. Hambleton [1760] (BL).

56pp. 8vo. 6d (tp).

CG(BL); EC 232:7; ESTC t057456.

BL

* N

553.

TACITURNA AND JOCUNDA : Or, Genius Alaciel's Journey through those two Islands. A Satirical Work. Translated from the French.

London : Printed for R. Withy, at the Dunciad in Cornhill; and J. Cook in May-Fair. 1760.

206pp. 8vo.

BB; CG(BB); EC 9:2; ESTC t088560.

BL HU UP

* N/M

554.

+THE THEATRE OF LOVE. A Collection of Novels None of which were ever Printed before.

Dublin : Printed by W. Smith. 1760.

120pp. 12mo.

1st edn, 1758 [435].

UM

C

555.

+THE UNFORTUNATE LOVERS : The History of Argalus and Parthenia. In Four Books adorned with Cuts.

London : Printed for Henry Woodgate and Samuel Brooks [1760?] (UI).

119pp. 12mo.

ESTC t128764; LO 144 (UI); McB 923.

A prose version of Francis Quarle's *Argalus and Parthenia*, based on Sir Philip Sidney's *Arcadia*. 1st edn, 1700, with 1715 edn at EC 173:2. Also, 1703, 1760 [556], 1765 [895].

BL UI

* N/M

556.

+THE UNFORTUNATE LOVERS; Or, the History of Argalus and Parthenia. In Four Books. Adorn'd with cuts. Fifth Edition.

London : Printed for C. Hitch and L. Hawes, in Pater-noster Row; S. Crowder, on London-Bridge; C. Ware, on Ludgate-hill; and H. Woodgate and S. Brooks, in Pater-noster Row [1760?] (BL).

167pp. 12mo.

ESTC t050415.

1st edn, 1700. Edns listed, 1760 [555].

BL

* N/M

557.
THE WORLD LOST AND REGAINED BY LOVE. An Allegorical Tale. To which is added, Iphis and Amaranta, Or, Cupid Revenged.
London : Printed for J. Burd, opposite St. Dunstan's Church, Fleet-street. 1760.
159pp. 12mo. 2s (BB) 2s6d sewed (MR).
MR XXII 460-464 (June 1760).
BB; CG(MR).
Dublin edn, 1760 [558].
YU
* N

558.
+THE WORLD LOST AND REGAINED BY LOVE. An Allegorical Tale. To which is added, Iphis and Amaranta, Or, Cupid Revenged.
Dublin : Printed for S. Smith, at Mr. G. Faulkner's. 1760.
112pp. 12mo.
EC 34:14; ESTC t075676.
1st edn, 1760 [557].
BL
* N

559.
[B. W.]
+TWELVE DELIGHTFUL NOVELS, Displaying the Stratagems of Love and Gallantry; Giving An account of the various Accidents, Intrigues and Events, which have happen'd to several Persons in the pursuance of their Amorous Inclinations. Very entertaining for Gentlemen, Ladies and others, in their Vacant Hours.
[12 titles follow]
By a Person of Quality.
Dublin : Printed by Ann Law, at the Rein-deer in Mountrath-street. 1760.
174pp. 12mo.
ESTC t118260.
Preface signed 'W.B.'
1st edn, 1719.
BL
* C

560.
[BERNARD Jean Frédéric]
THE PRAISE OF HELL : Or, A View of the Infernal Regions. Containing Some Account of the Advantages of that Place, with respect to its Antiquity, Situation, and Stability. Together with a Description of its Inhabitants; their Dresses, Manners, Amusements, and Employments. To which is added A detail of the Laws, Government, and Constitution of Hell. Adorned with Cuts; and illustrated with Notes, Critical, and Historical. In Two Volumes. Translated from the French.
London : Printed for G. Kearsley. Successor to the late Mr. Robinson, at the Golden Lion in Ludgate Street. 1760.
2 vols. 8vo. 6s (MR).
MR XXII 329 (Apr. 1760).
BB; CG(BL,HU); ESTC t106210.
A trans. of Eloge de l'enfer attributed to Bernard.
Also 1760 [561], 1770, 1775 edns.
BL CUL UI
* M

561.
[BERNARD Jean Frédéric]
+THE PRAISE OF HELL : Or, A View of the Infernal Regions. Containing Some Account
of the Advantages of that Place, with respect to its Antiquity, Situation, and Stability.
Together with a Description of its Inhabitants; their Dresses, Manners, Amusements, and
Employments. To which is added A detail of the Laws, Government, and Constitution of
Hell. Adorned with Cuts; and illustrated with Notes, Critical, and Historical. In Two
Volumes. Translated from the French.
London : Printed for M. Cooper. 1760.
2 vols. 12mo.
LO 131 (UP).
1st English edn and edns listed, 1760 [560].
HU LC PU UC UP YU
M

562.
[CARR John]
THE LIFE AND OPINIONS OF TRISTRAM SHANDY, GENTLEMAN.
London : Printed in the Year 1760.
223pp. 8vo.
CR X 237-238 (Sept. 1760); MR XXIII 327 (Oct. 1760) recognizing work as fraudulent.
CG(BL,MR); EC 239:6; ESTC t040935.
MR gives publisher as Scott.
504 copies printed, Wlm Bowyer Ledger, KM p.23. Purporting to be vol III of Tristram Shandy. Sterne's vols
III and IV, published 1761 [673]. Cf edns listed, 1759 [507].
BL YU
* N

563.
[CHETWOOD William Rufus]
+THE VOYAGES AND ADVENTURES OF CAPTAIN ROBERT BOYLE, In Several
Parts of the World
[9 more lines]
The Sixth Edition.
London : Printed in the Year. 1760.
269pp. 12mo.
1st edn, 1726. Edns listed, 1759 [478].
Bn
N

564.
[CHETWOOD William Rufus]
+THE VOYAGES, TRAVELS AND ADVENTURES OF WILLIAM OWEN GWIN
VAUGHAN, Esq.; with the History of his Brother Jonathon Vaughan, Six Years a Slave in
Tunis. Intermix'd with the Histories of Clerimont, Maria, Eleanora, and Others. Full of
Various Turns of Fortune. By the author of Captain Robert Boyle. The Second Edition.
London : Printed for T. Lownds at his Circulating Library, in Fleet Street. 1760.
2 vols. 12mo.
CG(BL); ESTC t057320; LO 132 (UP); McB 145.
1st edn, 1736. Also, 1754 [232].
BL UI UP
* N

565.
DAVYS Mrs [Mary]
+THE REFORM'D COQUET; OR, MEMOIRS OF AMORANDA. A NOVEL. By Mrs.
Davys, Author of the Humours of York. The Seventh Edition.
London : Printed for W. Cater in Holbourn; M. Cooper, in Pater-Noster- Row; and G. Woodfall,
at Charing Cross. 1760.
154pp. 12mo. 2s (tp).
CG(BL); ESTC t008501.
1st edn, 1724. Edns listed, 1752 [128].
BL
* N

566.
DAVYS Mrs [Mary]
+THE REFORM'D COQUET; OR, MEMOIRS OF AMORANDA. A NOVEL. By Mrs.
Davys, Author of the Humours of York. The Seventh Edition.
London : Printed for F. Noble [1760] (PU).
154pp. 12mo.
1st edn, 1724. Edns listed, 1752 [128].
PU
N

567.
[DEFOE Daniel]
+THE FORTUNES AND MISFORTUNES OF THE FAMOUS MOLL FLANDERS The
Seventh Edition.
London : C. Sympson [176-].
330pp. 12mo.
1st edn, 1722. Edns listed, 1750 [20].
Bn
N

568.
[DEFOE Daniel]
+THE LIFE AND MOST SURPRIZING ADVENTURES OF ROBINSON CRUSOE, Of
York, Mariner, Who Lived Eight and Twenty Years in an uninhabited island on the coast
of America, near the mouth of the great river Oroonoque. With an account of his
deliverance thence, and his after surprizing adventures. Also his Vision to the Angelic
World. The Ninth Edition.
Birmingham, Printed by J. Sketchley, Auctioneer, &c. [1760?] (BL).
408pp. 12mo.
CG(BL).
1st edn, 1719-20. Edns listed, 1752 [129].
BL
* N/M

569.
[DEFOE Daniel]
+ROBINSON CRUSOE.
Belfast : Daniel Blow [c.1760] (CG).
CG (possibly chapbook).
1st edn, 1719-20. Edns listed, 1752 [129].
M

570.
[FIELDING Henry]
(+)THE HISTORY OF AMELIA.
London : R. Snagg [1760] (BL).
12mo.
CG(BL).
An abridged version, called the 4th edn, LJM. Edns of full work listed, 1751 [83].
BL [copy missing]
N

571.
[FIELDING Sarah]
THE HISTORY OF OPHELIA. Published by The Author of David Simple. In Two Volumes.
London : Printed for R. Baldwin, at the Rose, in Pater-Noster-Row. 1760.
2 vols. 12mo. 6s (CR,MR).
CR IX 318 (Apr. 1760); MR XXII 328 (Apr. 1760).
AB(ELG,Pi); ESTC t132237; LO (HU,UI,UP); McB 316; SG 332.
Also, 1763 [775], 1785, 1787.
BL CUL FL HL HU NLC UI UM UP YU
* N

572.
[FORD Emanuel]
+THE FAMOUS AND PLEASANT HISTORY OF PARISMUS, THE VALIANT AND RENOWNED PRINCE OF BOHEMIA. In Three Parts. [14 more lines] The Eighth Edition.
London : Printed for Henry Woodgate and Samuel Brooks, at the Golden-Ball, in Pater-noster-row. [1760?] (BL).
114pp. 12mo.
ESTC t071888.
1st edn, 1637. Edns from 1700 include 1701, 1704, 1713, 1724, 1734. Also, 1770, 1790.
BL
* N/M

573.
[GRIFFITH Richard and Elizabeth]
+A SERIES OF GENUINE LETTERS BETWEEN HENRY AND FRANCES. The Second Edition, Revised, Corrected and Improved, By the Authors.
Dublin : Printed by S. Powell, in Crane-lane, for the Authors. 1760.
2 vols. 12mo. Subn.
EC 505:1; ESTC t111109.
1st edn and edns listed, 1757 [412].
BL HU UI YU
* E

574.
[HECQUET Madame]
THE HISTORY OF A SAVAGE GIRL, CAUGHT WILD IN THE WOODS OF CHAMPAGNE. Newly Translated from the French of Madam H——t.
London : Sold by R. Davidson, in the Strand [1760] (CG,LC).
116pp. 12mo.
AB(RI,St) as 1750, CG(HU).
'Published by Madame Hecquet', BL. Sometimes attributed to Charles Marie de la Condamine. Further edn, 1760 [575].
HU LC YU
* N/M

575.
[HECQUET Madame]
+THE HISTORY OF A SAVAGE GIRL, CAUGHT WILD IN THE WOODS OF
CHAMPAGNE. Newly Translated From the French of Madam H——t.
London : Sold by R. Dursley, T. Davison, T. Manson, C. Bland, and P. Jones. [1760?] (BL).
155pp. 12mo.
ESTC t124060.
Also, 1760 [574].
BL LC
* N/M

576.
[JOHNSON Samuel]
+THE PRINCE OF ABISSINIA; A TALE. In Two Volumes. The Third Edition.
London : Printed for R. and J. Dodsley, in Pall-Mall; and W. Johnston in Ludgate Street. 1760.
2 vols in 1. 8vo.
CG(HU); ESTC t139511.
1st edn and edns listed, 1759 [495].
BL CUNY HU NLC Tx UC UI UW
* N

577.
[JOHNSTON Charles]
CHRYSAL; OR, THE ADVENTURES OF A GUINEA. Wherein are exhibited Views of
several striking Scenes, With Curious and interesting Anecdotes of the most Noted Persons
in every Rank of Life, whose Hands it passed through in America, England, Holland,
Germany, and Portugal. By an Adept.
London : Printed for T. Becket, at Tully's Head, near Surry Street, in the Strand. 1760.
2 vols. 12mo. 6s (MR).
CR IX 419 (May 1760); MR XXIII 157-158 (May 1760).
BB; ESTC t089195; LO 138 (UI,YU); McB 493.
Variant spelling, Johnstone.
Also, 1760 [578], 1761 [657] [658], 1762 [722], 1764 [846], 1766 [1016], 1768 [1218] [1219]. Vols III-IV,
1765 [922] [923], 1767 [1109].
1st complete edn, 1767 [1108]. Also, 1771, 1775, 1783, 1785, 1791, 1794(3x).
BL Bod FL HU NYPL UI YU
* N

578.
[JOHNSTON Charles]
+CHRYSAL; OR, THE ADVENTURES OF A GUINEA. Wherein are exhibited Views of
several striking Scenes, With Curious and interesting Anecdotes of the most Noted Persons
in every Rank of Life, whose Hands it passed through, in America, England, Holland,
Germany, and Portugal. By an Adept.
Dublin : Printed by Dillon Chamberlaine, in Smock-Alley. 1760.
2 vols. 12mo.
McB 495.
1st edn and edns listed, 1760 [577].
Bod HL UI UW
* N

579.
[LUSSAN Marguerite de]
THE LIFE AND HEROIC ACTIONS OF BALBE BERTON, Chevalier de Grillon. Translated from the French by a Lady, And revised by Mr. Richardson, Author of Clarissa, &c. In Two Volumes.
London : Printed for H. Woodgate and S. Brooke, at the Golden Ball in Paternoster-Row. [1760] (MR).
2 vols. 12mo. 6s bound (MR,WS).
Printed by Samuel Richardson.
CR IX 342-353 (Apr. 1760); MR XXIII 156-157 (Aug. 1760).
CG; EC 50:8; ESTC t130968; WS 50.
A trans. of *Vie de Louis Balbe-Berton de Crillon* by Marguerite de Lussan.
Advertised as to be published, Nov. 1759. A 2nd issue as '2nd edn' in 1761, but only the tp was new, the work then distributed by Withy, WS.
BL DU HU NLC PU RFP YU
* N

580.
PIPER John
THE LIFE OF MISS FANNY BROWN (A Clergyman's Daughter) with the History and Remarkable Adventures of Mrs Julep, an Apothecary's Wife. The whole interspersed with a great Variety of Characters, Moral, Instructive, and Entertaining. To which is added, A Description of the most elegant Monuments in Westminster Abbey; the Curiousities in and about London; and Remarks on Several Cathedrals by John Piper Esq. of Lichfield.
Birmingham : Printed for the Author and sold by him at Lichfield; Mr. Ross in Middle Row, London; T. Aris at Birmingham; or by all Booksellers in Town and Country. 1760.
352pp. 8vo/12mo(HU). 2s6d sewed (MR). Subn.
MR XXXIV 469 (App. 1761i).
AB(WB); BB (as 1761); ESTC erroneously as 1740 t060020; CG; FB; LO 141 (FB,HU).
Subscription proposals first announced 30 Jan. 1756, *London Evening Post*. The collection of subscribers seems to have taken 4 years.
BL Bod HU UM
* M

581.
[PRÉVOST D'EXILES Abbé Antoine François]
+THE LIFE AND ENTERTAINING ADVENTURES OF MR. CLEVELAND, Natural Son of Oliver Cromwell, Written by Himself. Giving a particular Account of his Unhappiness in Love, Marriage, Friendship, &c. and his great Sufferings in Europe and America. Intermixed with Reflections, describing the Heart of Man in all its Variety of Passions and Disguises. Also, some curious Particulars of Oliver's History and Amours, and several remarkable Passages in the Reign of King Charles II never before made publick. The Third Edition corrected. In Four Volumes.
London : Printed for James Rivington and J. Fletcher, and R. Baldwin, in Pater-noster-Row; S. Crowder, on London-Bridge; and P. Davey and B. Law, in Ave-Mary-Lane. 1760.
4 vols. 12mo.
CG(BCat); PBG p.280.
1st English edn, 1734. Edns listed, 1750 [35].
Bn CUNY PU UP YU
* N

582
[RICCOBONI Marie Jeanne]
[BROOKE Mrs Frances Moore *trans.*]
+LETTERS FROM JULIET LADY CATESBY, TO HER FRIEND LADY HENRIETTA
CAMPLEY. Translated from the French. The Second Edition.
London : Printed for R. and J. Dodsley, in Pall-Mall. 1760.
252pp. 12mo. 3s (CR).
CR IX 420 (May 1760); MR XXII 521 (June 1760).
AB(McM,Pi); CG(GM,HU); ESTC t119372; FB 686; LO 142 (HU); SG 889.
1st edn and edns listed, 1759 [502].
BL HU NLC OU UP
* E

583.
[le SAGE Alain René]
+THE FIRST PART OF THE COMICAL ADVENTURES OF GIL BLAS OF
SANTILLANE. Containing His Comical Adventures, to his meeting with the Strolling
Players; with many uncommon and laughable Incidents. Second Edition.
London : Printed for R. Snagg, No.29, Pater-noster Row [1760] (BL).
72pp. 12mo.
1st edn, 1749. Edns listed, 1750 [36].
BL
* N

584.
[SMOLLETT Tobias]
+THE ADVENTURES OF RODERICK RANDOM. In Two Volumes. The Fifth Edition.
London : Printed for A. Millar, W. Strahan, John Rivington, J. Rivington and J. Fletcher, R.
Baldwin, J. Ward, J. Richardson, S. Crowder, P. Davey and B. Law, T. Caslon, T. Hope, T.
Becket, and M. Cooper. 1760.
2 vols. 12mo.
ESTC t055370; not the '5th' edn of 1756 and not listed in MW.
1st edn, 1748. Edns listed, 1750 [40].
BL Bod YU
* N

585.
[STERNE Laurence]
+THE LIFE AND OPINIONS OF TRISTRAM SHANDY, GENTLEMAN. The Second
Edition.
London : Printed for R. and J. Dodsley in Pall-Mall. 1760.
2 vols. 16mo. 4s sewed (adv cit KM).
ESTC t014790.
1st edn and edns listed, 1759 [507].
BL CUNY HU IU NLC NYPL OU PU UV YU
* N

586.
[STERNE Laurence]
+THE LIFE AND OPINIONS OF TRISTRAM SHANDY, GENTLEMAN. The Third
Edition.
London : Printed for R. and J. Dodsley in Pall-Mall. 1760.
2 vols. 12mo.
ESTC t014792.
1st edn and edns listed, 1759 [507].
BL UP YU
* N

587.
[STERNE Laurence]
**+THE LIFE AND OPINIONS OF TRISTRAM SHANDY, GENTLEMAN. The Third
Edition.**
Dublin : Printed for D. Chamberlaine, in Smock-Alley, and S. Smith, at Mr. Faulkner's in Essex-
Street. 1760.
2 vols. 12mo. 2s81/2ad.
ESTC t014717.
Published, Apr. 'Almost certainly the first Dublin edn', KM p.23. With variants. The Dublin edn of Lynch, incl.
vols dated 1760, actually printed in 1767 [1143].
1st edn and edns listed, 1759 [507].
BL NLI TCD
* N

588.
[STERNE Laurence]
**+THE LIFE AND OPINIONS OF TRISTRAM SHANDY, GENTLEMAN. In Two
Volumes.**
Dublin : Printed by D. Chamberlaine, in Smock-alley. 1760.
2 vols. 12mo.
Not the '2nd edn', 1760 [589].
1st edn and edns listed, 1759 [507].
CUL
* N

589.
[STERNE Laurence]
**+THE LIFE AND OPINIONS OF TRISTRAM SHANDY, GENTLEMAN. In Two
Volumes. The Second Edition.**
Dublin : Printed by D. Chamberlaine, in Smock-alley. 1760.
2 vols. 12mo.
ESTC t014712.
1st edn and edns listed, 1759 [507].
BL
N

590.
[STERNE Laurence]
**+THE LIFE AND OPINIONS OF TRISTRAM SHANDY, GENTLEMAN. The Fourth
Edition.**
London : Printed for R. and J. Dodsley in Pall-Mall. 1760.
2 vols. 8vo.
ESTC t014812.
1st edn and edns listed, 1759 [507].
BL Bod
* N

591.
[STEVENS George Alexander]
THE HISTORY OF TOM FOOL.
London : Printed for T. Waller opposite Fetter Lane, Fleet Street. 1760.
2 vols. 12mo. 6s (CR,MR).
CR IX 494 (June 1760); MR XXIII 163-164 (Aug. 1760).
AB(BL,T,WB); BB; CG(bkslip); DNB xviii p.1116 with authorship attribution; EC 288:4; ESTC t071398.
BL HL LC LU NYSL(HC - but lost)
* N

592.
VOLTAIRE François Marie Arouet de
CANDIDUS, OR ALL FOR THE BEST. Translated from the French of M. de Voltaire. In Two Parts.
London : Printed for M. Cooper. [1760?] (CUNY).
162pp. 12mo.
1st English edn and edns listed, 1759 [510].
CUNY
N/M

593.
VOLTAIRE François Marie Arouet de
+ZADIG : OR, THE BOOK OF FATE. An Oriental History, Translated from the French Original of Mr. Voltaire.
London : Printed for H. Serjeant, at the Black Swan, without Temple Bar [1760?] (CG).
242pp. 12mo.
CG.
1st English edn, 1749. Also, 1775, 1780, 1782, 1784, 179¬ 1794, 1795(2x), 1798, 1800.
N

594.
[WOODFIN Mrs A.]
THE AUCTION : A Modern Novel. In Two Volumes.
London : Printed for T. Lownds, near the Corner of Salisbury-Court, Fleet-Street. 1760.
2 vols 12mo.
AB(BsB); BB (as 1759); CG; EC 63:2; ESTC t010037 as 1770; LO(UP).
BL PU UP YU
* N

Miscellanies

595.
+Æsop's Fables. With Instructive Morals and Reflections, Abstracted from all Party Considerations, Adapted To All Capacities; And design'd to promote Religion, Morality, and Universal Benevolence.
[4 more lines]
London : Printed for J. Rivington, R. Baldwin, L. Hawes, W. Clarke, & R. Collins, S. Crowder, T. Longman, B. Law, R. Withy, J. Dodsley, G. Keith, G. Robinson, & J. Roberts & T. Cadell. [1760?] (BL).
192pp. 12mo.
ESTC t118432.
Edns listed, 1753 [199].
BL
* M/C

596.
An Answer to the Clockmaker.
London. n.d. [1760] (CG).
8vo (CG).
CG(-).
Cf 1759 [507] & 1760 [598].
M

597.
A Chronicle of the War between the Felicianites, the Gallianites; And of the Downfall of George the Son of the Lion. Together with the Book of his Lamentations.
London : Printed for J. Wilkie, in the St. Paul's Church-Yard; W. Lewis, in Russel Street, Covent Garden; and J. Robson, in Bond Street. 1760.
39pp. 8vo. 1s (tp).
CG(BL); ESTC t102483.
BL YU
* M (sat)

598.
The Clockmakers Outcry Against The Author of The Life and Opinions of Tristram Shandy. Dedicated to the Most Humble of Christian Prelates.
London : Printed for J. Burd, near the Temple Gate, Fleet-Street. 1760.
44pp. 8vo. 1s (tp & CR).
CR IX 413 (May 1760).
BB (as 'Coachmaker's Outcry'); CG(L); ESTC t126145.
Cf 1759 [507] & 1760 [596].
BL Bod FL UM YU
* M

599.
Education. A Fairy Tale. Taken from the French.
London : Printed by J. Mechell, at his Printing-Office, the King's-Arms, Fleet-Street. Sold by C. Corbett, at Addison's-Head, against St. Dunstan's-Church. [1760] (BL).
BL copy imperfect - 60pp only surviving. 8vo. 1s (tp).
CG(BL); ESTC t130924.
BL
* M

600.
Explanatory Remarks upon the Life and Opinions of Tristram Shandy; Wherein, the Morals and Politics of the Piece are clearly laid open, by Jeremiah Kunastrokius, M.D. [pseud].
London : Printed for E. Cabe in Ave-mary-Lane, Ludgate-street. 1760.
59pp. 8vo (CR) 12mo (BL). 3s (CR).
CR IX 319-320 (Apr. 1760).
CG(L); EC 765:4; ESTC t128379.
A 2nd vol. published, 1761 [684]. Cf 1759 [507].
BL Bod CUL FL HU IU NLC YU
* M

601.
+Fables of Æsop and Others, translated into English. With instructive applications; and a print before each fable. By Samuel Croxall, D.D. The Seventh Edition, carefully revised, and improved.
London : Printed for J. & R. Tonson. 1760.
329pp. 12mo.
ESTC t127929.
1st Croxall edn 1747. Edns listed, 1753 [199].
BL
M/C

602.
The Genuine Adventures of Sarah P——L.
London : Ranger [1760] (MR).
8vo. 6d (MR).
MR XXII 522 (June 1760).
N

603.
Genuine Memoirs of the Celebrated Miss Nancy Dawson. Adorned with a Beautiful Frontispiece.
London : Stevens [1760] (CR,MR).
12mo. 1s (CR,MR).
CR X 327 (Oct. 1760); MR XXIII 327 (Oct. 1760).
BB; CG(MR).
MR suggests by the author of *Great News From Hell* [604].
N

604.
Great News from Hell, Or The Devil Foil'd by Bess Weatherby. In a Letter from the late Celebrated Miss Betsy Wemyss, The little Squinting Venus, To the no less Celebrated Miss Lucy C——r.
London : Printed for J. Williams on Ludgate-hill; and sold by J. Dixwell in St. Martin's Lane, near Charing-Cross. 1760.
52pp. 8vo. 1s (tp).
CR X 328 (Oct. 1760); MR XXIII 327 (Oct. 1760).
CG(MR); EC 836:6; ESTC t128585; FB; LO 134 (FB,MR).
BL Bod
* M/N

605.
+The Histories of Some of the Penitents in the Magdalen-House, as supposed to be related by Themselves. In Two Volumes.
Dublin : Printed for P. Wilson and J. Potts. 1760.
2 vols. 12mo.
ESTC t057347.
1st edn, 1759 [516].
BL
M

606.
+The History of a Pickle-Herring, Or The Adventures of Butter-Milk Jack. The Second Edition With Additions.
Dublin : Printed by the Worshipful Fraternity of News-Hawkers. 1760.
16mo (CG).
CG.
1st edn not located.
M

607.
The Life and Opinions of Jeremiah Kunastrokius, Doctor of Physic &c &c &c.
London : Printed for E. Cabe, in Ave-mary Lane, Ludgate-Street. 1760.
156pp. [p.156, 'End of Volume I', but apparently no more volumes printed] 12mo. 2s6d (CR).
CR X 79 (July 1760).
BB; CG(CR).
Cf 1759 [507].
YU
M

608.
New Fairy Tales.
Belfast : Daniel Blow [c.1760] (CG).
CG(-).
C

609.
+The Secret History of Betty Ireland Who was trepanned into marriage at the age of fourteen, and debauched by Beau M-te, at fifteen, by whom she had one son; the vile injury she did to that gentleman, and her turning prostitute; he ramour (sic) with Lord M-d, when she came to London; and her ingratitude to that noble gentleman. [25 more lines] The Fifth Edition.
London : Printed for T. Sabine, No.81, Shoe Lane. [1760?] (BL).
63pp. 8vo.
CG(BL).
1st edn and edns listed, 1750 [50].
BL
* M

610.
Tristram Shandy at Ranelaugh : Containing some Remarkable Transactions that passed between that gentleman and Lady ****.
London : Printed for J. Dunstan. 1760.
38pp. 8vo. 1s (MR).
MR XXII 548 (App. 1760i).
BB; CG(MR).
Cf 1759 [507].
UMin
N/M

611.
Tristram Shandy in a Reverie. Containing among other choice Things, his Thoughts on the two late remarkable Trials of the Delinquents - An Answer to the Clock-maker - Adventure at Bedford - Hints upon Matrimony, etc etc. To which is added, The Litera Infernalis, or Poor Yorick. Recorded by Himself. And by him Addressed to the Admirers of his Life and Opinions.
London : Williams [1760] (CR).
8vo. 1s (CR,MR).
CR IX 493 (June 1760); MR XXII 549 (App. 1760i).
BB.
Cf 1759 [507].
M

612.
Tristram Shandy's Bon Mots, Repartees, Odd Adventures, And Humourous Stories; Being taken from Actual Conversations; Or collected from the most Authentick Intelligence. To which are added, by Way of Appendix; A Story of a Cock and a Bull, in the Shandy Stile; A Poetical Epistle, never before printed; A Discourse well worth the Perusal of all who are curious in the Sermon Way; and a New Dialogue of the Dead, between Dean Swift and Henry Fielding Esq.
London : Printed for E. Cabe in Ave-mary-Lane, Ludgate-street. 1760.
72pp. 12mo. 1s6d (tp).
Bod WCL YU
Cf 1759 [507].
* M

613.
An Unfortunate Mother's Advice to her Absent Daughters; In a Letter to Miss Pennington.
London : Printed by S. Chandler, And Sold by W. Bristow, next the Great Toy-Shop, St Paul's Church-Yard; and C. Etherington, Bookseller in York. 1761 [1760].
96pp. 8vo. 1s6d (tp).
CR X 401-402 (Nov. 1760); MR XXIII 523 (App. 1760ii).
BB; ESTC t079252.
Also, 1761 [692] [693], 1767 [1160], 1770, 1773. Cf 1766 [1045].
BL LC NYPL PU YU
* M

614.

Yorick's Meditations upon Various Interesting and Important Subjects. Viz. [24 titles follow].
London : Printed for R. Stevens, at Pope's-Head, in Pater-Noster-Row. 1760.
110pp. 12mo.
BB; ESTC t128380.
Dublin edn, 1760 [615]. Cf 1759 [507].
BL CUL HU IU
* M

615.

+Yorick's Meditations upon Various Interesting and Important Subjects. Viz [23 titles follow]
Dublin : Printed for James Hunter, in Sycamore-Alley. 1760.
71pp. 12mo.
1st edn, 1760 [614]. Cf 1759 [507].
CUL
* M

616.

Draper Charles *trans.*
(+)Fables Translated from Æsop, and other Authors. To which are subjoined, a Moral in Verse, and an Application in Prose, adapted to each Fable. Embellished with Cuts from the best Designs. By Charles Draper Esq.
London : W. Bristow [1760] (MR).
12mo. 3s (CR,MR).
CR X 240 (Sept. 1760); MR XXIII 162-163 (Aug. 1760).
BB (as 1761).
Edns and versions listed, 1753 [199].
BL
M/C

617.

[Goadby Robert]
+An Apology for the Life of Mr. Bampfylde-Moore Carew, Commonly call'd the King of beggars; being an impartial account of his life, from his leaving Tiverton school, at the age of fifteen, and entering into a society of gypsies, to the present time with his travels twice through great part of America. A particular account of the original government, language, laws, and customs of the gypsies. And a parallel dream after the manner of Plutarch, between Mr. B-M C and Mr. Thomas Jones. The Fifth Edition.
London : Printed for R. Goadby [Sherborne] and W. Owen [1760?] (BL). CUL has [176-].
344pp. 12mo.
CG has 8vo. [1760] '2nd edn'. 1st edn, London 1749, as version of edn of 1745. Edns listed, 1750 [54].
BL CUL
* M

618.

[Goadby Robert]
+An Apology for the Life of Mr. Bampfylde-Moore Carew, Commonly call'd the King of beggars; being an impartial account of his life, from his leaving Tiverton school, at the age of fifteen, and entering into a society of gypsies, to the present time with his travels twice through great part of America. A particular account of the original government, language, laws, and customs of the gypsies. And a parallel dream after the manner of Plutarch, between Mr. B-M C and Mr. Thomas Jones. The Sixth Edition.
London : Printed for R. Goadby [Sherborne] and W. Owen [1760] (BL).
CG has [1765?] (HU).
350pp. 12mo.
ESTC t110645.
1st edn, London 1749, as version of edn of 1745. Edns listed, 1750 [54].
BL
* M

619.
[Hamilton Anthony]
+Memoirs of the Life of Count de Grammont : Containing the Amorous intriques of the Court of
England in the Reign of Charles II. Translated from the French.
London : Printed for T. Payne. 1760.
327pp. 3s (GM)
CG(GM Apr. 1761).
1st English edn, 1714. Earlier edn, 1753 [207]. Cf 1760 [620].
BU RU UI YU
M

620.
[Hamilton Anthony]
[Goldsmith Oliver *trans.*]
Select Tales of Count Hamilton, Author of the Life and Memoirs of the Count De Grammont. Translated
from the French. In Two Volumes.
London : Printed for J. Burd, near Temple-Gate, Fleet-Street. 1760.
2 vols. 12mo. 6s (CR,MR).
CR IX 413 (May 1760); MR XXII 523-524 (June 1760).
AB(BsB,BL,Do); CG(BL); EC 50:2; ESTC t110854.
1st English edn of *Memoires de la vie du comte de Grammont*, 1714. Cf 1753 [207].
BL NLC UCLA YU
* M/C

621.
Hughes John *trans.*
+Letters of Abelard and Heloise. To which is prefix'd a particular Account of their Lives, Amours, and
Misfortunes : Extracted chiefly from Monsieur Bayle. Translated from the French by the late John
Hughes, Esq. To which is now first added, The poem of Eloisa to Abelard, by Mr. Pope. The Ninth
Edition.
London : Printed for P. Davey and B. Law, T. Lownds, and T. Caslon. 1760.
186pp. 12mo.
1st English edn, 1718. Edns listed, 1751 [112].
Tx
M/E

622.
M'Carthy Mrs Charlotte
+Fair Moralist; or, Love and Virtue. A Novel. By Mrs Charlotte M'Carthy.
2s (CG).
CG.
1st edn, 1745. Also, 1746.
M/N

623.
[Montesquieu Charles Louis de Secondat Baron de]
+Persian Letters. Translated from the French of M. De Secondat, Baron de Montesquieu, Author of The
Spirit of the Laws.
Glasgow : Printed for Robert Urie. 1760.
310pp. 8vo.
1st English edn, 1722. Edns listed, 1751 [113].
BL CUL
* M/E

624.

Rowe Mrs Elizabeth Singer

+Friendship in Death : In Twenty Letters from the Dead to the Living. To which are added, Letters Moral and Entertaining, In Prose and Verse. In Three Parts. By Mrs. Elizabeth Rowe.

Glasgow : Printed by James Knox, and sold at his Shop near the Head of the Salt-mercat. 1760.

292pp. 12mo.

ESTC t134497.

1st edn, 1728. Edns listed, 1750 [60].

BL

* M

625.

Rowe Mrs Elizabeth Singer

+Friendship in Death : In Twenty Letters from the Dead to the Living. To which are added, Letters Moral and Entertaining. In Prose and Verse. In Three Parts. By Mrs. Elizabeth Rowe.

London : Printed for R. Baldwin, J. Richardson, S. Crowder and Co. P. Davey and B. Law, T. Caslon and T. Field. 1760.

292pp. 12mo.

ESTC t134485.

1st edn, 1728. Edns listed, 1750 [60].

BL

* M

626.

[le Sale Antoine de]

The Fifteen Comforts of Matrimony. With the Addition of Three Comforts More. Wherein The Various Miscarriages of the Wedded State, and the miserable Consequences of Rash and Inconsiderate Marriages are laid open and detected.

London : Printed for H. Woodgate and S. Brooks, at the Golden Ball in Pater-noster-Row. 1760.

120pp. 12mo.

CG(BL); ESTC t128695.

'A trans. of *Les Quinze Joies de Mariage*, a work attributed to le Sale' BL.

BL

* M

627.

[Stevenson John Hall]

A Supplement to the Life and Opinions of Tristram Shandy, Gent. Serving to elucidate that Work. By the Author of Yorick's Meditations.

London : Printed for the Author, in the Year. 1760.

84pp. 12mo. 1s6d ($\frac{1}{2}$tp).

CR X 485 (Dec. 1760); MR XXIII 522 (App. 1760ii).

CG(MR); EC 160:2; ESTC t108022.

Cf 1759 [507].

BL

* M/N

628.
+THE ADVENTURES AND AMOURS OF THE MARQUIS DE NOAILLES, AND MADEMOISELLE TENCIN. To which is Added, the History of the Chevalier de Mirmont, and Miss Biron. Translated from a French Manuscript. In Two Volumes.
London : Printed for F. Noble at his Circulating Library, opposite Gray's-Inn-Gate, Holborn; And J. Noble, at his Circulating Library, in St. Martin's Court, near Leicester Square. 1761.
2 vols. 12mo.
CG(as 1767).
Sometimes attributed to 'Felicité de Biron'.
1st edn, 1746 (EC 6:1). Also, 1764 [804].
YU
* N/E

629.
ALMIRA, BEING THE HISTORY OF A YOUNG LADY OF GOOD BIRTH AND FORTUNE, BUT MORE DISTINGUISH'D MERIT.
London : Printed for W. Owen, near Temple-Bar, 1762 [1761].
2 vols. 12mo. 5s (MR) 6s (CR).
CR XII 480 (Dec. 1761); MR XXV 503 (App. 1761ii).
BB.
Cf 1758 [426] and 1769 [1271].
LC UM YU
* N

630.
THE AMOURS AND ADVENTURES OF TWO ENGLISH GENTLEMEN IN ITALY.
London. 1761.
CG(-).
NUC ref in later American edn (1795) to a London edn of 1761.
N

631.
ANGELICUS AND FERGUSIA. A TALE.
London : Printed for J. Johnson, at Mead's-Head, opposite the Monument. 1761.
67pp. 8vo. 1s (tp).
CR XIII 78 (Jan, 1762); MR XXV 501 (App. 1761ii).
AB(BL); BB(as Johnston); CG(BB,BL); ESTC t088358.
BL Bod YU
* N/M

632.
+THE HISTORY OF FREDERICK THE FORSAKEN. Interspersed with Anecdotes relative to several Personages of Rank and Fashion in England. In Two Volumes.
Dublin : Printed by J. Potts, at Swift's Head, in Damestreet. 1761.
2 vols. 12mo. 2s.8½d (adv-1763 [789]).
Adv-1763 [789]; CG(HU).
1st edn, 1760 [535].
HU NLC YU
* N

633.
THE KEPT MISTRESS.
London : Printed for J. Morgan, in Pater-noster Row. 1761.
141pp. 8vo. 2s (CR,MR).
CR XII 310-311 (Oct. 1761); MR XXV 393 (Nov. 1761).
AB(BL,Pi,WB); BB; CG(MR); ESTC t057445.
BL PU
* N

634.
THE LIFE AND OPINIONS OF BERTRAM MONTFICHET, ESQ; Written by Himself. In
Two Volumes.
London : Printed for C. G. Seyffert in Pall-Mall [1761] (HU).
2 vols. 8vo. 5s (CR) 6s (MR).
CR XI 393-395 (May 1761); MR XXIV 276 (Apr. 1761).
CG(HU); EC 161:2; ESTC t108026; LO 118 (as 1758).
BL CNY HU PU (UP as 1765)
* N

635.
THE LIFE AND SURPRIZING ADVENTURES OF DON ANTONIO DE TREZZANIO,
Who was Self-educated, and lived Forty-five Years in an uninhabited Island, in the East-
Indies. Written by Salandio the Hermit
[16 more lines]
London : Printed for H. Serjeant, at the Star, without Temple-Bar [1761?] (BL).
158pp. 8vo. 2s6d (MR).
MR XXV 472 (Dec. 1761).
AB(Pi) as 1766; CG(MR); ESTC t062081; McB 592.
An abridgment of Abu Jaafer Ebn Tophail, *Philosophus Autodidactus, or the History of Hai Ebn Yokdham*,
trans. Simon Ockley.
BL Bn UI
* N/M

636.
MEMOIRS OF MISS BETSY F. T.; Author of the Address to Old Maids and Bachelors
&c. Containing a Series of Adventures as well as Tragical as Comical, Gay and Amorous,
Serious and Jocose. Intermixed with the Characters of some of the most Eminent Beaux
and Belles of the Present Age. Being a Real History. Written by Herself.
London : Withy. 1761.
2 vols. 12mo. 5s sewed (MR) 6s (CR).
CR XI 335 (Apr. 1761); MR XXIV 351 (May 1761).
CG.
N/M

637.
MEMOIRS OF MR. CHARLES GUILDFORD. In a regular Series of Letters, Wrote by
Himself to a Friend. The whole founded on real Facts. In Two Volumes.
London : Printed for R. Withy, at the Dunciad, in Cornhill. 1761.
2 vols. 12mo. 6s (BB,CR).
CR XII 480 (Dec. 1761); MR XXV 503 (App. 1761ii).
BB; CG; EC 91:3; ESTC t108369; LO 153 (BL,UP).
BL UP
* E

638.
+THE SCOTCH MARINE; OR, MEMOIRS OF THE LIFE OF CELESTINA; A Young
Lady, who, secretly deserting her family, spent two years in strict amity, as a man, with
her beloved Castor.
[11 more lines]
Dublin : James Potts. 1761.
2 vols in 1. 12mo.
AB(Pi); CG(-).
1st edn, 1754 [226].
NLC
N

639.
SOPHRONIA : OR, LETTERS TO THE LADIES.
London : Printed for William Johnston, in Ludgate-street. 1761.
245pp. 12mo. 2s6d (MR) 3s (CR).
CR XI 420 (May 1761); MR XXIV 352 (May 1761).
AB(BL); ESTC t117042; LO 156 (HU,UP).
Also 1763 [767] and 1775 edns. Cf 1764 [815].
BL Bod HU (as 1762) IU NLC PU UCLA UM UP
* E

640.
THE WISE ONES BUBBLED; OR, LOVERS TRIUMPHANT, after a Series of above
Twenty years separation, and residence in divers foreign parts, most of the time subject to
the acutest difficulties. With an account of their miraculous meeting and adventures, till
they happily enjoyed the blessed fruits of their toils for each other. Printed from Mrs
Parsons's own Manuscript.
London : Wren [1761] (CR,MR).
2 vols. 12mo. 6s (CR,MR).
CR XI 163 (Feb. 1761); MR XXIV 349 (May 1761).
AB(WB) as 1760; CG(-).
N/M

641.
[BRET Antoine]
LYCORIS : OR, THE GRECIAN COURTEZAN. Translated from the French. By a
Gentleman.
London : Brotherton. 1761.
12mo. 2s (BB,MR).
CR XI 338 (Apr. 1761); MR XXIV 351 (May 1761).
BB; CG(MR).
Also, 1779 edn [EC 8:8].
(*) N

642.
BUTTON Edward
+THE PERSIAN TALES. A New Translation, From an Original Version of the Indian
Comedies of Mocles. Wherein All the Stories, formerly printed in Three Volumes, are
reduced into One. By Edward Button, Gent.
Dublin : Printed for G. and A. Ewing, W. Smith, and P. Wilson, in Dame-street. 1761.
300pp. 12mo.
1st edn, 1754 [230].
Bod
* C

643.
CERVANTES SAAVEDRA Miguel de
SMOLLETT Tobias *trans.*
+THE HISTORY AND ADVENTURES OF THE RENOWNED DON QUIXOTE.
Translated from the Spanish Miguel de Cervantes Saavedra. To which is prefixed, Some
Account of the Author's Life. By T. Smollett M.D. Illustrated with Twenty-eight new
Copper-Plates, designed by Hayman, and elegantly engraved. The Second Edition,
Corrected. In Four Volumes.
London : Printed for T. Osborne, C. Hitch and L. Hawes, A. Millar, H. Woodfall, John
Rivington, R. Baldwin, S. Crowder and Co. T. Longman, H. Payne, T. Lowndes, T. Caslon, and
G. Kearsley. 1761.
4 vols. 12mo.
Caslon and Kearsley omitted from tp of vol. III.
EC 97:3; ESTC t059495; MW 604.
1st edn of this trans, and edns listed, 1755 [302].
BL Bod CUL HU LC UCLA UW YU
* N

644.
[COVENTRY Francis]
+THE HISTORY OF POMPEY THE LITTLE. Or, The Life and Adventures of A Lap-
Dog. The Fourth Edition.
London : Printed for R. and J. Dodsley in Pallmall. 1761.
291pp. 12mo.
CG; ESTC t064744.
1st edn and edns listed, 1751 [77].
BL CUL HU NLC NYPL UF YU
* N

645.
[DEFOE Daniel]
+THE FORTUNES AND MISFORTUNES OF THE FAMOUS MOLL FLANDERS. Who
was born in Newgate and During a life of continu'd variety for threescore years... Written
from her own Memorandums. The Sixth Edition.
London : Printed by C. Sympson and J. Millar. 1761.
336pp. 12mo.
1st edn, 1721-2. Edns listed, 1750 [20].
VU YU
N

646.
[DEFOE Daniel]
+THE LIFE AND STRANGE SURPRISING ADVENTURES OF ROBINSON CRUSOE;
OF YORK, MARINER :
[7 more lines]
The Twelfth Edition, Adorned with Cuts. In Two Volumes.
London : Printed for C. Hitch and L. Hawes, J. Buckland, B. Dod, J. Rivington, R. Baldwin, W.
Johnston, T. Longman, T. Caslon, S. Crowder and Co. B. Law and Co. and J. Morgan. 1761.
Vol II as 'The Farther Adventures of Robinson Crusoe'.
2 vols. 12mo.
EC 175:7; ESTC t072281.
1st edn, 1719-20. Edns listed, 1752 [129].
BL IU RFP UM YU
* N/M

647.
[DEFOE Daniel]
+THE LIFE AND MOST SURPRISING ADVENTURES OF ROBINSON CRUSOE, OF
YORK MARINER... The Whole Three Volumes faithfully abridged. The Sixth Edition.
London : Printed for C. Hitch, L. Hawes and S. Crowder. 1761.
336pp.
1st edn, 1719-20. Edns listed, 1752 [129].
SU YU
N/M

648.
[FIELDING Sarah]
+THE ADVENTURES OF DAVID SIMPLE : Containing an Account of his Travels
Through the Cities of London and Westminster, In the Search of A Real Friend. By a
Lady. In Two Volumes. The Fourth Edition.
Dublin : Printed for Peter Wilson, in Dame-Street. 1761.
2 vols. 12mo.
CG(RI,St); ESTC t118991.
1st edn, 1744. Edns listed, 1753 [183]. Cf 1752 [133].
BL UP
* N

649.
[FORD Emanuel]
+THE FAMOUS HISTORY OF MONTELION, KNIGHT OF THE ORACLE, Son to the
True Mirror of Princes, The Most Renowned Persicles, King of Assyria. Shewing His
Strange Birth, unfortunate love, perilous Adventures in Arms; and how he came to the
Knowledge of his Parents. Intermixed with Variety of Pleasant and Delightful Discourse.
Dublin : Printed for Thomas Brown, at the Bible in High-street, where Country Chapmen, and
others, may be furnished with all Sorts of School-Books, at the most Reasonable Rates. 1761.
180pp. 24mo.
CG(HU); EC 2:4; ESTC t128324.
1st edn, 1637. Edns listed, 1759 [489].
BL Bod HU
* N/M

650.
[FORD Emanuel]
+THE FAMOUS HISTORY OF MONTELION, KNIGHT OF THE ORACLE; Son to the
true Mirrour of princes, the most renowned Persicles, king of Assyria. First Edition with
many alterations and additions, never before printed.
London printed and Dublin reprinted by A. Law. 1761.
180pp. 12mo.
1st edn, 1637. Edns listed, 1759 [489].
HU
N/M

651.
[GRIFFITH Richard and Elizabeth]
+A SERIES OF GENUINE LETTERS BETWEEN HENRY AND FRANCES. The Second
Edition, Revised, Corrected, Enlarged, and Improved, By the Author.
London, Printed for W. Johnston in Ludgate Street. 1761.
2 vols. 12mo. Subn.
CG(HU,BL); ESTC t11108.
1st edn and edns listed, 1757 [412].
BL Bod NLC UV
* E

652.
[GUTHRIE William]
+THE MOTHER; OR, THE HAPPY DISTRESS. A Novel. By the Author of The Friends.
In Two Volumes.
London : Printed for the Author: and sold by J. Wilkie, at the Bible, in St. Paul's Church-Yard.
1761.
2 vols. 12mo.
1st edn, 1759 [493].
HU YU
* N

653.
[HAWKESWORTH John]
ALMORAN AND HAMET : AN ORIENTAL TALE. In Two Volumes.
London : Printed for H. Payne, and W. Cropley, at Dryden's Head in Pater-noster Row. 1761.
2 vols. 8vo. 5s bound (CR,MR).
CR XI 469-474 (June 1761); MR XXIV 415-435 (May 1761).
BB; CG(HU); ESTC t068578; LO 149 (UI,UP); McB 408.
Also 1761 [654] [655], 1764 [920] and 1780.
BL Bod CNY CUL HL HU IU NLC PU UF UI UP WCL YU
* N

654.
[HAWKESWORTH John]
+ALMORAN AND HAMET : AN ORIENTAL TALE. In Two Volumes. The Second
Edition.
London : Printed by C. Say : For H. Payne and W. Cropley, at Dryden's Head in Pater-noster-
Row. 1761.
2 vols in 1. 8vo.
AB(BL,CB); CG(-); EC 238:1; ESTC t057815; McB 409.
1st edn, 1761 [653].
BL CUL DU UI UM UP UV YU
* N

655.
[HAWKESWORTH John]
+ALMORAN AND HAMET : AN ORIENTAL TALE. In Two Volumes.
Dublin : Printed for W. Smith, H. Saunders, R. Watts, H. Bradley, J. Potts, and T. and J.
Whitehouse, Booksellers. 1761.
2 vols in 1. 240pp. 8vo.
CG; McB 410.
1st edn, 1761 [653].
CUL NLC UI
* N

656.
HAYWOOD Mrs Eliza
+THE FORTUNATE FOUNDLINGS : Being the Genuine History of Colonel
M—rs, and his Sister, Madam du P—y, the issue of the Hon. Ch—es M—rs, son of the
late Duke of R—l—d. Containing many wonderful Accidents that befel them in their
travels. The whole calculated for the entertainment and improvement of the Youth of both
sexes. The Fifth Edition.
London : Printed for T. Gardner. 1761 [BB & CG, nd].
331pp. 12mo.
1st edn, 1744. Edns listed, 1758 [436].
OU
N

657.
[JOHNSTON Charles]
+CHRYSAL: OR, THE ADVENTURES OF A GUINEA. Wherein are exhibited Views of several striking Scenes, With Curious and interesting Anecdotes, of the most Noted Persons in every Rank of Life, whose Hands it passed through, In America, England, Holland, Germany and Portugal. By an Adept. The Second Edition greatly inlarged and corrected.
London : Printed for T. Becket, at Tully's Head, near Surry-street, in the Strand. 1761.
2 vols. 12mo. 6s (CR).
Rev of 2nd edn, CR XI 336 (Apr. 1761).
CG; ESTC t057342.
1st edn and edns listed, 1760 [577].
BL CUL FL NLC Tx UNC
* N

658.
[JOHNSTON Charles]
+CHRYSAL: OR, THE ADVENTURES OF A GUINEA. Wherein are exhibited Views of several striking Scenes, With Curious and interesting Anecdotes of the most Noted Persons in every Rank of Life, whose Hands it passed through, in America, England, Holland, Germany and Portugal. By an Adept. The Second Edition greatly inlarged and corrected.
Dublin : Printed for Henry Saunders, in High Street, and Hulton Bradley, in Dame Street. 1761.
2 vols. 12mo.
1st edn and edns listed, 1760 [577].
Bod CUL
* N

659.
[JONES Henry]
THE HISTORY OF THE TRAVELS AND ADVENTURES OF THE CHEVALIER JOHN TAYLOR, Opthalmiater;
[13 more lines] Written by Himself.
[15 more lines] Addressed to his only Son.
London : Printed for J. Williams, on Ludgate-Hill. 1761.
3 vols. 8vo. 7s6d (BB,CR,MR). Vols II and III, 'Printed for Mrs. Williams, on Ludgate-Hill, 1762'. tp of vol II closes 'Addressed to David Garrick, Esq'; tp of vol III closes 'Addressed to the Merchants of London'.
CR XIII 138-148 (Feb, 1762); MR XXVI 112-113 (Feb, 1762).
BB; CG(BL); ESTC t145526.
Dublin edn, 1762 [725]. Cf 1750 [44] and 1761 [660] [661].
BL
* N/M

660.
[JONES Henry]
THE LIFE AND EXTRAORDINARY HISTORY OF THE CHEVALIER JOHN TAYLOR. Member of the most celebrated Academies, Universities, and Societies of the Learned [24 more lines] Written from Authentic Materials and Published by his Son, John Taylor, Oculist. In Two Volumes.
London : Printed for M. Cooper, in Paternoster-Row. 1761.
2 vols. 8vo. 6s (CR,MR).
CR XI 474-480 (June 1761); MR XXV 106-112 (Aug. 1761).
CG; ESTC t096749; LO 152 (UP).
Dublin edn, 1761 [661]. Cf 1761 [659].
BL CUL YU
* N

661.
[JONES Henry]
+THE LIFE AND EXTRAORDINARY ADVENTURES OF THE CHEVALIER JOHN TAYLOR.
[25 more lines] **Written from Authentic Materials, and published by his Son, Joe Taylor, Oculist. In Two Volumes.**
Dublin : Printed for D. Chamberlain in Smock-Alley. 1761.
162pp, 2 vols in 1. 12mo.
ESTC t040926.
Probably the edn advertised by Hoey (2s2d bound or 1s7½d sewed), 1763 [786]. 1st edn, 1761 [660].
BL Bod
* N

662.
LENNOX Mrs Charlotte Ramsay
+HENRIETTA. By Mrs. Charlotte Lennox. In Two Volumes. The Second Edition. Corrected.
London : Printed for A. Millar, in the Strand. 1761.
2 vols. 8vo.
CG(HU); ESTC t139652.
1st edn and edns listed, 1758 [441].
BL Bod HL HU NLC PU
* N

663.
[RICCOBONI Marie Jeanne]
MEMOIRS OF LADY HARRIOT BUTLER : Now First Published From Authentic Papers, in the Lady's own hand-writing.
London : Printed for R. Freeman, near St. Paul's, 1741 [1761 - tp error].
Vol I of 2 vols. 12mo. 5s (MR) 6s (CR).
CR XII 363-370 (Nov. 1761); MR XXV 472 (Dec. 1761).
AB(as 1741); BB; CG; ESTC t066383; FB; LO 154 (FB,UO).
Vol II published 1762 [733] and Dublin edn, 1762 [734].
BL DU LC
* N

664.
RICHARDSON Samuel
+PAMELA; OR VIRTUE REWARDED. In a Series of Familiar Letters from a beautiful young damsel to her parents [&c.] In Four Volumes. The Eighth Edition.
London : Printed for Henry Woodfall, John Rivington, William Johnston, Joseph Richardson and Stanley Crowder and Co., 1762 [1761].
4 vols. 12mo. 12s bound (WS).
CG(HU); WS 14.
Published 28 Oct. 9th edn of vols I-II and 4th edn of the *Continuation*. 1st edn, 1741. Edns listed, 1754 [250].
CUNY IU WCL HU
* E

665.
[RIDLEY James]
THE HISTORY OF JAMES LOVEGROVE, ESQ; In Four Books.
London : Printed for John Wilkie, at the Bible in St. Paul's Church-Yard. 1761.
2 vols. 12mo. 6s (CR,MR).
CR XI 420 (May 1761); MR XXIV 352 (May 1761).
BB; CG(HU); EC 124:2; ESTC t057349.
BL HU LC
* N

666.
ROUSSEAU Jean Jacques
[KENRICK William *trans.*]
ELOISA : OR, A SERIES OF ORIGINAL LETTERS. Collected and published by J. J. Rousseau. Translated from the French. In Four Volumes.
London : Printed for R. Griffiths, at the Dunciad, and T. Becket and P. A. De Hondt, at Tully's Head, in the Strand. 1761.
4 vols. 12mo. 12s bound (CR,MR) & 1st 2 vols 5s sewed (MR).
CR XII 203-211 (Sept. 1761); MR XXIV 227-235, XXV 192-214, 241-260 (Apr, Sept, Oct. 1761).
AB(BL,RI); BB; CG; ESTC t132300; McB 777.
A trans. of *Julie ou la nouvelle Héloïse*, 1761.
Also 1761 [667] [668], 1764 [864], 1767 [1130], 1769 [1330] [1331], 1776, 1784, 1795(2x).
BL Bod HU NLC PU UCLA UI UV UW YU
* E

667.
ROUSSEAU Jean Jacques
[KENRICK William *trans.*]
+ELOISA: OR, A SERIES OF ORIGINAL LETTERS. Collected and Published by J. J. Rousseau. Translated from the French. In Four Volumes. The Second Edition.
London : Printed for R. Griffiths, at the Dunciad, and T. Becket and P. A. De Hondt, at Tully's Head, in the Strand. 1761.
4 vols. 12mo.
ESTC t132304.
1st English edn and edns listed, 1761 [666].
BL CUL UW YU
* E

668.
ROUSSEAU Jean Jacques
+ELOISA : OR, A SERIES OF ORIGINAL LETTERS Collected and Published By J. J. Rousseau. Translated from the French. In Four Volumes.
Dublin : Printed for James Hunter, in Sycamore-alley. 1761.
4 vols. 12mo.
AB; ESTC t136488.
The volumes seem to have been issued in stages : verso of vol I tp announces that vols III & IV 'are in great forwardness, and will speedily be published'.
1st English edn and edns listed, 1761 [666].
BL
* E

669.
[le SAGE Alain René]
[SMOLLETT Tobias *trans.*]
+THE ADVENTURES OF GIL BLAS OF SANTILLANE. A New Translation. By the Author of Roderick Random. Adorned with Thirty-three Cuts, neatly engraved. In Four Volumes. The Second Edition.
London : Printed for J. Rivington, R. Baldwin, T. Longman, R. Horsefield, S. Crowder and Co. B. Law, C. and R. Ware, and T. Caslon. 1761.
4 vols. 12mo.
CG(-); ESTC t119362; McB 552.
1st edn, 1749. Edns listed, 1750 [36].
BL CUL OU UCB UI
* N

670.
[SHERIDAN Mrs Frances Chamberlaine]
**MEMOIRS OF MISS SIDNEY BIDULPH, Extracted from her own Journal, And now
First Published. In Two Volumes.**
London : Printed for R. and J. Dodsley in Pall-Mall. 1761.
3 vols. 8vo. 9s (CR,MR).
CR XI 186-198 (Mar. 1761); MR XXIV 260-266 (Apr. 1761).
BB; CG; FB; LO 155 (FB,HU,UI,UP); McB 819.
Also 1761 [671] [672], 1767 [1136]. *The Conclusion*, published 1767 [1137] [1138]. Also, 1770, 1771, 1772,
1786, 1796.
Bod CUL CUNY HU IU MU NLC NYPL OU UI UV YU
* N

671.
[SHERIDAN Mrs Frances Chamberlaine]
**+MEMOIRS OF MISS SIDNEY BIDULPH. Extracted from Her Own Journal, And now
First Published. In Three Volumes. The Second Edition.**
London : Printed for R. and J. Dodsley, in Pall-Mall. 1761.
3 vols. 12mo.
CG(-); ESTC t142760.
1st edn and edns listed, 1761 [670].
BL
* N

672.
[SHERIDAN Mrs Frances Chamberlaine]
**+MEMOIRS OF MISS SIDNEY BIDULPH, Extracted from Her Own Journal, And now
First Published. In Two Volumes.**
Dublin : Printed by and for G. Faulkner. 1761.
2 vols. 12mo.
CG(HU); EC 242:3; ESTC t064723; McB 820.
1st edn and edns listed, 1761 [670].
BL CUL HU UI
* N

673.
[STERNE Laurence]
THE LIFE AND OPINIONS OF TRISTRAM SHANDY, GENTLEMAN.
London : Printed for R. and J. Dodsley in Pall-Mall. 1761.
Vols III and IV. 2 vols. 8vo. 5s (CR).
Rev of these vols, CR XI 314-317 (Apr. 1761).
ESTC t014705.
Vols I-II published and edns of all vols listed, 1759 [507].
BL HU LC NLC Tx UP
* N

674.
[STERNE Laurence]
+THE LIFE AND OPINIONS OF TRISTRAM SHANDY, GENTLEMAN.
London : Printed for R. and J. Dodsley in Pall-Mall. 1761.
Vols III and IV. 2 vols. 8vo.
1st edn [673] published Jan. 1761, but in May Dodsley advertised the 2 vols again. Certainly a 2nd edn of
vol.III did appear and at least 'a second issue' of vol.IV, KM, p.24.
Vols III-IV 1st published, 1761 [673]. Vols I-II published and edns of all vols listed, 1759 [507].
N

675.
[STERNE Laurence]
+THE LIFE AND OPINIONS OF TRISTRAM SHANDY, GENTLEMAN.
Dublin : Printed for H. Saunders, at the Corner of Christ-Church-Lane, in High-street. 1761.
Vols I-IV. 4 vols in 1. 305pp. 12mo. 2s8½d.
ESTC t014735; RCC p.74.
2nd edn of this set, 1765 [941]. Vols I-II published and edns of all vols listed, 1759 [507].
BL CUL NLC YU
* N

676.
[STERNE Laurence]
+THE LIFE AND OPINIONS OF TRISTRAM SHANDY, GENTLEMAN.
Dublin : Printed for D. Chamberlaine, in Smock-Alley, and S. Smith, at Mr. Faulkner's in Essex-Street. 1761.
Vols III and IV. 2 vols.
ESTC t014691.
Vols II-III 1st published, 1761 [673]. Vols I-II published and edns of all vols listed, 1759 [507].
BL CUL
* N

677.
[STERNE Laurence]
THE LIFE AND OPINIONS OF TRISTRAM SHANDY, GENTLEMAN.
London : Printed for T. Becket and P. A. Dehondt, in the Strand, 1762 [1761].
Volumes V and VI. 2 vols. 12mo. 5s (CR,MR).
Rev of vols V & VI, CR XIII 66-69 (Jan, 1762); MR XXVI 31-41 (Jan. 1761).
ESTC t014706; KM.
Published Dec. 1761, KM p.25. Edns of all vols listed, 1759 [507].
BL HU UF YU
* N

678.
[TIPHAIGNE DE LA ROCHE Charles François]
GIPHANTIA : OR A VIEW OF WHAT HAS PASSED, WHAT IS NOW PASSING, And during the Present Century, What Will Pass In The World; Translated from the original French, With explanatory Notes.
London : Printed for Robert Horsfield, in Ludgate-Street. 1761.
126pp. 12mo. 2s6d (CR) 3s (BB,MR). Vol II, dated 1760.
CR XI 109-115 (Feb. 1761); MR XXIV 222-226 (Apr. 1761).
BB; CG; EC 770:24; ESTC t099917; LO 157 (UI); McB 914.
A trans. of *Giphantié*. Also, Dublin edn, 1761 [679].
BL Bod CUL DU HU LC NYPL OU UCB UI UNC YU
* N

679.
[TIPHAIGNE DE LA ROCHE Charles François]
+GIPHANTIA; OR, A VIEW OF WHAT HAS PASSED, WHAT IS NOW PASSING, And, during the Present Century, What Will Pass, in the World. Translated from the original French, With explanatory Notes.
Dublin : Printed for G. Faulkner, in Essex Street, and J. Potts, in Dame Street. 1761.
2 pts in 1 vol. 101pp & 88pp. 12mo.
ESTC t118994.
1st edn, 1761 [678].
BL Bod
* N

680.
VOLTAIRE François Marie Arouet de
+CANDIDUS : OR, ALL FOR THE BEST. Translated from the French of M. de Voltaire.
Edinburgh : Printed by A. Donaldson and J. Reid for Alex. Donaldson. 1761.
108pp.
1st English edn and edns listed, 1759 [510].
AAS UW YU
N/M

681.
VOLTAIRE François Marie Arouet de
+CANDIDUS : OR, ALL FOR THE BEST. Translated from the French of M. de Voltaire.
Edinburgh : Printed in the Year 1761.
8d (tp).
1st English edn and edns listed, 1759 [510].
N/M

682.
[WILKINSON James]
HAU KIOU CHAOAAN OR THE PLEASING HISTORY. A Translation from the Chinese
Language. [4 more lines] In Four Volumes. With Notes.
London : Printed for R. and J. Dodsley in Pall-mall. 1761.
4 vols. 12mo. 10s bound (CR,MR).
CR XII 373-381 (Nov. 1761); MR XXV 427-436 (Dec. 1761).
AB(AR,BL,RI); CG(MR); ESTC t141065.
This trans. edited by Bishop Thomas Percy. BL also suggests a re-issue of the 1761 edn.
BL CUL CUNY DU HU NLC OU PU UW YU
* N

Miscellanies

683.
A Book Without a Title Page.
London : Jones [1761] (MR).
12mo. 6d (MR).
MR XXIV 351-352 (May 1761).
M

684.
Explanatory Remarks on the Third and Fourth Volumes of Tristram Shandy. Vol. II By the Author of
the First.
London : Printed for E. Cabe. 1761.
1s (MR).
MR XXIV 275-276 (Apr. 1761).
1st vol printed in 1760 [600]. Cf 1759 [507].
FL
M

685.
Genuine Memoirs Of the Late Celebrated Jane D****s.
London : Printed for J. Simpson. at Shakespear's Head in Paul's Alley, St. Paul's Church-yard. 1761.
128pp. 12mo. 2s sewed (½tp).
MR XXV 229 (Sept. 1761).
CG(BL); ESTC t073178.
BL
* M/N

686.
+The History of Mademoiselle de St. Phale. Giving a Full Account of the Miraculous Conversion of a Noble French Lady and her Daughter to the Reformed Religion. The Eighth Edition.
London : Printed for J. Beecroft, at the Bible and Crown in Pater-Noster-Row. 1761.
227pp. 12mo.
CG(BL); ESTC t127368.
1st edn, 1702. Also, 1707, 1712, 1722, 1738, 1787.
BL Bn
* M

687.
A Journal of the Travels of Nathaniel Snip, a Methodist Preacher of the Word, Containing an Account of the many marvellous Adventures which befel him, in his Way from the Town of Kingston upon Hull to the City of York.
London : Bristow and Cooper. 1761.
8vo. 6d (CR,MR).
CR XI 79 (Jan. 1761); MR XXIV 162 (Feb. 1761).
CG(BL)
[BL copy destroyed in WWII] HU
M

688.
The Life and Amours of Hafen Slawkenbergius, Author of the Institute of Noses.
London : Flexney, [1761] (MR).
12mo. 1s (MR).
CR XIII 76 (Jan, 1762); MR XXV 503 (App. 1761ii).
Cf 1759 [507].
M

689.
The Picture of Human Life, Or, The Way of the World; Represented in a Series of Instructive and Entertaining Examples : Or, The Mental Optician. In Two Volumes.
London : Printed for D. Steel, Book-Seller and Binder, at the Bible and Crown, near the Minories, DCCLXI [sic] [1761].
2 vols. 12mo.
CG(BL); EC 765:6; ESTC t128583.
BL UC WCL
* M/N

690.
+Select Fables of Esop and other Fabulists. In Three Books.
Birmingham : Printed by John Baskerville for R. and J. Dodsley in Pall Mall. 1761.
204pp. 8vo. 3s (CR,MR). 5s (tp).
CR XI 122-127 (Feb. 1761); MR XXIV 150-156 (Mar. 1761).
CG; ESTC t084696.
Also, 1761 [691], 1764 [873], 1765 [955]. Other versions listed, 1753 [199].
BL Bn CUL DU HU LC NLC PU UM UNC UV WCL YU
* M/C

691.
+Select Fables of Esop And Other Fabulists. In Three Books.
London : Printed for R. and J. Dodsley in Pallmall. 1761.
204pp. 8vo. 3s bound (tp).
Dodsley edn 1st published, 1761 [690]. Other edns and versions listed, 1753 [199].
CUL
* C

692.
+An Unfortunate Mother's Advice to her Absent Daughters; In a Letter to Miss Pennington. The Second
Edition.
London : Printed by S. Chandler, And Sold by W. Bristow, next the Great Toy-Shop, St Paul's Church-Yard;
and C. Etherington, Bookseller in York. 1761.
96pp. 8vo. 1s6d (tp).
ESTC t065158.
1st edn and edns listed, 1760 [613].
BL CUL
* M

693.
+An Unfortunate Mother's Advice to her Absent Daughters; In a Letter to Miss Pennington. The Third
Edition.
London : Printed by S. Chandler, And Sold by W. Bristow, next the Great Toy-Shop, St Paul's Church-Yard;
and C. Etherington, Bookseller in York. 1761.
96pp. 8vo. 1s6d (tp).
ESTC t069313.
1st edn and edns listed, 1760 [613].
BL
* M

694.
[Crébillon Claude Prosper Jolyot de]
+The Memoirs of Ninon de l'Enclos, With her letters to Monsr. de St. Evremond and to the Marquis de
Sevigne. Collected and Translated from the French. By a Lady. In Two Volumes.
London : Printed for R. and J. Dodsley, in Pall-mall. 1761.
2 vols. 12mo. 6s (CR,MR).
CR XII 445-449 (Dec. 1761); MR XXV 475 (Dec. 1761).
CG(MR); ESTC t061467.
A trans. of Douxménil's Mémoires et lettres pour servir a l'histoire de la vie de mademoiselle de l'Enclos.
Elizabeth Griffith sometimes suggested as translator.
1st English version, 1751 [108].
BL CUL
* M

695.
[Crébillon Claude Prosper Jolyot de]
The Secret History of Zeckineful, King of the Kofirans.
London : Thrush [1761] (CR).
8vo. 2s (CR).
CR XI 500 (June 1761).
CG(-).
A trans. of Les amours de Zeokinizul, 1746.
M

696.
[Montesquieu Charles Louis de Secondat Baron de]
+Letters from a Persian in England To his Friend at Isaphan. The Sixth Edition. Corrected and altered
by the Author.
Dublin : Printed for Geo. and Alex. Ewing. 1761.
228pp. 12mo.
1st English edn, 1722. Edns listed, 1751 [113].
CUL
* E/M

697.
+THE ADVENTURES OF A BLACK COAT. Containing a Series of Remarkable
Occurences and entertaining Incidents, That it was a Witness to in its Peregrinations
through the Cities of London and Westminster, in Company with Variety of Characters. As
related by Itself.
Dublin : Printed for Robert Bell, Bookseller and Auctioneer, at his great Auction-Rooms On
Cork-Hill, opposite to Lucas's Coffee-House. 1762.
188pp. 12mo. 1s1d sewed, 1s8d bound (tp).
CG as Dublin, Richard Watts and William Whitestone. 1762.
ESTC t086017.
1st edn and edns listed, 1760 [524].
BL Bod
* N

698.
ALL FOR LOVE; OR THE WORLD WELL LOST. A New Romance, Founded Entirely
on Fiction.
London : Printed for R. Freeman, Near St.Paul's. 1762.
155pp. 12mo. 8vo (BL). 2s (MR).
MR XXVI 319 (Apr. 1762).
AB(BL); BB; CG(HU); ESTC t079234.
Title derived from Dryden's play.
BL HU
* N

699.
THE COUNTRY SEAT; OR, SUMMER EVENINGS ENTERTAINMENTS. Translated
from the French. In Two Volumes.
London : Printed : And Sold by T. Lownds in Fleet Street. 1762.
2 vols. 12mo. 5s bound (MR).
CR XIV 156 (Aug. 1762); MR XXVII 71-72 (July 1762).
CG(HU,LC); EC 54:5; ESTC t092965.
Dublin edn, 1763 [757].
BL LC PU
* C

700.
+THE DEVIL UPON CRUTCHES IN ENGLAND; OR NIGHT SCENES IN LONDON.
Edinburgh : 1762.
12mo.
1st edn and edns listed, 1755 [285].
Bod
N

701.
A HISTORY OF THE MATRIMONIAL ADVENTURE OF A BANKER'S CLERK, WITH
THE PRETENDED LADY ANN FRANCES CAROLINE BOOTHBY : Otherwise sister to
the Duke of Beaufort; otherwise Miss Trevor; otherwise Miss Schudemore; otherwise Polly
Barns; otherwise Mrs Errington. In a Series of Letters addressed to Mr. George N—— at
Newcastle upon Tine.
London : Printed for C. Henderson under the Royal-Exchange. 1762.
176pp. 8vo. 2s6d (CG).
AB; ESTC t132194; FB; LO 151 (FB,HU).
CUL HU PU UCLA UI
* E

702.
LETTERS FROM SOPHIA TO MIRA : Containing the Adventures of a Lady; in which the several Situations, most common in Female Life, are naturally described.
London : Printed for R. & J. Dodsley, in Pall-mall, 1763 [1762].
253pp. 12mo. 2s6d (GM) 3s (CR,MR). Millar as bookseller, GM Dec. 1762.
CR XV 77 (Jan, 1763); MR XXVII 472-473 (Dec. 1762).
BB; CG(BL,GM,MR); ESTC t070914; FB; LO 162 (FB,MR).
BL Bod
* E

703.
THE MATRONS. Six Short Histories.
London : Printed for R. and J. Dodsley, in Pall-mall. 1762.
241[233]pp. 8vo. 3s (CR).
CR XIV 153-154 (Aug. 1762).
EC 218:1; ESTC t077680.
BL Bod BU CUL HU NLC UNC WCL
* C

704.
THE ROMANCE OF A NIGHT; OR, A COVENT-GARDEN ADVENTURE.
London : Nicoll. 1762.
8vo / 12mo. 1s (CR/MR).
CR XIV 319 (Oct. 1762); MR XXVII 386-387 (Nov. 1762).
Cf 1764 [827].
N

705.
[ARGENS Jean Baptiste de Boyer, Marquis d']
THE LIFE AND AMOURS OF COUNT DE TURENNE. Originally Wrote in French. By the Author of The Jews Letters &c.
London : Printed for J. Williams, The Corner of the Mitre Tavern, Fleet-Street. 1762.
12mo. 2s (BB,CR).
CR XIII 270 (Mar. 1762).
BB; CG.
N

706.
[ARGENS Jean Baptiste de Boyer, Marquis d']
+THE LIFE AND AMOURS OF COUNT DE TURENNE, Originally wrote in French By the Author of the Jews Letters. The Second Edition.
London : Printed for J. Williams, The Corner of the Mitre Tavern, Fleet-Street. 1762.
152pp. 12mo.
EC 204:4; ESTC t131037.
BL
* N

707.
[CHETWOOD William Rufus]
+THE VOYAGES AND ADVENTURES OF CAPTAIN ROBERT BOYLE, In several Parts of the World [8 more lines] The Sixth Edition.
London : Printed for T. Lownds, in Fleet-Street. 1762.
295pp. 12mo.
ESTC t119326; PBG p.249.
1st edn, 1726. Edns listed, 1759 [478].
BL CUNY
* N

708.
[COOPER Maria Susanna]
LETTERS BETWEEN EMILIA AND HARRIET.
London : Printed for R. and J. Dodsley in Pall-Mall. 1762.
175pp. 12mo. 2s (CR) 3s (MR).
CR XIII 159 (Feb. 1762); MR XXVI 154-155 (Feb. 1762).
AB(BL); CG(-); ESTC t081162; FB; LO 158 (FB,BL).
Dublin edn, 1762 [709]. Later edn of 1775 retitled 'The Daughter; Or, The History of Miss Harriet Ayres'.
BL YU
* E

709.
[COOPER Maria Susanna]
+LETTERS BETWEEN EMILIA AND HARRIET.
Dublin : 1762.
1st edn, 1762 [708].
UP YU
E

710.
[DEFOE Daniel]
+THE LIFE AND MOST SURPRISING ADVENTURES OF ROBINSON CRUSOE, OF
YORK, MARINER [&c.]
The Seventh Edition.
Edinburgh : Printed by A. Donaldson and J. Reid for Alexander Donaldson. 1762.
308pp. 12mo.
1st edn, 1719-20. Edns listed, 1752 [129].
SU
N/M

711.
[DEFOE Daniel]
+THE WONDERFUL LIFE AND MOST SURPRISING ADVENTURES OF ROBINSON
CRUSOE, OF YORK, MARINER.
Glasgow : R. Smith. 1762.
140pp.
1st edn, 1719-20. Edns listed, 1752 [129].
LC
N/M

712.
[DUNTON John]
(+)THE LIFE, TRAVELS AND ADVENTURES OF CHRISTOPHER WAGSTAFF,
GENTLEMAN, Grandfather to Tristram Shandy. Originally published In the latter End of
the last Century. Interspersed with A suitable Variety of Matter, By the Editor
[3 more lines]
London : Printed for J. Hinxman, in Pater-noster Row. 1762.
2 vols. 12mo. 5s bound (MR) 6s (BB,CR).
CR XIII 519 (June 1762); MR XXVI 474 (June 1762).
BB; CG(BL); EC 228:6; ESTC t071528; LO 163 (UI); McB 594.
Former version, 1691. 2nd edn, 1763 [773]. Cf 1759 [507].
BL Bod CUL FL Tx UCB UI
* N

713.
FIELDING Henry
+THE HISTORY OF THE ADVENTURES OF JOSEPH ANDREWS, And his Friend Mr.
Abraham Adams. Written in Imitation of the Manner of Cervantes, Author of Don
Quixote. By Henry Fielding, Esquire. The Sixth Edition, Revised and Corrected. In Two
Volumes.
London : Printed for A. Millar, in the Strand. 1762.
2 vols. 12mo.
CG; ESTC t089902.
1st edn, 1742. Edns listed, 1751 [84].
BL YU
* N

714.
FIELDING Henry
THE WORKS OF HENRY FIELDING, ESQ; With the Life of the Author. In Four
Volumes.
London : Printed for A. Millar, opposite Catharine-Street, in the Strand. 1762.
4 vols. 4to. £5.5s bound and gilt (MR).
MR XXVI 364-375, 481-494, XXVII 49-56 (May 1762, App 1762i, July 1762).
ESTC t089839.
Editor and author of the 'Life', Arthur Murphy.
Also 1762 [715], 1766 [1006], 1767 [1097], 1769 [1309], 1771 (3x), 1775 (2x), 1780, 1783, 1784.
BL Bod DU HL HU IU NLCPU UI UV WCL YU
* C/N

715.
FIELDING Henry
+THE WORKS OF HENRY FIELDING, ESQ; With a Life of the Author. In Eight
Volumes. The Second Edition.
London : Printed for A. Millar, in the Strand. 1762.
8 vols. 8vo. £2.12s6d (CR,MR).
CR XIV 1-21 (July 1762); and noted in MR rev.s listed 1762 [714].
ESTC t089840.
1st edn and edns listed, 1762 [714].
BL PU UNC UV YU
* C/N

716.
[GOLDSMITH Oliver]
THE CITIZEN OF THE WORLD; Or Letters From A Chinese Philosopher, Residing in
London, To His Friends in the East.
London : Printed for the Author and Sold by J. Newbery and W. Bristow, in St. Paul's Church-
yard; J. Leake and W. Frederick, at Bath; B. Collins, at Salisbury; and A. M. Smart and Co. at
Reading. 1762.
2 vols. 12mo. 6s (CR,MR).
CR XIII 397-400 (May 1762); MR XXVI 477 (June 1762).
AB(BL); BB; CG(HU); ESTC t146033; LO 159 (HU,RL,UI); TS pp.70-75 noting variant issue.
Published, May 1762.
Also 1762 [717] [718], 1769 [1312], 1774, 1775, 1776, 1782, 1785, 1790, 1792, 1793, 1794, 1799.
BL CUNY HU LC PU Tx UCLA UI UM UNC UV UW YU
* E/M

717.
[GOLDSMITH Oliver]
+THE CITIZEN OF THE WORLD; Or, Letters from a Chinese Philosopher, Residing in London, To His Friends in the East.
London : Printed for J. Newbery, at the Bible and Sun, in St. Paul's Church-yard. 1762.
2 vols. 12mo.
ESTC t146035; McB 349.
1st edn and edns listed, 1762 [716].
BL Bod CUL
* E/M

718.
[GOLDSMITH Oliver]
+THE CITIZEN OF THE WORLD; Or, Letters from a Chinese Philosopher, Residing in London, To his Friends in the East.
Dublin : Printed for George and Alex. Ewing. 1762.
2 vols in 1. 12mo. 5s5d.
CG(HU); ESTC t146034.
Published Nov. 1762, RCC p.115.
1st edn and edns listed, 1762 [716].
BL CUL CUNY HU NLI TCD YU
* E/M

719.
[GRIFFITH Richard]
+SOMETHING NEW. In Two Volumes. The Second Edition, Revised and Corrected by the Author.
London : Printed for E. and C. Dilly in the Poultry. 1762.
2 vols. 12mo.
ESTC t069140.
'1st' edn, if issued, also in 1762?. Also, 1772 edn.
BL Bod YU
* N

720.
[HAYWOOD Mrs Eliza]
+THE HISTORY OF MISS BETSY THOUGHTLESS.
1762.
4 vols. 8vo.
CG(-).
1st edn and edns listed, 1751 [85].
DU UNH
N

721.
[HAYWOOD Mrs Eliza]
+THE WIFE. By Mira, one of the authors of the Female Spectator, and Epistles for the Ladies. The Second Edition.
London : Printed for T. Gardner. 1762.
282pp.
CG(-).
1st edn, 1756 [373].
Bn FL PU UI UW
N/M

722.
[JOHNSTON Charles]
+CHRYSAL: OR, THE ADVENTURES OF A GUINEA. Wherein are exhibited Views of
several striking Scenes, With Curious and interesting Anecdotes of the most Noted Persons
in every Rank of Life, whose Hands it passed through, in America, England, Holland,
Germany and Portugal. By an Adept. The Third Edition, greatly inlarged and corrected.
London : Printed for T. Becket and P. A. de Hondt. 1762.
2 vols. 12mo.
1st edn and edns listed, 1760 [577].
Tx
N

723.
[JOHNSTON Charles]
THE REVERIE; OR, A FLIGHT TO THE PARADISE OF FOOLS. By the Editor of the
Adventures of a Guinea. In Two Volumes.
Dublin : Printed by Dillon Chamberlaine, in Smock-alley. 1762.
2 vols. 12mo.
An unauthorized 1st edn.
AB(AR,BL,St); EC 90:2; ESTC t066926.
Also, 1762 [724], 1767 [1110], 1776.
BL HL HU LC UO YU
* N

724.
[JOHNSTON Charles]
+THE REVERIE: OR A FLIGHT TO THE PARADISE OF FOOLS. Published by the
Editor of The Adventures of a Guinea. In Two Volumes.
London : Printed for T. Becket and P. A. Da [sic] Hondt, in the Strand, 1763 [1762].
2 vols in 1. 286pp. 12mo. 5s in boards (CR) 6s (MR).
CR XIV 440-445 (Dec. 1762); MR XXVII 471-472 (Dec. 1762).
AB(as 1763); BB; CG(BB,HU); ESTC t126192 LO 168 (UP,UI); McB 501.
1st (unauthorized) edn and edns listed, 1762 [723].
BL Bod BU CUL CUNY DU HU IU NYSL(HC) OU PU Tx UI UM YU
* N

725.
[JONES Henry]
+THE HISTORY OF THE TRAVELS AND ADVENTURES OF THE CHEVALIER JOHN
TAYLOR.
Dublin : 1762? (Bod).
1st edn, 1761 [659].
Bod
N

726.
[LANGHORNE John]
SOLYMAN AND ALMENA.
London : Printed for H. Payne and W. Cropley, at Dryden's Head in Pater-Noster-Row. 1762.
198pp. 12mo. 2s (MR) 3s (CR).
CR XIII 148-154 (Feb. 1762); MR XXVI 254-264 (Apr. 1762).
AB(LHW,McL,Pi); CG(BL,HU); EC 192:9; ESTC t134591;
LO 160 (UI,UP); McB 526.
Also 1762 [727], 1764 [850], 1780, 1781, 1784, 1787, 179- 1790, 1795(2x).
BL Bod CUL CUNY HU NLC OU UI UP YU
* N

727.
[LANGHORNE John]
+SOLYMAN AND ALMENA.
Dublin : Printed by W. Smith, Sen. and J. Potts, Booksellers, in Dame-street. 1762.
175pp. 12mo.
ESTC t107265.
1st edn and edns listed, 1762 [726].
BL CUL
* N

728.
[LELAND Thomas]
LONGSWORD, EARL OF SALISBURY. An Historical Romance.
London : Printed for W. Johnston, in Ludgate-Street. 1762.
2 vols. 12mo. 5s (CR) 6s bound (MR).
CR XIII 252-257 (Mar. 1762); MR XXVI 236-237 (Mar. 1762).
BB; CG(BB,HU); JT; LO 161 (UI); McB 541 (as by John Leland).
Also, Dublin edn 1762 [729], 1766 [1022], 1775, 1790.
BU CUL LC NLC UC UI UM UNC WCL
* N

729.
[LELAND Thomas]
+LONGSWORD, EARL OF SALISBURY. An Historical Romance.
Dublin : Printed for G. Faulkner, in Essex-Street. 1762.
2 vols. 12mo.
ESTC t119302.
BL UO
* N

730.
LENNOX Mrs Charlotte Ramsay
SOPHIA. By Mrs Charlotte Lennox. In Two Volumes.
London : Printed for James Fletcher, in St. Paul's Church-Yard. 1762.
2 vols. 12mo. 6s bound (CR,MR).
CR XIII 434-435 (May 1762); MR XXVII 73-74 (July 1762).
AB(AR,BL,St); BB(as 1763); CG; EC 208:1; ESTC t066924.
Dublin edn, 1762 [731].
BL Bod CUL CUNY IU UC YU
* N

731.
LENNOX Mrs Charlotte Ramsay
+THE HISTORY OF SOPHIA. By the Celebrated Mrs Lennox, Author of the Female Quixote, Henrietta, &c.
Dublin : Printed by James Hoey. [1762?] (adv-1764 [822]).
1s7½d sewed 2s2d bound in calf & lettered.
Adv- 1764 [822] & 1763 [786].
1st edn, 1762 [730].
N

732.
MARIN Michel-Ange
FARFALLA, OR THE CONVERTED ACTRESS.
BB & CG as 'Tartalla', 1762. 12mo.
A trans. of Marin's *La Farfala; ó La Cómica convertida.*
N

733.
[RICCOBONI Marie Jeanne]
MEMOIRS OF LADY HARRIOT BUTLER : Now First Published From Authentic Papers,
in the Lady's own hand-writing.
London : Printed for R. Freeman, near St. Paul's. 1762.
Volume II
186pp. 12mo.
Unlike 1761 vol. tp does not say 'In Two Volumes'.
EC 334:2; ESTC t066383.
Vol I, published 1761 [663].
BL
* N

734.
[RICCOBONI Marie Jeanne]
+MEMOIRS OF LADY HARRIOT BUTLER : Now First Published From Authentic
Papers, in the Lady's own hand-writing.
Dublin : Printed by John Exshaw, and James Potts, Booksellers, in Dame-street. 1762.
2 vols. 12mo.
ESTC t118814.
1st edn of each vol, 1761 [663] and 1762 [733].
BL CUL
* N

735.
RICHARDSON Samuel
+THE HISTORY OF SIR CHARLES GRANDISON. In a Series of Letters. By Mr Samuel
Richardson, Author of Pamela and Clarissa. In Seven Volumes. The Fourth Edition.
London : Printed (by Assignment from Mr. Richardson's Executors) for J. Rivington, in St.
Paul's Church-Yard; C. Hitch and L. Hawes, R. Baldwin, J. Richardson, S. Crowder and Co. and
J. Coote, in Pater-noster-Row. 1762.
7 vols. 8vo. Vol I, 2s6d sewed (WS).
CG; ESTC t058999; WS 42.
Vol I published 1 Feb. Remaining vols published in monthly installments. Vol VII of an abortive 1756 issue
reissued in this edn. Also a variant, suggested but not proven as a piracy, WS 43.
1st edn and edns listed, 1753 [191].
AAS BL Bn Bod CUNY CUL UW YU
* E

736.
[SCOTT Mrs Sarah Robinson and
MONTAGU Lady Barbara]
A DESCRIPTION OF MILLENIUM HALL, AND THE COUNTRY ADJACENT :
Together with the Characters of the Inhabitants, And such Historical Anecdotes and
Reflections, as May excite in the Reader proper Sentiments of Humanity, and Lead the
Mind to the Love of Virtue. By a Gentleman on his Travels.
London : Printed for J. Newbery, at the Bible and Sun, in St. Paul's Church-yard. 1762.
2 vols in 1. 262pp. 12mo. 2s6d (CR) 3s (MR).
CR XIV 463-464 (Dec. 1762); MR XXVII 389-390 (Nov. 1762).
BB; CG(HU); EC 224:5; ESTC t107679; FB; LO 164 (FB,HU,UI,UP); McB 803.
Sometime attributed to Goldsmith and Smart. Probably written in collaboration with Lady Barbara Montagu,
'The Life and Writing of Mrs Sarah Scott' unpublished dissertation by M. Crittenden.
Also 1763 [791], 1764 [866] [867], 1767 [1133], 1778.
BL Bod CUL DU HL HU IU NLC PU UC UI UM UP YU
* N

737.
[SMOLLETT Tobias]
+THE ADVENTURES OF RODERICK RANDOM. The Fifth Edition.
Dublin : Printed and sold by T. Dyton. 1762.
MW 37.
1st edn, 1748. Edns listed, 1750 [40].
N

738.
[SMOLLETT Tobias]
THE ADVENTURES OF SIR LAUNCELOT GREAVES. By the Author of Roderick Random. In Two Volumes.
London : Printed for J. Coote. 1762.
2 vols. 12mo. 6s (CR,MR).
CR XIII 427-429 (May 1762); MR XXVI 391 (May 1762).
AB(ELG,BL,Pi); BB; CG(HU); ESTC t055384; LO 165 (UI); McB 850; MW 236; newSG.
1st appeared in monthly installments in *The British Magazine* Jan. 1760 - Dec. 1761 (Rivington and Fletcher).
Also 1762 [739], 1763 [795], 1767 [1139], 1774-9, 1775, 1780-3, 1782, 1783, 1786, 1792, 1793(2x), 1795, 1796, 1797, 1800.
BL Bod CUL CUNY HU NLC Tx UI UP WCL YU
* N

739.
SMOLLETT Tobias
+THE ADVENTURES OF SIR LAUNCELOT GREAVES. Illustrated with Copper Plates. By the Author of Roderick Random.
Dublin : Printed by James Hoey, junior. 1762.
264pp. 12mo. 2s2d sewed 2s8½d bound [advs- 1763 [786] 1764 [786]).
ESTC t055385; MW 237.
1st complete edn and edns listed, 1762 [738].
BL CUL IU
* N

740.
STAYLEY George
THE LIFE AND OPINIONS OF AN ACTOR. A real History, in Two real Volumes. By Mr. George Stayley, Late of Smock-Alley, Comedian.
Dublin : Printed for the Author. And sold by G. Faulkner, in Dublin; J. Hinton, Bookseller, at the King's Arms in Newgate-street, London; and all the Author's Friends in England and Ireland. 1762.
2 vols. 12mo.
CG; ESTC t068222.
In imitation of Sterne. Cf 1759 [507].
BL HU
* N

741.
[STERNE Laurence]
+THE LIFE AND OPINIONS OF TRISTRAM SHANDY, GENTLEMAN.
Dublin : Printed by H.[enry] Saunders, at the Salmon in Castle-Street. 1762.
Vols V & VI, as cont. of vols I-IV published, 1761.
2 vols in 1. 120pp. 12mo.
CG; ESTC t014695.
Vols V-VI 1st published, 1761 [677]. Vols I-II published and edns of all vols listed, 1759 [507].
BL Bod
* N

742.
WOODFIN Mrs A.
THE HISTORY OF MISS HARRIOT WATSON. In Two Volumes. By Mrs Woodfin,
Author of the Auction.
London : Printed for T. Lownds, at his Circulating Library, in Fleet-Street. 1762.
2 vols. 8vo. 5s (BB).
CR XV 62-66 (Jan, 1763); MR XXVIII 162 (Feb, 1763).
AB; BB; both as 1763.
Dublin edn, 1763 [797].
YU
* N

                                Miscellanies

743.
A Collection of Ridiculous Stories.
London : Hinxman. 1762.
12mo. 1s6d (CR).
CR XIII 523 (June 1762).
M/C

744.
Four Genuine Letters which lately passed between a Noble Lord and a young Woman of Fashion.
London : Williams. 1762.
4to. 2s (MR).
MR XXVI 319 (Apr. 1762).
Other edns and responses incl. 1762 [745].
LC (with variants) Tx YU
M

745.
+Four Genuine Letters, which lately passed between a Noble Lord and a young Woman of Fashion. To
which is added, a Letter from a Lady to Miss ******.
[Dublin] London : Printed, and Dublin reprinted by Matthew Williamson, in Dame-street. 1762.
10pp. 8vo.
CG(BL); ESTC t063258.
1st edn, 1762 [744].
BL CUL
* M

746.
Genuine Letters to a Young Lady of Family, Figure, and Fortune : Previous to Her Intended Espousals.
To which are Added, Three Poems, by the Same Author
[10 more lines]
London : Printed for J. Wilkie, at the Bible, in St. Paul's Church-Yard. 1762.
148pp. 12mo. 2s (MR).
MR XXV 502 (App 1761ii).
CG; FB; LO 149 (FB,MR).
CUL NLC
* M

747.

Gisbal, An Hyperborean Tale : Translated From the Fragments of Ossian, the Son of Fingal. The Second Edition.

London : Printed for the Author, and Sold by J. Pridden, at the Feathers in Fleet-Street, near Fleet-Bridge. 1762. 44pp. 8vo. 1s (CR,MR).

CR XIV 76 (July 1762); MR XXVII 156 (Aug. 1762).

BB, CG(BL).

BL HU NYPL YU

* M/N (sat)

748

Letters to a Young Nobleman.

London : Printed for A. Millar, in the Strand. 1762. 230pp. 8vo.

ESTC t063764.

BL CUL DU NYPL Tx UP

* M

749.

[d'Auborn A.]

+The French Convert. Being a true Relation of the happy Conversion of a Noble French Lady, from the Errors and Superstitions of Popery, to the Reformed Religion, by Means of a Protestant Gardener her Servant.

[13 more lines]

Glasgow : Printed for Robert Smith, and sold at his shop, at the sign of the Gilt-Bible, near the head of the Salt-mercat. 1762. 119pp. 12mo.

CG(BL); ESTC t089432.

1st edn, [17-]. Edns listed, 1757 [421].

BL

* M/N

750.

[Mitchell John]

The Female Pilgrim, or, the Travels of Hephzibah, Under the Similitude of a Dream : In which is given,
[26 more lines]

London : Printed for the Author, and Sold by J. Johnson, at Mead's Head, opposite the Monument. 1762. 438pp. 8vo. 7s bound (BB,MR).

MR XXVII 219 (Sept. 1762).

AB(BL); BB; CG(BL); ESTC t118155.

'Published in 9 parts', BL.

Also 1762 [751], 1793 and 1800 edns.

BL Bod CUL NLC PU UC YU

* M

751.

Mitchell John

+The Female Pilgrim, Or, the Travels of Hephzibah, Under the Similitude of a Dream : In which is given,

[13 more lines]

By John Mitchell.

London : Printed for the Author, and Sold by J. Johnson, at Mead's Head, opposite the Monument. 1762. 438pp. 8vo.

1st edn, 1762 [750].

CUL

* M

752.
Montesquieu Charles Louis de Secondat Baron de
Flloyd Thomas *trans.*
+Persian Letters. By M. De Montesquieu. Translated from the French, By Mr. Flloyd. In Two Volumes. The Fourth Edition. With several new Letters and Notes.
London : Printed for J. and R. Tonson, in the Strand. 1762.
2 vols. 12mo.
1st English edn, 1722. Edns listed, 1751 [113].
CUL LC UNC UV
* E/M

753.
Rowe Mrs Elizabeth Singer
+Friendship in Death : In Twenty Letters from the Dead to the Living. To which are added, Letters Moral and Entertaining, in Prose and Verse : In Three Parts. By Mrs Elizabeth Rowe.
Edinburgh : Printed by A. Donaldson and J. Reid, for Alexander Donaldson. 1762.
292pp. 12mo.
ESTC t134487.
1st edn, 1728. Edns listed, 1750 [60].
BL Bn PU
* M

1763

754.
THE ADVENTURES OF JACK FITZPATRICK, Embellished with a copper-plate frontispiece of a Night-Scene.
Dublin : Printed for James Hoey [1763?] (adv -1763 [775]).
2s 2d sewed 2s 8½d bound in calf and lettered.
Adv-1763 [775].
N

755.
THE ADVENTURES OF MARK THE RAMBLER. Written by Himself.
London : Williams. 1763.
12mo. 3s (MR) 3s6d (CR).
CR XV 322 (Apr. 1763); MR XXVIII 404 (May 1763).
BB; CG(CR,MR).
N

756.
THE ADVENTURES OF PATRICK O'DONNEL, In His Travels Through England and Ireland. Written by Himself.
London : J. Williams. 1763.
12mo. 2s6d (CR,GM,MR).
CR XVI 138-142 (Aug. 1763); MR XXIX 236 (Sept. 1763).
AB(Pi); BB; CG(BB,GM).
N

757.
+THE COUNTRY SEAT; OR, EVENINGS ENTERTAINMENTS. Translated from the Spanish, And carefully compared with the Original, found among the Papers of Don Velasco, Late Governor of the Moro Castle, at the Havannah.
Dublin : Printed by James Hoey, at the Mercury in Skinner-Row. 1763.
233pp. 12mo.
ESTC t107623.
Adv in 1763 [789] as published by James Potts.
1st edn (as 'Summer Evenings'), 1762 [699].
BL Bod CUL
* C

758.
EACH SEX IN THEIR HUMOUR : Or, the Histories of the Families of Brightley, Finch, Fortescue, Shelburne, and Stevens. Written by a Lady of Quality, Whilst she was abroad on her Travels, and found among her Papers, since her Decease. In Two Volumes.
London : Printed for the Editor; And Sold by F. Noble, at his Circulating Library, opposite Grays's-Inn-Gate, Holborn; And J. Noble, at his Circulating Library, in St. Martin's Court, near Leicester Square, 1764 [1763].
2 vols. 12mo. 6s (CR,MR).
CR XVI 449-452 (Dec. 1763); MR XXX 75 (Jan, 1764).
AB(as 1764); CG(CR,HU); EC 207:5; ESTC t027894.
Preface signed M. C.
Dublin edn, 1764 [809].
BL CUL HU NLC UMin YU
* N

759.
THE HISTORY OF THE GAY BELLARIO AND THE FAIR ISABELLA, Founded on Facts and Illustrated with Adventures in Real Life.
London : Printed for W. Morgan. 1763.
12mo (BB). 2s6d sewed (MR).
MR XXX 77-78 (Jan, 1764).
BB; CG(BB,HU).
Also, 1766 [983].
HU
N

760.
THE LIFE AND ADVENTURES OF A REFORMED MAGDALEN. In a Series of Letters to Mrs *** of Northampton. Written by Herself. In Two Volumes.
London : Nicoll (CR) or Griffin (BB,MR).
2 vols. 12mo. 4s sewed (BB,MR) 5s (CR).
CR XVII 36-37 (Jan, 1764); MR XXX 77 (Jan, 1764).
BB; CG(BB).
N

761.
THE LIFE AND ADVENTURES OF PETER WILLIAMSON.
Dublin : Printed by James Hoey [1763?] (Adv - 1763 [775] and 1764 [851]).
10d.
Advs-1763 [775] 1764 [851]; CG.
'Authentic Instances of French and Indian Cruelty, exemplified in the Sufferings of Peter Williamson' had been published in *The Grand Magazine*, 1758.
N/M

762.
THE LOVES OF CARMI AND IPHIS; A Novel, Founded on the Story of Jepthah's Vow.
London : Printed for J. Denham : and sold by T. Field, at the corner of Pater-noster row,
Cheapside. 1763.
143pp. 8vo. 1s6d (BB).
MR XXVIII 245-246 (Mar. 1763).
BB; CG.
HU
N

763.
MEMOIRS OF THE CHEVALIER PIERPOINT. In Two Volumes.
London : Printed for R. and J. Dodsley in Pall-Mall. 1763.
2 vols. 12mo. 4s sewed (MR) 5s (CR).
CR XV 11-13 (Jan. 1763); MR XXVIII 78 (Jan. 1763).
AB(Pi,St); CG.
BB has 1762, 'Memoirs of the Chevalier Pierropaint'.
Vols III & IV, 1764 [820]. Dublin edn, 1765 [890].
HU IU LC YU
* N

764.
MEMOIRS OF THE LIFE AND ADVENTURES OF TSONNONTHOUAN, A KING OF
THE INDIAN NATION CALLED ROUNDHEADS. Extracted from Original Papers and
Archives. In Two Volumes.
London : Printed for the Editor, and sold by J. Knox. 1763.
2 vols. 12mo. 5s (MR) 6s bound (CR).
CR XV 378-388 (May 1763); MR XXVIII 492-493 (June 1763).
CG(CR).
CNY HU LC YU
N

765.
THE PEREGRINATIONS OF JEREMIAH GRANT, ESQ; A WEST INDIAN.
London : Printed for G. Burnet, at Bishop Burnet's-head, near Arundel-street, in the Strand.
1763.
327pp. 12mo. 3s (CR,MR).
CR XV 13-21 (Jan. 1763); MR XXVIII 162 (Feb. 1763).
BB; CG(HU); LO 171 (UP).
Bn HU UP
N

766.
THE SCHOOL FOR WIVES. In a Series of Letters.
London : Printed for R. and J. Dodsley, in Pall-mall. 1763.
184pp. 8vo. 3s (CR,MR).
CR XV 130-135 (Feb. 1763); MR XXVIII 326-327 (Apr. 1763).
AB(BL,TDW,WB); CG(HU); EC 218:3; ESTC t072466; LO 172 (BL).
BL Bod CUL CUNY HU NLC PU UC UCLA
* E

767.
+SOPHRONIA; OR, LETTERS TO THE LADIES.
Dublin : Printed for D. Chamberlaine in Smock-Alley, James Hunter and J. Mitchell, in Sycamore-Alley. 1763.
237pp. 8vo.
CG; ESTC t107101.
1st edn and edns listed, 1761 [639].
BL CUL YU
* E

768.
[AMORY Thomas]
+THE LIFE OF JOHN BUNCLE ESQ : Containing Various Observations and Reflections, made in several parts of the World; and many extraordinary relations.
London : J. Johnson. 1763.
1 vol.
CG.
Vol I published, 1756 [362]. Vol II not published until 1766 [990].
LC
N

769.
[BROOKE Mrs Frances Moore]
THE HISTORY OF LADY JULIA MANDEVILLE. In Two Volumes. By the Translator of Lady Catesby's Letters.
London : Printed for R. and J. Dodsley in Pall-Mall [1763].
2 vols. 12mo. 6s (CR,MR).
CR XVI 41-45 (July 1763); MR XXIX 159-160 (Aug. 1763).
AB(BL,ELG,McGoff); BB; ESTC t065262; JT; LO 166 (HU,UI,UP); McB 104.
Also, 1763 [770] [771] [772], 1764 [824], 1765 [899], 1766 [992], 1767 [1089], 1769 [1299], 1773, 1775, 1782(2x), 1788.
BL UI UP
* E

770.
[BROOKE Mrs Frances Moore]
+THE HISTORY OF LADY JULIA MANDEVILLE. In Two Volumes. By the Translator of Lady Catesby's Letters. The Second Edition.
London : Printed for R. and J. Dodsley in Pall-Mall. 1763.
2 vols. 12mo.
ESTC t132105.
1st edn and edns listed, 1763 [769].
BL CUL OU Tx YU
* E

771.
[BROOKE Mrs Frances Moore]
+THE HISTORY OF LADY JULIA MANDEVILLE. In Two Volumes. By the Translator of Lady Catesby's Letters. A New Edition.
London : Printed for R. Dodsley, in Pall-Mall [1763] (BL).
2 vols. 12mo.
ESTC t031406.
1st edn and edns listed, 1763 [769].
BL Bod
* E

772.
[BROOKE Mrs Frances Moore]
+THE HISTORY OF LADY JULIA MANDEVILLE. In Two Volumes. By the Translator
of Lady Catesby's Letters.
Dublin : Printed by J. Potts, at Swift's Head in Dame-street. 1763.
2 vols. 8vo.
ESTC t102390.
BL BU UC
1st edn and edns listed, 1763 [769].
* E

773.
[DUNTON John]
+THE LIFE, TRAVELS AND ADVENTURES OF CHRISTOPHER WAGSTAFF,
GENTLEMAN, Grandfather to Tristram Shandy.
London : Hinxman. 1763.
8vo.
1st version, 1691, and 1st edn of this version, 1762 [712].
Bod
N

774.
FIELDING Henry
+THE HISTORY OF TOM JONES, A FOUNDLING. In Four Volumes. By Henry
Fielding, Esq.
London : Printed for A. Millar, over-against Catherine-street in the Strand. 1763.
4 vols. 12mo.
CG; EC 286:3; ESTC t001946; McB 294.
1st edn, 1749. Edns listed, 1750 [24].
BL [imperf] HU UCB UI YU
* N

775.
[FIELDING Sarah]
+THE HISTORY OF OPHELIA. Published by the Author of David Simple. In Two
Volumes. The Second Edition, with Additions.
Dublin : Printed by James Hoey Junior. 1763.
337pp. 12mo. '2s8½d bound together or 2s2d sewed' (adv-1763 [786]).
ESTC t134299
1st edn and edns listed, 1760 [571].
BL UI
* N

776.
[KIMBER Edward]
+THE LIFE AND ADVENTURES OF JOE THOMPSON. A Narrative founded on Fact.
Written by Himself. The Third Edition.
London : Printed for John Hinton, at the King's-Arms, in Newgate-Street; And W. Frederick,
Bookseller, in Bath. 1763.
2 vols. 12mo.
CG(HU); PBG 319.
1st edn and edns listed, 1750 [27].
CUL HU (imperf) LC YU
N

777.
[LANGHORNE John]
THE EFFUSIONS OF FRIENDSHIP AND FANCY. In Several Letters to and from Select Friends.
London : Printed for T. Becket and P. A. De Hondt, in the Strand. 1763.
2 vols. 8vo. 4s sewed (BB,MR).
MR XXVIII 481-483 (June 1763).
AB(BkB); BB; ESTC t137491.
2nd edn, 1766 [1020].
BL CUL FL PU UCLA UF YU
* E

778.
[LANGHORNE John]
THE LETTERS THAT PASSED BETWEEN THEODOSIUS AND CONSTANTIA, AFTER SHE HAD TAKEN THE VEIL. Now First Published from the Original Manuscripts.
London : Printed for T. Becket and P. A. DeHondt, in the Strand. 1763.
165pp. 8vo. 2s6d (CR,MR).
CR XVI 11-16 (July 1763); MR XXIX 147-153 (Aug. 1763).
AB(Bk,EM,RI); BB; CG(HU); ESTC t107275; FB; LO 169 (FB,HU,UI).
Also 1763 [779] [780], 1764 [849], 1766 [1021], 1770(2x), 1782. Cf 1765 [926] with edns listed.
BL CUL HU NLC UC UI
* E

779.
[LANGHORNE John]
+THE LETTERS THAT PASSED BETWEEN THEODOSIUS AND CONSTANTIA; AFTER SHE HAD TAKEN THE VEIL. The Second Edition.
London : Printed for T. Becket and P. A. De Hondt, in the Strand, 1764 [1763].
185pp. 8vo. 2s6d sewed 3s bound ($\frac{1}{2}$tp).
Rev of 2nd edn, CR XVII 80 (Jan, 1764); MR XXIX 477 (Dec. 1763).
ESTC t057346; McB 523.
1st edn and edns listed, 1763 [778].
CUNY BL Bod CUNY DU IU OU UF UI UM UV UW
* E

780.
[LANGHORNE John]
+THE LETTERS THAT PASSED BETWEEN THEODOSIUS AND CONSTANTIA; AFTER SHE HAD TAKEN THE VEIL. Now first published from the Original Manuscripts.
Dublin : Printed for J. Potts, at Swift's-Head, in Dame-street. 1763.
144pp. 8vo.
1st edn and edns listed, 1763 [778].
Bod
* E

781.
LENNOX Charlotte Ramsay
+THE FEMALE QUIXOTE; OR, THE ADVENTURES OF ARABELLA. The Third Edition.
Dublin : W. Whitestone. 1763.
2 vols in 1.
CG
1st edn and edns listed, 1752 [139].
NYPL UC
N

782.
[LONGUEVILLE Peter]
+THE HERMIT : OR, THE UNPARALLEL'D SUFFERINGS AND SURPRISING
ADVENTURES OF MR. PHILIP QUARLL. [&c.]
The Fourth Edition.
London : Printed for J. Wren, S. Crowder, H. Woodgate, J. Fuller, and J. Warcus. 1768.
263pp. 12mo.
1st edn, 1727. Edns listed, 1751 [93].
A '4th' edn was issued by these booksellers in 1768 [1220]. A re-issue?
NLC UM
N/M

783.
[MADDEN Samuel]
+THE REIGN OF GEORGE VI.
London : Printed for W. Nicoll, at the Paper-Mill, in St. Paul's Church-Yard. 1763.
192pp. 12mo. 2s6d (CG).
CG(BL); ESTC t070919.
From his 1733 *Memoirs of the Twentieth Century*.
BL
* N/M

784.
[MARMONTEL Jean François]
[ROBERTS Miss R. *trans.*]
SELECT MORAL TALES. Translated from the French By a Lady.
Glocester [sic] : Printed by R. Raikes, for the editour. 1763.
196pp. 8vo.
AB(BL); CG(BL,HU); EC 166:6; ESTC t064649.
Also, *Moral Tales*, 1764 [852] [853], with vol. III 1765 [931], 1766 [1025] [1026], 1768 [1223], 1781,
1792(4x), 1795, 1800.
BL HU
* C

785.
MINIFIE Margaret and Susannah
THE HISTORIES OF LADY FRANCES S——, AND LADY CAROLINE S——. Written
by the Miss Minifies, Of Fairwater, in Somersetshire.
London : Printed for R. and J. Dodsley, in Pall-Mall. 1763.
3 vols. 12mo. 9s (CR,MR). Subn.
CR XVI 108-117 (Aug. 1763); MR XXIX 160 (Aug. 1763).
AB(BL); CG(HU); ESTC t068575; FB; JT; LO 167 & 170 (FB,HU,UP).
Dublin edn, 1763 [786]. Vol. IV published, 1764 [856].
BL [imperf] Bod CUL HU NLC OU UM UP YU
* E

786.
MINIFIE Margaret and Susannah
+THE HISTORIES OF LADY FRANCES S——, AND LADY CAROLINE S——. Written
by the Miss Minifies, Of Fairwater, in Somersetshire.
Dublin : Printed for James Hoey, junior, and James Potts. 1763.
276pp. 12mo. 2s2d sewed 2s8½d bound (Adv-1764 [822]).
ESTC t124909.
1st edn, 1763 [785].
BL PU UP
* E

787.
RAMSAY Andrew Michael
+THE TRAVELS OF CYRUS. To which is annexed, A Discourse upon the Theology and Mythology Of the Pagans. By the Chevalier Ramsay. The Ninth Edition.
London : Printed by James Bettenham : And Sold by L. Hawes, W. Clarke, and R. Collins, in Pater-noster Row. 1763.
356pp. 12mo.
ESTC t082614.
1st English edn, 1727. Edns listed, 1752 [146].
BL HU UCo
* M/N

788.
RAMSAY Andrew Michael
+THE TRAVELS OF CYRUS. To which is annexed, A Discourse upon the Theology and Mythology Of the Pagans. By the Chevalier Ramsay. The Ninth Edition.
Dublin : Printed for William Smith and Son, Booksellers, at the Hercules in Dame-Street. 1763.
311pp. 12mo.
1st English edn, 1727. Edns listed, 1752 [146].
CUL UV
* M/N

789.
[RICCOBONI Marie Jeanne]
[BROOKE Mrs Frances Moore *trans.*]
+LETTERS FROM JULIET, LADY CATESBY, TO HER FRIEND HENRIETTA CAMPLEY. Translated from the French. The Second Edition.
Dublin : Printed by J. Potts, at Swift's Head, in Dame-street. 1763.
167pp. 12mo.
ESTC t084636.
1st edn and edns listed, 1759 [502].
BL Bod
* E

790.
[RICCOBONI Marie Jeanne]
[BROOKE Mrs Frances Moore *trans.*]
+LETTERS FROM JULIET, LADY CATESBY, TO HER FRIEND HENRIETTA CAMPLEY. Translated from the French. The Third Edition.
London : Printed for R. and J. Dodsley, in Pall-Mall. 1763.
252pp. 12mo.
1st edn and edns listed, 1759 [502].
Bod IU Tx UCLA UP
E

791.
[SCOTT Mrs Sarah Robinson and
MONTAGU Lady Barbara]
+A DESCRIPTION OF MILLENIUM HALL, AND THE COUNTRY ADJACENT : Together with the Characters of the Inhabitants, And such Historical Anecdotes and Reflections, As May excite in the Reader proper Sentiments of Humanity, and lead the Mind to the Love of Virtue. By a Gentleman on his Travels.
Dublin : Printed for Peter Wilson, in Dame-street. 1763.
282pp. 12mo.
ESTC t059855.   1st edn and edns listed, 1762 [736].
BL
* N

792.
[SHEBBEARE John]
+LYDIA, OR FILIAL PIETY. A NOVEL. By the Author of the Marriage Act, A Novel; and Letters on the English Nation.
Dublin : Printed for Sarah Cotter. 1763.
4 vols in 2. 8vo.
CG.
1st edn and edns listed, 1755 [324].
UM
N

793.
[SMOLLETT Tobias]
+THE ADVENTURES OF PEREGRINE PICKLE. In which are included, Memoirs of a Lady of Quality. In Four Volumes. The Second Edition, Revised, Corrected, and Altered by the Author.
Dublin : Printed by Henry Saunders in Castle-Street, James Potts in Dame-Street, and Thomas Richey in Essex-Street, Booksellers. 1763.
4 vols. 12mo.
ESTC t055346; MW 139.
1st edn and edns listed, 1751 [99].
BL CUL
* N

794.
[SMOLLETT Tobias]
+THE ADVENTURES OF RODERICK RANDOM The Sixth Edition.
London : Printed for A. Millar, W. Strahan, J. Rivington, R. Baldwin, W. Johnson, J. Richardson, T. Caslon, T. Hope, T. Becket, and P. A. DeHondt and J. Hinxman. 1763.
2 vols. 12mo.
CG; MW 38.
1st edn, 1748. Edns listed, 1750 [40].
YU
N

795.
[SMOLLETT Tobias]
+THE ADVENTURES OF SIR LAUNCELOT GREAVES. By the Author of Roderick Random. The Second Edition.
Dublin : Printed by James Hoey, Junior. 1763.
264pp. 12mo.
MW 238.
1st complete edn and edns listed, 1762 [738].
IU UW
N

796.
[STERNE Laurence]
+THE LIFE AND OPINIONS OF TRISTRAM SHANDY, GENTLEMAN.
London : [Dodsley] 1763.
2 vols. 12mo.
A 5th edn of vols I & II, noted, KM p.23.
1st edn and edns of all vols listed, 1759 [507].
N

797.
WOODFIN Mrs A.
+THE HISTORY OF MISS HARRIOT WATSON. In Two Volumes. By Mrs Woodfin, Author of The Auction.
Dublin : Printed by James Hoey [1763?] (adv-1766 [822]).
2 vols. 2s2d sewed 2s8½d (adv-1764 [822]).
Adv-1764 [822].
1st edn, 1762 [742].
N

Miscellanies

798.
+Select Fables of Esop and other Fabulists. The Third Edition.
London : Printed for R. and J. Dodsley. 1763.
204pp. 12mo.
1st Dodsley edn, 1761 [690]. Edns listed, 1753 [199].
YU [and University of Rochester, NY, as 1762]
M/C

799.
[Collier John]
Tim Bobbin's Toy-Shop open'd or, his Whimsical Amusements. Containing his view of the Lancashire dialect
[15 more lines]
Embellished with Copper-plates designed by the Author, and engraved by Mr. Barlow, of Bolton.
Manchester : Printed and Sold by Joseph Harrop, and by the Booksellers throughout England and Wales. 1763.
180pp. 12mo.
CG; ESTC t116628.
BL LC NLC UIC
* M

800.
[Cruden Alexander]
The History of Richard Potter, A Sailor, and Prisoner in Newgate, who was tried at the Old-Bailey in July 1763 and received sentence of Death for attempting, at the instigation of another Sailor, to receive Thirty-five Shillings of Prize-money, due to a third Sailor
[20 more lines]
London : Printed for J. and W. Oliver, in Bartholomew Close : For G. Keith, in Gracechurch street; E. Dilly, in the Poultry; M. Lewis; in Pater-noster-Row; G. Freer, in Bell-yard near Temple-Bar; and J. Ridley, near St. James's Palace. 1763.
68pp. 8vo.
BB; ESTC t000571.
BL CUL
* M

801.
[Goadby Robert]
+An Apology for the Life of Mr. Bampfylde-Moore Carew, Commonly call'd The King of the Beggars.
[16 more lines]
The Seventh Edition.
London : Printed for R. Goadby, and W. Owen, Bookseller, at Temple-Bar. 1763.
348pp. 12mo.
CG.
1st London edn 1749 as version of an edn of 1745. Edns listed, 1750 [54].
CUL UMin YU
* M

802.
[Shebbeare John]
(+)Select Letters on the English Nation : By Batista Angeloni, A Jesuit, Who resided many years in London. Translated from the Original Italian.
Dublin : Printed for Wlm. Williamson, Bookseller and Whole-Sale Stationer, at Mecænas's [sic] Head in Bride-street. 1763.
292pp. 8vo.
ESTC t088374.
1st edn of full version, 1755 [345].
BL CUNY Tx
* M/E

803.
[Stevens George Alexander]
The Dramatic History of Master Edward, Miss Ann, Mrs Llwhuddwhydd, And Others, the Extraordinaries of these Times. Collected from Zaphaniel's Original Papers. Illustrated with Copper-Plates.
London : Printed for T. Waller, opposite Fetter-Lane, Fleet-Street, 1743 [1763].
192pp. 12mo. 3s6d sewed (CR,MR).
CR XV 373-377 (May 1763); MR XXVIII 328 (Apr. 1763).
CG(GM Mar 1763); ESTC t116476.
A series of dialogues in the style of a play.
BL CNY HU IU NLC UC YU
* M

1764

804.
+THE ADVENTURES OF THE MARQUIS DE NOAILLES, AND MADEMOISELLE TENCIN. A Narrative founded on Truth, Translated from the French. In Two Volumes.
Dublin : Printed for W. Sleater at Pope's-Head on Cork-Hill, and J. Williams in Skinner-Row. 1764.
2 vols. 12mo.
Vol II tp has 'Wil. Sleater'.
1st edn, 1761 [628].
'By Felicité de Biron, pseud' BL.
CUL
* N/E

805.
THE AMOURS AND ADVENTURES OF CHARLES CARELESS, ESQ; Interspersed with a Variety of curious and entertaining Anecdotes; Critical and Moral Reflections, Droll and surprising Scenes; Familiar and interesting Descriptions; And some humourous and important Characters. Drawn from Real Life. In Two Volumes. Written by Himself.
London : Printed for James Fletcher and Co. in St. Paul's Church-Yard. 1764.
2 vols. 12mo. 6s (CR,MR).
CR XVII 479-480 (June 1764); MR XXX 328-329 (Apr. 1764).
AB(Backus); BB; CG(MR); LO 174 (UP)
Dublin edn, 1764 [806].
Bod UP
* N

806.
+THE AMOURS AND ADVENTURES OF CHARLES CARELESS, ESQ.
Dublin : H. Saunders [1764?] (adv-1767 [1084]).
2 vols. 4s4d.
Adv-1767 [1084].
1st edn, 1764 [805].
N

807.
CLEANTHES AND SEMANTHE. A Dramatic History. By the Author of Leonora. In Two
Volumes.
London : Printed for T. Davies in Russel-Street, Covent-Garden; and J. Fletcher, in St. Paul's
Church-yard. 1764.
2 vols in 1. 12mo. 6s (CR,MR).
CR XVIII 75-76 (July 1764); MR XXXI 159-160 (Aug. 1764).
BB; CG(BB,HU); FB; LO 176 (FB,HU).
HU
* N

808.
+THE DEVIL UPON CRUTCHES IN ENGLAND : OR NIGHT SCENES IN LONDON, A
Satirical Work Written upon the Plan of the celebrated Diable Boiteux of M. Le Sage. In
Two Parts. By a Gentleman of Oxford. The Sixth Edition.
London : Printed for F. Noble, opposite Gray's Inn Gate [1764] (LC).
CG.
1st edn of this version, and edns listed, 1755 [285].
LC
N

809.
+EACH SEX IN THEIR HUMOUR : Or, The Histories of the Families of Brightley, Finch,
Fortescue, Shelburne, and Stevens. Written by a Lady of Quality, Whilst she was abroad
on her Travels, and found among her Papers, since her Decease. In Two Volumes.
Dublin : Printed for P. Wilson, S. Price, and J. Potts, Booksellers, in Dame-street. 1764.
2 vols in 1. 12mo.
1st edn, 1763 [758].
YU
N

810.
THE HISTORY OF EMILY WILLIS, A Natural Daughter, Very Entertaining.
Dublin : 'Lately published by James Williams, Bookseller at the Paper and Parchment Ware-
House in Skinner-Row near Fishamble-Street [?1764) (adv-1764 [804]).
2s8½d bound.
Adv - 1764 [804].
By the same author, *Memoirs of a Coquet*, 1765 [889].
'Third' edn, 1768 [1183].
N

811.
THE HISTORY OF MISS CHARLOTTE SEYMOUR. In Two Volumes.
London : Burnet. 1764.
2 vols. 12mo. 5s sewed (MR).
CR XVII 309 (Apr. 1764); MR XXX 244 (Mar. 1764).
BB(erroneously as 1754); CG(MR).
N

812.
THE HISTORY OF MISS LUCINDA COURTNEY; In a Series of Original Letters,
Written by Herself, To her Friend Miss Constantia Bellmour. In Three Volumes.
London : Printed by W. Hoggard, For Francis Noble, at his Circulating Library, opposite Gray's-
Inn-Gate, Holborn : and John Noble, at his Circulating Library, in St. Martin's Court near
Leicester Square [1764?] (YU).
3 vols. 12mo. 9s bound (tp).
CR XVIII 350-353 (Nov. 1764); MR XXXI 398 (Nov. 1764).
AB(ELG); BB; CG(GM Nov, 1767); LO 179 (YU).
YU
* E

813.
+THE HISTORY OF MISS LUCINDA COURTNEY; In a Series of Original Letters,
Written by Herself, To her Friend Miss Constantia Bellmour. In Three Volumes..
Dublin : Printed for A. Leathley, J. Hoey, senior, P. Wilson, H. Saunders, S. Cotter, E. Watts, J.
Hoey, junior, J. Potts, S. Watson, J. Williams, and J. Sheppard. 1764.
3 vols. 12mo.
ESTC t084640.
BL
* E

814.
THE HISTORY OF MISS OAKLEY.
London : Printed for the Author. 1764.
And sold by Bladon (CR,MR).
95pp. 12mo. 2s sewed (CR/MR).
CR XVII 400 (May 1764); MR XXX 488 (June 1764).
BB; CG as 2 vols; FB; LO 180 (FB,YU).
YU
* E

815.
THE HISTORY OF SOPHRONIA, A Novel Founded on Truth.
Dublin : 'Lately published by James Williams, Bookseller at the Paper and Parchment Ware-
House in Skinner-Row near Fishamble-Street [?1764] (adv-1764 [804]).
2s8½d bound.
Adv-1764 [804].
Possibly a piracy of Sophronia, 1761 [639].
E?

816.
THE LOVES OF CHÆREAS AND CALLIRRHOE. Written originally in Greek By
Chariton of Aphrodisios. Now first translated into English. In Two Volumes.
London : Printed for T. Becket and P. A. De Hondt, in the Strand. 1764.
2 vols. 8vo. 5s sewed (MR) 6s (CR).
CR XVII 37-39 (Jan. 1764); MR XXX 61-63 (Jan. 1764).
BB; AB(BB,GBF,Pi); CG(BB,MR,BL); ESTC t069302.
BL Bod
* N

817.
MEMOIRS OF ****, COMMONLY KNOWN BY THE NAME OF GEORGE
PSALMANAZAR; A Reputed Native of Formosa. Written by himself in order to be
published after his Death. Containing an Account of his Education, Travels, Adventures,
Connections, Literary Productions, and Pretended conversion from Heathenism to
Christianity.
London : Printed for the Executrix. Sold by R. Davis, in Piccadilly; J. Newbery, in St. Paul's
Church-Yard; L. Davis, and C. Reymers in Holborn. 1764.
364pp. 8vo. 4s sewed (MR) 5s (CR).
CR XVII 366-371 (Nov. 1764); MR XXI 364-385 (Nov. 1764).
BB; ESTC t066823.
The work is often associated with Goldsmith, TS, pp.121-123. Cf *An Enquiry into the Objections against*
George Psalmanazar, London 1710. Also, 1765 [887] [888].
BL Bod CUL
* N/M

818.
THE MEMOIRS OF MISS D'ARVILLE, OR THE ITALIAN FEMALE PHILOSOPHER.
In a Series of Adventures founded on Fact. Translated from the Italian.
London : Printed for J. Pridden and T. Jones. 1764.
2 vols. 12mo. 5s sewed (BB,CR,MR).
CR XIX 160 (Feb, 1765); MR XXX 243 (Mar. 1764).
AB(Lowe); BB; CG.
2nd edn, 1764 [819].
BU
N

819.
+THE MEMOIRS OF MISS D'ARVILLE, OR THE ITALIAN FEMALE PHILOSOPHER.
In a Series of Adventures founded on Fact. Translated from the Italian. The Second
Edition.
London : Printed for J. Pridden and T. Jones. 1764.
2 vols. 12mo.
1st edn, 1764 [818].
DU UM
N

820.
MEMOIRS OF THE CHEVALIER PIERPOINT.
Volumes III and IV.
London : Printed for R. and J. Dodsley. 1764.
12mo. 4s sewed (MR) 5s (CR).
Revs of vols III & IV, CR XVII 478-479 (June 1764); MR XXX 244 (Mar. 1764).
1st 2 vols, 1763 [763]. Dublin edn, 1765 [890].
BL Bod
N

821.
(+)MEMOIRS OF THE PRINCESS OF MONPENSIER, AND THE DUKE OF BALAFRE.
Translated from the French.
London : Printed for, and Sold by J. Wilkie, at the Bible in St. Paul's Church Yard. 1764.
158pp. 12mo. 2s sewed (CR,MR)
CR XVIII 157-158 (Aug. 1764); MR XXX 489 (June 1764).
CG(MR).
Original edn, 1675.
CUL
* N/M

822.
THE ORIENTALIST : A Volume of Tales After The Eastern Taste. By the Author of
Roderick Random, Sir Launcelot Greaves, &c And Others.
Dublin : Printed by James Hoey, junior. 1764.
281pp. 12mo.
MW refs, p.96.
Not by Smollett.
CUL
* C

823.
THE RISE AND SURPRIZING ADVENTURES OF DONALD M'GREGOR. A Novel. In
Two Volumes.
London : Williams. 1764.
2 vols. 8vo. 4s (CR,MR).
CR XVII 478 (June 1764); MR XXX 488 (June 1764).
BB; CG(MR).
2nd edn, 1765 [894].
N

824.
[BROOKE Mrs Frances Moore]
+THE HISTORY OF LADY JULIA MANDEVILLE. In Two Volumes. By the Translator
of Lady Catesby's Letters. The Third Edition.
London : Printed for R. and J. Dodsley in Pall-Mall. 1764.
2 vols. 12mo.
1st edn and edns listed, 1763 [769].
ULPA UNC
E

825.
[BROOKE Mrs Frances Moore]
(+)THE OLD MAID. By Mary Singleton, Spinster. A New Edition, Revised and corrected
by the Editor.
London : Printed for A. Millar in the Strand. 1764.
304pp. 12mo. 3s (CR).
CR XVII 398-399 (May 1764).
ESTC t135042; LO 175 (UP)
First issued in a periodical paper of 37 no's, 1755-56.
BL BU CUL NYPL UM UP
* E

826.
[CHETWOOD William Rufus]
+THE VOYAGES, DANGEROUS ADVENTURES, AND IMMINENT ESCAPES OF
CAPT. RICHARD FALCONER. The Fifth Edition, Corrected.
London : Printed for G. Keith. 1764.
PBG p.228.
1st edn, 1719-20. Edns listed, 1752 [126].
N

827.
[CLELAND John]
THE SURPRIZES OF LOVE, EXEMPLIFIED IN THE ROMANCE OF A DAY, Or; an Adventure in Greenwich-Park, last Easter; the Romance of a Night, or, a Covent-garden Adventure; the second edition; with the Addition of two stories, never before in Print, entitled The Romance of a Morning; or, the Chance of a Sport; the Romance of an Evening, or, Who would have thought it?
London : Lowndes. 1764.
12mo. 2s6d sewed (CR) 3s (GM)
CR XVIII 480 (Dec. 1764).
CG(GM Dec. 1764).
Dublin edn, 1764 [828]. Also, 1765 [904]. Cf 1762 [704].
N

828.
[CLELAND John]
+THE SURPRIZES OF LOVE, EXEMPLIFIED IN THE ROMANCE OF A DAY, Or; an Adventure in Greenwich-Park, last Easter; the Romance of a Night, or, a Covent-Garden Adventure.
Dublin : Printed by James Hoey Jr. 1764.
1st edn, 1764 [827].
UV
N

829.
CRONZECK Cristoph Otto von Schoenaich, Baron
ARMINIUS : OR, GERMANIA FREED. Translated From the Third Edition of the German Original, Written by Baron Cronzeck. With an Historical and Critical Preface, By the Celebrated Gottsched of Leipsic.
London : Printed for T. Becket and P. A. De Hondt in the Strand; and W. Nicoll, in St. Paul's Church-yard. 1764.
2 vols. 8vo. 5s (BB,CR).
CR XVIII 253-360 (Nov. 1764).
AB(BB,RJ); BB; CG(-); ESTC t100452.
BL LC NYPL YU
* N/M

830.
[FAUQUES Marianne Agnés Pillement, Dame de]
+ABBASSAI : AN EASTERN TALE.
Dublin : Printed for J. Potts and J. Shepard. 1764.
2 vols in 1. 12mo.
McB 260.
1st English edn, 1759 [484].
NLC UI
N

831.
[FAUQUES Marianne Agnés Pillement, Dame de]
ORIENTAL ANECDOTES; OR, THE HISTORY OF HAROUN ALRACHID.
London : Printed for W. Nicoll and T. Durham. 1764.
2 vols. 12mo. 6s (CR,MR).
CR XVII 296-298 (Apr. 1764); MR XXXI 160 (Aug. 1764).
AB(LC); McB 261.
Dublin edn, 1764 [832].
LC UCB UI
N

832.
[FAUQUES Marianne Agnés Pillement, Dame de]
+ORIENTAL ANECDOTES; OR, THE HISTORY OF HAROUN ALRACHID.
Dublin : Printed for Peter Wilson, James Potts, Alex. M'Culloh and Jam. Williams. 1764.
2 vols in 1. 12mo.
CG; McB 262.
1st edn, 1764 [831].
CUL UI
* N

833.
[FÉNELON François de Salignac de La Mothe]
+THE ADVENTURES OF TELEMACHUS, THE SON OF ULYSSES.
Dublin : Printed for Peter Wilson. 1764.
444pp. 12mo.
ESTC t134909.
1st English edn, 1699. Edns listed, 1755 [312].
BL
N/M

834.
FIELDING Henry
+THE HISTORY OF THE ADVENTURES OF JOSEPH ANDREWS, AND HIS FRIEND,
MR. ABRAHAM ADAMS. Written in Imitation of The Manner of Cervantes, Author of
Don Quixote. By Henry Fielding, Esquire. The Seventh Edition, revised and corrected. In
Two Volumes.
London : Printed for A. Millar, in the Strand. 1764.
2 vols. 12mo.
CG(HU); ESTC t133839.
1st edn, 1742. Edns listed, 1751 [84].
BL Bod CUNY HU YU
* N

835.
[GENTLEMAN Francis]
A TRIP TO THE MOON. Containing an Account of the Island of Noibla. Its Inhabitants,
Religious and Political Customs, &c. By Sir Humphrey Lunatic, Bart.
York : Printed by A. Ward for S. Crowder in Pater-noster-Row; W. Bristow in St. Paul's
Church-Yard; J. Pridden and W. Griffin in Fleet-street; G. Burnet, in the Strand; G. Woodfall, at
Charing-Cross; and J. Johnson, opposite the Monument, London; C. Etherington, in York; and
W. Charnley, in Newcastle upon Tyne. 1764.
205pp. 8vo. 2s (BB,MR) 2s6d (CR).
CR XVII 429-432 (June 1764); MR XXX 354-358 (May 1764).
CG(BB); ESTC t124808.
2nd vol. issued 1765 [915]. 2nd edn, 1765 [916].
BL Bod FL UMin YU
* N

836.
[GIBBES Phoebe]
THE HISTORY OF LADY LOUISA STROUD, AND THE HONOURABLE MISS CAROLINE STRETTON. In Two Volumes.
London : Printed for, and Sold by, F. Noble, at his Circulating Library, opposite Gray's-Inn-Gate, Holborn : And J. Noble, at his Circulating Library, in St. Martin's Court, near Leicester Square. 1764.
2 vols. 12mo. 5s (BB,MR) 6s (CR).
CR XVII 307-308 (Apr. 1764); MR XXX 244 (Mar. 1764).
AB(BL); BB; CG(BL); EC 206:1; ESTC t066899; FB; LO 177 (BL,CR,FB).
Also, 1764 [837] [838].
BL
* E

837.
[GIBBES Phoebe]
+**THE HISTORY OF LADY LOUISA STROUD, AND THE HONOURABLE MISS CAROLINE STRETTON. In Two Volumes. The Second Edition.**
London : Printed for, and Sold by, F. Noble, at his Circulating Library, Opposite Gray's-Inn-Gate, Holborn : And J. Noble, at his Circulating Library, in St. Martin's Court, near Leicester Square. 1764.
2 vols. 12mo.
1st edn, 1764 [836].
UC UP YU
* E

838.
[GIBBES Phoebe]
+**THE HISTORY OF LADY LOUISA STROUD, AND THE HONOURABLE MISS CAROLINE STRETTON.**
Dublin : Printed for P. Wilson, J. Exshaw, H. Saunders [etc] 1764.
2 vols in 1.
newSG
1st edn, 1764 [836].
UP
E

839.
[GIBBES Phoebe]
THE LIFE AND ADVENTURES OF MR. FRANCIS CLIVE. In Two Volumes.
London : Printed for T. Lownds, at his Circulating Library, in Fleet-street. 1764.
2 vols. 12mo. 5s sewed (CR,MR).
CR XVII 307 (Apr. 1764); MR XXX 243-244 (Mar. 1764).
BB.
Dublin edn, 1764 [840].
CUL HU
* N

840.
[GIBBES Phoebe]
+**THE LIFE AND ADVENTURES OF MR. FRANCIS CLIVE. In Two Volumes.**
Dublin : Printed for E. Watts, J. Potts, A. M'Culloh and J. Williams. 1764.
2 vols. 12mo. Vol.II 'Printed for J. Exshaw, E. Watts, J. Potts, A. M'Culloh, and J. Williams'.
AB(Dublin edn, BL); CG(HU).
1st edn, 1764 [839].
CUL HU NLC
* N

841.
[GRIFFITH Richard]
[GRAFIGNY Françoise d'Issembourg d'Happoncourt de]
THE TRIUMVIRATE : OR, THE AUTHENTIC MEMOIRS OF A. B. AND C. In Two Volumes.
London : Printed for W. Johnston, in Ludgate-street. 1764.
2 vols. 12mo. 6s (MR).
CR XIX 235-237 (Mar, 1765); MR XXXII 316-317 (Apr, 1765).
AB(AR,RI); BB; EC 368:1; ESTC t077690; JT.
Dublin edn, 1764 [842].
BL BU HU IU LC NLC YU
* N

842.
[GRIFFITH Richard]
[GRAFIGNY Françoise d'Issembourg d'Happoncourt de]
+THE TRIUMVIRATE : OR, THE AUTHENTIC MEMOIRS OF A. B. AND C.
Dublin : H. Saunders [1764?] (adv-1767 [1084]).
2s8½d.
Adv-1767 [1084].
1st edn, 1764 [841].
N

843.
[GUEULETTE Thomas Simon]
[HUMPHREYS Samuel *trans.*]
+PERUVIAN TALES, Related in One Thousand and One Hours, By One of the Select Virgins of Cusco, to the Ynca of Peru, To dissuade him from a Resolution he had taken to destroy himself by Poison. Interspersed with Curious and Historical Remarks.
[3 more lines]
Translated from the Original French By Samuel Humphreys, Esq; In Three Volumes. The Fourth Edition.
London : Printed for Charles Rivington; And Sold by John Rivington, in St. Paul's Church-yard. 1764.
3 vols. 12mo.
Vol.III tp has 'Continued by John Kelly, Esq' not 'Translated... By Samuel Humphreys'.
CG(BL); ESTC t114268; McB 389.
1st English edn, 1734. Also, 1734, 1739, 1749, 1784, 1786.
BL UI LC NYPL
* N/C

844.
GUEULETTE Thomas Simon
FLLOYD Thomas *trans.*
+TARTARIAN TALES; Or, A Thousand and One Quarters of Hours. Written in French by the celebrated Mr. Gueuletee [sic], Author of the Chinese, Mogul and other Tales. With Historical and Geographical Notes. The Whole now for the first Time translated into English, By Thomas Flloyd.
Dublin : Printed for William Williamson, Bookseller, and Wholesale-Stationer, at Mecænas's-Head [sic] in Bride-Street. 1764.
318pp. 12mo.
CG; ESTC t131490.
1st edn and edns listed, 1759 [491].
BL
* N/C

845.
[HAYWOOD Mrs Eliza]
+THE CITY JILT : Or, The Alderman turn'd Beau. A Secret History.
London : Printed by T. Bailey, at the Ship and Crown, Leaden-hall street, where Tradesmens Bills are Printed at the Letter-press, and off Copper-plates *** Where Maredant's Antiscorbatic Drops are Sold at Six Shillings the Bottle, which Cures the most inveterate Scurvy, Leprosy, &c. [1764?] (BL).
56pp. 8vo.
ESTC t057429.
1st edn, 1726. Also, 1726(2x).
BL
* N/M

846.
[JOHNSTON Charles]
+CHRYSAL : OR, THE ADVENTURES OF A GUINEA. Wherein are exhibited Views of several striking Scenes, with Curious and Interesting Anecdotes of the Most Noted Persons in every Rank of Life, whose Hands it passed through, in America, England, Holland, Germany and Portugal. By an Adept. The Fourth Edition Greatly Enlarged and Corrected.
London : Printed for T. Becket, at Tully's Head, near Surry-Street, in the Strand. 1764.
2 vols. 12mo.
AB(ELG,RI); CG(HU); ESTC t119016; McB 496.
1st edn and edns listed, 1760 [577].
AAS BL HU UI YU
* N

847.
[KIMBER Edward]
MARIA : THE GENUINE MEMOIRS OF AN ADMIRED LADY OF RANK AND FORTUNE, And of Some of her Friends. In Two Volumes.
London : Printed for T. Baldwin, in Pater-noster-Row, and T. Lownds in Fleet-Street. 1764.
2 vols. 12mo. 4s sewed (BB,MR) 8vo 6s (CR).
CR XVIII 313 (Oct. 1764); MR XXX 243 (Mar. 1764).
BB; CG(MR).
Dublin edn, 1764 [848]. 2nd edn, 1765 [925].
N

848.
[KIMBER Edward]
+MARIA : THE GENUINE MEMOIRS OF AN ADMIRED LADY OF RANK AND FORTUNE, And of Some of her Friends.
Dublin : Printed for P. Wilson, H. Saunders [etc] 1764.
2 vols in 1. 8vo. 2s8½d (adv-1767 [1084] and 1764 [851]).
Adv-1764 [851] 1767 [1084]; CG(HU).
1st edn, 1764 [847].
HU UNC
N

849.
[LANGHORNE John]
+THE LETTERS THAT PASSED BETWEEN THEODOSIUS AND CONSTANTIA; AFTER SHE HAD TAKEN THE VEIL. The Third Edition.
London : Printed for T. Becket and P. A. De Hondt, in the Strand. 1764.
185pp. 12mo.
1st edn and edns listed, 1763 [778].
Bod YU
* E

850.
[LANGHORNE John]
+SOLYMAN AND ALMENA. An Oriental Tale. The Second Edition.
London : Printed for T. Becket. 1764.
198pp. 12mo.
1st edn and edns listed, 1762 [726].
LCP
N

851.
LENNOX Mrs Charlotte Ramsay
+THE HISTORY OF THE MARQUIS OF LUSSAN AND ISABELLA. By Mrs Lennox,
Author of the Female Quixote, and Sophia.
Dublin : Printed by James Hoey, Junior. 1764.
197pp. 12mo.
CG(-).
Bod YU
* N

852.
MARMONTEL [Jean François]
(+)MORAL TALES, BY M. MARMONTEL.
London : Printed for T. Becket and P. A. De Hondt, near Surry-Street, in the Strand. 1764.
2 vols. 5s (MR) 6s (CR).
CR XVII 43-49 (Jan. 1764); MR XXX 59-61 (Jan. 1764).
ESTC t090767; LO 181 (UP); CG (as Vol II).
1st English edn and edns listed, 1763 [784].
BL DU UP YU
* C

853.
MARMONTEL [Jean François]
DENIS Charles and LLOYD Robert *trans.*
(+)THE MORAL TALES OF M. MARMONTEL. Translated from the French by C. Denis
and R. Lloyd.
London : Printed for G. Kearsley. 1764.
2 vols. 5s (MR).
AB(as Denis & Lloyd trans. by Becket & De Hondt 1764); McB 637.
Noted in rev.s of other trans. of 1764 - [784].
UI
C

854.
[MINIFIE Susannah (later Gunning)]
FAMILY PICTURES, A NOVEL. Containing Curious and Interesting Memoirs of several
Persons of Fashion in W——re. By a Lady. In Two Volumes.
London : Printed for W. Nicoll, in St. Paul's Church-Yard; and T. Durham, in the Strand. 1764.
2 vols. 12mo. 4s sewed (MR) 5s (CR).
CR XVIII 313 (Oct. 1764); MR XXX 243 (Mar. 1764).
CG(HU); ESTC t125278; LO 178 (HU,UP)
Dublin edn, 1764 [855].
BL HU UP
* E

855.
[MINIFIE Susannah (later Gunning)]
+FAMILY PICTURES, A NOVEL. Containing Curious and Interesting Memoirs of several
Persons of Fashion in W——re. By a Lady. In Two Volumes.
Dublin : Printed for P. Wilson, J. Exshaw, S. Price, and J. Potts. 1764.
2 vols. 12mo.
AB(Bk); CG(HU).
1st edn, 1764 [854].
CUL HU UP
* E

856.
MINIFIE Margaret and Susannah
THE HISTORIES OF LADY FRANCES S—— AND LADY CAROLINE S——. Written
by the Miss Minifies Of Fairwater, in Somersetshire.
London : Printed for R. and J. Dodsley, in Pall-Mall. 1764.
Volume IV. 12mo. 3s (CR).
Rev of vol.IV, CR XVIII 158 (Aug. 1764).
Vols I-III, published 1763 [785].
E

857.
RICCOBONI Marie Jeanne
THE HISTORY OF MISS JENNY SALISBURY; Addressed to the Countess of
Roscommond. Translated from the French of the celebrated Madame Riccoboni. In Two
Volumes.
London : Printed for T. Becket and P. A. De Hondt, at Tully's Head, in the Strand. 1764.
2 vols. 12mo. 6s (CR,MR).
CR XVIII 313-314 (Oct. 1764); MR XXXI 475-478 (Dec. 1764).
BB; CG; EC 132:5; ESTC t133748; FB; LO 182 (FB,MR,Peabody); McB 750.
A trans. of *Histoire de Miss Jenny.* 1764.
Dublin edn, 1764 [858].
BL UI
* N

858.
RICCOBONI Marie Jeanne
+THE HISTORY OF MISS JENNY SALISBURY; Addressed to the Countess of
Roscommond. Translated from the French of the celebrated Madame Riccoboni.
Dublin : Printed for A. Leathley etc. nd.
Booksellers incl. H. Saunders (adv-1767 [1084]).
2 vols in 1. 2s8½d.
Adv-1767 [1084].
1st edn, 1764 [857].
Bod [as 1770?] UNC as [1760?]
N

859.
[RICCOBONI Marie Jeanne]
[BROOKE Mrs Frances Moore *trans.*]
+LETTERS FROM JULIET LADY CATESBY, To her Friend Lady Henrietta Campley.
Translated from the French. The Fourth Edition.
London : Printed for R. and J. Dodsley, in Pall-Mall. 1764.
CG; ESTC t066375.
1st edn and edns listed, 1759 [502].
BL CNY LC YU
* E

860.
RICHARDSON Samuel
+CLARISSA. OR, THE HISTORY OF A YOUNG LADY : Comprehending The most
Important Concerns of Private Life. By Mr. Richardson, Author of Pamela and Sir Charles
Grandison. In Eight Volumes. The Fifth Edition.
London : Printed for J. Rivington, in St. Paul's Church-yard; W. Johnston, in Ludgate-street; C.
Rivington, in Staining-lane; R. Withy, in Cornhill; J. Coote, and M. Richardson, in Paternoster-
row; and T. Lowndes, in Fleet-street. 1764.
8 vols. 12mo.
CG; ESTC t058972.
Vols II-VIII have additional title lines.
1st edn, 1747-48. Edns listed, 1751 [96].
BL Bod CUL DU UMo UCLA YU
* E

861.
[RICHARDSON Samuel]
+THE PATHS OF VIRTUE DELINEATED; OR, THE HISTORY IN MINIATURE OF
THE   CELEBRATED   PAMELA,   CLARISSA   HARLOW   AND   SIR   CHARLES
GRANDISON.
London : Printed for R. Baldwin and B. Collins. 1764.
239pp. 12mo.
CG(BC).
1st edn and edns listed, 1756 [377].
YU
N/C

862.
[RIDLEY James]
THE TALES OF THE GENII: OR, THE DELIGHTFUL LESSONS OF HORAM, SON
OF ASMAR. Faithfully Translated from the Persian Manuscript; and Compared with the
French and Spanish Editions Published at Paris and Madrid. By Sir Charles Morell,
Formerly Ambassador from the British Settlements in India to the Great Mogul.
London : Printed for J. Wilkie, in St. Paul's Church-Yard. 1764.
2 vols. 8vo. 'Published in numbers at 1s each' (MR) 6s (CR).
CR XVIII 34-41 (July 1764); MR XXXI 478-479 (Dec. 1764). Rev. of vol II, CR XIX 136-137
(Feb, 1765).
BB; CG(BL); EC 202:2; ESTC t070073; LO 183 (UI,UP); McB 762.
Also, 1764 [863] [863a], 1765 [937], 1766 [1035], 1770, 1780(2x), 1786, 1793, 1794.
BL Bod DU HU NLC PU UCLA UI UNC YU
* C

863.
[RIDLEY James]
+THE TALES OF THE GENII: OR THE DELIGHTFUL LESSONS OF HORSAM, THE
SON OF ASMAR. Faithfully translated from the Persian Manuscript and Compared with
the French and Spanish editions published at Paris and Madrid. By Sir Charles Morell.
The Second Edition.
London : Printed for J. Wilkie. 1764.
2 vols. 8vo.
CG.
1st edn and edns listed, 1764 [862].
UF UW
N/C

863a.
[RIDLEY James]
+THE TALES OF THE GENII : OR THE DELIGHTFUL LESSONS OF HORSAM, THE SON OF ASMAR.
Dublin : Printed for and sold by James Hoey Junior. [?1764] (adv-1764 [851]).
6s6d sewed 8s1½d bound (adv-1764 [851]).
Adv-1764 [851].
1st edn and edns listed, 1764 [862].
N/C

864.
[ROUSSEAU Jean Jacques]
[KENRICK William *trans.*]
+ELOISA : Or, a Series of Original Letters Collected and published By J. J. Rousseau. Translated from the French. In Four Volumes. The Third Edition.
London : Printed for T. Becket and P. A. De Hondt, at Tully's Head, in the Strand. 1764.
4 vols. 12mo.
ESTC t136475; McB 778.
1st edn and edns listed, 1761 [666].
BL HU NLC UCLA UI
* E

865.
[le SAGE Alain René]
[SMOLLETT Tobias *trans.*]
+THE HISTORY AND ADVENTURES OF GIL BLAS OF SANTILLANE. In Four Volumes.
Edinburgh : Printed by A. Donaldson and J. Reid. For A. Donaldson, and J. Wood. 1764.
4 vols. 12mo.
ESTC t130464.
1st edn, 1749. Edns listed, 1750 [36].
BL
* N

866.
[SCOTT Mrs Sarah Robinson and
MONTAGU Lady Barbara]
+A DESCRIPTION OF MILLENIUM HALL, AND THE COUNTRY ADJACENT : Together with the Characters of the Inhabitants, And such Historical Anecdotes and Reflections as May excite in the Reader proper Sentiments of Humanity, and lead the Mind to the Love of Virtue. By a Gentleman on his Travels. The Second Edition Corrected.
London : Printed for J. Newbery, at the Bible and Sun in St. Paul's Church-Yard. 1764.
264pp. 12mo.
BB; CG; ESTC t070076; LO 184 (citing YU which is 1762).
1st edn and edns listed, 1762 [736].
BL Bod CUL
* N

867
[SCOTT Mrs Sarah Robinson and
MONTAGU Lady Barbara]
+A DESCRIPTION OF MILLENIUM HALL, AND THE COUNTRY ADJACENT :
Together with the Characters of the Inhabitants, And such Historical Anecdotes and
Reflections, As May excite in the Reader proper Sentiments of Humanity, and lead the
Mind to the Love of Virtue. By A Gentleman on his Travels. The Second Edition.
Dublin : Printed for Peter Wilson, in Dame-street. 1764.
282pp. 12mo.
1st edn and edns listed, 1762 [736].
CUL
* N

868.
[WALPOLE Horace]
THE CASTLE OF OTRANTO, A STORY. Translated by William Marshal, Gent. From
the Original Italian of Onuphrio Muralto Canon of the Church of St. Nicholas at Otranto.
London : Printed for Tho. Lownds in Fleet-Street, 1765 [1764].
200pp. 8vo. 3s (CR).
CR XIX 50-51 (Jan, 1765).
ESTC t063198; ATH p.52.
Published, 24 Dec. 1764, ATH. Also, 1765 [943] [944] [945] [946], 1766 [1041], 1769 [1347], 1782, 1786,
1791(2x), 1793, 1795, 1796, 1797, 1800.
BL Bod FL HU LWL IU NLC UI UV YU
* N

869.
WOODFIN Mrs A.
THE DISCOVERY : OR, MEMOIRS OF MISS MARIANNE MIDDLETON. By Mrs
Woodfin, Author of Harriot Watson, Sally Sable, and of The Auction, a Modern Novel. In
Two Volumes.
London : Printed for T. Lownds, at his Circulating Library in Fleet-street. 1764.
2 vols. 12mo. 5s sewed (CR) 6s (MR).
CR XVII 398 (May 1764); MR XXX 488-489 (June 1764).
AB(BL,SA); BB; CG(BB); EC 199:6; ESTC t068567; LO 186 (UP).
Dublin edn, 1764 [870].
BL NLC UP
* N

870.
[WOODFIN Mrs A.]
+THE DISCOVERY; OR, MEMOIRS OF MISS MARIANNE MIDDLETON.
Dublin : W. Smith. 1764.
2 vols in 1. 135pp.
CG.   1st edn, 1764 [869].
N

Miscellanies

871.
The New Story-Teller : or, Universal Entertainer. Being a certain Method to cast off Care, an infallible
cordial for low-spirits, and a Help to Conversation. By Thomas Tell-Tale, Esq. In Two Volumes.
Dublin : Printed for James Hoey, Junior [1764?]. (adv-1764 [822]).
2 vols. 4s4d sewed 5s5d bound. Adv-1764 [822].
Also, 1782 edn (BL).
M

872.
The School of Virtue, or Polite Novelist. Consisting of Novels, Tales, Fables, Allegories, &c &c, Moral and Entertaining in Prose and Verse.
London : Cooke. 1764.
12mo. 2s (BB,MR).
MR XXXI 399 (Nov. 1764).
AB(CB, and as printed by E. Sumpter, 1763); BB; CG(-).
C

873.
+Select Fables of Esop and Other Fabulists. In Three Books.
London : Printed by John Baskerville, for R. and J. Dodsley in Pall-mall. 1764.
186pp. 12mo.
CG(BL); ESTC t084993.
Dodsley edn 1st published, 1761 [690]. Other edns listed, 1753 [199].
BL Bn CUL HU IU NYPL YU
* M/C

874.
[Goudar Ange de]
The Chinese Spy, or Secret Envoy from the Court of Pekin, to examine into the present State of Europe. Translated from the Chinese.
London : Printed for T. Becket and P. A. De Hondt. 1764.
6 vols. 8vo. 18s (BB).
MR XXXI 534-538 (App. 1764ii).
AB(ELG).
Later ref. in MR XXXIII 165-167 suggests this is an edn in French, but original rev. does not say so.
Cf 1751 [107]. Also, 1765 [962], 1766 [1052].
M

875.
[Hughes John trans.]
+Letters of Abelard and Heloise. Extracted Chiefly from Monsieur Bayle.
London : 1764.
1st English edn, 1718. Edns listed, 1751 [112].
RU
M/E

876.
[Lesuire Robert Martin]
[Andrews J. P.trans.]
The Savages of Europe. From the French.
London : Printed by D. Leach for T. Davies. 1764.
144pp. 12mo.
A trans. of Les Sauvages de l'Europe, Berlin 1760. Dublin edn, 1764 [877].
HU LC PU Tx UI UP YU
M (sat)

877.
[Lesuire Robert Martin]
[Andrews J. P.trans.]
+The Savages of Europe. From the French.
Dublin : Printed for P. Wilson, J. Hoey, Jun. J. Potts, A. M'Cullogh and J. Williams. 1764.
120pp. 12mo.
1st edn, 1764 [876].
CUL
* M (sat)

878.
Limbourg Jean Philippe de
New Amusements of the German Spa. Written in French, in the Year 1763, By J. P. De Limbourg, M.D.
[5 more lines]
London : Printed for L. Davis and C. Reymers, in Holborn; W. Owen, near Temple-Bar; W. Sandby, against St. Dunstan's Church, Fleet Street; and R. Baldwin, in Pater-Noster-Row. 1764.
2 vols. 12mo. Vol.II tp, 'To which are added Novels, Containing Certain Histories, Anecdotes and Adventures'.
ESTC t110523.
Dublin edn, 1765 [964].
BL PU UC UNC YU
* M

879.
[Rowe Mrs Elizabeth Singer]
+**Friendship in Death : In Twenty Letters from the Dead to the Living. To which are added, Letters Moral and Entertaining, in Prose and Verse : In Three Parts.**
Glasgow : Printed for Robert Aitken, Bookseller in Paisley. 1764.
292pp. 8vo.
1st edn, 1728. Edns listed, 1750 [60].
Provincial Library, Victoria, BC Canada. DU has 1764 286pp. copy.
M

880.
[Stewardson William]
Spiritual Courtship; or the Rival Quakeresses. A True Narrative in Westminster.
1764.
CG(-). Haverford College, PA.
M

1765

881.
+**EASTERN STORIES.**
Belfast : Joy (CG).
CG.
C/M

882.
THE FRUIT-SHOP, A TALE.
London : Printed for C. Moran, in Covent Garden. 1765.
2 vols. 8vo(BL)/12mo(CG,MR). 4s sewed (CR) 5s (MR).
CR XIX 475 (June 1765); MR XXXIII 86 (July 1765).
AB(Ashbee Collection); CG(MR); ESTC t106047.
Also, 1765 [883].
BL
* N

883.
+**THE FRUIT SHOP, A TALE.**
Dublin : 1765.
12mo (CG).
CG has Dublin edn of 1765 by Thomas Peach. 1st edn, 1765 [882].
N

884.
THE HISTORY OF MISS INDIANA DANBY. In Two Volumes. By a Lady.
London : Printed for J. Dodsley, in Pall-mall. 1765.
2 vols. 12mo (BB,MR). 5s (CR) 6s (BB,MR).
CR XIX 467-469 (June 1765); MR XXXII 480-481 (June 1765).
BB; AB(BL,ELG); CG(HU); FB; JT; LO 190 (FB,HU).
Dublin edn, 1765 [885]. Vols III & IV published 1767 [1071]. Also, 1772.
By the author of *Eliza*, 1766 [975].
BL Bn HU PU UCLA YU
* E

885.
+THE HISTORY OF MISS INDIANA DANBY. By a Lady.
Dublin : Printed for J. Hoey, H. Saunders etc. 1765.
2 vol. 3s3d bound (adv-1767 [1084]).
Adv-1767 [1084]; CG(HU).
1st edn, 1765 [884].
HU
E

886.
LOVE IN HIGH LIFE; OR THE AMOURS OF A COURT.
London : Printed for T. Knowles, next the Chapter-House in St. Paul's Church-Yard. n.d. [BL
has ?1760, but rev.s suggest 1765].
189pp. 12mo. 2s6d (MR,CR,BB).
CR XIX 476 (June 1765); MR XXXII 235 (Mar. 1765).
BB; CG(MR); ESTC t066910.
BL FL
* N

887.
+MEMOIRS OF ** COMMONLY KNOWN BY THE NAME OF GEORGE
PSALMANAZAR; A Reputed Native of Formosa. Written by himself, In order to be
published after his Death :**
[7 more lines]
The Second Edition.
London : Printed for R. Davies, in Piccadilly, J. Newbery in St. Paul's Church-Yard, L. Davis
and C. Reymers, in Holborn. 1765.
307pp. 8vo (BB).
BB; ESTC t136711.
1st edn, 1764 [817].
BL Bod CUL DU HU LC NLC NYPL PU UC UI UP UV UW YU
* N/M

888.
+MEMOIRS OF ** COMMONLY KNOWN BY THE NAME OF GEORGE
PSALMANAZAR; A Reputed Native of Formosa. Written by himself. In Order to be
published after his Death.**
[8 more lines]
Dublin : Printed for P. Wilson, J. Exshaw, E. Watts, S. Cotter, J. Potts, and J. Williams. 1765.
234pp. 12mo.
CG; ESTC t136712; TS p.122-123 (Goldsmith association).
1st edn, 1764 [817].
BL CUL UI WCL
* N/M

889.
MEMOIRS OF A COQUET; OR, THE HISTORY OF MISS HARRIOT AIRY By the
Author of Emily Willis, Or the History of a Natural Daughter.
London : Printed by W. Hoggard for Francis Noble and John Noble. 1765.
195pp. 8vo. 3s (CR,MR).
CR XIX 236 (Mar. 1765); MR XXXII 394 (May 1765).
AB(BL,Pi); CG(BL,HU); ESTC t074447.
BL HU [missing] NLC OU UP
* N

890.
+MEMOIRS OF THE CHEVALIER PIERPOINT, AND THE COUNTESS MELESINDA.
In Four Volumes.
Dublin : Printed by J. Potts, at Swift's-Head in Dame-Street. 1765.
4 vols. 12mo.
ESTC t119318.
1st edns of the vols, 1763 [763] and 1764 [820].
BL
* N

891.
NUTREBIAN TALES, Or the Strange and Surprising Adventures Of A Captive Queen,
Wonderful Deliverance of her Children; Curious Metamorphosis of a Monkey, Butterfly,
&c. Anecdotes of a Convent, History of the Prince de Barnaville and the Count. The whole
Interspersed with many entertaining Amours and Secret Histories. In Two Volumes.
London : Printed for R. Dodsley, Pall-Mall. 1765.
2 vols. 12mo.
CG(HU); ESTC t057811.
BL HU NYSL
* C/M

892.
THE PARASITE.
London : Burnet. 1765.
2 vols. 12mo (BB). 5s sewed (MR,BB) 6s6d (CR).
CR XIX 236 (Mar. 1765); MR XXXII 235 (Mar. 1765).
BB.
Dublin edn, 1765 [893].
N

893.
+THE PARASITE.
Dublin : Printed for P. Wilson, J. Exshaw, S. Cotter, H. Saunders, E. Watts, J. Potts, and J.
Williams. 1765.
2 vols in 1. 228pp. 8vo.
AB(EM); CG(BL); EC 334:5; ESTC t067640.
Final page of vol.II states 'End of Vol II' not 'Finis'.
1st edn, 1765 [892].
BL UP YU
* N

894.
+THE RISE AND SURPRISING ADVENTURES OF DONALD M'GREGOR A Novel. The Second Edition.
London : Printed for J. Williams, next the Mitre-Tavern, Fleet-Street. 1765.
102pp. 12mo.
LO 194 (UP).
1st edn, 1764 [823].
UP
* N

895.
+THE UNFORTUNATE LOVERS : The History of Argalus and Parthenia. In Four Books. Adorn'd with Cuts.
London : Printed for Henry Woodgate, and Samuel Brooks, at the Golden-Ball, in Pater-noster-Row [1765] (BL).
119pp. 12mo.
1st edn, 1700. Edns listed, 1760 [555].
BL
* N/M

896.
THE WANDERER : OR, MEMOIRS OF CHARLES SEARLE, ESQ; Containing His Adventures by Sea and Land. With Many remarkable Characters, and interesting Situations in Real Life; and a variety of surprizing Incidents. In Two Volumes.
London : Printed for T. Lowndes, at his Circulating Library, in Fleet-street, 1766 [1765].
2 vols. 12mo. 5s sewed (CR) 6s (MR,BB).
CR XX 476 (Dec. 1765); MR XXXIII 490 (Dec. 1765).
BB; CG(MR); ESTC t116560; LO 207 (UP,BL); PBG p.355.
Dublin edn, 1766 [989].
BL UP
* N

897.
THE WILTSHIRE BEAU : OR, THE LIFE AND ADVENTURES OF BEN BARNARD.
London : Moran (MR) or Nicoll (CR) 1765.
2 vols 12mo. 5s (CR) 6s bound (MR).
CR XIX 471 (June 1765); MR XXXII 394 (May 1765).
AB(ELG); CG(GM Mar. 1765).
N

898.
[BEHN Mrs Aphra]
+LOVE-LETTERS BETWEEN A NOBLEMAN AND HIS SISTER. With the History of their Adventures. In Three Parts. The Eighth Edition.
London : Printed for L. Hawes and Co. S. Crowder, W. Johnston, B. Law, and R. Withy. 1765.
2 vols. 12mo.
tp of vol II has 'The Amours of Philander and Sylvia : Being the third and last Part of Love-Letters between a Nobleman and his Sister. To which is added, The Trial of Ford Lord Grey. The Eighth Edition'.
CG(BL); ESTC t071304.
1st edn, 1684. Edns listed, 1759 [477].
BL
* E

899.
[BROOKE Mrs Frances Moore]
+THE HISTORY OF LADY JULIA MANDEVILLE. In Two Volumes. By the Translator
of Lady Catesby's Letters. The Fourth Edition.
London : Printed for J. Dodsley, in Pall-Mall. 1765.
2 vols 12mo.
CG; ESTC t071300.
1st edn and edns listed, 1763 [769].
BL NLC UF UP
* E

900.
CERVANTES SAAVEDRA Miguel de
SMOLLETT Tobias *trans.*
+THE HISTORY AND ADVENTURES OF THE RENOWNED DON QUIXOTE.
Translated from the Spanish of Miguel de Cervantes Saavedra. To which is prefixed, Some
Account of the Author's Life. By T. Smollett, M.D. Illustrated with Twenty-eight new
Copper-Plates, designed by Hayman, and elegantly engraved. The Third Edition, Corrected.
In Four Volumes.
London : Printed for T. Osborne, C. Hitch and L. Hawes, A. Millar, H. Woodfall, John
Rivington, R. Baldwin, S. Crowder, T. Longman, T. Lowndes, T. Caslon, J. Knox, and
Richardson and Urquhart. 1765.
4 vols. 12mo.
CG(BL); ESTC t059494; MW 605.
1st Smollett trans. and edns listed, 1755 [302].
BL HU LC NLC UIC YU
* N

901.
CERVANTES SAAVEDRA Miguel de
SMOLLETT Tobias *trans.*
+THE HISTORY AND ADVENTURES OF THE RENOWNED DON QUIXOTE.
Translated from the Spanish of Miguel de Cervantes Saavedra. To which is prefixed, Some
Account of the Author's Life. By T. Smollett, M.D.
London : Printed for the Proprietors and Sold by All Booksellers in Town and Country. 1765.
MW 606.
1st Smollett trans. and edns listed, 1755 [302].
N

902.
[CHETWOOD William Rufus]
+THE VOYAGES AND ADVENTURES OF CAPTAIN ROBERT BOYLE, In several Parts
of the World. [8 more lines] The Seventh Edition.
Dublin : Printed for Peter Wilson, in Dame street, and Elizabeth Watts, in Skinner-row. 1765.
264pp. 12mo.
CG(BL)
1st edn, 1726. Edns listed, 1759 [478].
BL [unlocated] CUL
* N

903.
[CHETWOOD William Rufus]
+THE VOYAGES, DANGEROUS ADVENTURES AND MIRACULOUS ESCAPES OF
CAPT. RICHARD FALCONER.
Manchester : 1765.
1st edn, 1719-20. Edns listed, 1752 [126]
N

904.
[CLELAND John]
(+)THE SURPRIZES OF LOVE, Exemplified in the Romance of a Day and the Romance
of a Night. The Second Edition; with the Addition of Two Stories, never before in Print,
entitled, The Romance of a Morning, and the Romance of an Evening.
London : Printed for T. Lownds and W. Nicoll. 1765.
274pp. 12mo. 3s (MR).
MR XXXII 156-157 (Feb. 1765).
AB(L); McB 877; LO 196 (UP,UI).
1st edn and edns listed, 1764 [827].
HL FL IU LC OU UI UP
N

905.
[COLLYER Mrs Mary]
+FELICIA TO CHARLOTTE : BEING LETTERS FROM A YOUNG LADY IN THE
COUNTRY TO HER FRIEND IN TOWN. Containing A Series of the most interesting
Events, interspersed with Moral Reflections, Chiefly tending to prove that the Seeds of
Virtue are implanted in the Mind of every Reasonable Being. In Two Volumes. By the
Editor of the Death of Abel.
Dublin : Printed for D. Chamberlain, in Dame-street; and J. Williams in Skinner-row. 1765.
171pp. 8vo.
1st edn, 1744. Edns listed, 1755 [308].
Bod
* E

906.
CROXALL Samuel
THE NOVELLIST : OR, TEA-TABLE MISCELLANY. Containing the Select Novels of Dr.
Croxall; With other Polite Tales, and Pieces of Modern Entertainment. The whole designed
for Instruction and Amusement. Ornamented with Cuts. In Two Volumes.
London : Printed for T. Lownds, in Fleet-Street, 1766 [1765].
2 vols. 12mo. 6s (CR,MR).
CR XX 400 (Nov. 1765); MR XXXIII 491 (Dec. 1765).
CG; ESTC t128555.   Cf 1769 [1306].
BL LC NLC PU UC
* C

907.
[DEFOE Daniel]
+THE LIFE AND ADVENTURES OF ROXANA, THE FORTUNATE MISTRESS, OR,
MOST UNHAPPY WIFE. In Three Parts [19 more lines]
London : Printed for S. Crowder, in Pater-noster Row, and S. Gamidge, in Worcester. 1765.
144pp. 12mo.
CG; EC 1:3; ESTC t070633.
An abridgment of 1st edn of 1742. Edns listed, 1750 [21].
BL
* N

908.
[DEFOE Daniel]
+THE LIFE AND ADVENTURES OF THE FAMOUS MOLL FLANDERS [&c.]
London : Printed for J. Cooke. 1765.
358pp. 16mo.
1st edn, 1721-2. Edns listed, 1750 [20].
NYPL
N

909.
[DEFOE Daniel]
+THE LIFE AND MOST SURPRISING ADVENTURES OF ROBINSON CRUSOE, OF
YORK, MARINER [7 more lines] The Ninth Edition.
Birmingham : Printed by J. Sketchley, Auctioneer, &c. [1765] (BL).
408pp. 12mo.
EC 53:4; ESTC t072307.
1st edn, 1719-20. Edns listed, 1752 [129].
BL
* N/M

910.
[DEFOE Daniel]
+THE LIFE AND MOST SURPRISING ADVENTURES OF ROBINSON CRUSOE, OF
YORK, MARINER; Who lived eight and twenty years in an uninhabited island on the
coast of America, near the mouth of the great river Oroonoque. With an account of his
deliverance thence, and his after surprising adventures. The Eighth Edition.
Edinburgh : Printed for A. Donaldson and J. Reid : For Alexander Donaldson, and sold at his
shops in London and Edinburgh. 1765.
328pp. 12mo.
ESTC t072306.
1st edn, 1719-20. Edns listed, 1752 [129]. A further edn, *The Wonderful Life*, formerly attributed to 1765, now
dated c.1770.
BL YU
* N/M

911.
ÉLIE DE BEAUMONT Marie Anne Louise Morin-Dumesnil
THE HISTORY OF THE MARQUIS DE ROSELLE. In a Series of Letters. By Madam
Elie de Beaumont. Translated from the French. In Two Volumes.
London : Printed for T. Becket and P. A. De Hondt in the Strand. 1765.
2 vols. 12mo. 5s (MR) 6s (CR).
CR XIX 350-354 (May 1765); MR XXI 515-522 (App. 1764ii) & MR XXXII 480 (June 1765).
AB(BL,LC,McL); CG(BL,HU); EC 60:3; ESTC t107004; LO 187 (FB,HU,UI); McB 249.
Dublin edn, 1765 [912]. 2nd edn, 1766 [1003].
BL Bod HU LC OU UCB UI
* E

912.
ÉLIE DE BEAUMONT Marie Anne Louise Morin-Dumesnil
+THE HISTORY OF THE MARQUIS DE ROSELLE.
Dublin : H. Saunders [1765?] (adv-1767 [1084]).
3s3d
Adv-1767 [1084].
1st edn, 1765 [911].
E

913.
[FÉNELON François de Salignac de La Mothe]
+THE ADVENTURES OF TELEMACHUS, THE SON OF ULYSSES, Written by The
Archbishop of Cambray : A New Translation. In Two Volumes.
Berwick : Printed for R. Taylor. 1765.
2 vols in 1. 215pp. 12mo.
ESTC t139009.
1st English edn, 1699. Edns listed, 1755 [312].
BL CUL
* N/M

914.
FIELDING Henry
+THE HISTORY OF TOM JONES, A FOUNDLING. By Henry Fielding, Esq:
London : Printed for A. Millar, over-against Catherine-street in the Strand. 1765.
4(?) vols. 12mo.
CG; ESTC t142205.
1st edn, 1749. Edns listed, 1750 [24].
BL [imperf] HU UI YU
* N

915.
[GENTLEMAN Francis]
A TRIP TO THE MOON. Containing an Account of the Island of Noibla, Its Inhabitants,
Religious and Political Customs, &c. By Sir Humphrey Lunatic, Bart. Volume II.
London : Printed for S. Crowder, in Pater-noster-Row; W. Nicoll, and W. Bristow, in St. Paul's
Church-Yard; and C.Etherington, in York. 1765.
242pp. 12mo. 2s6d (vol II, CR,MR).
Rev of vol II, CR XIX 137-139 (Feb. 1765); MR XXXII 159 (Feb. 1765).
ESTC t139565.
Vol. I published 1764 [835].
BL NLC
* N

916.
[GENTLEMAN Francis]
+A TRIP TO THE MOON. Containing an Account of the Island of Noibla, Its Inhabitants,
Religious and Political Customs, &c. By Sir Humphrey Lunatic, Bart. The Second Edition.
London : Printed for S. Crowder, in Pater-noster-Row; W. Nicoll, and W. Bristow, in St. Paul's
Church-Yard; and C.Etherington, in York. 1765.
2 vols. 12mo.
'Undoubtedly... printed by Ann Ward [of York]', KM p.20.
CG.
1st edn of each vol, 1764 [835] and 1765 [915].
CUL UM UNC YU
* N

917.
GOMEZ Madeleine Angélique Poisson de
[HAYWOOD Mrs Eliza trans.]
+LA BELLE ASSEMBLÉE : Being a Curious Collection of Some Very Remarkable
Incidents Which happen'd to Persons of the First Quality in France.
[6 more lines]
By Madam de Gomez. Adorn'd with Copper-Plates. In Four Volumes. The Eighth Edition.
London : Printed for H. Woodfall, W. Strahan, J. Rivington, R. Baldwin, W. Johnston, C.
Rivington, R. Horsfield, G. Keith, W. Nichols, C. and R. Ware, M. Richardson, J. and T. Pote,
and T. Burnet. 1765.
4 vols. 12mo.
McB 369.
1st English edn, 1725. Edns listed, 1754 [239].
CUL LC UI
* N/M

918.
[GUÉRIN DE TENCIN Madame Claudine Alexandrine]
THE FEMALE ADVENTURERS. A Novel, In Two Volumes.
London : Printed for M. Folingsby and J. Wilkie. 1765 (MR,CG).
2 vols. 12mo (CG). 4s sewed (adv-1766 [973]) 5s (BB,MR).
MR XXXIII 490 (Dec. 1765).
AB(ELG); CG.
A trans. of de Tencin's *Les malheurs d'amours.* Dublin edn, 1766 [1014].
N

919.
[GUEULETTE Thomas Simon]
**+CHINESE TALES : Or, the Wonderful Adventures of the Mandarin Fum-Hoam. Related
by Himself, To divert the Sultana, upon the Celebration of her Nuptials. Written in French
by M. Gueulette. And Translated by the Rev. Mr. Stackhouse**
[5 more lines]
Dublin : Printed and Sold by W. Sleater, at Pope's-Head on Cork-Hill. 1765.
239pp. 12mo.
A trans. of *Les avantures merveilleuses du mandarin Fum-Hoam,* 1723.
1st English edn, 1725. Also, 1726, 1740, 1745, 1781(2x), 1791, 1793, 1795, 1798.
CUL PU UM
* N/C

920.
[HAWKESWORTH John]
+ALMORAN AND HAMET.
Belfast : Joy [c.1765] (CG).
CG.
1st edn and edns listed, 1761 [653].
N

921.
[HAYWOOD Mrs Eliza]
+THE HISTORY OF MISS BETSY THOUGHTLESS.
Dublin : Oliver Nelson. 1765.
4 vols. 12mo (CG).
CG(Whicker 28).
1st edn and edns listed, 1751 [85].
UNC YU
N

922.
[JOHNSTON Charles]
**CHRYSAL : OR, THE ADVENTURES OF A GUINEA. Wherein are exhibited Views of
several striking Scenes, with Curious and Interesting Anecdotes of the Most Noted Persons
in every Rank of Life, whose Hands it passed through, in America, England, Holland,
Germany and Portugal. By an Adept.**
London : Printed for T. Becket and P. A. De Hondt, at Tully's Head, near Surry-Street, in the
Strand. 1765.
Volumes III & IV. 2 vols. 12mo. 6s (CR,MR).
Rev of these vols, CR XX 120-124 (Aug. 1765); MR XXXIII 87 (July 1765).
ESTC t128716.
Vols I-II published and edns listed, 1760 [577].
BL HU NYPL PU YU
* N

923.
[JOHNSTON Charles]
+CHRYSAL : OR, THE ADVENTURES OF A GUINEA. Wherein are exhibited Views of
several striking Scenes, with Curious and Interesting Anecdotes of the Most Noted Persons
in every Rank of Life, whose Hands it passed through, in America, England, Holland,
Germany and Portugal. By an Adept.
Dublin : Printed by Dillon Chamberlaine. 1765.
Volume III (& IV?).
Probably 2 vols. 12mo.
CG(BL).
Vols III-IV 1st published, 1765 [922]. Vols I-II published and edns listed, 1760 [577].
BL unlocated
* N

924.
[KIMBER Edward]
THE GENEROUS BRITON; OR, THE AUTHENTIC MEMOIRS OF WILLIAM
GOLDSMITH, ESQ; In Two Volumes.
London : Printed for C. Henderson, under the Royal Exchange. 1765.
2 vols. 12mo. 5s (CR) 6s (MR).
CR XIX 466-467 (June 1765); MR XXXIII 86 (July 1765).
ESTC t062265.
Dublin edn, 1766 [1018]. Also, 1792.
BL Bod BU CUL UI
* N

925.
[KIMBER Edward]
+MARIA; THE GENUINE MEMOIRS OF A YOUNG LADY OF RANK AND FORTUNE.
By the Author of The Life and Adventures of Joe Thompson. The Second Edition,
corrected.
London : Printed for R. Baldwin in Pater-noster-Row, and T. Lownds in Fleet-Street. 1765.
2 vols. 12mo.
CG(BL); EC 286:5; ESTC t070736.
1st edns (under variant title), 1764 [847].
BL YU
* N

926.
[LANGHORNE John]
THE CORRESPONDENCE OF THEODOSIUS AND CONSTANTIA, From their first
acquaintance to the departure of Theodosius. Now first published from the Original
Manuscripts. By the Editor of the Letters that passed between Theodosius and Constantia,
after she had taken the Veil.
London : Printed for T. Becket and P. A. Dehondt, at Tully's Head, in the Strand. 1765.
152pp. 12mo. 2s6d sewed (MR).
CR XIX 169-173 (Mar. 1765); MR XXXII 19-29 (Jan. 1765).
CG; ESTC t119399; FB; LO 191 (UP,HU,FB).
Also, 1765 [927], 1766 [1019], 1770, 1796, 1799. Cf 1763 [778] with edns listed.
BL CUL DU NYPL OU PU UC UF UI UP YU
* E

927.
[LANGHORNE John]
+THE CORRESPONDENCE OF THEODOSIUS AND CONSTANTIA, From their first
acquaintance to the departure of Theodosius. Now first published from the Original
Manuscripts. By the Editor of the Letters that passed between Theodosius and Constantia
after she had taken the Veil.
Dublin : Printed for P. Wilson, S. Cotter, E. Watts, J. Potts, J. Williams, and J. Sheppard,
Booksellers. 1765.
144pp. 8vo.
1st edn and edns listed, 1765 [926].
CUL
* E

928.
[MARISHALL Jean]
THE HISTORY OF MISS CLARINDA CATHCART, AND MISS FANNY RENTON.
London : Printed by W. Hoggard. For Francis Noble, at his Circulating Library, opposite Gray's-
Inn-Gate, Holborn; And John Noble, at his Circulating Library, in St. Martin's Court, near
Leicester-Square, 1766 [1765].
2 vols. 12mo. 5s sewed (BB,MR) 6s (CR).
CR XX 288-292 (Oct. 1765); MR XXXIII 405 (Nov. 1765).
AB(BL,MH) as 1766; BB; CG(BB); ESTC t073524; FB; LO 192 (FB,HU).
Also, 1766 [1023] [1024], 1767 [1114].
BL CUNY PU YU
* E

929.
[MARIVAUX Pierre Carlet de Chamblain de]
+THE FORTUNATE VILLAGER : OR, MEMOIRS OF SIR ANDREW THOMPSON. In
Two Volumes.
Dublin : Printed for Sarah Cotter, and James Williams, in Skinner-Row. 1765.
2 vols in 1. 12mo.
CG(HU); ESTC t105238.
1st English version, 1735. Also, 1757 [415].
BL CUL HU
* N

930.
[MARIVAUX Pierre Carlet de Chamblain de]
[COLLYER Mrs Mary ? *trans.*]
+THE VIRTUOUS ORPHAN; Or The Life, Misfortunes, and Adventures, of Indiana.
Written by Herself. In Two Volumes. The Fourth Edition.
London : Printed for L. Hawes, W. Clarke, and R. Collins, at the Red-Lion in Pater-Noster-Row.
1765.
2 vols. 12mo.
Vol II, dated 1766.
CG; ESTC t118966.
1st English edn, 1746. Edns listed, 1755 [322].
BL
* N

931.
MARMONTEL Jean François
[DENNIS Charles and LLOYD Robert *trans.*]
MORAL TALES. By M. Marmontel.
London : Printed for T. Becket and P. A. de Hondt, near Surry-Street, in the Strand. 1765.
Volume III. 1 vol. 12mo. 3s (MR).
Rev of vol.III, CR XX 448-450 (Dec. 1765); MR XXIV 234 (Mar. 1766).
CG; ESTC t090767.
1st 2 vols and edns listed, 1763 [784].
BL Bod YU
* C

932.
[MARTEILHÉ Jean]
[GOLDSMITH Oliver *trans.*]
+THE MEMOIRS OF A PROTESTANT, Condemned to the Galleys of France, For His Religion. Written by Himself. [11 more lines] In Two Volumes. Translated from the Original, just published at the Hague. By James Willington.
Dublin : Printed for Wm. Fleming and S. Brown. 1765.
2 vols in 1. 252pp. 12mo.
ESTC t062644.
1st edn, 1758 [443].
BL CUL
* N/M

933.
[OAKMAN John]
THE LIFE AND SURPRISING ADVENTURES OF BENJAMIN BRASS, An Irish Fortune-Hunter. In Two Volumes.
London : Printed for W. Nicoll, in St. Paul's Church-Yard. 1765.
2 vols. 12mo. 5s (CR,MR).
CR XIX 74-75 (Jan. 1765); MR XXXII 76-77 (Jan. 1765).
EC 236:5; ESTC t057358.
BL
* N

934.
RAMSAY Andrew Michael
+THE TRAVELS OF CYRUS : To which is annexed, A Discourse upon the Theology and Mythology of the Pagans. By the Chevalier Ramsay.
Berwick upon Tweed : Printed for R. Taylor. 1765.
2 vols. 12mo.
CG(BL); ESTC t082618.
1st edn, 1727. Edns listed, 1752 [146].
BL
M/N

935.
[RICCOBONI Marie Jeanne]
+HISTORY OF THE MARQUIS DE CRESSY. Translated from the French.
London : Printed for T. Becket and P. A. de Hondt in the Strand, and J. Balfour in Edinburgh. 1765.
172pp. 8vo. 2s6d (MR).
MR XXXIII 87 (July 1765).
AB(BL); CG(BC); EC 56:3; ESTC t131024.   1st edn(?), 1759 [501].
BL NYPL UI YU [possible variant]
* N

936.
RICHARDSON Samuel
+CLARISSA. OR, THE HISTORY OF A YOUNG LADY; Comprehending The most
Important Concerns of Private Life; And particularly shewing, The Distresses that may
attend the Misconduct Both of Parents and Children, In Relation to Marriage. By Mr.
Samuel Richardson. The Fourth Edition.
Dublin : Printed by J. Potts at Swift's Head in Dame-street. 1765.
7 vols. 12mo. 19s6d (RCC).
ESTC t059001; RCC p.240.
The above tp (usual title of the later vols) taken from vol. V - vols I & II missing from BL set & vols III-IV,
dated 1766.
1st edn, 1747-48. Edns listed, 1751 [96].
BL [imperf] NYPL
* E

937.
[RIDLEY James]
+THE TALES OF THE GENII : OR THE DELIGHTFUL LESSONS OF HORAM, SON
OF ASMAR. Faithfully Translated from the Persian Manuscript; and Compared with the
French and Spanish Editions Published at Paris and Madrid. By Sir Charles Morell,
Formerly Ambassador from the British Settlements in India to the Great Mogul. The Third
Edition.
London : Printed for J. Wilkie, in St. Paul's Church-Yard. 1765.
2 vols. 8vo.
1st edn and edns listed, 1764 [862].
HL NYPL
C

938.
[le SAGE Alain René]
[DILWORTH W. H. trans.]
+THE ADVENTURES OF GIL BLAS DE SANTILLANE. Published for the Improvement
and Entertainment of the British Youth of both sexes. By W. H. Dilworth, A.M.
Glasgow : Printed, and Sold by J. Galbraith and Company. 1765.
115pp. 8vo.
1st English version, 1735. Edns listed, 1750 [36].
CUL
* N

939.
[SMOLLETT Tobias]
+THE ADVENTURES OF PEREGRINE PICKLE. In which are included, Memoirs of a
Lady of Quality. In Four Volumes. The Third Edition.
London : Printed for R. Baldwin, and M. Richardson, in Pater-noster-Row. 1765.
4 vols. 12mo.
CG(BL); ESTC t055347; MW 140.
1,000 copies, Strahan ledgers.
1st edn and edns listed, 1751 [99].
BL UC YU
* N

940.
[STERNE Laurence]
THE LIFE AND OPINIONS OF TRISTRAM SHANDY, GENTLEMAN.
London : Printed for T. Becket and P. A. Dehondt, in the Strand. 1765.
Volumes VII & VIII. 2 vols. 8vo. 2s each (CR) 4s sewed (MR).
Rev of these vols, CR XIX 65-66 (Jan. 1765); MR XXXII 120-139 (Feb. 1765).
ESTC t014820.
The 1st edn of these vols, published Jan. 1765, comprising 4,000 copies, Strahan Ledgers, KM p.27. KM also
identifies a reissue or a 'concealed 2nd edn'. 1765. Vols I-II published and edns of all vols listed, 1759 [507].
BL DU HU IU NLC NYPL PU UF UP UV YU
* N

941.
[STERNE Laurence]
+THE LIFE AND OPINIONS OF TRISTRAM SHANDY, GENTLEMAN. The Second
Edition.
Dublin : Printed by Henry Saunders, in Castle-street, near the Castle Gate. 1765.
Volumes I-IV. 4 vols in 1. 305pp. 12mo.
ESTC t014744; RCC p.74.
Vols I-II published and edns of all vols listed, 1759 [507]. Vols III-IV published 1761 [673] and 1st set of vols
I-IV, 1761 [675].
BL YU
* N

942.
[STERNE Laurence]
+THE LIFE AND OPINIONS OF TRISTRAM SHANDY, GENTLEMAN.
Dublin : Printed by Henry Saunders, in Castle-street, near the Castle Gate. 1765.
Volumes V-VIII. 4 vols. 12mo.
ESTC t014738.
Vols V-VI 1st published 1761 [677]; vols VII-VIII 1765 [940]; vols I-II and edns of all vols listed, 1759 [507].
5 Dublin booksellers also advertising edn in Feb. (RCC, p.74) but issue uncertain.
CUL NLC YU
* N

943.
[WALPOLE Horace]
+THE CASTLE OF OTRANTO, A GOTHIC STORY. The Second Edition.
London : Printed for William Bathoe in the Strand, and Thomas Lownds in Fleet-Street. 1765.
200pp. 12mo.
Rev of 2nd edn, CR XIX 469 (June 1765); MR XXXII 394 (May 1765).
CG; ATH pp.54-5.
1st edn and edns listed, 1764 [868].
BL Bod CUNY IU LWL OU Tx
* N

944.
[WALPOLE Horace]
+THE CASTLE OF OTRANTO, A STORY. Translated by William Marshal, Gent. From
the Original Italian of Onuphrio Muralto, Canon of the Church of St. Nicholas at Otranto.
Dublin : Printed by J. Hoey, J. Exshaw, P. Wilson, S. Cotter, W. Sleater, J. Potts, S. Watson, J.
Hoey junior, J. Williams, and J. Sheppard [1765] (LWL,Bod).
203pp. 12mo.
CG.
1st edn and edns listed, 1764 [868].
Bod LWL
* N

945.
[WALPOLE Horace]
+THE CASTLE OF OTRANTO, A STORY. Translated by William Marshal, Gent. From
the Original Italian of Onuphrio Muralto, Canon of the Church of St. Nicholas at Otranto.
Dublin : Printed for J. Hoey, P. Wilson, J. Exshaw, S. Cotter, W. Sleater, J. Potts, S. Watson, J.
Hoey junior, J. Williams, and J. Sheppard. [1765] (LWL).
146pp. 12mo.
ESTC t063185; ATH p.54.
1st edn and edns listed, 1764 [868].
BL CUNY LWL NLC NYPL Tx UI YU
* N

946.
[WALPOLE Horace]
+THE CASTLE OF OTRANTO, A STORY. Translated by William Marshal, Gent. From
the Original Italian of Onuphrio Muralto, Canon of the Church of St. Nicholas at Otranto.
Dublin : Printed for Elizabeth Watts, in Skinner-Row. 1765.
215pp. 12mo.
ESTC t100478; ATH p.54.
1st edns and edns listed, 1764 [868].
BL LWL
* N

947.
[WOODFIN Mrs A.]
+THE HISTORY OF MISS SALLY SABLE. By the Author of the Memoirs of a Scotch
Family.
Dublin : 1765 (UF).
1st edn and edns listed, 1757 [417].
UF
N

Miscellanies

948.
+Æsop's Fables.
Belfast : Joy [1765] (CG).
CG(adv).   Edns listed, 1753 [199].
M/C

949.
The Female Barbers; An Irish Tale, after the Manner of Prior.
London : Williams. 1765 (MR).
4to. 6d (CR,MR)
CR XX 235 (Sept. 1765); MR XXXIII 248 (Sept. 1765).
Various edns from 1750 in verse. Rev suggests this edn not in verse.
M

950.
The History of the Life and Sufferings of Henry Grace, of Basingstoke in the County of Southampton.
Being a Narrative Of the Hardships he underwent during several Years Captivity among the Savages in
North America. [7 more lines] Written by Himself.
Sold by the Author in Basingstoke, and by Wilson and Fell in London, 1765 (MR).
56pp. 8vo. 1s (MR).
MR XXXII 239-240 (Mar. 1765).
2nd edn, 1765 [951].
N

951.
+The History of the Life and Sufferings of Henry Grace, of Basingstoke in the County of Southampton. Being a Narrative Of the Hardships he underwent during several Years Captivity among the Savages in North America. [7 more lines] Written by Himself. The Second Edition.
[Reading] : Printed for the Author : And Sold at his House in Basingstoke, at the Printing-Office in Reading, and by J. Cooke, at Shakespear's-Head, in Pater-noster-Row, London. 1765.
56pp. 8vo. 1s (tp).
ESTC t068598.
1st edn, 1765 [950].
BL
* N/M

952.
Memoirs of the Court of Portugal, And of the Administration of the Count of D'Oeyras. Taken from a Series of Original Letters. Written in French.
London : Printed for William Bingley, opposite Durham-Yard, in the Strand [1765] (BL).
104pp. 8vo.
CG(BL); ESTC t095291.
BL
* M

953.
Miss C——y's Cabinet of Curiosities; or, the Green-Room Broke Open. By Tristram Shandy Gent.
Utopia [London], Printed for William Whirligig, at the Maiden's Head, in Wind-mill-street. 1765.
48pp. 8vo(BL)/12mo(CG). [Price an English Six-pence] (tp).
AB(BL), CG(BL); ESTC t039508.
Cf 1759 [507].
BL
* M

954.
+The Secret History of Betty Ireland, Who was trepann'd into Marriage at the Age of Fourteen, and debauched by Beau M–te at Fifteen, by whom she had one Son; the vile Injury she did to that Gentleman, and her turning Prostitute [28 more lines] The Sixth Edition.
London : Printed for John Lever, at Little Moorgate, next London Wall, near Moorfields [1765?] (BL).
47pp. 8vo. 6d (tp).
CG(BL); ESTC t109761.
1st edn ?1741. Edns listed, 1750 [50].
BL
* M

955.
+Select Fables of Esop and Other Fabulists. In Three Books. By R. Dodsley. A New Edition.
London : Printed for J. Dodsley in Pall-mall. 1765.
204pp. 12mo. 3s bound (tp).
CG(BL); ESTC t084998.
1st Dodsley edn, 1761 [690]. Other edns listed, 1753 [199].
BL [missing since 1984] DU NYPL UC
* M/C

956.
+Venus Unmasked : Or an Inquiry into the Nature and Origin of the Passion of Love. Interspersed with curious and entertaining accounts of several modern amours. In Two Volumes.
London : Printed for the Author, and Sold by M. Thrush. 1765.
2 pts. 1st edn, 1759 [519].
YU
M

957.
d'Argens Jean Baptiste de Boyer, Marquis
+The Jewish Spy : Being a Philosophical, Historical, and Critical Correspondence, which lately passed between certain Jews in Turkey, Italy, France, &c. Translated from the Originals into French, by the Marquis d'Argens, and now done into English. The Third Edition.
London : Printed for A. Millar, J. Rivington, R. Baldwin, W. Johnston, and A. Shuckburgh. 1765.
5 vols. 12mo.
ESTC t131033.
1st edn and edns listed, 1753 [205].
M

958.
[Billardon de Sauvigny Edmé Louis]
Oriental Apologues; or Instructive Fables. Translated from the French.
London : Printed for T. Davies, in Russel-Street, Covent-Garden; Richardson and Urquhart, under the Royal Exchange; and I. Walter, at Homer's Head, Charing-Cross. 1765.
204pp. 12mo. 2s6d sewed (CR,MR).
CR XIX 47-50 (Jan. 1765); MR XXXII 95-97 (Feb. 1765).
CG(MR); ESTC t031402; FB; LO 193 (FB,MR).
BL LC YU
* M/C

959.
[Donneau de Visé Jean]
+The Husband Forced to be Jealous : Or, The Good Fortune of Those Women That Have Jealous Husbands. Being The Secret History of several Noble Persons; a very Entertaining History, and founded on real Facts, and not the Result of an inventive Fancy, as many Books are. Translated from the French. The Second Edition.
London : Printed for John Lever, Bookseller, Stationer, and Printseller, at Little Moorgate, next to London Wall, and near Moorfields. 1765.
62pp. 8vo. 1s (tp).
EC 8:2; ESTC t099448; McB 472.
A prose trans. of *Le jaloux par force*, 1688. A trans. by 'N.H.' of a work also attributed to Marie Catherine Hortense des Jardins, Calling herself Madame de Villedieu.
BL UI
* M/N

960.
[Fielding Sarah]
+The Governess; Or, The Little Female Academy. Calculated for the Entertainment and Instruction of Young Ladies in their Education. By the Author of David Simple.
London : Printed for T. Clarke and F. Brookes. 1765.
166pp. 12mo.
CG(HU).
1st edn, 1749. Edns listed, 1751 [110].
CUL FL HU UMin
* M/C

961.
[Goadby Robert]
+An Apology for the Life of Mr. Bampfylde Moore-Carew. The Sixth Edition. With Additions.
London : Printed for R. Goadby, and W. Owen, [1765] (LC,YU).
Possibly the same, or reissue of 1760 [618].
1st edn and edns listed, 1750 [54].
LC YU
M

962.
[Goudar Ange de]
+The Chinese Spy; or, Emissary from the Court of Pekin, Commissioned to examine into The Present State of Europe. Translated from the Chinese. In Six Volumes.
London : Printed for S. Bladon, in Pater-noster Row. 1765.
6 vols. 12mo. 18s (MR,BB).
MR XXXIII 165-167 (Aug. 1765).
BB, ESTC t097973; FB; LO 189 (MR,FB); CG(HU).
1st edn and edns listed, 1764 [874].
BL Bod CUL HU UNC
* M

963.
Hughes John *trans*.
+Letters of Abelard and Heloise. To which is prefix'd, a particular account of their lives, amours and misfortunes. By the late John Hughes, Esq. To which is now first added, the poem of Eloisa to Abelard. By Mr. Pope. Tenth Edition, ornamented with cuts.
London : Printed for W. Johnston, B. Law, T. Lownds, and T. Caslon. 1765.
180pp. 12mo.
CG(BL); ESTC t038496.
1st English edn, 1718. Edns listed, 1751 [112].
BL
* M/E

964.
Limbourg Jean Philippe de
+New Amusements of the German Spa. Written in French in the Year 1763 by J. P. de Limbourg.
Dublin : Printed for S. Cotter etc. 1765.
2 vols. 16mo.
CG(NUC); NUC.
1st edn, 1764 [878].
LC UI
M

965.
Somis Ignazio
An Historical Narrative of a most Extraordinary Event which happened at the village of Bergemoletto in Italy; where three women were saved out of the ruins of a stable, in which they had been buried thirty-seven days by a heavy fall of snow. By Ignazio Somis. Translated from the Italian.
London : Printed for T. Osborne. 1765.
208pp. 12mo.
CG; ESTC t136714.
Also, 1768 [1257].
CUL BL
M

966.
[Witherspoon John]
The History of a Corporation of Servants. Discovered a few Years ago in the Interior parts of South America.
London : Dilly. 1765.
8vo. 1s (CR,MR).
CR XX 154 (Aug. 1765); MR XXXIII 243-244 (Sept. 1765).
Also, 1765 [967].
M (sat)

967.
[Witherspoon John]
+The History of a Corporation of Servants. Discovered a few Years ago in the interior parts of South America. Containing some very surprising events and extraordinary characters.
Glasgow : Printed for J. Gilmour, and sold by him and other booksellers in town and country. 1765.
76pp. 8vo.
CG; ESTC t054874.
1st edn, 1765 [966].
BL LC PU YU
* M

968.
[Woodcock Thomas]
+An Account of some Remarkable Passages in the Life of a Private Gentleman.
Glasgow : Trent. 1765.
CG.
1st(?) edn, 1708. Also, 1711.
M

1766

969.
THE ADOPTED DAUGHTER; OR, THE HISTORY OF MISS CLARISSA B—. In Two Volumes.
London : Printed for Francis Noble, at his Circulating Library, opposite Gray's-Inn-Gate, Holborn; And John Noble, at his Circulating Library, in St. Martin's Court, near Leicester Square, 1767 [1766].
2 vols. 8vo. 6s (CR,MR).
CR XXII 469 (Dec. 1766); MR XXXV 485 (Dec. 1766).
BB; CG(BB); ESTC t075325; LO 209 (YU).
Dublin edn, 1767 [1058].
BL YU
* E

970.
THE ADVENTURES OF CHARLES VILLIERS, AN UNFORTUNATE COURT DEPENDENT.
London : Bladon. 1766.
2 vols. 12mo. 5s (CR) 6s (MR).
CR XXII 379 (Nov. 1766); MR XXXVI 173 (Feb, 1767).
AB(ELG,WB); BB; CG(BB).
N

971.
THE ADVENTURES OF JACK WANDER. Written by Himself. Interspers'd with Some Humorous Anecdotes, and Original Memoirs.
London : Printed for T. Jones, at his Circulating Library, in Great Mary's-Buildings, St. Martin's-Lane [1766] (YU).
160pp. 12mo. 2s6d (CR,MR).
CR XXI 470-471 (June 1766); MR XXXIV 407 (May 1766).
BB; CG(BB,MR); EC 64:7; ESTC t057424.
BL HU YU
* N

972.
THE ADVENTURES OF MISS HARRIET SPRIGHTLY, A LADY OF PLEASURE.
Interspersed with the Histories and Characters, the Amours and Intrigues of several
Personages well known in the polite World.
London : Serjeant. 1766.
2 vols. 12mo. 5s sewed (BB,MR) 6s (CR).
CR XXI 237 (Mar. 1766); MR XXXIV 241 (Mar. 1766).
BB.
N

973.
THE AMOURS OF LAIS : OR THE MISFORTUNES OF LOVE.
London : Printed for M. Folingsby, in Fleet-Street; and J. Wilkie, in St. Paul's Church-Yard.
1766.
230pp. 12mo. 2s6d (BB,MR) 3s (CR).
CR XXI 157 (Feb. 1766); MR XXXIV 241 (Mar. 1766).
AB(BL); BB; CG(as 1761); ESTC t117010.
BL CUL
* N

974.
THE CONFLICT : OR, THE HISTORY OF MISS SOPHIA FANBROOK. In Three
Volumes.
London : Printed for Francis Noble, at his Circulating Library, near Middle-Row, Holborn; And
John Noble, at his Circulating Library, in St. Martin's Court, near Leicester-Square, 1767 [1766].
3 vols. 12mo. 9s (BB,CR,MR).
CR XXII 380 (Nov. 1766); MR XXXVI 173 (Feb, 1767).
AB(BL,Pi); BB; CG(BB,BL,HU); ESTC t074439.
BL Bod HU UC
* N

975.
ELIZA : OR, THE HISTORY OF MISS GRANVILLE. By the Author of Indiana Danby.
In Two Volumes.
London : Printed by W. Hoggard, for Francis Noble, at his Circulating Library, opposite Gray's-
Inn-Gate, Holborn; and John Noble, at his Circulating Library, in St. Martin's Court, near
Leicester Square. 1766.
2 vols. 12mo. 5s (CR) 6s (BB,MR).
CR XXI 156-157 (Feb. 1766); MR XXXIV 82 (Jan. 1766).
BB (as 1765); CG; EC 223:3; ESTC t068743; FB; LO 198 (CR,FB).
Dublin edn, 1766 [976].
BL Bod
* E

976.
+ELIZA : OR, THE HISTORY OF MISS GRANVILLE. By the Author of Indiana Danby.
In Two Volumes.
Dublin : Printed for P. Wilson, E. Watts, J. Hoey Junior, and J. Potts. 1766.
2 vols in 1.
1st edn, 1766 [975].
Grosvenor Ref. Div. and Erie Co. Library, Buffalo, NY.
E

977.
THE FAITHFUL FUGITIVES: OR, ADVENTURES OF MISS TERESA M——. In a Series
of Letters to a Friend.
London : Printed for T. Vernor, and J. Chater, at their Circulating Library, on Ludgate-Hill.
1766.
237pp. 12mo. 2s6d (BB,MR) 3s (CR).
CR XXXI 219-221 (Mar. 1766); MR XXXIV 241 (Mar. 1766).
BB; CG(BB); FB; LO 199 (CR,FB,UP).
UP YU
* E

978.
THE HISTORY OF ELIZA. WRITTEN BY A FRIEND. In Two Volumes.
London : Printed for J. Dodsley, in Pall-Mall. 1767 [1766].
141pp. 12mo. 6s.
CR XXII 434-438 (Dec. 1766); MR XXXVI 172-173 (Feb. 1767).
AB(BL,Pi); BB; CG(BL); ESTC t092326; FB; LO 219 (FB,UP).
Possibly by Charlotte Lennox, DWW, p.197.
Dublin edn, 1767 [1070].
BL IU OU PU
* N

979.
THE HISTORY OF LA RIVIÉRE. Translated from the French.
London : Printed for W. Flexney, near Gray's-Inn Gate, Holborn; and A. and C. Corbett,
opposite St. Dunstan's Church, Fleet-Street. 1766.
271pp. 12mo. 3s bound (tp).
AB(BL); CG(BL); EC 56:11; ESTC t075795.
BL NYSL(HC).
* N

980.
THE HISTORY OF MISS DELIA STANHOPE. In a Series of Letters to Miss Dorinda
Boothby. In Two Volumes.
London : Lownds. 1767 [1766].
2 vols. 12mo. 6s (CR,MR).
MR XXXV 485 (Dec. 1766); CR XXII 359-362 (Nov. 1766).
BB; CG(MR); FB; LO 202 (FB).
Also, 1767 [1073] [1074].
UCLA NYPL
E

981.
THE HISTORY OF MISS HARRIOT FITZROY, AND MISS EMILIA SPENCER. By the
Author of Lucinda Courtney.
London : Printed by W. Hoggard, for F. and J. Noble. 1767 [1766].
2 vols. 8vo. 6s (CR,MR).
CR XXII 354-359 (Nov. 1766); MR XXXV 407 (Nov. 1766).
AB(ELG,Pi); BB; CG(MR); FB; LO 221 (CR,FB,UP,HU).
Dublin edn, 1767 [1076].
CUNY HU UC UP
E

982.
THE HISTORY OF SIR CHARLES BEAUFORT. Containing the Genuine and Interesting Memoirs of a Family of Distinction in the South of England. Displaying the Miseries that may arise from acting contrary to that peculiar character which nature has given to both the sexes.
London : Printed for T. Lownds in Fleet-Street, and W. Nicoll, in St. Paul's Church-yard. 1766.
2 vols. 12mo. 6s (CR,MR).
CR XXI 139-140 (Feb. 1766); MR XXXIV 240-241 (Mar. 1766).
AB(Pi); BB; CG(HU); LO 203 & 208; McB 460.
HU UI PU YU
* N

983.
(+)THE HISTORY OF THE GAY BELLARIO, AND THE FAIR ISABELLA, Founded on Facts, and Illustrated with Adventures in Real Life.
London : Printed for J. Cooke at the Shakespear's-Head in Pater-Noster Row. 1766.
240pp. 12mo.
CG(YU).
An edn also issued in 1763 [759].
YU
* N

984.
THE LIFE AND OPINIONS OF TRISTRAM SHANDY, GENTLEMAN. Vol. IX.
London : Printed for T. Durham, at Charing-Cross, and T. Caslon, in Pater-noster Row. 1766.
[not by Sterne].
143pp. 8vo. 2s6d (CR,MR).
CR XXI 141 (Feb. 1766); MR XXXIV 168 (Feb. 1766).
Sterne's vol. IX, published, 1767 [1140].
Also, 1766 [985].
Bod CUL
* N

985.
+THE LIFE AND OPINIONS OF TRISTRAM SHANDY, GENTLEMAN. Vol. IX. The Second Edition.
London : Printed for T. Durham, at Charing-Cross, and T. Caslon, in Pater-noster Row. 1766.
[not by Sterne].
8vo. 2s6d.
KM p.30.
1st edn, 1766 [984]. Cf Sterne's vol.IX, 1767 [1140].
N

986.
MEMOIRS OF MR WALLCOT, A GENTLEMAN (OF YORKSHIRE) AND HIS FAMILY. A Narrative Founded on Real Facts.
London : Printed for T. Jones. [1766] (CR,MR).
2 vols. 12mo. 5s sewed (adv-1766 [970], CR,MR).
CR XXI 157 (Feb. 1766); MR XXXIV 241 (Mar. 1766).
Adv-1766 [970]; BB.
OU
N

987.
THE PROGRESS OF VANITY AND VIRTUE, OR, THE HISTORY OF TWO SISTERS.
In Two Volumes.
London : Printed for J. Fletcher and Co. in St Paul's Church-Yard. 1766.
2 vols. 12mo. 5s (BB,CR) 6s (GM,MR).
CR XXI 470 (June 1766); GM 287 (June 1766); MR XXXV 146 (Aug. 1766).
BB; CG(BL,MR).
Dublin edn, 1766 [988].
BL
* N

988.
+THE PROGRESS OF VANITY AND VIRTUE, OR, THE HISTORY OF TWO SISTERS.
Dublin : H. Saunders. [1766?] (adv-1767 [1084]).
2s8½d.
Adv-1767 [1084].
1st edn, 1766 [987]
N

989.
+THE WANDERER : OR, MEMOIRS OF CHARLES SEARLE, ESQ; Containing his
Adventures by Sea and Land. With many remarkable Characters, and interesting situations
in real life; and a variety of surprizing incidents.
Dublin : Printed for H. Saunders, J. Hoey, jun. and J. Williams. 1766.
2 vols in 1. 2s8½d (adv-1767 [1084]).
Adv-1767 [1084].
1st edn, 1765 [896].
NLC UP
N

990.
[AMORY Thomas]
(+)THE LIFE OF JOHN BUNCLE, ESQ; Containing Various Observations and Reflections
Made in several Parts of the World, And Many Extraordinary Relations.
London : Printed for J. Johnson and B. Davenport, at the Globe in Pater-Noster Row. 1766.
2 vols. 8vo. 6s (MR) 10s [both vols] (CR).
Rev of vol.II, CR XXI 470 (June 1766); MR XXXV 33-43, 100-123 (July, Aug. 1766).
CG(BB,HU); ESTC t128392; McB 21.
Vol I. published 1756 [362].
BL Bod CUL HU NYPL PU UI WCL
* N

991.
BACULARD d'ARNAUD François Marie Thomas de
FANNY; OR, THE HAPPY REPENTANCE. From the French of Mr. D'Arnaud.
London : Becket. 1766.
8vo. 2s (CR,MR).
CR XXII 80 (July 1766); MR XXXV 97-100 (Aug. 1766).
CG(MR).
A trans. of Fanni; ou L'heureux repentir, histoire angloise, 1764.
Dublin edn, 1767 [1084].
N

992.
BROOKE Mrs Frances Moore
+THE HISTORY OF LADY JULIA MANDEVILLE. By the Translator of Lady Catesby's
Letters. The Third Edition.
Dublin : J. Potts. 1766.
2 vols in 1.
1st edn and edns listed, 1763 [769].
HU UP
E

993.
BROOKE Henry
THE FOOL OF QUALITY; OR, THE HISTORY OF HENRY EARL OF MORELAND. In
Four Volumes. By Mr. Brooke.
London : Printed for W. Johnston, in Ludgate-Street. 1766.
Volumes I & II.
2 vols. 12mo. 3s each (CR).
CR XXII 197-204 (Sept. 1766); vol I, MR XXXV 145-146 (Aug. 1766) and vol II, MR XXXV
286-297, 346-356 (Nov. 1766).
AB(AR,BL); BB; ESTC t057311; LO 197 (UI,UP); McB 106.
Also, 1767 [1090] [1091]; vol III, 1768 [1202]; vol IV, 1769 [1300]. Vol V published, 1770. Further edns,
1776, 1777, 1781, 1782, 1784, 1792, 1793, 1796, 1798(2x).
BL [imperf] HU LU OU PU Tx UI UP YU
* N

994.
CERVANTES SAAVEDRA Miguel de
JARVIS Charles *trans.*
+THE LIFE AND EXPLOITS OF THE INGENIOUS GENTLEMAN DON QUIXOTE DE
LA MANCHA. Translated from the Original Spanish of Miguel Cervantes de Saavedra. By
Charles Jarvis, Esq. The Fourth Edition.
London : Printed for J. and R. Tonson, in the Strand, and J. Dodsley, in Pall-Mall. 1766.
4 vols. 12mo.
CG; ESTC t059888; McB 134.
1st edn of Jarvis trans, 1742. Edns listed, 1756 [367]. Cf Smollett trans. with edns listed, 1755 [302], and Ozell
trans. with edns listed, 1757 [409].
BL HU LC UI
* N

995.
CERVANTES SAAVEDRA Miguel de
OZELL John *trans.*
+THE HISTORY OF THE RENOWNED DON QUIXOTE. Written in Spanish by Miguel
de Cervantes Saavedra. Translated by Several Hands : and Published by The Late Mr.
Motteux. Revised a-new from the best Spanish Edition, By Mr. Ozell.
[3 more lines]
Edinburgh : Printed by A. Donaldson, and sold at his Shops in London and Edinburgh. 1766.
4 vols. 12mo.
ESTC t059493; RCC p.79.
1st Motteux trans, 1700. Ozell revision, 1719. Edns listed, 1757 [409]. Cf Smollett trans. with edns listed, 1755
[302], and Jarvis trans. with edns listed, 1756 [367].
BL LC
* N

996.
CERVANTES SAAVEDRA Miguel de
SMOLLETT Tobias *trans.*
+THE HISTORY OF THE RENOWNED DON QUIXOTE. Translated from the Spanish of
Miguel de Cervantes Saavedra. To which is prefixed, Some Account of the Author's Life.
By T. Smollett M.D. Illustrated with Copper-Plates. In Four Volumes.
Dublin : Printed for Thomas Ewing in Dame-street, 1766.
4 vols. 12mo.
ESTC t059492; MW 607; RCC p.79.
1st edn of Smollett trans. and edns listed, 1755 [302].
BL Bod CUL NYPL
* N

997.
[CHAIGNEAU William]
+THE HISTORY OF JACK CONNOR. In Two Volumes. The Fourth Edition Corrected
and Improved.
Dublin : Printed for Hulton Bradley, at the King's Arms and Two Bibles in Dame-street. 1766.
2 vols. 12mo.
Vol.II tp, 'The History of Jack Connor, now Conyers' as in earlier edns. 1st edn and edns listed, 1752 [124].
CUL HU NYSL(HC) PU Tx
* N

998.
[CLELAND John]
GENUINE MEMOIRS OF THE CELEBRATED MISS MARIA BROWN. Exhibiting The
Life of a Courtezan in the most Fashionable Scenes of Dissipation. Published by the Author
of the Woman of Pleasure. In Two Volumes.
London : Printed for I. Allcock, near St. Paul's. 1766.
2 vols. 12mo. 6s (BB,MR).
MR XXXIV 406 (May 1766).
BB; CG; EC 192:3; ESTC t084799.   Also, 1766 [999].
BL
* N/M

999.
[CLELAND John]
+GENUINE MEMOIRS OF THE CELEBRATED MISS MARIA BROWN. Exhibiting The
Life of a Courtezan in the most Fashionable Scenes of Dissipation. Published by the Author
of a W** of P*** In Two Volumes.
London : Printed for I. Allcock, near St. Paul's. 1766.
2 vols. 12mo.
ESTC t084798.   Also, 1766 [998].
BL
* N/M

1000.
[CLELAND John]
+MEMOIRS OF A WOMAN OF PLEASURE. From the Original Corrected Edition. With
a Set of Elegant Engravings.
London : Printed in the Year 1766.
2 vols. 8vo.
ESTC t133517.
1st edn, 1749. Edns and versions listed, 1750 [19].
BL
* N/M

1001.
[CRÉBILLON Claude Prosper Jolyot de]
[HUMPHREYS Samuel *trans.*]
+LETTERS FROM THE MARCHIONESS DE M*** TO THE COUNT DE R***.
Translated from the Original French, By Mr. Humphreys.
Dublin : Printed by James Hoey, junior, on the West-Side of Parliament-Street, near Essex-Bridge. 1766.
242pp. 12mo.
ESTC t106781; McB 165.
1st edn and edns listed, 1758 [437].
BL UI
* E/M

1002.
[DEFOE Daniel]
+THE LIFE AND STRANGE SURPRISING ADVENTURES OF ROBINSON CRUSOE,
MARINER, OR YORK. The Thirteenth Edition.
London : Printed for J. Buckland, W. Strahan, J. Rivington, R. Baldwin, L. Hawes and W.
Clarke and R. Collins, W. Johnston, T. Caslon, T. Longman, B. Law, J. Wilkie, T. Lowndes, W.
Nicoll, and the Executors of B. Dod. 1766.
2 vols. 12mo. Vol II, 'The Farther Adventures... The Thirteenth Edition'.
EC 175:7; ESTC t072281.
1st edn, 1719-20. Edns listed, 1752 [129].
BL [vol.I only] NYPL RFP YU
* N/M

1003.
[ÉLIE DE BEAUMONT Marie Anne Louise Morin-Dumesnil]
+THE HISTORY OF THE MARQUIS DE ROSELLE. In A Series of Letters. By Madame
Elie de Beaumont. Translated from the French. The Second Edition, Corrected.
London : Printed for T. Becket and P. A. De Hondt in the Strand. 1766.
2 vols. 12mo.
CG(BL); ESTC t107005; McB 250.
1st edn, 1765 [911].
BL UI UNC UP YU
* E

1004.
[FÉNELON François de Salignac de La Mothe]
+THE ADVENTURES OF TELEMACHUS, THE SON OF ULYSSES. The Eighteenth
Edition.
London : Printed for J. Brotherton. 1766.
2 vols. 8vo.
1st English edn, 1699. Edns listed, 1755 [312].
Bn [imperf]
N/M

1005.
FIELDING Henry
+THE HISTORY OF TOM JONES, A FOUNDLING. With the Life of the Author, By
Arthur Murphy, of Lincoln's Inn, Esq; In Three Volumes. By Henry Fielding, Esq.
Dublin : Printed for W. and W. Smith, P. Wilson, J. Exshaw, and H. Bradley. 1766.
3 vols. 12mo.
ESTC t133821; RCC pp.68,239.
1st edn, 1749. Edns listed, 1750 [24].
BL NLI YU
* N

1006.
FIELDING Henry
+THE WORKS OF HENRY FIELDING ESQ; With The Life of the Author. In Twelve
Volumes. The Third Edition.
London : Printed for A. Millar, in the Strand. 1766.
12 vols. 12mo.
ESTC t089841; McB 304.
1st edn of collected works and edns listed, 1762 [714].
BL Bod HU UC UCo UV YU
* C/N

1007.
[GOLDSMITH Oliver]
THE VICAR OF WAKEFIELD : A TALE. Supposed to be written by Himself.
Salisbury : Printed by B. Collins, For F. Newbery, in Pater-Noster-Row, London. 1766.
2 vols. 12mo. 6s (MR).
MR XXXIV 407 (May 1766).
AB(BL,Mgs,Q); BB; ESTC t146175; LO 200 (RL,UI,YU); TS; McB 352.
Published 27 Mar. 1766. 4 variants [A-D] of this 1st, authorized edn, TS pp.173-175. Also 1766 [1008] [1009]
[1010] [1010a] [1011] [1012], 1767 [1099] [1100], 1769 [1313], 1770, 1772, 1773, 1774, 1774-5, 1776,
1777(2x), 1778, 1779, 1780(2x), 1781(3x), 1782(2x), 1783(2x), 1784, 1785(2x), 1786, 1787, 1789, 1790(4x),
1791(6x), 1792(5x), 1793(4x), 1797, 1798(2x), 1799(3x), 1800(6x).
BL Bod Bn CUNY HL HU NLC PU UI UV YU
* N

1008.
[GOLDSMITH Oliver]
+THE VICAR OF WAKEFIELD : A TALE. Supposed to be written by Himself. The
Second Edition.
London : Printed for F. Newbery, in Pater-Noster-Row. 1766.
2 vols. 12mo. 6s (CR).
Rev of 2nd edn, CR XXI 439-441 (June 1766).
ESTC t146180; McB 354; TS p.175.
1st edn and edns listed, 1766 [1007].
BL CUL FL HU LC UC UI UMin UW
* N

1009.
[GOLDSMITH Oliver]
+THE VICAR OF WAKEFIELD : A TALE. Supposed to be written by Himself. The Third
Edition.
London : Printed for F. Newbery, in Pater-Noster-Row. 1766.
2 vols. 12mo.
McB 355; TS p.176.   1st edn and edns listed, 1766 [1007].
Bod HL HU UC UI
N

1010.
[GOLDSMITH Oliver]
+THE VICAR OF WAKEFIELD : A TALE. Supposed to be written by Himself.
Dublin : Printed for W. and W. Smith, A. Lethly, J. Hoey, sen. P. Wilson, J. Exshaw, E. Watts,
H. Saunders, J. Hoey, jun. J. Potts, and J. Williams. [1766] (BL,CUL and vol.II dated 1766).
2 vols. 12mo. 3s3d bound in 1 vol (adv-1767 [1084]). Vol II has 'Leathley'.
ESTC t146177; McB 356; RCC p.116; TS p.178.
Published 27 May. 1st edn and edns listed, 1766 [1007].
BL Bod CUL HU NLI TCD UCLA UI UNC
* N

1010a.
[GOLDSMITH Oliver]
+THE VICAR OF WAKEFIELD : A TALE. Supposed to be written by Himself.
Dublin : Printed for W. and W. Smith, A. Lethley, J. Hoey, sen. P. Wilson, J. Exshaw, E. Watts,
H. Saunders, J. Hoey, jun. J. Potts, and J. Williams. 1766.
2 vols. 12mo.
A 2nd edn or issue, almost sold out by July, RCC, p.116.
1st edn and edns listed, 1766 [1007].
YU
N

1011.
[GOLDSMITH Oliver]
+THE VICAR OF WAKEFIELD : A TALE. Supposed to be written by Himself. In Two
Volumes.
'Corke : Printed by Eugene Swiney, in the Year 1766'.
2 vols. 12mo.
ESTC t146179; TS p.177.
TS suggests made up from sheets of a pirated issue printed in London, but does not exclude the possibility of
some printing in Cork.
1st edn and edns listed, 1766 [1007].
BL HU
* N

1012.
[GOLDSMITH Oliver]
+THE VICAR OF WAKEFIELD : A TALE. Supposed to be written by Himself. In Two
Volumes. [Cork] London : Printed in the Year 1766.
2 vols. 12mo.
ESTC t146802; TS pp.179-180.
A press variant of the Eugene Swiney edn, 1766 [1011].
1st edn and edns listed, 1766 [1007].
BL Bod HU YU
* N

1013.
[GRIFFITH Richard and Elizabeth]
A SERIES OF GENUINE LETTERS BETWEEN HENRY AND FRANCES.
London : Printed for W. Johnston, in Ludgate-Street. 1766.
Volumes III & IV. 2 vols. 12mo. Subn.
CR XXIII 30-36 (Jan. 1767); MR XXXVI 154-155 (Feb. 1767).
BB; CG(BB); ESTC t111107.
Vols I-II and edns listed, 1757 [412].
BL Bod CUL DU HU LC YU
* E

1014.
[GUÉRIN DE TENCIN Madame Claudine Alexandrine]
+THE FEMALE ADVENTURERS.
Dublin : Printed for P. Wilson and J. Potts. 1766.
2 vols in 1.
CG(TW).
1st edn, 1765 [918].
HU
N

1015.
[JOHNSON Samuel]
+THE PRINCE OF ABISSINIA. A Tale. In Two Volumes. The Fourth Edition.
London : Printed for W. Strahan, W. Johnston, and J. Dodsley. 1766.
2 vols. 8vo.
CG(AR); EC 221:4; ESTC t139512.
1st edn and edns listed, 1759 [495].
BL Bod Tx UC
* N

1016.
[JOHNSTON Charles]
+CHRYSAL : OR, THE ADVENTURES OF A GUINEA. Wherein are exhibited Views of
several striking Scenes, with Curious and Interesting Anecdotes of the Most Noted Persons
in every Rank of Life, whose Hands it passed through, in America, England, Holland,
Germany and Portugal. By an Adept. The Fifth Edition, greatly inlarged and corrected.
London : Printed for T. Becket and P. A. De Hondt, at Tully's Head, near Surry-Street, in the
Strand. 1766.
Volumes I & II. 2 vols. 12mo.
ESTC t119101.
1st edn and edns listed, 1760 [577].
BL CUL CUNY UP YU
* N

1017.
[KELLY Hugh]
MEMOIRS OF A MAGDALEN : OR, THE HISTORY OF LOUISA MILDMAY. Now first
published from a Series of Original Letters. In Two Volumes.
London : Printed for W. Griffin, in Catherine-Street, in the Strand. 1767 [1766].
2 vols. 8vo. 6s (BB,CR).
CR XXII 373-375 (Nov. 1766); MR XXXVI 30 (Mar. 1767).
BB; CG(GM); EC 218:7; ESTC t072182; FB; LO 204 (BL,FB,HU).
Dublin edn, 1767 [1111]. Also, 1782, 1784, 1792, 1795.
BL HU NLC Tx UC
* E

1018.
[KIMBER Edward]
+THE GENEROUS BRITON; OR, THE AUTHENTIC MEMOIRS OF WILLIAM
GOLDSMITH. In Two Volumes.
Dublin : Exshaw. 1766.
8vo.
AB; CG.
1st edn and edns listed, 1765 [924].
N

1019.
[LANGHORNE John]
+THE CORRESPONDENCE OF THEODOSIUS AND CONSTANTIA, From her first
acquaintance to the departure of Theodosius. Now first published from the Original
Manuscripts. By the Editor of the Letters that passed between Theodosius and Constantia
after she had taken the Veil. The Second Edition.
London : Printed for T. Becket and P. A. De Hondt, at Tully's Head, in the Strand. 1766.
152pp. 12mo.
1st edn and edns listed, 1765 [926].
Bod NLC YU
* E

1020.
[LANGHORNE John]
+THE EFFUSIONS OF FRIENDSHIP AND FANCY. In Several Letters to and from Select
Friends. The Second Edition with large Additions and Improvements.
London : Printed for T. Becket and P. A. De Hondt, in the Strand. 1766.
2 vols. 8vo. 6s (BB,CR,MR).
Rev of 2nd edn, CR XXII 316 (Oct. 1766); MR XXXIV 313-314 (Apr. 1766).
BB; ESTC t136779.
1st edn, 1763 [777].
BL UMin YU
* E

1021.
[LANGHORNE John]
+THE LETTERS THAT PASSED BETWEEN THEODOSIUS AND CONSTANTIA; After
she had Taken the Veil. The Fourth Edition.
London : Printed for T. Becket and P. A. De Hondt, at Tully's Head, in the Strand. 1766.
182pp. 8vo.
CG; ESTC t068338; McB 525.
1st edn and edns listed, 1763 [778].
BL Bod UI UNC
* E

1022.
[LELAND Thomas]
+LONGSWORD, EARL OF SALISBURY. An Historical Romance. In Two Volumes. The
Second Edition.
Dublin : Printed by George Faulkner, in Parliament Street. 1766.
2 vols in 1. 173pp. 12mo.
ESTC t118910.
1st edn and edns listed, 1762 [728].
BL
* N

1023.
[MARISHALL Jean]
+THE HISTORY OF MISS CLARINDA CATHCART, AND MISS FANNY RENTON. In
Two Volumes. The Second Edition.
London : Printed for Francis Noble, at his Circulating Library, opposite Gray's-Inn-Gate,
Holborn; And John Noble, at his Circulating Library, in St. Martin's Court, near Leicester-
Square. 1766.
2 vols. 12mo.
1st edn and edns listed, 1765 [928].
UF [imperf]
E

1024.
M[ARISHALL] J[ean]
+THE HISTORY OF MISS CLARINDA CATHCART AND MISS FANNY RENTON. In
Two Volumes.
Dublin : P. Wilson. 1766.
2 vols.
CG(HU).
1st edn and edns listed, 1765 [928].
HU
E

1025.
MARMONTEL Jean François
+MORAL TALES BY M. MARMONTEL.
London : Printed for T. Becket and P. A. De Hondt, near Surry-Street, in the Strand. 1766.
Volume III. 251pp. 8vo.
CG(MR).
1st edn of vol.III, 1765 [931]. 1st edn of vols I-II and edns listed, 1763 [784].
YU
* C

1026.
MARMONTEL Jean François
+MORAL TALES, BY M. MARMONTEL. The Second Edition.
London : Printed for T. Becket and P. A. De Hondt, near Surry-Street, in the Strand. 1766.
3 vols. 12mo.
1st edn (vols I-II) and edns listed, 1763 [784].
CUL
* C

1027.
[MÉNARD Léon]
THE AMOURS OF CALISTHENES AND ARISTOCLEA; A NOVEL.
London : 1766.
12mo.
BB; CG(BB).
A trans. of Les Amours de Callisthène et d'Aristoclée.
N

1028.
MINIFIE Margaret and Susannah
THE PICTURE. A NOVEL. By The Miss Minifies, Of Fairwater in Somersetshire; Authors
of the History of Lady Frances S——, and Lady Caroline S——.
London : Printed for the Authors, And Sold by J. Johnson and Co. at the Globe, in Pater-Noster-
Row. 1766.
3 vols. 12mo. 9s (CR,MR).
CR XXI 288-290 (Apr. 1766); MR XXXIV 406 (May 1766).
AB(Pi); BB; CG(GM); ESTC t125288; LO 201 (CR,HU,UP,UI).
BL HU NYSL(HC) UI UP
* N

1029.
le PRINCE DE BEAUMONT Jeanne Marie
+THE HISTORY OF A YOUNG LADY OF DISTINCTION. In a Series of Letters between
Madame du Montier, and the Marchioness de ***, her Daughter. Translated from the
French of Madame de Beaumont.
London : Nobles. 1766.
2 vols. 12mo. 6s (MR).
MR XXXV 328 (Oct. 1766).
BB; CG.
BL & ESTC has given earlier edn as by Élie de Beaumont, from attribution by MR rev. of this edn, but see
1758 [445] and note to 1st edn, 1754 [245].
E

1030.
le PRINCE DE BEAUMONT Madam [Jeanne Marie]
LETTERS FROM EMERANCE TO LUCY. Translated from the French of Madame Le Prince De Beaumont. In Two Volumes.
London : Printed for J. Nourse, in the Strand, Bookseller to His Majesty. 1766.
2 vols. 12mo. 5s (BB,CR) 6s (MR).
CR XXI 432-438 (June 1766); MR XXV 147 (Aug. 1766).
AB(BL); BB; ESTC t067329.
A trans. of *Lettres d'Émérance à Lucie*, 1765. 1st London edn in French, 1765. Dublin edn, 1766 [1031].
BL
* E

1031.
le PRINCE DE BEAUMONT Madam [Jeanne Marie]
+LETTERS FROM EMERANCE TO LUCY. Translated from the French of Madame Le Prince De Beaumont.
Dublin : H. Saunders [1766?] (adv-1767 [1084]).
4s4d.
Adv-1767 [1084].
1st English edn, 1766 [1030].
E

1032.
le PRINCE DE BEAUMONT Madam [Jeanne Marie]
THE VIRTUOUS WIDOW : OR MEMOIRS OF THE BARONESS DE BATTEVILLE, Translated from the French of Madam le Prince de Beaumont.
London : Printed for J. Nourse, in the Strand. 1766.
12mo. 3s bound (CR,MR).
CR XXI 438-439 (June 1766); MR XXV 27-30 (July 1766).
BB; CG(MR).
Dublin edn, 1767 [1126].
N

1033.
RICCOBONI Marie Jeanne
THE CONTINUATION OF THE LIFE OF MARIANNE. To which is added The History of Ernestina, With Letters and Other Miscellaneous Pieces. Translated from the French of Madame Riccoboni.
London : Printed for T. Becket and P. A. de Hondt, near Surry-Street, in the Strand. 1766.
226pp. 12mo.
CG(GM); ESTC t065512; LO 227 (as 1766).
A trans. of *Recueil de pièces détachées*, 1765. Later included in Lane's 1781, *Select Novels*.
BL
* N

1034.
RICHARDSON Samuel
+THE HISTORY OF SIR CHARLES GRANDISON. In a Series of Letters. By Mr. Samuel Richardson, Author of Pamela and Clarissa. In Seven Volumes. The Fifth Edition.
London : Printed (by Assignment from Mr Richardson's Executors) for J. Rivington, in St. Paul's Church-Yard; R. Baldwin, S. Crowder, J. Coote, and Mr. Richardson, in Pater-noster-Row. 1766.
7 vols. 12mo.
EC 220:1; ESTC t058987; McB 756.
1st edn and edns listed, 1753 [191].
BL Bod CUL UI UMo
* E

1035.
[RIDLEY James]
+THE TALES OF THE GENII : OR, THE DELIGHTFUL LESSONS OF HORAM, THE
SON OF ASMAR. Faithfully Translated from the PersiAn Manuscript; and Compared with
the French and Spanish Editions Published at Paris and Madrid. The Third Edition. In
Two Volumes. By Sir Charles Morell, Formerly Ambassador from the British Settlements
in India to the Great Mogul.
London : Printed for J. Wilkie, in St. Paul's Church-Yard. 1766.
2 vols. 12mo.
CG(HU); ESTC t129380.
1st edn and edns listed, 1764 [862].
Bod CUL HL HU NCU YU
* C

1036.
[ROBINSON John]
THE HISTORY OF MR. CHARLES CHANCE, AND MISS CLARA VELLUM.
London : Printed by Cæsar Ward, For Francis Noble, at his Circulating Library, near Middle-
Row Holborn; And John Noble, at his Circulating Library, in St. Martin's Court, near Leicester-
Square. 1767 [1766].
231pp. 12mo. 3s (CR,MR).
CR XXII 468-469 (Dec. 1766); MR XXXVI 173 (Feb. 1767).
BB; CG(BB,MR); ESTC t071397.
BL BU
* N

1037.
[le SAGE Alain René]
[SMOLLETT Tobias *trans.*]
+THE ADVENTURES OF GIL BLAS OF SANTILLANE. A New Translation, By the
Author of Roderick Random. Adorned with Thirty-three Cuts, Neatly engraved. In Four
Volumes. The Third Edition.
London : Printed for T. Osborne, J. Rivington, R. Baldwin, W. Strahan, W. Johnston, T.
Longman, B. Law, R. Horsfield, T. Caslon, C. and R. Ware, Z. Stuart, and W. Nicoll. 1766.
4 vols. 12mo.
CG; ESTC t130468.
1st edn, 1749. Edns listed, 1750 [36].
BL DU HU YU
* N

1038.
[SCOTT Mrs Sarah Robinson]
THE HISTORY OF SIR GEORGE ELLISON. In Two Volumes.
London : Printed for A. Millar, in the Strand. 1766.
2 vols. 12mo. 6s (CR,MR).
CR XXI 281-288 (Apr. 1766); MR XXXV 43-46 (July 1766).
AB(BL,ELG,RI); BB(as 1776); CG; EC 229:4; ESTC t071399.
2nd edn, 1770.
BL CUL DU HL NLC OU UCLA UP YU
* N

1039.
[SHEBBEARE John]
+MATRIMONY, A NOVEL; Containing a Series of Interesting Adventures. In Two
Volumes. The Third Edition.
London : Printed for T. Lowndes, in Fleet-Street; J. Knox, in the Strand; and B. Collins, at
Salisbury. 1766.
2 vols. 12mo.
CG; ESTC t064745.
1st edn and edns listed, 1754 [253]. 1st edn of this title, 1755 [325].
BL CUL CUNY UNC UP YU
* N

1040.
[SMOLLETT Tobias]
+THE ADVENTURES OF RODERICK RANDOM. In Two Volumes. The Seventh Edition.
London : Printed for A. Millar, W. Strahan, J. Rivington, R. Baldwin, W. Johnston. T. Caslon,
B. Law, T. Becket and P. A. De Hondt, T. Lowndes, J. Knox, W. Nicoll, T. Durham, and M.
Richardson. 1766.
2 vols. 12mo.
ESTC t055371; MW 39.
1st edn, 1748. Edns listed, 1750 [40].
BL UI YU
* N

1041.
[WALPOLE Horace]
+THE CASTLE OF OTRANTO, A GOTHIC STORY. The Third Edition.
London : Printed for William Bathoe in the Strand. 1766.
200pp. 8vo. 4s sewed (*London Chronicle*, Jan. 1767)
ATW pp.44-56.
1st edn and edns listed, 1764 [868].
Bod CUL CUNY LWL NLC Tx YU
* N

Miscellanies

1042.
The Adventure of a Bale of Goods from America, in consequence of the Stamp Act.
London : Printed for J. Almon. 1766.
23pp. 8vo. 6d (BB,MR).
CR XXI 142 (Feb. 1766); MR XXXIV 157 (Feb. 1766).
BB(as 1765); CG(HU).
BU HL HU
M

1043.
The Entertaining Fabulist: Containing a Variety of Diverting Tales and Novels in Prose and Verse. To
which is Prefixed a short Tractate in Story-telling.
London : Bladon [1766] (MR).
2s6d sewed (MR).
MR XXXIV 82 (Jan. 1766).
BB(as 1765); CG(MR).
Also, 1770 edn.
C

1044.
+Fables of Æsop And Others, Translated into English. With instructive Applications; and a Print before each Fable. By Samuel Croxall, D.D. The Eighth Edition, carefully revised, and improved.
London : Printed for J. and R. Tonson. 1766.
329pp. 12mo.
McB 13.
Croxall's edn 1st published, 1747. Edns listed, 1753 [199].
Bn CUL UI
* M/C

1045.
Letters on Different Subjects, Amongst which are Interspers'd The Adventures of Alphonso, after the Destruction of Lisbon. By the Author of The Unfortunate Mother's Advice to her Absent Daughters.
London : To be had by the Subscribers at those Booksellers to whom they have subscribed, and at W. Bristow's in Roll's Buildings, Fetter-Lane. 1766.
2 vols. 8vo. Vols I-II 6s (CR).
CR XXII 214-220 (Sept. 1766).
CG; FB; LO 206 (FB,HU,UP).
Vols III-IV published in 1767, with edns [1153] [1154] [1155]. Also, 1770.
Bod HU NLC PU UP UNC
M/C

1046.
The Midnight Spy, Or, A View of the Transactions of London and Westminster, From The Hours of Ten in the Evening, till Five in the Morning; Exhibiting a great Variety of Scenes in High and Low Life, With the Characters of some Well known Nocturnal Adventurers of both Sexes.
[8 more lines]
London : Printed for J. Cooke, at the Shakespear's Head in Pater-noster Row. 1766.
147pp. 12mo. 2s (CR,MR).
CR XXI 313 (Apr. 1766); MR XXXIV 315 (Apr. 1766).
CG(BL).
BL Bod CUL IU NLC UCLA YU
* M

1047.
+The Secret History of Betty Ireland. The Seventh Edition.
London : Printed for John Lever [1766?] (CUNY,YU).
48pp. 12mo.
1st edn, [1741]. Edns listed, 1750 [50].
CUNY YU
M

1048.
[d'Argens Jean Baptiste de Boyer, Marquis]
+The Jewish Spy : Being a Philosophical, Historical, And Critical Correspondence, By Letters, which lately passed between Certain Jews in Turkey, Italy, France &c. Translated from the Originals into French, By the Marquis D'Argens; And now done into English. The Third Edition.
London : Printed for A. Miller [sic], J. Rivington, R. Baldwin, W. Johnston and A. Shuckburgh. 1766.
5 vols. 12mo.
CG(BL); ESTC t131033.
Vol V, dated 1765.
1st edn, 1739-40. Edns listed, 1753 [205].
BL BU CUNY HU PU Tx UI UV YU
* M

1049.

d'Aulnoy Marie Catherine La Mothe (Jumelle de Berneville) Countess

(+)A Collection of Novels and Tales of the Fairies. Written By That Celebrated Wit of France, the Countess D'Anois. In Three Volumes. Containing [11 titles follow]

The Fifth Edition. Translated from the best Edition of the Original French, by several Hands.

London : Printed for J. Brotherton, R. Baldwin, H. Woodfall, B. Law, C. and R. Ware, and G. Burnett. 1766.

3 vols. 8vo.

CG; ESTC t082647.

1st edn and similar edns listed, 1758 [452].

BL CUL [vol.II has '3rd Edn', 1766] NLC

* C/M

1050.

[Cervantes Saavedra Miguel de]

A Dialogue between Scipio and Bergansa, Two Dogs belonging to the City of Toledo. Giving an Account of their Lives and Adventures. [3 more lines] To which is annexed The Comical History of Rincon and Cortado. Both Written by the Celebrated Author of Don Quixote; and now first Translated From the Spanish Original.

London : Printed by Cæsar Ward; For Messrs. Richardson and Urquhart, at the Royal Exchange; and C. Etherington, at York. 1766.

180pp. 12mo.

EC 87:4; ESTC t075709.

Also, 1767 [1162].

* M

1051.

[Crisp Stephen]

+A Short History of a Long Travel from Babylon to Bethel. The Seventh Edition.

London : Printed and Sold at the Bible in George-Yard, Lombard-street. 1766.

28pp. 12mo.

CG(BL).

1st edn, 1720. Also, 1771, 1777, 1784.

BL [missing since 1986] Tx

M

1052.

[Goudar Ange de]

+The Chinese Spy; or Emissary from the Court of Pekin, commissioned to examine into the Present State of Europe. Translated from the Chinese.

Dublin : H. Saunders. 1766

6 vols in 3. 16mo. 8s1½d (adv-1767 [1084]).

Adv-1767 [1084]; CG

'1st Dublin edn', CG.

1st edn, 1764 [874]. Cf work by d'Argens, 1751 [107].

DU

M

1053.

[Haywood Mrs Eliza]

+The Female Spectator. The Sixth Edition.

London : Printed for T. Gardner. 1766.

4 vols.

CG(HU)

1st edn, 1744. Edns listed, 1750 [57].

BU HU OU

C/M

1054.
Montesquieu Charles Louis de Secondat, Baron de
+The History of the Troglodites; Translated from the French of Mr. de Montesquieu.
Chelmsford : Printed and Sold by T. Toft and R. Lobb : Sold also by J. Buckland at the Buck, and J. Payne at the Feathers, in Paternoster-Row; and W. Griffin in Catherine Street in the Strand, London. 1766.
23pp. 8vo.
From *Lettres Persianes* of 1721. Ozell trans, 1722; Flloyd trans, 1762.
Cf edns listed, 1751 [113].
Bod
* M

1055.
Montesquieu Charles Louis de Secondat, Baron de
The History of the Troglodites; Translated from the French of Mr. de Montesquieu.
London : Griffin [1766] (GM).
CR XXI 312 (Apr. 1766); MR XXXIV 473 (June 1766).
London re-issue.
CG(GM Apr. 1766).
From *Lettres Persianes* of 1721. Ozell trans, 1722; Flloyd trans, 1762.
Cf edns listed, 1751 [113].
M

1056.
Schouten Hendrik
Gent P. M. *trans.*
(+)The Hairy Giants: Or, A Description of Two Islands in the South Sea, Called by the Names of Benganga and Coma, Discovered by Henry Schooten, of Harlem, In a Voyage begun January 1699 and finished October 1671.
[9 more lines]
Written in Dutch by Henry Schooten, And Englished by P. M. Gent.
London : Printed in the Year 1671. Reprinted in the Year 1761, and Sold by J. Spilsbury, in Russel-Court, Covent-Garden.
24pp. 8vo. 6d (CR).
CR XXII 397-398 (Nov. 1766).
CG; EC 232:3; ESTC t069291.
1st edn, 1671.
BL CUL
* M

1057.
Thompson Edward
Sailor's Letters. Written to his Select Friends in England during his Voyages and Travels in Europe, Asia, Africa, and America, from the Years 1754 to 1759. By Edward Thompson. In Two Volumes.
London : T. Becket. 1766.
2 vols. 12mo.
Also, 1767 [1168] [1169].
FL NLC NYPL YU
M/E

1058.
+THE ADOPTED DAUGHTER; OR THE HISTORY OF MISS CLARISSA BEAUMONT.
Dublin : Printed for J. Williams. 1767-8.
2 vols in 1.
1st edn, 1766 [969].
DU
E

1059.
THE ADVENTURES OF A KIDNAPPED ORPHAN.
London : Printed for M. Thrush, at the King's-Arms, in Salisbury-Court, Fleet-Street, 1747 [1767].
252pp. 12mo. 2s6d sewed (CR) 3s (MR).
CR XXIV 345-349 (Nov. 1767); MR XXXVII 470 (Dec. 1767).
CG; EC 239:5; ESTC t068055; LO 211 (BL,UP); PBG 357(with note on dating).
BL FL HU IU NLC UP YU
* N

1060.
THE ADVENTURES OF AN AUTHOR. Written by Himself and a Friend. In Two Volumes.
London : Printed for Robinson and Roberts, No 25 in Paternoster-Row. 1767.
2 vols. 12mo. 6s (CR,MR).
CR XXIII 216-217 (Mar. 1767); MR XXXVI 238-239 (Mar. 1767).
AB(HWD); CG(HU); ESTC t085909; FB; LO 210 & 212 (FB,NYSL,UP).
BL FL HU NYSL UP
* N

1061.
+ARABIAN NIGHTS' ENTERTAINMENTS. Translated into English from the French of M. Galland.
London. 1767.
4 vols. 12mo.
CG(-).
1st English edn of this version, 1706. Edns listed, 1753 [167].
C

1062.
THE CONVENT : OR, THE HISTORY OF JULIA. In Two Volumes.
London : Printed for T. Lowndes, at his Circulating Library, in Fleet-street. 1767.
2 vols. 12mo. 6s (CR,MR).
CR XXIII 145-146 (Feb. 1767); MR XXXVI 172 (Feb. 1767).
AB(BL,WTS); EC 11:2; ESTC t108206; FB; LO 213 (BL,FB).
Dublin edn, 1767 [1063].
HU
* E

1063.
+THE CONVENT; OR, THE HISTORY OF JULIA. In Two Volumes.
Dublin : Printed for W. and W. Smith, P. Wilson, J. Exshaw, H. Saunders, J. Murphy, W. Sleater, D. Chamberlaine, J. Potts, J. Hoey, jun., S. Watson, J. Williams, and J. Mitchell. 1767.
2 vols in 1. 250pp. 12mo.
London edn, 1767 [1062].
YU
* E

1064.
THE COUNTRY COUSINS : OR, A JOURNEY TO LONDON. A Novel. In Two Volumes.
London : Printed by W. Hoggard, For Francis Noble, at his Circulating Library, near Middle-Row, Holborn; And John Noble, at his Circulating Library, in St. Martin's Court, near Leicester-Square, 1767.
2 vols. 12mo. 6s (MR).
MR XXXVI 173 (Feb. 1767).
AB(F); CG(-).
YU
* N

1065.
THE CRUEL DISAPPOINTMENT; OR, THE HISTORY OF MISS EMMELINE MERRICK; A Novel, Founded on Fact. In Two Volumes.
London : Printed for S. Bladon. 1767.
2 vols. 12mo. 6s (CR,MR).
CR XXIII 464 (June 1767); MR XXXVI 410 (May 1767).
CG(GM); LO 232 (UI) as 1768; McB 173.
UI
N

1066.
THE ENTERTAINING AMOUR OF SYLVANDER AND SYLVIA, A Fashionable Buck, And A Delicate Edinburgh Belle. Contained in Twenty-Four Genuine Letters. Wrote in the Year 1766.
Edinburgh : 1767.
89pp. 12mo.
CG(BL); EC 231:6; ESTC t064718.
BL
* E

1067.
THE FEMALE AMERICAN; OR, THE ADVENTURES OF UNCA ELIZA WINKFIELD. Compiled by Herself. In Two Volumes.
London : Printed for Francis Noble, at his Circulating Library, opposite Gray's-Inn-Gate, Holbourn; And John Noble, at his Circulating Library, in St. Martin's-Court, near Leicester-Square. 1767.
2 vols. 12mo. 5s (MR) 6s (CR).
CR XXIII 217 (Mar. 1767); MR XXXVI 238 (Mar. 1767).
CG(-); ESTC t066366; LO 214 (BL,NYPL) PBG 356.
BL NYPL YU
* N

1068.
THE FORCE OF NATURE; OR, THE HISTORY OF CHARLES LORD SOMMERS : In Two Volumes. By the Editor of the Wanderer.
London : Printed for Francis Noble, at his Circulating Library, near Middle-Row, Holbourn; And John Noble, at his Circulating Library, in St. Martin's Court, near Leicester Square. 1768 [1767].
2 vols. 12mo. 5s (CR) 6s (MR).
CR XXIV 430-436 (Dec. 1767); MR XXXVIII 150 (Feb. 1768).
CG(CR,MR,UnM); ESTC 111144; FB; LO 215 (CR,FB).
BL
* E

1069.
THE GENEROUS GUARDIAN : OR, THE HISTORY OF HORATIO SAVILLE, ESQ,
AND MISS LOUISA C****. In Two Volumes.
London : Printed for T. Vernor and J. Chator, at their Circulating Library, on Ludgate-hill. 1767.
2 vols. 12mo. 5s (CR).
CR XXIV 472 (Dec. 1767); MR XXXVIII 151 (Feb. 1768).
CG(MR,ScM).
HU
N

1070.
+THE HISTORY OF ELIZA. Written by a Friend.
Dublin : Printed for G. Faulkner, P. Wilson. 1767.
2 vols in 1. 12mo.
McB 453.
Possibly by Charlotte Lennox, DWW, p.197.
1st edn, 1766 [978].
UI UM UP
E

1071.
THE HISTORY OF INDIANA DANBY. By a Lady. Volumes III and IV.
London : Lownds. 1767.
2 vols. 12mo. 6s (CR,MR).
CR XXIII 278-280 (Apr. 1767); MR XXXVI 77 (July 1767).
CG(ScM).
Vols I-II, published 1765 [884]. Also, Dublin edn, 1772.
UCLA YU
E

1072.
THE HISTORY OF MAJOR BROMLEY AND MISS CLIFFEN.
London : Printed for J. Wilkie, in St. Paul's Church-Yard, and T. Lownds, in Fleetstreet. 1767.
2 vols. 12mo. 6s (CR,MR).
CR XXIV 300-304 (Oct. 1767); MR XXXVII 394 (Nov. 1767).
AB; CG(BL); EC 163:2; ESTC t066901; newSG.
BL UP YU
* N

1073.
+THE HISTORY OF MISS DELIA STANHOPE. In a Series of Letters to Miss Dorinda
Boothby. In Two Volumes.
Dublin : Printed for William Smith and Son, and William Colles, Booksellers in Dame-street.
1767.
2 vols in 1. 171pp & 126pp. 12mo.
ESTC t125602.
1st edn, 1766 [980].
BL CUL
* E

1074.
+THE HISTORY OF MISS DELIA STANHOPE. In a Series of Letters to Miss Dorinda
Boothby. In Two Volumes. The Second Edition.
London : Printed for T. Lowndes, at his Circulating Library, in Fleet-street. 1767.
CG.
1st edn, 1766 [980].
E

1075.
THE HISTORY OF MISS EMILIA BEVILLE. In Two Volumes.
London : Printed by W. Hoggard, for Francis Noble, at his Circulating Library, near Middle-row,
Holborn; and John Noble, at his Circulating Library, in St. Martin's Court, near Leicester-square.
1768 [1767].
2 vols. 12mo. 6s (CR,MR).
CR XXIV 296-300 (Oct. 1767); MR XXXVII 393 (Nov. 1767).
CG(CR); FB; LO 220 (FB,HU,UP).
HU UP
E

1076.
+THE HISTORY OF MISS HARRIOT FITZROY AND MISS EMILIA SPENCER.
Written after the Manner of Mr. Richardson's Clarissa, by the Author of Lucinda
Courtney.
Dublin : Printed by J. Williams. 1767.
2 vols in 1. 272pp.
1st edn, 1766 [981].
DU UP
E

1077.
THE HISTORY OF MISS PITTBOROUGH. In a Series of Letters. By a Lady. In Two
Volumes.
London : Printed for A. Millar, and T. Cadell, in the Strand; and J. Johnson and Co. in Pater-
noster Row. 1767.
2 vols. 12mo. 6s (CR,MR).
CR XXIII 131-135 (Feb. 1767); MR XXXVI 238 (Mar. 1767).
CG(Clapp); EC 234:5; ESTC t108052; FB; LO 222 (CR,FB,UI,UP); McB 458.
BL DU FL UC UCLA UI UNC UP
* E

1078.
THE HISTORY OF MR. BYRON AND MISS GREVILLE. In Two Volumes.
London : Printed for Francis Noble, at his Circulating Library, near Middle-Row, Holborn; and
John Noble, at his Circulating Library, in St. Martin's Court, near Leicester-Square. 1767.
2 vols. 12mo. 6s (CR,MR).
CR XXIII 157-158 (Mar. 1767); MR XXXVII 151 (Aug. 1767).
CG(BL); EC 210:2; ESTC t066904.
Dublin edn, 1768 [1184].
BL
* N

1079.
THE HISTORY OF MRS DRAYTON AND HER TWO DAUGHTERS. In Three Volumes.
London : Printed for F. Noble, at his Circulating Library, near Middle-Row, Holborn; and J.
Noble, at his Circulating Library, in St. Martin's Court, near Leicester Square. 1767.
3 vols. 12mo. 7s6d sewed or 9s bound (CR,MR).
CR XXIII 463-464 (June 1767); MR XXXVI 410 (May 1767).
CG(MR); ESTC t126597.
'Sometimes attributed to Adolphus Bannac' BL.
BL
* N

1080.
THE MEMOIRS OF GEORGE TUDOR, Wrote by Several Hands, But Revised and Set in Order wholly by Himself.
London : Pridden. 1767.
2 vols. 12mo. 5s (CR,MR).
CR XXIV 205-212 (Sept. 1767); MR XXXVII 314 (Oct. 1767).
CG(MR).
N

1081.
MEMOIRS OF THE REMARKABLE LIFE OF MR. CHARLES BRACHY. In a Series of Adventures, in Europe, Africa, &c. To which is added, The Hermit; Or, the History of Cloalde.
Dublin : Printed by James Hoey, Senior, at the Sign of the Mercury in Skinner-Row [1767?] (BL).
2 vols in 1. 12mo.
Vol II entitled 'Cloalde or the Hermit'.
ESTC t069917.
BL
* N

1082.
THE NUNNERY; OR, THE HISTORY OF MISS SOPHIA HOWARD.
London : Nobles. 1767.
2 vols. 12mo. 5s (MR) 6s (CR).
CR XXIII 146 (Feb. 1767); MR XXXVI 171-172 (Feb. 1767).
CG(-); LO 223 (UP).
The work is *not* by Edward Jermingham, author of a play, 'The Nunnery', confused with this novel.
NLC UP
N

1083.
THE PERPLEXED LOVERS : OR, THE HISTORY OF SIR EDWARD BALCHEN, BART. In Three Volumes.
London : Printed by W. Hoggard, for Francis Noble, at his Circulating Library, near Middle-Row, Holborn; and John Noble, at his Circulating Library, in St. Martin's Court near Leicester Square. 1768 [1767].
3 vols. 12mo. 7s6d (CR) 9s (MR).
CR XXIV 355-356 (Nov. 1767); MR XXXVII 469-470 (Dec. 1767).
CG(HU); EC 236:3; ESTC t055910; LO 241 (UP).
BL HU UP YU
* N

1084.
BACULARD d'ARNAUD François Thomas Marie de
+FANNY : OR, THE HAPPY REPENTENCE. From the French of M. D'Arnaud.
Dublin : Printed by and for H. Saunders, in Castle-street. 1767.
69pp. 12mo.
AB(as 1777); CG; ESTC t016498.
1st edn, 1766 [991].
BL Bod
* N

1085.
[BOSWELL James]
DORANDO, A SPANISH TALE.
London : Printed for J. Wilkie at the Bible in St. Paul's Church-Yard. Sold Also by J. Dodsley in Pall-Mall, T. Davies in Russel-Street Covent-Garden, And by the Booksellers of Scotland. 1767
50pp. 8vo. 1s (CR).
CR XXIV 80 (July 1767).
AB(BL,Hunt); CG(BL); ESTC t034841.
Also, 1767 [1086] [1087] [1088].
BL HL HU YU
* N

1086.
[BOSWELL James]
+DORANDO, A SPANISH TALE. The Second Edition.
London : Printed for J. Wilkie at the Bible in St. Paul's Church-Yard. Sold Also by J. Dodsley in Pall-Mall, T. Davies in Russel-Street Covent-Garden, And by the Booksellers of Scotland. 1767
50pp. 8vo.
1st edn, 1767 [1085].
CUL
* N

1087.
[BOSWELL James]
+DORANDO, A SPANISH TALE. The Third Edition with Corrections and Alterations.
Edinburgh : Printed for J. Wilkie, London; sold also by Drummond, Edinburgh; and by all the booksellers in Scotland. 1767.
50pp. 8vo.
CG; ESTC t137140.
1st edn, 1767 [1085].
BL YU
* N

1088.
[BOSWELL James]
+DORANDO. A SPANISH TALE. The Fourth Edition, with Corrections, Alterations and Additions.
London : J. Wilkie. 1767.
50pp. 8vo.
1st edn, 1767 [1085].
NYPL
N

1089.
[BROOKE Mrs Frances Moore]
+THE HISTORY OF LADY JULIA MANDEVILLE. In Two Volumes. The Third Edition.
Dublin : Printed for J. Potts. 1767.
CG(HCL).
1st edn and edns listed, 1763 [769]. A re-issue of 1766 [992].
HU UP
E

1090.
BROOKE Henry
+THE FOOL OF QUALITY; OR, THE HISTORY OF HENRY EARL OF MORELAND.
In Four Volumes. The Second Edition. By Mr. Brooke.
London : Printed for W. Johnston, in Ludgate-Street. 1767.
Volumes I & II. 2 vols. 12mo.
CG; ESTC t117246.
1st edn and edns listed, 1766 [993]. Vol III, 1768 [1202]. Vol IV, 1769 [1300].
BL CUL NLC Tx UF UI UM
* N

1091.
BROOKE Henry
+THE FOOL OF QUALITY; OR, THE HISTORY OF HENRY EARL OF MORELAND.
In Four Volumes. The Third Edition. By Mr. Brooke.
London : Printed for W. Johnston, in Ludgate-Street. 1767.
2 vols. Vol. I dated 1770. Vol. II, 1767.
ESTC t095737.
1st edn and edns listed, 1766 [993].
BL
* N

1092.
[DEFOE Daniel]
+THE LIFE AND STRANGE SURPRISING ADVENTURES OF ROBINSON CRUSOE,
OF YORK, MARINER [7 more lines]
Written by Himself. In Two Volumes.
London : Printed for T. Thompson, R. Damper, L. Burch, H. Shoram, T. Clitch, B. Blossom, D.
Lord, F. Fritchet, G. Townwold, J. Dwarf, J. Liblond and W. Blanchard. 1767.
2 vols. 12mo. Vol II, 'The Farther Adventures'.
EC 224:3; ESTC t072283.
1st edn, 1719-20. Edns listed, 1752 [129].
BL Bn CUL RFP YU
* N/M

1093.
FIELDING Henry
+THE HISTORY OF THE ADVENTURES OF JOSEPH ANDREWS, AND HIS FRIEND
MR. ABRAHAM ADAMS. Written in Imitation of the Manner of Cervantes, Author of
Don Quixote. By Henry Fielding Esq. The Fourth Edition.
Dublin : Printed for D. Chamberlaine and J. Potts. 1767.
344pp.
1st edn, 1742. Edns listed, 1751 [84].
CG(-); RCC pp.64,239.
YU
N

1093a.
FIELDING Henry
+THE HISTORY OF THE ADVENTURES OF JOSEPH ANDREWS, AND HIS FRIEND
MR. ABRAHAM ADAMS.
Dublin : Printed for W. and W. Smith, G. Faulkner, and T. Ewing, Booksellers. 1767.
1 vol.
RCC pp64,239.
1st edn, 1742. Edns listed, 1751 [84].
NLI TCD
N

1094.
FIELDING Henry
+THE HISTORY OF THE ADVENTURES OF JOSEPH ANDREWS, AND HIS FRIEND
MR. ABRAHAM ADAMS. Written in Imitation of the Manner of Cervantes, Author of
Don Quixote. By Henry Fielding Esq. The Fourth Edition.
Edinburgh : Printed by Martin & Wotherspoon. 1767.
12mo.
1st edn, 1742. Edns listed, 1751 [84].
HU
N

1095.
FIELDING Henry
+THE HISTORY OF TOM JONES, A FOUNDLING. By Henry Fielding, Esq;
Edinburgh : Printed by Martin & Wotherspoon. 1767.
3 vols. 12mo.
CG; ESTC t133822.
1st edn, 1749. Edns listed, 1750 [24].
BL YU
* N

1096.
FIELDING Henry
+THE HISTORY OF TOM JONES, A FOUNDLING.
Dublin : Printed for James Hoey, sen. James Hoey jun. D. Chamberlaine, and James Potts. 1767.
3 vols. 12mo.
CG; RCC pp.68-69,239.
1st edn, 1749. Edns listed, 1750 [24].
YU
N

1097.
FIELDING Henry
+THE WORKS OF HENRY FIELDING ESQ... With a Life of the Author. The Fourth
Edition.
Edinburgh : Printed by Martin & Wotherspoon. 1767.
12 vols. 12mo.
1st edn and edns listed, 1762 [714].
Bod BU HU NLC PU UW YU
C/N

1098.
[GIBBES Pheobe]
THE WOMAN OF FASHION; OR, THE HISTORY OF LADY DIANA DORMER. In Two
Volumes.
London : Printed for J. Wilkie, in St. Paul's Churchyard. 1767.
2 vols. 12mo. 6s (CR,MR).
CR XXIII 465 (June 1767); MR XXXVII 151 (Aug. 1767).
CG(HU); LO 217 (HU).
HU PU
* N

1099.
[GOLDSMITH Oliver]
+THE VICAR OF WAKEFIELD : A TALE. Supposed to be written by Himself. The
Fourth Edition.
Dublin : Printed in the Year. 1767.
1st edn and edns listed, 1766 [1007].
HU YU
N

1100.
[GOLDSMITH Oliver]
+THE VICAR OF WAKEFIELD : A TALE. Supposed to be written by Himself.
Dublin : Printed for W. and W. Smith, A. Leathley, J. Hoey sen. P. Wilson, J. Exshaw, E.
Watts, H. Saunders, J. Hoey jun. J. Potts, and J. Williams. 1767.
2 vols in 1. 182pp. 12mo.
ESTC t146181.
1st edn and edns listed, 1766 [1007].
BL CUL HU UNC YU
* N

1101.
[GOMEZ Madeleine Angélique Poisson de]
THE LONDON MERCHANT, A TALE. From the French of Madame de Gomez.
London : Almon. 1767.
12mo. 1s6d (CR,MR).
CR XXIV 157-158 (Aug. 1767); MR XXXVII 393 (Nov. 1767).
CG(GM).
N

1102.
[GRIFFITH Richard and Elizabeth]
+A SERIES OF GENUINE LETTERS BETWEEN HENRY AND FRANCES. The Third
Edition, Revised, Corrected, Enlarged, and Improved, By the authors.
London : Printed for W. Johnston, in Ludgate-Street. 1767.
Vols I-II.
2 vols. 12mo. 6s (CR,MR).
ESTC t111105.
1st edn and edns listed, 1757 [412].
BL DU HU LC YU
* E

1103.
[HAYWOOD Mrs Eliza]
+THE FRUITLESS ENQUIRY. Being A Collection Of several entertaining Histories and
Occurences, Which fell under the Observation of A Lady in her Search after Happiness. By
the Author of the History of Miss Betsy Thoughtless. The Second Edition.
London : Printed for T. Lowndes, in Fleet-Street. 1767.
278pp. 12mo.
CG; ESTC t059700; PBG 258.
1st edn, 1727. Also, 1769 [1315].
BL NLC YU
* N/C

1104.
[HAYWOOD Mrs Eliza]
+THE INVISIBLE SPY. By Explorabilis. In Two Volumes. The Third Edition.
London : Printed for L. Gardner, at Cowley's-Head, facing St. Clement's-Church in the Strand.
1767.
2 vols. 12mo.
ESTC t135554.
1st edn (as 'Exploralibus') and edns listed, 1755 [316].
BL UM
* N/M

1105.
[HIGGS Henry]
HIGH LIFE : A NOVEL. OR, THE HISTORY OF MISS FAULKLAND. In Two Volumes.
London : Printed for T. Lowndes, at his Circulating Library, in Fleet-Street, 1768. [1767].
2 vols. 12mo. 6s (CR,MR).
CR XXIV 350-355 (Nov. 1767); MR XXXVII 394 (Nov. 1767).
CG(Clapp); LO 218 (HU [in fact Dublin edn] FB).
Dublin edn, 1768 [1216].
YU
* E

1106.
[JENNER Charles]
LETTERS FROM ALTAMONT IN THE CAPITAL, TO HIS FRIENDS IN THE
COUNTRY.
London : Printed for T. Becket and P. A. De Hondt, in the Strand. 1767.
272pp. 12mo. 3s (CR,MR).
CR XXIV 63-66 (July 1767); MR XXXVII 146-147 (Aug. 1767).
ESTC t057337.
Dublin edn, 1767 [1107]. Also, 1776. YU suggests possibility of an earlier, 1764 edn.
BL DU OU YU
* E/M

1107.
[JENNER Charles]
+LETTERS FROM ALTAMONT IN THE CAPITAL, TO HIS FRIENDS IN THE
COUNTRY.
Dublin : Printed for W. Sleator [sic] J. Potts, and J. Williams, Booksellers. 1767.
219pp. 8vo.
CG.
BU CUL HU NLC UCLA UP
* E/M

1108.
[JOHNSTON Charles]
+CHRYSAL : OR, THE ADVENTURES OF A GUINEA. Wherein are exhibited several
striking Scenes, with curious and interesting Anecdotes of the most noted Persons in every
Rank of Life, whose Hands it passed through, in America, England, Holland, Germany and
Portugal. By an Adept. The Third Edition, greatly enlarged and corrected. In Four
Volumes.
London : Printed for John Hill in the Strand. 1767.
4 vols. 12mo.
ESTC t061908.
The first complete edn. Vols I-II published and edns listed, 1760 [577]. Vols III-IV 1st published, 1765 [922].
BL Bod NYPL PU Tx UM UV
* N

1109.
[JOHNSTON Charles]
+CHRYSAL : OR, THE ADVENTURES OF A GUINEA. Wherein are exhibited several
striking Scenes, with curious and interesting Anecdotes of the most noted Persons in every
Rank of Life, whose Hands it passed through, in America, England, Holland, Germany and
Portugal. By an Adept. The Second Edition.
London : Printed for T. Becket and P. A. De Hondt, in the Strand. 1767.
Volumes III and IV. 2 vols. 12mo.
ESTC t140679.
Vols III-IV 1st published, 1765 [922]. Vols I-II published and edns listed, 1760 [577].
BL UP
* N

1110.
[JOHNSTON Charles]
+THE REVERIE: OR, A FLIGHT TO THE PARADISE OF FOOLS. Published by the
Editor of The Adventures of a Guinea. In Two Volumes.
London : Printed for T. Becket, and P. A. De Hondt, in the Strand. 1767.
2 vols. 12mo.
ESTC t061908.
1st edn and edns listed, 1762 [723].
BL BU HU OU Tx UP UW YU
* N

1111.
[KELLY Hugh]
+MEMOIRS OF A MAGDALEN : OR, THE HISTORY OF LOUISA MILDMAY. Now
First Published from a Series of Original Letters. In Two Volumes.
Dublin : Printed for P. Wilson, J. Exshaw, J. Murphy, H. Saunders, W. Sleater, J. Potts, D.
Chamberlain, J. Hoey, jun., J. Williams, and T. Ryder. 1767.
2 vols. 12mo.
AB; CG has a '2nd edn' by Griffin, but without source.   1st edn, 1766 [1017].
YU
* E

1112.
[KIMBER Edward]
+THE LIFE, EXTRAORDINARY ADVENTURES, VOYAGES, AND SURPRIZING
ESCAPES OF CAPT. NEVILLE FROWDE, OF CORK. In Four Parts.
London : Printed for J. Brown. 1767.
220pp. 12mo.
1st edn and edns listed, 1758 [440].
BU UCB
N/M

1113.
[MARISHALL Jean]
THE HISTORY OF ALICIA MONTAGUE. By the Author of Clarinda Cathcart. In Two
Volumes.
London : Printed for the Author : and sold by Robinson and Roberts, in Pater-noster-Row;
Richardson and Urquhart, at the Royal Exchange; and T. Cadell, (Successor to Mr. Millar) in the
Strand. 1767.
2 vols. 12mo. 6s (CR,MR).
CR XXIII 210-214 (Mar. 1767); MR XXXVII 76 (July 1767).
CG; ESTC t138872; LO 225 (UP,FB); FB.
BL IU NLC UP YU
* E

1114.
[MARISHALL Jean]
+THE HISTORY OF MISS CLARINDA CATHCART, AND MISS FANNY RENTON. In
Two Volumes. The Third Edition.
London : Printed for Francis Noble, at his Circulating Library, opposite Gray's-Inn Gate,
Holborn; and John Noble, at his Circulating Library, in St. Martin's Court, near Leicester-Square.
1767.
2 vols. 12mo. 6s. (tp).
ESTC t064749.
1st edn and edns listed, 1765 [928].
BL
* E

1115.
MARMONTEL Jean François
BELISARIUS. By M. Marmontel, Member of the French Academy.
London : Printed for and Sold by P. Vaillant, in the Strand; and by Robinson and Roberts, in
Pater-noster Row. 1767.
240pp. 12mo. 3s (CR,MR).
CR XXIII 168-179 (Mar. 1767); MR XXXVI 290-298 (Apr. 1767).
CG; EC 57:5; ESTC t090758; LO 226 (UP).
Trans. of *Bélisaire*, 1767. Also, 1767 [1116] [1117] [1118] [1119] [1120], 1768 [1221] [1222], 1773, 1783,
1784, 1786, 1789, 1794(4x), 1796. Cf 1759 [523].
BL CUL UP
* N

1116.
MARMONTEL Jean François
+BELISARIUS. By M. Marmontel, Member of the French Academy. The Second Edition.
London : Printed for and Sold by P. Vaillant, in the Strand; and by Robinson and Roberts, in
Pater-noster Row. 1767.
240pp. 12mo.
ESTC t090758.
1st edn and edns listed, 1767 [1115].
BL CUL
* N

1117.
MARMONTEL Jean François
+BELISARIUS. By M. Marmontel, Member of the French Academy. The Third Edition.
London : Printed for and Sold by P. Vaillant, in the Strand; and by Robinson and Roberts, in
Pater-noster Row. 1767.
240pp. 12mo.
ESTC t090760.
1st edn and edns listed, 1767 [1115].
BL DU LU OU RU Tx UF UP UV YU
* N

1118.
MARMONTEL Jean François
+BELISARIUS. By M. Marmontel. Member of the French Academy.
Dublin : Printed for P. Wilson, J. Exshaw, H. Saunders, J. Murphy, W. Sleater, D.
Chamberlaine, J. Potts, J. Hoey jun. and J. Williams. 1767.
240pp. 8vo.
CG; ESTC t119692.   1st edn and edns listed, 1767 [1115].
BL
* N

1119.
MARMONTEL Jean François
+BELISARIUS. By M. Marmontel. Member of the French Academy. The Second Edition.
Dublin : Printed for P. Wilson, J. Exshaw, H. Saunders, J. Murphy, W. Sleater, D. Chamberlaine, J. Potts, J. Hoey jun. and J. Williams. 1767.
240pp. 8vo.
ESTC t132083.
1st edn and edns listed, 1767 [1115].
BL
* N

1120.
MARMONTEL Jean François
+BELISARIUS. By M. Marmontel, Member of the French Academy. To which are added, Fragments of Moral Philosophy by the same Author.
Edinburgh : Printed for A. Kincaid and J. Bell, and W. Gordon. 1767.
276pp. 12mo.
ESTC t120071.
1st edn and edns listed, 1767 [1115].
BL WCL
N

1121.
[MINIFIE Susannah (later Gunning)]
BARFORD ABBEY; A Novel in a Series of Letters. In Two Volumes.
London : Printed for T. Cadell (Successor to Mr. Miller) [sic] in the Strand; and J. Payne, in Paternoster-Row. 1768 [1767].
2 vols. 12mo. 6s (CR,MR).
CR XXIV 422-430 (Dec. 1767); MR XXXVIII 335 (Apr. 1768).
BB; CG(BB,HU); ESTC t072174; LO 236 (UP,UI,HU); McB 395.
BL HU UI UP YU
* E

1122.
MOUHY Charles de Fieux, Chevalier de
+THE FORTUNATE COUNTRY MAID. Being the Entertaining Memoirs Of the present celebrated Marchioness of L—— V——; [10 more lines] From the French of the Chevalier De Mouhy. In Two Volumes. The Sixth Edition.
London : Printed for J. Rivington, in St. Paul's Church Yard; Hawes, Clarke and Collins, and R. Baldwin, in Pater-noster-Row; E. Johnson and B. Law, Ave Mary Lane; R. Ware, on Ludgate-Hill; T. Lowndes and C. Corbett, in Fleet-Street. 1767.
2 vols. 12mo.
ESTC t075668.
1st edn, 1740. Edns listed, 1758 [444].
BL Tx
* N/M

1123.
PENN Rev. James
THE FARMER'S DAUGHTER OF ESSEX. By James Penn, Vicar of Clavering cum Langley, in the County of Essex, and Lecturer of St. Ann and Agnes, Aldersgate.
London : Printed for the Author; and to be had at his House, in Christ's Hospital. 1767.
223pp. 12mo. '2s6d unbound and 3s bound' (tp).
CR XXIII 464 (June 1767); MR XXXVII 76 (July 1767).
CG(BL,MR); EC 91:1; ESTC t108403; JT.
BL NYSL(HC) UC
* N

1124.
[PRÉVOST D'EXILES Abbé Antoine François]
(+)THE HISTORY OF THE CHEVALIER DES GRIEUX : Written by himself Translated from the French.
London : Printed for B. White, at Horace's Head, in Fleet-street. 1767.
2 vols. 8vo. 4s (CR) / 12mo. 5s (MR).
CR XXIV 141-143 (Aug. 1767); MR XXXVII 76-77 (July 1767).
MR notes as a new version. A trans. of *Manon Lescaut*, 1731.
HU PU
N

1125.
[le PRINCE DE BEAUMONT Jeanne Marie]
+THE HISTORY OF A LADY OF DISTINCTION : IN A SERIES OF LETTERS. In Two Volumes. The Third Edition.
Dublin : Printed by James Hoey, at the Mercury in Skinner-Row. 1767.
2 vols in 1. 240pp. 12mo.
CG; ESTC t127686 (with alternative authorship as noted, 1754 [245]).
1st edn and edns listed, 1754 [245].
BL
* E

1126.
le PRINCE DE BEAUMONT Jeanne Marie
+THE VIRTUOUS WIDOW : OR, MEMOIRS OF THE BARONESS DE BATTEVILLE.
Translated from the French of Madame le Prince de Beaumont.
Dublin : Printed for J. Williams, Bookseller, in Skinner-Row. 1767.
267pp. 12mo.
ESTC t103376.
Trans. of *Mémoires de Madame la baronne de Batteville, ou La veuve parfaite*, 1766. 1st English edn, 1766 [1032].
BL
* N

1127.
RICCOBONI Marie Jeanne
LETTERS FROM THE COUNTESS DE SANCERRE, TO COUNT DE NANCÉ, HER FRIEND. By Madam Riccoboni. Translated from the French.
London : Printed for T. Becket and P. A. De Hondt, in the Strand. 1767.
2 vols. 8vo.
BB; CG(BB); EC 93:2; ESTC t131028; LO 228 (HU)
Trans. of *L'Histoire d'Adelaide d'Dammartin, Comtesse de Sancerre*, 1766. Dublin edn, 1768 [1228].
BL HU LC OU UC UV YU
* E

1128.
RICHARDSON Samuel
+THE HISTORY OF SIR CHARLES GRANDISON. In A Series of Letters. By Mr. Samuel Richardson. The Fourth Edition.
London : Printed (by assignment from Mr Richardson's executors) for J. Rivington etc.
7 vols. 12mo.
CG.
1st edn and edns listed, 1753 [191].
Tx
E

1129.
RICHARDSON Samuel
+PAMELA : OR, VIRTUE REWARDED. The Eighth Edition. To which are prefixed,
extracts from several curious Letters written to the Editor on the Subject.
London : Printed for H. Woodfall, J. Rivington, W. Strahan, R. Baldwin, W. Johnston, M.
Richardson and B. Collins. 1767.
4 vols. 12mo.
Noted in WS 14. Earlier 'Eighth' edn issued 1761 [664]. 1st edn, 1740. Edns listed, 1754 [250].
UCo UMo
E

1130.
ROUSSEAU Jean Jacques
+ELOISA, OR A SERIES OF ORIGINAL LETTERS COLLECTED AND PUBLISHED
BY J. J. ROUSSEAU. Translated from the French. The Fifth Edition.
Dublin : Printed for P. Wilson. 1767.
4 vols. 12mo.
1st English edn and edns listed, 1761 [666].
HU SI
E

1131.
[le SAGE Alain René]
[SMOLLETT Tobias *trans.*]
+THE ADVENTURES OF GIL BLAS OF SANTILLANE.
London : Printed for T. Osborn, J. Rivington, R. Baldwin. 1767.
4 vols. 12mo.
McB 553.   1st edn, 1749. Edns listed, 1750 [36].
UI
N

1132.
[le SAGE Alain René]
[SMOLLETT Tobias *trans.*]
+THE ADVENTURES OF GIL BLAS OF SANTILLANE. A New Translation. By Tobias
Smollet M.D. Author of Roderick Random &c. Adorned with a new Set of Cuts, neatly
Engraved. In Four Volumes.
Dublin : Printed for Peter Wilson, in Dame-street. 1767.
4 vols in 2. 12mo.
ESTC t120582; RCC p.79.
1st edn, 1749. Edns listed, 1750 [36].
BL CUL
* N

1133.
[SCOTT Mrs Sarah Robinson]
[MONTAGU Lady Barbara]
+A DESCRIPTION OF MILLENIUM HALL, AND THE COUNTRY ADJACENT :
Together with the Characters of the Inhabitants, And such Historical Anecdotes and
Reflections, As may Excite in the Reader Proper Sentiments of Humanity, And Lead the
Mind to the Love of Virtue. By a Gentleman on his Travels. The Third Edition.
London : Printed for J. Newbery, at the Bible and Sun in St. Paul's Church-Yard. 1767.
262pp. 12mo.
CG(BL); ESTC t064713; McB 804 (as 1762).
1st edn and edns listed, 1762 [736].
BL Bod CUL HU UI UP UW
* N

1134.
[SHERIDAN Mrs Frances Chamberlaine]
THE HISTORY OF NOURJAHAD. By the Editor of Sidney Bidulph.
London : Printed for J. Dodsley in Pall-Mall. 1767.
240pp. 12mo. 3s (CR,MR).
CR XXIV 34-41 (July 1767); MR XXXVII 314 (Oct. 1767).
CG(HU); ESTC t147336; LO 229 (UP,UI); McB 817.
Also Dublin edn, 1767 [1135], and 1788, 1792, 1798.
BL CUL CUNY DU HU NLC OU UC UI UNC UP UWYU
* N

1135.
[SHERIDAN Mrs Frances Chamberlaine]
+THE HISTORY OF NOURJAHAD. By the Editor of Sidney Bidulph.
Dublin : Printed for P. Wilson, J. Murphy, W. Sleater, D. Chamberlaine, J. Potts, J. Mitchell, J.
Williams, and W. Colles. 1767.
222pp. 12mo.
CG(HU); ESTC t118782; McB 818.
1st edn and edns listed, 1767 [1134].
BL UI YU
* N

1136.
[SHERIDAN Mrs Frances Chamberlaine]
**+MEMOIRS OF MISS SIDNEY BIDULPH. Extracted from her own Journal, And now
first published. In Three Volumes. The Third Edition.**
London : Printed for J. Dodsley, in Pall-Mall. 1767.
Volumes I-III. 3 vols. 12mo.
CR XXIII 274-278 (Apr. 1767).
CG(HU); ESTC t119361.
Vols IV & V, published 1770. 1st edn and edns listed, 1761 [670].
BL HU UP YU
* N

1137.
[SHERIDAN Mrs Frances Chamberlaine]
**THE CONCLUSION OF THE MEMOIRS OF MISS SYDNEY BIDULPH, As Prepared for
the Press by the late Editor of the former Part.**
London : Printed for J. Dodsley, in Pall-mall. 1767.
Volumes III & IV. 2 vols. 12mo. 6s (MR).
MR XXXVII 238 (Sept. 1767).
Also Dublin edn, 1767 [1138]. Edns of full work listed, 1761 [670].
HU
* N

1138.
[SHERIDAN Mrs Frances Chamberlaine]
+THE CONCLUSION OF THE MEMOIRS OF MISS SYDNEY BIDULPH.
Dublin : 1767.
3 vols in 2.
CG(BC).
1st vols published and edns listed, 1761 [670].
N

1139.
SMOLLETT Tobias
+THE ADVENTURES OF SIR LAUNCELOT GREAVES. By Tobias Smollett. M.D. The
Fourth Edition.
Cork : Printed for the Proprietor. 1767.
270pp. 12mo.
CG(HU); ESTC t055387; MW 239.
1st complete edn and edns listed, 1762 [739].
BL HU UIC
* N

1140.
[STERNE Laurence]
THE LIFE AND OPINIONS OF TRISTRAM SHANDY, GENTLEMAN. Vol.IX.
London : Printed for T. Becket and P. A. Dehondt, in the Strand. 1767.
145pp. 8vo.
CR XXIII 135-138 (Feb. 1767); MR XXXVI 93-102 (Feb. 1767).
ESTC t014824.
Vols I-II published and edns of all vols listed, 1759 [507]. Cf spurious vol.IX, 1766 [984].
BL
* N

1141.
[STERNE Laurence]
+THE LIFE AND OPINIONS OF TRISTRAM SHANDY, GENTLEMAN. Vol.IX.
Dublin : Printed for W. and W. Smith, J. Exshaw, H. Saunders, S. Watson, and W. Colles. 1767.
95pp. 12mo.
Vol.IX 1st published, 1767 [1140]. Edns of all vols listed, 1759 [507].
CUL
* N

1142.
[STERNE Laurence]
+THE LIFE AND OPINIONS OF TRISTRAM SHANDY, GENTLEMAN. Vol.IX.
Dublin : Printed for H. Saunders, in Castle-street, near Castle Gate. 1779 [1769].
48pp. 12mo.
ESTC t014786.
Vol.IX 1st published, 1767 [1140]. Edns of all vols listed, 1759 [507].
BL
* N

1143.
[STERNE Laurence]
+THE LIFE AND OPINIONS OF TRISTRAM SHANDY, GENTLEMAN.
Dublin : Printed for D. Lynch. 1760-1767. [1767].
8 vols in 3. 8vo.
Vol I & II, dated 1760; vols II-VI, 1761; vols VII & VIII, 1765.
ESTC t014740.
Almost certainly all vols printed in 1767. KM p.23.
Edns of all vols listed, 1759 [507].
BL
* N

1144.
[STERNE Laurence]
+THE LIFE AND OPINIONS OF TRISTRAM SHANDY, GENTLEMAN. The Second
Edition.
London : Printed for T. Becket and P. A. Dehondt, in the Strand. 1767.
Volumes V & VI. 2 vols. 12mo.
KM p.36, noting variant issues.
Vols V-VI 1st published, 1761 [677]. Vols I-II published and edns of all vols listed, 1759 [507].
N

1144a.
[STERNE Laurence]
+THE LIFE AND OPINIONS OF TRISTRAM SHANDY, GENTLEMAN. The Sixth
Edition.
London : Printed for R. Dodsley. 1767.
Volumes I & II. 2 vols. 12mo.
'Probably the edn of 500 copies printed by William Bowyer for Dodsley in the winter of 1766-67', KM p.23.
1st edn and edns of all vols listed, 1759 [507].
N

1145.
[PFEIL Johann Gottlob Benjamin]
STREIT F. W. *trans.*
THE MEMOIRS OF THE COUNT OF P—; Shewing at Once The Dreadful Consequences
of Vice, and the Happiness in being Virtuous. A Novel. Translated from the German By F.
W. Streit, F. Ducal S. at Jena. In Two Volumes.
London : Printed for the Translator by William Franklin, in Bartlett's Buildings, And Sold by J.
Dodsley, in Pall-Mall, S. Bladon, in Pater-Noster-Row, and R. Dymott, opposite Somerset-House,
in the Strand. 1767.
2 vols. 12mo. 6s (CR,MR).
CR XXXIV 194-198 (Sept. 1767); MR XXXVII 151-152 (Aug. 1767).
AB; CG(HU); ESTC t091508; newSG.
Dublin edn, 1767 [1146].
BL HU UC UP
* N

1146.
[PFEIL Johann Gottlob Benjamin]
STREIT F. W. *trans.*
+MEMOIRS OF THE COUNT OF P–, A Novel Translated from the German by F. W.
Streit.
Dublin : Printed for P. Wilson. [1767?] (adv-1767 [1135]).
2 vols.
Adv-1767 [1135].   1st English edn, 1767 [1145]
N

1147.
[WITHERS Philip]
THE ANTS : A RHAPSODY. In Two Volumes.
London : Printed for L. Davies and C. Reymers, in Holborn; T. Davies, in Covent Garden; and
R. Baldwin, in Pater-noster-Row. 1767.
2 vols. 12mo. 4s (CR,MR).
CR XXXIV 32-34 (July 1767); MR XXXVII 147 (Aug. 1767).
AB(BL,Ri); CG(HU); ESTC t091059.
YU copy tp MS note, 'D. O'Pheilly, pseud'. MS note in HU copy, 'probably by Philip Withers'.
AAS BL HU IU LC OU UW YU
* N/M

1148.
[YOUNG Arthur]
THE ADVENTURES OF EMMERA, OR THE FAIR AMERICAN. Exemplifying The Peculiar Advantages of Society and Retirement. In Two Volumes.
London : Printed for W. Nicoll, at the Paper-Mill, No 51, in St. Paul's Church-yard. 1767.
2 vols. 8vo. 6s (CR,MR).
CR XXIII 272-274 (Apr. 1767); MR XXXVI 239 (Mar. 1767).
AB(WB); CG(HU); EC 238:3; ESTC t057422; LO 230 (HU).
BL HU LC YU
Dublin edn, 1767 [1149].
* E

1149.
[YOUNG Arthur]
+THE ADVENTURES OF EMMERA; OR, THE FAIR AMERICAN, Exemplifying the Peculiar Advantages of Society and Retirement.
Dublin : Printed by James Hoey. 1767.
2 vols in 1. 12mo.
CG; McB 5.
1st edn, 1767 [1148].
Bn BU HU NYPL UI
E

Miscellanies

1150.
+The Fables of Æsop, and Other Allegorical Writers. Translated into English : with proper applications, and a suitable design to each Fable. By Samuel Croxall. The Ninth Edition, Carefully revised and improved.
Dublin : Printed for J. Exshaw. 1767.
379pp. 12mo.
Edns listed, 1753 [199].
UMin
M/C

1151.
(+)Fables and Tales for the World, and Miscellanies for the Country. Patricia's Address. Being fit to be read in all Churches and Chapels throughout England; but not at Berwick upon Tweed nor Bedfordshire.
London : P. Stevens. 1767.
8vo. 2s6d (CR).
CR XXIV 158-159 (Aug. 1767).
Printed in 1750 as Fables and Tales for the Ladies [43].
M/C

1152.
The Instructive Novellist : A Collection of Moral, Entertaining and Improving Stories, on Various Subjects, compiled from the Best Authors.
London : Noble. 1767.
12mo. 1s6d (CG).
CG(MR).
M

1153.

+Letters on Different Subjects; In Four Volumes; Amongst which are interspers'd Adventures of Alphonso after the Destruction of Lisbon. By the Author of The Unfortunate Mother's Advice to her Absent Daughter's. The Second Edition.

London : To be had by the Subscribers at those Booksellers to whom they have subscribed, and at W. Bristow's in Roll's Buildings, Fetter-Lane. 1767.

4 vols. 8vo.

ESTC t093497.

1st edn and edns listed, 1766 [1045].

BL

M/C

1154.

+Letters on Different Subjects; In Four Volumes; Amongst which are interspers'd Adventures of Alphonso after the Destruction of Lisbon. By the Author of The Unfortunate Mother's Advice to her Absent Daughter's. The Third Edition.

London : To be had by the Subscribers at those Booksellers to whom they have subscribed, and at W. Bristow's in Roll's Buildings, Fetter-Lane. 1767.

4 vols. 8vo.

1st edn and edns listed, 1766 [1045].

UP

M/C

1155.

+Letters on Different Subjects; In Four Volumes; Amongst which are interspers'd Adventures of Alphonso after the Destruction of Lisbon. By the Author of The Unfortunate Mother's Advice to her Absent Daughter's.

London : To be had by the Subscribers at those Booksellers to whom they have subscribed, and at W. Bristow's in Roll's Buildings, Fetter-Lane. 1767.

4 vols. 8vo.

ESTC t093499. A further edn.

1st edn and edns listed, 1766 [1045].

BL

M/C

1156.

The Moral and Entertaining Story Teller : Being a Collection of Genuine Tales, Ancient and Modern. Calculated to promote virtue in youth, and render vice hateful to it, by striking examples of their several consequences.

London : Printed for J. Williams. 1767.

2 vols. 8vo.

CG.

LC Tx UC

M/C

1157.

The New Modern Story Teller, or Universal Entertainer : Being a Collection of Merry, Polite, Grave, Moral, Entertertaining [sic] and Improving Tales. In Two Volumes.

London : Printed for the Author and sold by David Steel, at the Bible and Crown, in King-Street, near Little Tower-hill; and by all the booksellers in town and country. 1767.

2 vols. 12mo. 6d bound (tp).

CG(HU); ESTC t010036.

BL HU UI

* C/M

1158.
The Polite Companion; or, Stories for the Ladies.
Dublin : Printed for W. Sleator. 1767.
1 vol.
CG(HU).
HU
M/C

1159.
+**Select Fables of Esop and Other Fabulists. In Three Books. By R. Dodsley. A New Edition.**
London : Printed for J. Dodsley, in Pall-Mall. 1767.
204pp. 12mo.
1st Dodsley edn, 1761 [690]. Other versions and edns listed, 1753 [199].
HU
M/C

1160.
+**An Unfortunate Mother's Advice to her absent Daughters; in a Letter to Miss Pennington. The Fourth Edition.**
London : Printed by J. Towers. And sold by Mr. Bristow; and Mr. Walter. 1767.
8vo. 5s (CR).
CR XXIII 434-439 (June 1767) as vols. III and IV.
ESTC t079364.
1st edn and edns listed, 1760 [613].
BL NLC
M

1161.
The Wooden Bowl. A Tale. To which is Added, A Love-March. Taken from Mr. Collet's four celebrated Pieces, viz, Courtship, Elopement, Honey-moon, and Matrimony.
London : Printed for C. Moran, in the Great Piazza, Covent Garden. 1767.
20pp. 4to. 1s (tp).
CR XXIV 384 (Nov. 1767).
Parody on Peregrine Pickle. Collet's 'Pieces' are prints.
HU YU
M

1162.
[Cervantes Saavedra Miguel de]
+**A Dialogue between Scipio and Bergansa, Two Dogs belonging to the City of Toledo. Giving an Account of their Lives and Adventures. With the Comical History of Rincon and Cortado.**
London : Printed for S. Bladon. 1767.
180pp. 12mo.
ESTC t075710.
1st edn and edns listed, 1766 [1050].
BL HU LC NLC UC UNC YU
M

1163.
[Haywood Mrs Eliza]
(+)**Twenty-Four Entertaining Histories Illustrated by Modern Characters in Real Life.**
London : Printed for J. Gardner. 1767.
2 vols. 12mo.
A version of 1753 [188].
YU
M/C

1164.
Montesquieu Charles Louis de Secondat Baron de
Flloyd Thomas *trans.*
+Persian Letters. By M. De Montesqiueu. Translated from the French, By Mr. Flloyd. In Two Volumes.
The Fifth Edition.
Dublin : Printed for J. Potts, and W. Colles, Booksellers, in Dame-street. 1767.
105pp. 12mo.
1st English edn, 1722. Edns listed, 1751 [113].
CUL
* M/E

1165.
[Paterson Samuel]
Another Traveller! Or Cursory Remarks and Tritical Observations made upon a Journey Through Part
of the Netherlands In the latter End of the Year 1766. By Coriat Junior. In Two Volumes.
London : Printed for Joseph Johnson, and J. Payne, in Pater-Noster-Row; And T. Cadell, in the Strand. 1767.
Volume I. 1 vol. 12mo. 5s sewed (MR).
MR XXXIX 434-448 (Dec. 1768).
ESTC t056853.
Vol II issued, 1768 [1254]. 2nd edn, 1769 [1360].
BL
* M

1166.
[Povey Charles]
+The Virgin in Eden; or, the State of Innocency. Deliver'd by way of Image and Description.
[18 more lines] The Fifth Edition.
London : Printed for J. Brown, in Holiday Yard, Creed Lane, in Ludgate-Street; and sold by all the Booksellers
in Town and Country. 1767.
119pp. 8vo.
CG(-); ESTC t133525; newSG. An attack on *Pamela.* 1st edns, 1741. Reissued with new tp, 1769 [1363].
BL UP WCL YU
* M/C

1167.
Richer Adrien
+Great Events from Little Causes. Or, A Selection of Interesting and Entertaining Stories, Drawn from
the Histories of different Nations. Wherein Certain Circumstances, seemingly inconsiderable, are
discovered to have been apparently productive of very Extraordinary Incidents. Translated from the
French of Monsieur A. Richer. [2 more lines]
London : Printed for F. Newbery, in Paternoster Row. 1767.
232pp. 12mo.
EC 173:2; ESTC t108008.
Dublin edn, 1768 [1255].
BL
* M/C

1168.
Thompson Edward
+Sailor's Letters. Written to his Select Friends in England during his Voyages and Travels in Europe,
Asia, Africa, and America, from the Years 1754 to 1759. By Edward Thompson. In Two Volumes. The
Second Edition, Corrected.
London : T. Becket. 1767.
2 vols. 12mo.
1st edn, 1766 [1057].
Bn LC NYPL UC UNC
M/E

1169.
Thompson Edward
+Sailor's Letters. Written to his Select Friends in England during his Voyages and Travels in Europe, Asia, Africa, and America, from the Years 1754 to 1759. By Edward Thompson. In Two Volumes.
Dublin : Printed by J. Potts. 1767.
2 vols in 1. 178pp. 12mo.
ESTC t132382.
1st edn, 1766 [1057].
BL
M/E

1768

1170.
(+)THE ADVENTURES OF EDMUND HERVEY AND MISS MATILDA ORBE, Wherein a Delicate Sense of the Tender Passion is displayed; Or, The Captain in Love, In a Series of Letters.
Dublin : 1768.
2 vols in 1. 8vo.
CG(BCat).
Possibly a pirated edition of 1768 [1175].
E

1171.
THE ADVENTURES OF MISS BEVERLY, Interspersed with Genuine Memoirs of a Northern Lady of Quality. In Two Volumes.
London : Printed for S. Bladon, in Pater-noster-Row. 1768.
2 vols. 12mo. 6s (CR,MR).
CR XXVI 209-212 (Sept. 1768); MR XXXVIII 411-412 (May 1768).
AB(BL); BB; CG(BB); ESTC t074440.
BL PU
* N

1172.
THE ADVENTURES OF OXYMEL CLASSIC ESQ; ONCE AN OXFORD SCHOLAR.
London : Printed for William Flexney, opposite Gray's-Inn-Gate, Holborn. 1768.
2 vols. 12mo. 6s (CR,MR).
CR XXV 464 (June 1768); MR XXXVIII 249 (Mar. 1768).
CG(MR).
HU YU
* N

1173.
THE AFFECTING HISTORY OF TWO YOUNG GENTLEWOMEN, Who were ruined by Their Excessive Attachment To The Amusements of the Town. To which is added, Many Practical Notes, By Dr. Typo, P.T.M.
London : Printed by T. Baldwin, in Great-May's Buildings; And Sold by W. Bingley, in the Strand, And H. Woodgate, in St. Paul's Church-Yard. [1768] (CR,MR).
86pp. 12mo. 1s (tp).
CR XXVI 360-363 (Oct. 1768); MR XXXIX 410 (Nov. 1768).
ESTC t068883.
BL [as ?1780]
* N/M

1174.
THE ARTLESS LOVERS. A Novel. In a Series of Letters From Miss Lucy Wheatly in Town, to Miss Annabell Grierson in the Country. In Two Volumes.
London : Printed for J. Wilkie, at No. 71, in St. Paul's Church-Yard. 1768.
2 vols. 12mo. 6s (MR).
CR XXVIII 372-373 (Nov. 1769); MR XL 258-259 (Mar. 1769).
CG(GM); ESTC t080390; FB; LO 250 (CR,FB).
BL
* E

1175.
THE CAPTAIN IN LOVE. A Tragi-Comical Novel. In Two Volumes.
London : Printed for S. Bladon, in Pater-noster-Row. 1768.
2 vols. 12mo. 5s (MR) 6s (CR as Lowndes).
CR XXVI 360-363 (Nov. 1768); MR XXXVIII 151 (Feb. 1768).
CG(MR); FB; LO 231 (CR,FB); McB 173.
Dublin edn, 1768 [1176].
Possible further version, 1768 [1170].
UI
E

1176.
+THE CAPTAIN IN LOVE. A Tragi-Comical Novel. In Two Volumes.
Dublin : Printed for J. Hoey, senior, J. Exshaw, H. Saunders, and W. Colles. 1768.
2 vols. 12mo.
ESTC t127877.
1st edn, 1768 [1175].
BL
* E

1177.
THE DISTRESSED LOVERS : OR, THE HISTORY OF EDWARD AND ELIZA. In a Series of Letters. In Two Volumes.
London : Printed for Robinson and Roberts, at No. 25, in Paternoster-Row. 1768.
2 vols. 8vo. 5s (CR).
CR XXV 54-57 (Jan. 1769).
CR; ESTC t139134; FB; LO 233 (CR,FB).
BL
* E

1178.
THE DISTREST WIFE, OR THE HISTORY OF ELIZA WYNDHAM; Related in a Journey from Salisbury. In Two Volumes.
London : Printed for W. Cooke, in May-Fair, And sold by J. Wilkie, in St. Paul's Church-yard. 1768.
2 vols. 12mo. 5s (MR).
CR XXV 294-295 (Apr. 1768); MR XXXIX 83 (July 1768).
BB; CG(BB,HU); LO 234 (HU).
Has been incorrectly attributed to Dumanoir, the translator of the work into French.
HU YU
* N

1179.
THE ENTANGLEMENT; OR, THE HISTORY OF MISS ELEONORA FRAMPTON, AND MISS ANASTASIA SHAFTOE.
London : Nobles. 1768.
2 vols. 12mo. 5s (CR) 6s (MR).
CR XXV 59 (Jan. 1768); MR XXXVIII 499 (July 1768).
NYSL(HC)
N

1180.
THE FARMER'S SON OF KENT. A Tale. In Two Volumes.
London : Printed for Francis Noble, at his Circulating Library near Middle Row, Holborn; And John Noble, at his Circulating Library in St. Martin's Court, near Leicester-Square. 1769 [1768].
2 vols. 12mo. 6s (MR).
MR XXXIX 412 (Nov. 1768).
BB; CG(BB,UnM); EC 11:4; ESTC t100068.
Dublin edn, 1769 [1263].
BL
* N

1181.
THE HAPPY EXTRAVAGANT : OR MEMOIRS OF CHARLES CLAIRVILLE, ESQ. In Two Volumes.
London : Nobles. 1768.
2 vols. 12mo. 6s (MR).
CR XXV 464 (June 1768); MR XXXIX 84 (July 1768).
CG(MR); LO 237 (UP).
RU UP
N

1182.
THE HISTORY OF A LATE INFAMOUS ADVENTURE, BETWEEN A GREAT MAN AND FAIR CITIZEN. In a Series of Letters from a Lady near St James's to her Friend in the Country.
London : Printed for W. Bingley. 1768.
46pp. 8vo. 1s (CR,MR).
CR XXV 65 (Jan. 1768); MR XXXVIII 69-70 (Jan. 1768).
CG; LO 238.
LC
E/M (sat)

1183.
THE HISTORY OF EMILY WILLIS, A NATURAL DAUGHTER. In Two Volumes. The Third Edition.
London : Printed for Francis Noble, at his Circulating Library near Middle Row, Holborn; And John Noble, at his Circulating Library in St. Martin's Court, near Leicester-Square. 1768.
2 vols. 12mo.
CG(BC); ESTC t094635; LO 239 (UP).
By the author of *Memoirs of a Coquet*, 1765 [889].
One edn (lost) 1764 [810].
BL UP
* N

1184.
+THE HISTORY OF MR. BYRON AND MISS GREVILLE. In Two Volumes.
Dublin : Printed for W. Colles, Bookseller, in Dame-street. 1768.
2 vols in 1. 261pp. 12mo.
CG(BL); ESTC t066374.
1st edn, 1767 [1078].
BL
* N

1185.
LIGHT SUMMER READING FOR THE LADIES; OR, THE HISTORY OF LADY LUCY
FENTON.
London : Robinson and Roberts. 1768.
3 vols. 12mo. 7s6d (CR) 9s (MR).
CR XXV 462-464 (June 1768); MR XXXIX 83 (July 1768).
BB; CG(MR); FB; LO 240 (MR,FB).
N

1186.
LOVE AT CROSS PURPOSES : Exemplified in Two Sentimental and Connected Histories
from Real Life. viz. I. The Forced Marriage; Or the History of Sir George Freemore and
Miss Emily Menel, In Two Volumes. II. Memoirs of Lady Frances Freemore, In Two
Volumes.
London : Nobles. 1768.
4 vols. 12mo. 6s (CR) 10s sewed (MR).
CR XXVIII 375-376 (Nov. 1769); MR XXXIX 501-503 (Dec. 1768).
Re-issued at discount in 1769?
C/N

1187.
MEMOIRS OF A SCOUNDREL. BY AN INJURED FAIR.
London : Cooke. 1768.
2 vols. 12mo. 6s (MR).
MR XXXIX 85 (July 1768).
CG(MR).
N

1188.
+MEMOIRS OF LYDIA TONGUE-PAD AND JULIANA CLACKIT.
London : Coote. 1768.
272pp. 12mo. 2s6d (MR).
CR XXVI 376 (Nov. 1768); MR XXXVIII 249 (Mar. 1768).
BB(but confusing with Thrush edn); CG(MR, & attributing to Southworth).
correctly identified this as 'an old book, newly vamp'd'. Earlier version, 1750 [13].
OU UP YU
N

1189.
MEMOIRS OF TWO YOUNG GENTLEMEN. Exhibiting The Most striking instances of
the seduction and snares to which young people are liable, the horrors consequent upon
vice and dissipation [15 more lines]
Edinburgh : Printed by J. Reid; and sold at his printing-office in Bailie Fyfe's close, and by all
the Booksellers in town and country. 1768.
386pp. 12mo.
CG(BL); ESTC t072358.
BL
* N/M

1190.
THE MODERN WIFE. A Novel. In Two Volumes.
London : Printed for T. Lowndes, at No. 77, in Fleet-Street. 1769 [1768].
2 vols. 12mo. 6s (CR,MR).
CR XXVI 452-457 (Dec. 1768); MR XXXIX 411 (Nov. 1768).
CG; ESTC t125304; FB; LO 243 (MR,FB).
Has been incorrectly attributed to John Stevens, bookseller of a play of this title in 1744. Also, 1769 [1286] [1287].
BL UP
* E

1191.
THE ORPHAN DAUGHTERS. A MORAL TALE.
London : Nobles. 1768.
2 vols. 12mo. 6s (MR).
CR XXVI 376 (Nov. 1768); MR XXXIX 84 (July 1768).
CG(BB).
N

1192.
THE POINT OF HONOUR. A NOVEL.
London : Nobles. 1768.
2 vols. 12mo. 6s (MR).
CR XXVI 376 (Nov. 1768); MR XXXIX 84-85 (July 1768).
CG(MR).
N

1193.
THE SUMMER-HOUSE : OR THE HISTORY OF MR. MORTAN AND MISS BAMSTED. In Two Volumes.
London : Printed by W. Hoggard, for Francis Noble, at his Circulating Library, near Middle-row, Holborn; And John Noble, at his Circulating Library, in St. Martin's Court, near Leicester-square. 1768.
2 vols. 12mo. 6s (MR).
CR XXXVI 60-62 (July 1768); MR XXXVIII 498-499 (June 1768).
CG(MR,ScM).
AAS HU
E

1194.
THE TEST OF FRIENDSHIP; Or, The History of Lord George B——, and Sir Harry Acton, Bart. In Two Volumes.
London : Printed by W. Adlard, for F. and J. Noble. 1769 [1768].
2 vols. 12mo. 6s (MR).
CR XXVI 312-313 (Oct. 1768); MR XL 86 (Jan. 1769).
CG(MR).
CUNY
N

1195.
THE TRIUMPH OF LOVE AND BEAUTY; OR, THE HISTORY OF MR. WALLACE AND HIS FAMILY.
London : Printed for Robinson and Roberts. 1768.
2 vols. 12mo.
LO 244 (UP).
PU UP
N

1196.
TRUE DELICACY; OR THE HISTORY OF LADY FRANCIS TYLNEY, AND HENRY CECIL, ESQ;
London : Printed by W. Adlard, Wine-Office-Court, Fleet-Street, For Francis Noble, at his Circulating Library, near Middle-Row, Holborn; And John Noble, at his Circulating Library, in St. Martin's Court, near Leicester-Square. 1769 [1768].
2 vols. 12mo. 6s (CR,MR).
CR XXVII 151 (Feb. 1769); MR XXXIX 163 (Aug. 1768).
CG(BL); EC 198:3; ESTC t057457.
Dublin edn, 1769 [1294].
BL
* N

1197.
THE UNEXPECTED WEDDING, IN A SERIES OF LETTERS.
London : Printed for T. Becket and P. A. De Hondt, near Surry-Street, in the Strand. 1768.
235pp. 8vo. 3s (MR).
MR XXXVIII 249 (Mar. 1768).
CG(HU); EC 129:2; ESTC t057459; LO 245 (UP,HU).
Dublin edn, 1768 [1198].
BL HL HU UC UI UP YU
* E

1198.
+THE UNEXPECTED WEDDING, IN A SERIES OF LETTERS.
Dublin : Printed for H. Saunders. 1768.
235pp. 12mo.
McB 921.
1st edn, 1768 [1197].
UI
E

1199.
THE VANITY OF HUMAN WISHES; OR, THE HISTORY OF SIR JAMES SCUDAMORE, BART.
London : Printed for Robinson and Roberts, in Pater-noster-row; and Richardson and Urquhart, at the Royal-Exchange. 1768.
2 vols. 12mo. 6s (MR).
CR XXV 52-53 (Jan. 1768); MR XXXVIII 248-249 (Mar. 1768).
CG(HU); FB; LO 246 (HU,FB).
Dublin edn, 1768 [1200].
HU
* N

1200.
+THE VANITY OF HUMAN WISHES; OR, THE HISTORY OF SIR JAMES SCUDAMORE, BART.
Dublin : Printed for W. Colles in Dame Street. 1768.
2 vols in 1. 299pp. 12mo.
ESTC t137678.
1st edn, 1768 [1199].
BL HU
* N

1201.
THE VISITING DAY. A NOVEL.
London : Printed for T. Lowndes, No.77. in Fleet-Street. 1768.
2 vols. 12mo. 6s (CR,MR).
CR XXVI 206-208 (Sept. 1768). MR XXXVIII 499 (June 1768).
CG(HU); LO 247 (HU).
CUL HL HU NLC
* N

1202.
BROOKE Henry
**THE FOOL OF QUALITY; OR THE HISTORY OF HENRY EARL OF MORELAND. In
Four Volumes. Volume III. By Mr. Brooke.**
London : Printed for W. Johnston, in Ludgate-Street. 1768.
12mo. 3s (MR).
MR XXXIX 410-411 (Nov. 1768).
ESTC t147806 (with 2 variants identified).
Vols I-II published and edns listed, 1766 [993]. Vol IV published, 1769 [1300].
BL HU OU Tx UI UP YU
* N

1203.
[CLELAND John]
THE WOMAN OF HONOR. In Three Volumes.
London : Printed for T. Lowndes, at No 77, in Fleet-street; And W. Nicoll, at No 51, in St.
Paul's Church-yard. 1768.
3 vols. 12mo. 9s (MR).
CR XXV 284-294 (Apr. 1768); MR XXXIX 83-84 (July 1768).
CG; ESTC t084797; FB; LO 248 (CR,FB,UP).
Dublin edn, 1768 [1204].
CUL DU UP
* N

1204.
[CLELAND John]
+THE WOMAN OF HONOR.
Dublin : 1768.
3 vols.
CG(BCat) '1st Dublin edn'. 1st edn, 1768 [1203].
N

1205.
[DEFOE Daniel]
**+THE LIFE AND MOST SURPRISING ADVENTURES OF ROBINSON CRUSOE, OF
YORK, MARINER.** [8 more lines]
Edinburgh : Printed for and sold by Alex. M'Caslon, Bookseller opposite to the Chapel of Ease,
Cross-causey. 1768.
116pp. 8vo.
EC 193:2; ESTC t137274.
1st edn, 1719-20. Edns listed, 1752 [129].
BL CNY
* N/M

1206.
[DEFOE Daniel]
+THE LIFE, REMARKABLE ADVENTURES AND PYRACIES, OF CAPTAIN
SINGLETON :
[14 more lines]
The Third Edition.
London : Printed for F. Noble, in Holborn; J. Noble, in St. Martin's Court; T. Lowndes, in Fleet-
Street; and J. Johnson and B. Davenport, in Pater-noster Row. 1768.
299pp. 12mo.
EC 175:8; ESTC t069686.
1st edn, 1720. Also, 1737, 1800.
BL BPL CUL UI WCL
* N

1207.
[DONALDSON William]
THE LIFE AND ADVENTURES OF SIR BARTHOLOMEW SAPSKULL, BARONET.
Nearly Allied to Most of the Great Men in the three Kingdoms. By Somebody.
London : Printed for J. Williams No. 38, next the Mitre Tavern, Fleet-Street. 1768.
2 vols. 12mo. 6s (MR).
CR XXVI 312 (Oct. 1768); MR XXXIX 83 (July 1768).
ESTC t127425; LO 235 (UI); McB 246.
BL NYSL(HC) UI
* N

1208.
FÉNELON François de Salignac de La Mothe
HAWKESWORTH John *trans.*
(+)THE ADVENTURES OF TELEMACHUS, THE SON OF ULYSSES. **Translated from
the French of Messire Francois Salignac de la Mothe-Fenelon, Archbishop of Cambray. By
John Hawkesworth, L.L.D.**
London : Printed for the Author, by W. and W. Strahan. 1768.
462pp. 4to. £1.1s (MR). Subn.
CR XXVII 170-178 (Mar. 1769); MR XXXIX 237 (Sept. 1768).
BB; CG(BB); McB 269.
CR gives Becket as bookseller.
Trans. of *Les Aventures de Télémaque*, 1699. Edns listed, 1755 [312].
BU CUL HL HU NLC NYPL UF UI
* N/M

1209.
FIELDING Henry
+THE HISTORY OF THE ADVENTURES OF JOSEPH ANDREWS, AND HIS FRIEND
MR. ABRAHAM ADAMS. **Written in Imitation of The Manner of Cervantes, Author of
Don Quixote. By Henry Fielding, Esquire. Illustrated with Cuts. The Eighth Edition,
revised and corrected. In Two Volumes.**
London : Printed for A. Millar, and Sold by T. Cadell, in the Strand. 1768.
2 vols. 12mo.
CG; EC 58:11; ESTC t089896.
1st edn, 1742. Edns listed, 1751 [84].
BL BU CUL HU UI Tx YU
* N

1210.
FIELDING Henry
+THE HISTORY OF TOM JONES, A FOUNDLING. In Four Volumes. By Henry Fielding Esq.
London : Printed for A. Millar and sold by T. Cadell, his Successor, in the Strand. 1768.
4 vols. 12mo.
CG; EC 204:6; ESTC t001945.
1st edn, 1749. Edns listed, 1750 [24].
BL NLC PU YU
* N

1211.
GESSNER Saloman
DAPHNIS : A POETICAL, PASTORAL NOVEL. Translated from the German of Mr. Gessner, The Celebrated Author of the Death of Abel. By an English Gentleman, who resided several Years at Hamburgh. [3 more lines]
London : Sold by J. Dodsley, in Pall-mall; T. Cadell, in the Strand; W. Owen, Temple-Bar; G. Kearsley, Ludgate-Street; J. Wilkie and W. Nicoll, in St. Paul's Church-yard; and W. Davenhill, at the Royal Exchange. 1768.
132pp. 12mo.
EC 232:5; ESTC t093830.
BL HU NLC UP
* N/M (is a prose work)

1212.
[GRAFIGNY Françoise d'Issembourg d'Happoncourt de]
+LETTERS WRITTEN BY A PERUVIAN PRINCESS. Translated from the French.
London : Printed for M. Cooper in the Strand. 1768.
186pp. 8vo.
ESTC t108401.
1st English edn, 1748. Edns listed, 1753 [185].
BL Bn HU NLC PU UI UP WCL YU
* E

1213.
[HAYWOOD Mrs Eliza]
(+)CLEMENTINA; OR THE HISTORY OF AN ITALIAN LADY, Who Made Her Escape From A Monastery, For The Love Of A Scots Nobleman.
London : Printed by W. Adlard, Wine-Office-Court, Fleet-Street, For Francis Noble, at his Circulating Library, near Middle-Row, Holborn; And John Noble, at his Circulating Library, in St. Martin's Court, near Leicester-Square. 1768.
240pp. 12mo. 3s (MR).
CR XXV 59 (Jan. 1768); MR XXXVIII 412 (May 1768).
CG; ESTC t075384. A revised edn of Haywood's The Agreeable Caledonian, the preface signed 'T.B.'
BL
* N

1214.
[HAYWOOD Mrs Eliza]
+THE HISTORY OF MISS BETSY THOUGHTLESS. In Four Volumes. The Fourth Edition.
London : Printed for L. Gardner, opposite St Clement's Church in the Strand. 1768.
4 vols. 8vo.
CG; ESTC t075389.
1st edn and edns listed, 1751 [85].
BL UM
* N

1215.
[HAYWOOD Mrs Eliza]
+THE INVISIBLE SPY. By Exploralibus. In Two Volumes.
Dublin : Printed by Henry Saunders, in Castle-street. 1768.
2 vols. 8vo.
BB; CG(BB,HU); ESTC t073515.
1st edn and edns listed, 1755 [316].
BL HU
* N/M

1216.
[HIGGS Henry]
+HIGH LIFE : A NOVEL, OR THE HISTORY OF MISS FAULKLAND. In Two
Volumes.
Dublin : Printed for J. Exshaw, H. Saunders, W. Sleater, D. Chamberlaine, J. Potts, J. Hoey jun.,
J. Williams, J. Mitchell, and W. Colles. 1768.
2 vols in 1. 298pp. 8vo.
1st edn, 1767 [1105].
YU
* E

1217.
'INAYĀT Allāh
[DOW Alexander trans.]
TALES, TRANSLATED FROM THE PERSIAN OF INATULLA OF DELHI.
London : Printed for T. Becket and P. A. De Hondt, in the Strand. 1768.
2 vols in 1. 8vo. 5s (CR) 6s (MR).
CR XXVII 136-139 (Feb. 1769); MR XL 221-232 (Mar. 1769).
AB; BB; CG(BB); ESTC t114551; McB 474; newSG.
Dublin edn, 1769 [1318].
BL LC Tx UCLA UI UP
C

1218.
[JOHNSTON Charles]
+CHRYSAL : OR, THE ADVENTURES OF A GUINEA. Wherein are exhibited Views of
several striking Scenes, With Curious and interesting Anecdotes of the most Noted Persons
in every Rank of Life, whose Hands it passed through, in America, England, Holland,
Germany, and Portugal. By an Adept. The Sixth Edition, greatly inlarged and corrected.
London : Printed for T. Becket and P. A. DeHondt, at Tully's-Head near Surry-Street, in the
Strand. 1768.
Volumes I & II. 2 vols. 12mo.
ESTC t069467.   1st edn and edns listed, 1760 [577].
BL CUL HU [imperf] Tx
* N

1219.
[JOHNSTON Charles]
+CHRYSAL : OR, THE ADVENTURES OF A GUINEA. Wherein are exhibited several
striking Scenes, with curious and interesting Anecdotes of the most noted Persons in every
rank of Life, whose Hands it passed through, in America, England, Holland, Germany and
Portugal. By an Adept. The Seventh Edition.
London : Printed for T. Becket and P. A. De Hondt. 1768.
Volumes I & II. 2 vols. 12mo.
1st edn and edns listed, 1760 [577].
HU [imperf] OU PU
* N

1220.
[LONGUEVILLE Peter]
+THE HERMIT : OR THE UNPARALLEL'D SUFFERINGS AND SURPRISING
ADVENTURES OF MR. PHILIP QUARLL [&c.]
The Fourth Edition.
London : Printed for J. Wren, S. Crowder, H. Woodgate, J. Fuller, and J. Warcus. 1768.
263pp. 8vo.
CG; McB 598.
Reissue of 1763 [782]? 1st edn and edns listed, 1751 [93].
UI UOr WCL
N/M

1221.
MARMONTEL Jean François
+BELISARIUS. By M. Marmontel, Member of the French Academy. A New Edition.
London : Printed for and sold by P. Vaillant, in the Strand; and by Robinson and Co. in
Paternoster Row. 1768.
240pp. 12mo.
ESTC t061500.
1st edn and edns listed, 1767 [1115].
BL CUL
* N

1222.
MARMONTEL Jean François
+BELISARIUS. By M. Marmontel. A New Edition.
London : Printed by M. Cooper. 1768.
232pp. 12mo.
CG(BL).
1st edn and edns listed, 1767 [1115].
BL [missing]
N

1223.
MARMONTEL Jean François
+MORAL TALES, BY M. MARMONTEL. In Three Volumes.
Edinburgh : Printed by A. Donaldson, and Sold at his Shops in London and Edinburgh. 1768.
3 vols. 12mo.
CG; ESTC t090769.
1st edn and edns listed, 1763 [784].
BL YU
* C

1224.
MULSO Thomas
CALLISTUS; OR, THE MAN OF FASHION. AND SOPHRONIUS; OR, THE COUNTRY
GENTLEMAN. In Three Dialogues. By Thomas Mulso Esq.
London : Printed for Benjamin White, at Horace's Head, in Fleet-street; and James Dodsley, in
Pall-mall. 1768.
213pp. 8vo. 2s6d (CR,MR).
CR XXV 213 (Mar. 1768); MR XXXVIII 367-355 (May 1768).
AB(WB ?variant title); CG(HU); ESTC t010230.
Also, 1768 [1225] and Dublin edn, 1769 [1323].
BL CUL DU HU LC OU Tx YU
* N

1225.
MULSO Thomas
+CALLISTUS; OR, THE MAN OF FASHION. AND SOPHRONIUS; OR, THE
COUNTRY GENTLEMAN. In Three Dialogues. By Thomas Mulso Esq. The Second
Edition.
London : Printed for Benjamin White, at Horace's Head, in Fleet-street; and James Dodsley, in
Pall-mall. 1768.
213pp. 8vo.
ESTC t011249.   1st edn, 1768 [1224].
BL CUL
* N

1226.
le PRINCE DE BEAUMONT Jeanne Marie
THE NEW CLARISSA : A TRUE HISTORY. By Madame de Beaumont.
London : Printed for J. Nourse, Bookseller to His Majesty, opposite Catherine-Street, in the
Strand. 1768.
2 vols. 12mo. 6s (CR,MR).
CR XXVI 355-359 (Nov. 1768); MR XXXIX 82-83 (July 1768).
CG(BL); EC 9:1; ESTC t102659; McB 551.
Trans. of La Nouvelle Clarice, histoire véritable, 1767. Dublin edn, 1769 [1325].
BL DU UI
* E

1227.
RICCOBONI Marie Jeanne
(+)THE CONTINUATION OF THE LIFE OF MARIANNE. To which is added, the
History of Ernistina; with Letters, and other Miscellaneous Pieces. Translated from the
French of Madame Riccoboni.
London : Printed for Becket and De Hondt. 1768.
12mo. 3s (MR).
MR XXXVIII 72-73 (Jan. 1768).
1st edn, 1766 [1033]. This might be a re-issue.
N/C

1228.
RICCOBONI Marie Jeanne
+LETTERS FROM THE COUNTESS DE SANCERRE, TO COUNT DE NANCÉ, HER
FRIEND. By Madam Riccoboni. Translated from the French.
Dublin : Printed for James Williams. 1768.
2 vols in 1. 8vo.
1st edn, 1767 [1127].
IU PU
E

1229.
RICHARDSON Samuel
+CLARISSA; OR, THE HISTORY OF A YOUNG LADY : Comprehending The Most
Important Concerns of Private Life. By Mr. Richardson, Author of Pamela and Sir Charles
Grandison. In Eight Volumes. The Sixth Edition.
London : Printed for J. Rivington, R. Baldwin, W. Johnston, S. Crowder, C. Rivington, T.
Lowndes, T. Davies, J. Johnson and J. Payne, W. Griffin, T. Becket, F. Newberry, T. Cadell,
and J. Knox. 1768.
8 vols. 12mo. Authorship given on tp to vols I & II only.
CG; ESTC t058973.   1st edn, 1747-48. Edns listed, 1751 [96].
AAS BL IU NYPL UP
* E

1230.
[RICHARDSON Samuel derived]
+VIRTUE REWARDED : Or, The History, In Miniature, Of the Celebrated Pamela. The
Third Edition.
London : Printed for James Ogden. 1768.
68pp. 12mo.
1st edn of original work, 1740. Full edns listed, 1754 [250].
CUL
* N/M

1231.
[SMOLLETT Tobias]
+THE ADVENTURES OF PEREGRINE PICKLE. In which are Included, Memoirs of a
Lady of Quality. In Four Volumes. The Third Edition, Revised, Corrected, and Altered by
the Author.
Dublin : Henry Saunders in Castle street, and James Potts in Dame-street, Booksellers. 1768.
4 vols in 2. 12mo.
Vols III and IV dated, 1769.
CG(BL); ESTC t055348; MW 141.
1st edn and edns listed, 1751 [99].
BL IU UIC YU
* N

1232.
[SMOLLETT Tobias]
+THE ADVENTURES OF RODERICK RANDOM. The Seventh Edition.
Dublin : T. Dyton. 1768.
2 vols.
CG; MW 40 (as 1786).
1st edn, 1748. Edns listed, 1750 [40].
UC
N

1233.
[STERNE Laurence]
+THE LIFE AND OPINIONS OF TRISTRAM SHANDY, GENTLEMAN. The Seventh
Edition.
London : Printed for J. Dodsley, in Pall-Mall, 1768.
Volumes I-IV. 4 vols. 12mo.
Vols issued at different times during the year. Vol II, dated 1769.
KM pp.23,25.
Vols III-IV 1st published, 1761 [673]. Vols I-II published and edns of all vols listed, 1759 [507].
CUL HU
* N

1234.
[STERNE Laurence]
A SENTIMENTAL JOURNEY THROUGH FRANCE AND ITALY. By Mr. Yorick.
London : Printed for T. Becket and P. A. De Hondt, in the Strand. 1768.
2 vols. 8vo. 5s sewed (MR). Subn.
CR XXV 181-185 (Mar. 1768); MR XXXVIII 174-185, 309-319 (Mar. & Apr. 1768)
CG; ESTC t014747; LO 242 (UP,UI,RL,YU).
Also, 1768 [1235] [1236] [1237] [1238], 1769 [1340] [1341], 1770, 1771, 1773, 1774(2x), 1775, 1776, 1778,
1780(4x), 1782(4x), 1783, 1784(2x), 1787, 1790(2x), 1791, 1792(3x), 1793, 1794, 1795, 1798, 1800.
BL Bn CUL DU HL HU LC Tx UI UP UV YU
* N/M

1235.
[STERNE Laurence]
+A SENTIMENTAL JOURNEY THROUGH FRANCE AND ITALY. By Mr. Yorick. The
Second Edition.
London : Printed for T. Becket and P. A. De Hondt, in the Strand. 1768.
2 vols. 8vo. Subn.
EC 219:2; ESTC t014750.
1st edn and edns listed, 1768 [1234].
BL CUL CUNY HU IU LC OU PU Tx UC UF UNC UW YU
* N/M

1236.
[STERNE Laurence]
+A SENTIMENTAL JOURNEY THROUGH FRANCE AND ITALY. By Mr. Yorick. A
New Edition.
London : Printed for T. Becket and P. A. De Hondt, in the Strand. 1768.
2 vols. 8vo.
EC 235:1; ESTC t014766.
1st edn and edns listed, 1768 [1234].
BL
* N/M

1237.
[STERNE Laurence]
+A SENTIMENTAL JOURNEY THROUGH FRANCE AND ITALY. By Mr. Yorick.
Dublin : Printed for G. Faulkner, J. Hoey sen. J. Exshaw, and H. Saunders. 1768.
2 vols. 12mo.
ESTC t014769; RCC p.77.
Published Apr. 1768.
1st edn and edns listed, 1768 [1234].
BL NLI
N/M

1238.
[STERNE Laurence]
+A SENTIMENTAL JOURNEY THROUGH FRANCE AND ITALY. By Mr. Yorick. The
Second Edition.
Dublin : Printed for G. Faulkner, J. Hoey sen. J. Exshaw, and H. Saunders. 1768.
2 vols. 12mo.
ESTC t014799; RCC p.77.
Published, Aug. 1768. Magee of Belfast also advertising edn at this time.
1st edn and edns listed, 1768 [1234].
BL TCD
N/M

1239.
VOLTAIRE François Marie Arouet de
L'INGENU; OR THE SINCERE HURON, A TRUE STORY; Translated from the French
of Mr. de Voltaire.
London : Bladon. 1768.
8vo. 3s6d sewed (MR).
MR XXXIX 161 (Aug. 1768).
Also, 1768 [1240], 1771 (variant title), 1786.
N

1240.
VOLTAIRE François Marie Arouet de
+L'INGENU: OR, THE SINCERE HURON. A TRUE HISTORY. Translated from the
French of M. de Voltaire.
Glasgow : Printed for Robert Urie. 1768.
189pp. 12mo.
ESTC t137681.
1st English edn and edns listed, 1768 [1239].
BL
* N

1241.
VOLTAIRE François Marie Arouet de
THE PRINCESS OF BABYLON. Translated from the French of M. de Voltaire.
London : Printed for S. Bladon, in Pater-noster-row. 1768.
8vo. 3s6d bound (MR).
MR XXXIX 124-126 (Aug. 1768).
newSG.
HL HU LU NLC UP YU
N

1242.
[YOUNG Arthur]
THE ADVENTURES OF MISS LUCY WATSON. A Novel.
London : Printed for W. Nicoll, at the Paper Mill, No 51, in St. Paul's Church Yard. 1768.
227pp. 12mo. 2s6d (CR) 3s (MR).
CR XXV 209-211 (Mar. 1768); MR XXXVIII 72 (Jan. 1768).
AB(BL); BB; CG(CR,MR); ESTC t116996; FB; LO 249 (BB,FB).
BL
* E

Miscellanies

1243.
An Account of a Savage Girl, Caught Wild in the Woods of Champagne. Translated from the French of
Madam de H———t. With A Preface, Containing several Particulars committed in the Original Account.
Edinburgh : Printed for A. Kincaid and J. Bell. 1768.
63pp. 12mo. 1s (MR).
CR XXV 471 (June 1768); MR XXXIX 69-70 (July 1768).
ESTC t146817.
MR has by Kincaid & Co [and] Sold by Richardson and Co. in London. 1768.
BL
* M

1244.
The Companion for the Fire-side : or Winter Evening's Amusement. Being A Curious Collection of
entertaining and instructive Stories, Tales, Fables, Allegories, Historical Facts, Eastern Tales, Novels,
Remarkable Events, and Singular Occurences. Selected from the best Writers in several Languages, many
of which never appeared in print before.
London : Printed for J. Cooke, No. 10. Pater-noster-Row. 1768.
236pp. 12mo.
MR XXXIX 83 (July 1768).
ESTC t128490.
Also Dublin edn, 1769 [1348], and 1772.
BL
* M/C

1245.
The Fig-Leaf - Veni, vidi, vici, ivi : or He's gone! Who? Yorick &c.
London : Tomlinson. 1768.
4to. 1s (MR).
MR XXXVIII 323 (Apr. 1768).
BB
Cf 1759 [507].
M

1246.
Memoirs of the Seraglio of the Bashaw of Merryland. By a Discarded Sultana.
London : Printed for S. Bladon. 1768.
50pp. 8vo. 1s6d (tp).
CR XXV 65 (Jan. 1768); MR XXXVIII 69 (Jan. 1768).
Also, 1768 [1247].
YU
M/N (sat)

1247.
+Memoirs of the Seraglio of the Bashaw of Merryland. By a Discarded Sultana. The Second Edition.
London : Printed for S. Bladon. 1768.
52pp. 8vo.
CG; ESTC t017571.
1st edn, 1768 [1246].
BL
* M/N

1248.
The Remarkable History of the Rise and Fall of Masaniello, the Fisherman of Naples.
[6 more lines]
London : Printed by J. Browne, No. 73, Shoe-Lane, and sold by the Booksellers in Town and Country. 1768.
210pp. 12mo 1s6d (tp).
Also, [?1770] edn.
CUL
* M

1249.
A True and Genuine Narrative of Mr. and Mrs. Tenducci. In a Letter to a Friend at Bath; Giving a full Account, from their Marriage in Ireland, to the Present Time.
London : Printed for J. Pridden. 1768.
8vo. 1s6d (MR).
MR XXXVIII 63 (Jan. 1768).
ESTC t117835.
BL
M (sat)

1250.
[Fielding Sarah]
+The Governess; Or, The Little Female Academy. Calculated for the Entertainment and Instruction of Young Ladies in their Education. By the Author of David Simple. The Fifth Edition. Revised and Corrected.
London : Printed for A. Millar; and Sold by T. Cadell, in the Strand. 1768.
146pp. 12mo. 18d bound (tp).
ESTC t100474.
1st edns, 1749. Edns listed, 1751 [110].
BL Bn UC
* M/C

1251.
[Goadby Robert]
+An Apology for the Life of Mr. Bamfylde-Moore Carew, Commonly call'd The King of Beggars, Being
an impartial Account of his Life. [&c.]
The Eighth Edition.
London : Printed for R. Goadby [Sherborne]; W. Owen; and J. Lee. 1768.
347pp. 12mo.
ESTC t110289.
1st London edn, 1749. Edns listed, 1750 [54].
BL IU YU
M

1252.
[Godwin Francis]
+The Strange Voyage and Adventures of Domingo Gonsales to the World in the Moon
[29 more lines]
With a Description of the Pike Teneriff, as travelled up by some English Merchants. The Second Edition.
London : Printed by John Lever, Bookseller, Stationer, and Print-seller, at Little Moorgate, next to London Wall,
near Moorfields. 1768.
[51]pp. 8vo. 1s (tp).
ESTC t090146
BL CUL
* M/N

1253.
[Mouhy Charles de Fieux Chevalier de]
+The Busy-Body; or, The Adventures of Monsieur Bigand; A Man Infinitely Inquisitive and Entertaining,
even to Rashness; which unhappy Faculties, nevertheless, instead of ruining, raised him from the lowest
Obscurity.
Dublin : Printed for J. Williams. 1768.
CG(HU).
Trans. of *La Mouche, ou Les aventures de M. Bigand*, 1742. 1st English edn, 1742.
HU
M

1254.
[Paterson Samuel]
Another Traveller! Or Cursory Remarks and Tritical Observations made upon a Journey through part of
the Netherlands, In the latter End of the year 1766. By Coriat Junior.
London : Johnson and Payne. 1768-69.
Volume II. 1 vol. 12mo.
CR XXVIII 261-267 (Oct. 1769).
CG.
Vol I issued, 1767 [1165]. 2nd edn, 1769 [1360].
M

1255.
Richer Adrien
+Great Events from Little Causes; a Selection of Interesting and Entertaining Stories, drawn from the
histories of different Nations. Translated from the French of Monsieur A. Richer.
Dublin : 1768.
CG(HU).
1st edn, 1767 [1167].
HU
M/C

1256.
Rowe Mrs Elizabeth Singer
+Friendship in Death : In Twenty Letters from the Dead to the Living. To which are added, Letters
Moral and Entertaining, in Prose and Verse. By Mrs. Elizabeth Rowe. In Two Parts.
Edinburgh : Printed by A. Donaldson, and sold at his Shops in London and Edinburgh. 1768.
336pp. 12mo.
ESTC t083332.
1st edn, 1728. Edns listed, 1750 [60].
BL
* M

1257.
Somis Ignazio
(+)A True and Particular Account, Of the Most Surprising Preservation and Happy Deliverance of Three
Women who were buried Thrity-seven Days. By Ignazio Somis.
London : Printed for H. Serjeant. 1768.
208pp. 12mo.
ESTC t136715.
A reissue of 1765 [965].
BL YU
M

1258.
[Stevenson John Hall]
A Sentimental Dialogue Between Two Souls, in the Palpable Bodies of an English Lady of Quality and an
Irish Gentleman.
[London?] 1768.
38pp. 8vo.
EC 172:6; ESTC t066916.
BL
* M

1259.
Voltaire François Marie Arouet de
The Man of Forty Crowns. Translated from the French of M. de Voltaire.
Glasgow : Printed for Robert Urie. 1768.
182pp. 12mo.
ESTC t137634.
A trans. of L'homme aux quarante ecus.
Also, 1770.
BL CUL
* M/N

1260.
CONSTANTIA AND HER DAUGHTER JULIA, AN ITALIAN HISTORY; With a Discourse on Romances.
London : Printed for Robinson and Co. 1769.
12mo. '2 Pamphlets, Price 4s stitched' (MR) 6s (CR).
CR XXVII 311 (Apr. 1769); MR XL 344-345 (Apr. 1769).
BB; CG(BB).
Dublin edn, 1769 [1261].
N

1261.
+CONSTANTIA AND HER DAUGHTER JULIA, AN ITALIAN HISTORY; With a Discourse on Romances.
Dublin : D. Chamberlaine, J. Potts, J. Hoey jun. J. Williams, and C. Ingham. 1769.
2 vols in 1.
newSG.   1st edn, 1769 [1260].
NLC UP
N

1262.
THE DELICATE EMBARRASSMENTS. A Novel. In Two Volumes.
London : Printed for Robinson and Roberts in Pater-noster-Row. 1769.
2 vols. 16mo. 6s (CR,MR).
BB; CG(BB,BL); EC 244:6; ESTC t070909.
CR XXVII 310 (Apr. 1769); MR XL 259 (Mar. 1769)
BL
* N

1263.
+THE FARMER'S SON OF KENT. A Tale. In Two Volumes.
Dublin : Printed for J. Williams in Skinner Row. 1769.
2 vols. 12mo.
1st edn, 1768 [1180].
CUL
* N

1264.
FATAL OBEDIENCE : OR, THE HISTORY OF MR. FREELAND. In Two Volumes, Written by Himself.
London : Printed for the Author; and sold by F. and J. Noble at their respective circulating libraries in Holborn and St. Martin's Court. [1769] (MR).
2 vols. 12mo. 5s bound (tp) 6s (MR).
CR XXVIII 369-372 (Nov. 1769); MR XLI 479 (Dec. 1769).
AB(BL,ELG); CG; ESTC t077677; LO 487; SG 306.
Introductory 'Letter' by 'T. Wilmot'. Variously dated (BL as ?1780), but rev. suggests 1769.
BL UP
* N

1265.
FEMALE CONSTANCY; OR, THE HISTORY OF MISS ARABELLA WALDEGRAVE.
London : Davies. 1769.
2 vols. 12mo. 5s sewed.
CR XXVII 471 (June 1769).
BB; CG(BB,GM May 1769).
N

1266.
THE FRENCH LADY. A NOVEL.
London : Lowndes. 1769.
2 vols. 12mo. 6s (CR,MR).
CR XXVIII 277-281 (Oct. 1769); MR XLI 480 (Dec. 1769).
BB; CG(BB).
N

1267.
THE FRUITLESS REPENTANCE; OR, THE HISTORY OF MISS KITTY LE FEVER. In Two Volumes.
London : Printed for F. Newbery, the Corner of St. Paul's Church Yard. 1769.
2 vols. 12mo. 5s sewed (MR).
CR XXIX 43-47 (Jan. 1770); MR XLII 72 (Jan. 1770).
CG(HU); EC 418:6; ESTC t107703; FB; LO 255 (FB,HU,UP).
Dublin edn, 1770.
Sometimes attributed to Mrs Inchbald.
BL HU UP
* E

1268.
(+)THE GENERAL LOVER, OR SMALL-TALKER; A Series of Letters from a Lady in the west of England to Lady Anne D—— abroad.
Dublin : Printed for J. Williams, and C. Ingham, Booksellers in Skinner-row. 1769.
179pp. 12mo.
CG(HU); ESTC t119254.
A Dublin edn of 1769 [1292].
BL HU YU
* E

1269.
(+)GENUINE MEMOIRS OF THE LIFE AND ADVENTURES OF THE CELEBRATED MISS ANN ELLIOT. Written by a Gentleman.
[5 more lines]
The Second Edition.
London : Printed for J. Roson, No.54, St. Martin's Le Grand; and J. Fell, No.14, Pater-noster-Row. 1769.
238pp. 12mo. 2s6d sewed (CR).
CR XXVIII 67-68 (July 1769).
CG(GM); FB; LO 256 (CR,FB).
A 1st edn not located.
CUL
* M/N

1270.
THE HAPPY DISCOVERY; OR, THE HISTORY OF MISS EMILY CRESWELL.
London : Printed for J. Wilkie, in St. Paul's Church-yard; and T. Lowndes, in Fleet-street. 1769.
2 vols. 12mo. 5s sewed (MR).
MR XLII 70 (Jan. 1770).
CG(HU); FB; LO 261 (FB,HU).
Dublin edn, 1770.
HU
N

1271.
THE HISTORY OF AMINTOR AND TERESA.
London : Printed for W. Owen in Fleet-street. 1769.
168pp. 8vo. 2s6d (CR) 3s (MR).
CR XXVII 152 (Feb. 1769); MR XL 86-87 (Jan. 1769).
CG(MR); ESTC t072455; LO 262 (UP).
A supplement to *Almira*, 1761 [629].
BL NYSL(HC) UP
* N

1272.
THE HISTORY OF ELIZA MUSGROVE.
London : Printed for W. Johnston. 1769.
2 vols in 1. 12mo. 4s sewed (CR) 4s6d sewed (MR).
CR XXVII 452-459 (June 1769); MR XLI 73-74 (July 1769).
CG; FB; LO 263 (CR,FB).
Dublin edn, 1770.
YU
N

1273.
THE HISTORY OF JACK WILKS, A LOVER OF LIBERTY. In Two Volumes.
London : Printed for H. Gardner, opposite St. Clement's Church, in the Strand. 1769.
2 vols. 12mo. 5s (CR) 6s (MR).
CR XXVII 151-152 (Feb. 1769); MR XL 258 (Mar. 1769).
CG; ESTC t072456.
BL
* N/M (sat)

1274.
THE HISTORY OF LORD CLAYTON AND MISS MEREDITH. In Two Volumes.
London : Printed for Robinson and Co. 1769.
2 vols. 12mo. 6s (MR).
CR XXVII 310-311 (Apr. 1769); MR XL 259 (Mar. 1769).
CG.
Dublin edn, 1769 [1275].
N

1275.
+THE HISTORY OF LORD CLAYTON AND MISS MEREDITH. In Two Volumes.
Dublin : Printed for P. and W. Wilson, H. Saunders, W. Sleater, D. Chamberlaine, J. Potts, J. Williams, and C. Ingham. 1769.
2 vols. 12mo.
CG(HU); EC 220:2; ESTC t107627.
1st edn, 1769 [1274].
BL HU
* N

1276.
THE HISTORY OF MISS SOMMERVILLE. Written by a Lady. In Two Volumes.
London : Printed for Newbery and Carnan, No. 65, the North-Side of St. Paul's Church-Yard. 1769.
2 vols. 8vo. 6s in vellum (MR).
CR XXVII 373-382 (May 1769); MR XLI 76-77 (July 1769).
BB; CG(BB,HU); ESTC t066903; LO 264 (HU,UP).
DU HU LC UC UNC UP
* E

1277.
HORTENSIA; OR, THE DISTRESSED WIFE. A Novel. By a Lady.
London : Printed for Robinson and Roberts. 1769.
2 vols. 12mo.
LO 265 (UI); McB 468.
UI
N

1278.
THE INJURED DAUGHTER : OR THE HISTORY OF MISS MARIA BEAUMONT. In Two Volumes.
London : Printed for F. Noble and J. Noble. 1769.
2 vols. 12mo. 5s sewed (MR) 6s (CR).
CR XXVII 151 (Feb. 1769); MR XL 86 (Jan. 1769).
BB; CG(MR).
PU
N

1279.
INJURED INNOCENCE : OR, VIRTUE IN DISTRESS. An Affecting Narrative; Founded on Facts. Containing the Memoirs of Mrs Adams and Lord Whatley. By His Lordship's Chaplain.
Wolverhampton : Printed for R. Sarjeant. 1769.
40pp. 8vo. 6d (tp).
ESTC t099974.
Also 1793 edn.
BL
* N/M

1280.
LETTERS OF AN ENGLISH LADY, WRITTEN TO ONE OF HER FEMALE FRIENDS.
London : Robinson and Roberts. 1769.
CG.
E

1281.
THE LIFE, OPINIONS, AND SENTIMENTAL JOURNAL OF GEORGE NOEL.
London : Woodgate. 1769.
12mo.
CG.
Imitation of Sterne. Cf 1759 [507].
N

1282.
THE MAN OF GALLANTRY; OR, THE HISTORY OF SIR WILLIAM LOVEDALE AND MISS SOPHIA DIGHTON. In a Series of Letters.
London : 1769
FB; LO 270 (FB,BL [Dublin edn]).
Also, Dublin 1769 [1283].
E

1283.
+THE MAN OF GALLANTRY, OR THE HISTORY OF SIR WILLIAM LOVEDALE AND MISS SOPHIA DIGHTON. In a Series of Letters.
Dublin : Printed by J. Potts, at Swift's Head, in Dame-street. 1769.
178pp. 12mo.
CG(BL); EC 198:8; ESTC t066381.
1st edn, 1769 [1282].
BL
* E

1284.
MARGARETTA, COUNTESS OF RAINSFORD : A SENTIMENTAL NOVEL.
London : Printed for Johnson and Payne. 1769.
2 vols. 8vo. 6s (MR).
CR XXVII 370-373 (May 1769); MR XL 345 (Apr. 1769).
AB; CG(LC); LO 271 (YU); newSG.
Dublin edn, 1770.
LC UCLA UP YU
N

1285.
THE MASQUERADE; OR, THE HISTORY OF LORD AVON AND MISS TAMEWORTH
London : Printed for Robinson and Roberts, at No.25, in Pater-noster-row. 1769.
2 vols. 12mo. 6s (CR,MR).
CR XXVIII 453-455 (Dec. 1769); MR LXII 71 (Jan. 1770).
CG(HU); FB; LO 272 (FB,HU).
Dublin edn, 1770.
HU UIC
N

1286.
+THE MODERN WIFE. A Novel.
Dublin : 1769.
2 vols in 1.
CG.
1st edn, 1768 [1190].
N

1287.
+THE MODERN WIFE. A Novel. In Two Volumes. The Second Edition.
London : 1769.
12mo.
CG.
1st edn, 1768 [1190].
N

1288.
PRIVATE LETTERS FROM AN AMERICAN IN ENGLAND TO HIS FRIENDS IN AMERICA.
London : Printed for J. Almon, opposite Burlington-House, in Piccadilly. 1769.
163pp. 8vo. 2s6d sewed (MR).
MR XLI 67-70 (July 1769).
CG; ESTC t055461; FB; LO 274 (FB,HU,MR).
BL CUL HU LC NYPL UCLA YU
* E/M (sat)

1289.

THE RATIONAL LOVERS; OR, THE HISTORY OF SIR CHARLES LEUSUM, AND MRS FRANCES FERMOR. In Two Volumes.
London : Printed for Francis Noble, at his Circulating Library, near Middle-Row, Holborn; And John Noble, at his Circulating Library, St. Martin's Court, Leicester-Square. 1769.
2 vols. 12mo. 6s (MR).
CG; EC 227:6; ESTC t067642.
BL PU
* N

1290.

THE REWARD OF VIRTUE; OR, THE HISTORY OF MISS POLLY GRAHAM. Intermixed with several curious and interesting incidents in the lives of several Persons of both Sexes, remarkable for the singular Adventures which befel them. To which is added, a brief Description of Bounty-Hall, and its Inhabitants.
London : Robson. 1769.
12mo. 2s6d (MR).
MR XLI 479 (Dec. 1769).
BB; CG(BB).
N

1291.

A SKETCH OF HAPPINESS IN RURAL LIFE AND OF THE MISERIES THAT ATTEND AN INDISCREET PASSION.
London : Millan. 1769.
8vo. 1s6d (MR).
MR XLI 74-76 (July 1769).
CG; FB; LO 277 (FB,MR).
N

1292.

THE SMALL TALKER : A SERIES OF LETTERS FROM A LADY IN THE WEST OF ENGLAND TO LADY ANNE D—— ABROAD.
London : Johnson and Payne. 1769.
2 vols. 12mo. 2s6d (CR,MR).
CR XXVII 388-389 (May 1769); MR LXI 74 (July 1769).
CG; LO 278 (HU).
Dublin edn, 1769 [1268].
HU
E

1293.

THE SYBIL. A Novel. By a Lady.
London : Johnson and Payne. 1769.
2 vols. 12mo. 5s sewed (MR).
CR XXVII 389 (May 1769); MR XLI 74 (July 1769).
CG(Bn).
Bn PL
N

1294.

+TRUE DELICACY; OR, THE HISTORY OF LADY FRANCES TYLNEY, AND HENRY CECIL, ESQ.
Dublin : Printed by D. Chamberlaine. 1769.
2 vols in 1. 12mo.
1st edn, 1768 [1196].
N

1295.
[ALENÇON Mons. de]
THE BONZE, OR, CHINESE ANCHORITE, An Oriental Epic Novel. Translated from the Mandarine Language of Hoamchi-Vam, a Tartarian Proselite, by Monsr D'Alenzon,
[8 more lines]
London : Sold by R. Dodsley Pall Mall, I. Walter Charing Cross, Messrs Becket & Hondt in the Strand, and F. Newbery, Facing St. Paul's Church. 1769.
2 vols. 8vo. 6s sewed (CR).
CR XXVII 178-181 (Mar. 1769); MR XL 370-373 (May 1769).
AB; BB; CG(BB); ESTC t126581; newSG.
LC NYPL UC UP YU
* N

1296.
[ATKYNS Lady]
THE HERMIT. A NOVEL. By a Lady.
London : Printed for Gardner. 1769.
2 vols. 12mo. 6s (CR,MR).
CR XXVIII 217-225 (Sept. 1769); MR XL 520 (June 1769).
CG(HU); LO 251 (UP).
Dublin edn, 1770.
HU UP
N

1297.
[BEHN Mrs Aphra]
+LOVE-LETTERS BETWEEN A NOBLEMAN AND HIS SISTER; With the History of Their Adventures. In Three Parts. The Seventh Edition.
London : D. Brown, C. Hitch and L. Hawes, A. Millar, J. and R. Tonson. 1769.
CG.
E/M

1298.
[BROOKE Mrs Frances Moore]
THE HISTORY OF EMILY MONTAGUE. In Four Volumes. By the Author of Lady Julia Mandeville.
London : Printed for J. Dodsley, in Pall Mall. 1769.
4 vols. 12mo. 10s sewed (CR,MR).
CR XXVII 300-302 (Apr. 1769); MR XLI 231-232 (Sept. 1769).
BB; CG(BB,HU); ESTC t072176; FB; LO 252 (FB,HU,UI,UO); McB 102.
Also, 1777, 1784, 1800.
BL CUL HU UI UO
* E

1299.
[BROOKE Mrs Frances Moore]
+THE HISTORY OF LADY JULIA MANDEVILLE. In Two Volumes. By the Translator of Lady Catesby's Letters. The Fifth Edition.
London : Printed for J. Dodsley, in Pall-Mall. 1769.
2 vols. 12mo.
ESTC t073525; McB 105.
1st edn and edns listed, 1763 [769].
BL Bn UI UP YU
* E

1300.
BROOKE Henry
THE FOOL OF QUALITY, OR THE HISTORY OF HENRY, EARL OF MORELAND.
London : Printed for W. Johnston, in Ludgate-Street. 1769.
Volume IV. 1 vol. 12mo. 3s (MR).
MR XLI 318 (Oct. 1769).
ESTC t147806 (with variants).
Vols I-II published and edns listed, 1766 [993]; vol III, 1768 [1202]. Vol V published, 1770.
BL
* N

1301.
CERVANTES SAAVEDRA Miguel de
KELLY George *trans.*
+THE HISTORY OF THE RENOWNED DON QUIXOTE DE LA MANCHA. Written
Originally in Spanish by Miguel de Cervantes Saavedra; And translated into English by
George Kelly, Esq. [4 more lines] In Four Volumes.
London : Printed for the Translator; And sold by E. Carpenter and A. Bridgman, at No.32,
Fetter-Lane, Fleet-Street. 1769.
4 vols. 12mo.
CG(BL); EC 86:3; ESTC t059472.
Other trans. with edns listed, 1755 [302].
BL HU LC
* N

1302.
CERVANTES SAAVEDRA Miguel de
WILMOT Charles Henry *trans.*
+THE HISTORY OF THE RENOWNED DON QUIXOTE DE LA MANCHA. Translated
from the Spanish of Miguel de Cervantes Saavedra By Charles Henry Wilmot, Esq. In Two
Volumes.
London : Printed for J. Cooke. [1769?] (BL).
2 vols. 8vo.
ESTC t087449.   Other trans. and edns listed, 1755 [302].
BL [imperf]
N

1303.
[CHETWOOD William Rufus]
+THE VOYAGES, DANGEROUS ADVENTURES, AND IMMINENT ESCAPES OF
CAPT. RICHARD FALCONER. The Sixth Edition, Corrected.
London : Printed for G. Keith and F. Blyth. 1769.
CG; PBG 228.
1st edn, 1719-20. Edns listed, 1752 [126].
N

1304.
[COOPER Maria Susanna]
THE EXEMPLARY MOTHER; OR, LETTERS BETWEEN MRS VILLARS AND HER
FAMILY. Published by a Lady from the Originals in her Possession. In Two Volumes.
London : Printed for T. Becket and P. A. De Hondt, in the Strand. 1769.
2 vols. 12mo. 5s sewed (CR,MR).
CR XXVII 297-299 (Apr. 1769); MR XL 476-480 (June 1769).
CG(MR); ESTC t131015; LO 252 (UI,YU); McB 153.
Dublin edn, 1769 [1305]. Also, 1784.
BL CUL UI YU
* E

1305.
[COOPER Maria Susanna]
+THE EXEMPLARY MOTHER: OR, LETTERS BETWEEN MRS VILLARS AND HER
FAMILY. Published by a Lady. From the Originals in her Possession. In Two Volumes.
Dublin : Printed for P. and W. Wilson, J. Exshaw, H. Saunders, W. Sleater, J. Potts, D.
Chamberlaine, B. Grierson, J. Williams and C. Ingham. 1769.
2 vols. 12mo.
CG.
1st edn, 1769 [1304].
CUL
* E

1306.
[CROXALL Samuel]
+A SELECT COLLECTION OF NOVELS AND HISTORIES. Written by the most
Celebrated Authors in several Languages. [4 more lines]
In Six Volumes. The Fourth Edition, with large Additions.
Dublin : Printed by James Hoey, Junior, in Parliament-Street. 1769.
6 vols. 12mo.
Vols II-VI, dated 1770.
2nd edn, 1729. Cf 1765 [906].
CUL
* C

1307.
[DEFOE Daniel]
+THE LIFE AND MOST SURPRISING ADVENTURES OF ROBINSON CRUSOE, OF
YORK, MARINER [5 more lines]
The Ninth Edition.
Edinburgh : Printed for A. Donaldson, and sold at his Shops in London and Edinburgh. 1769.
318pp. 12mo.
CG.
1st edn, 1719-20. Edns listed 1752 [129].
BL
* N/M

1308.
FÉNELON François de Salignac de La Mothe
HAWKESWORTH John *trans.*
+THE ADVENTURES OF TELEMACHUS, THE SON OF ULYSSES. Translated from the
French of Messire François Salignac de la Mothe-Fenelon, Archbishop of Cambray. By
John Hawkesworth, L.L.D.
Dublin : Printed for P. Wilson, H. Saunders, W. Sleater, D. Chamberlaine, J. Potts, B. Grierson,
J. Hoey, jun. J. Williams, and W. Colles. 1769.
448pp. 12mo.
1st edn of Hawkesworth trans, 1768 [1208]. 1st English version, 1699. Edns listed, 1755 [312].
BU CUL HU
* N/M

1309.
FIELDING Henry
+THE COLLECTED WORKS OF HENRY FIELDING.
London : 1769.
WLC iii 329.
1st edn and edns listed, 1762 [714].
C/N

1310.
FIELDING Henry
+THE HISTORY OF THE ADVENTURES OF JOSEPH ANDREWS. And his Friend Mr.
Abraham Adams. Written in Imitation of The Manner of Cervantes, Author of Don
Quixote. By Henry Fielding, Esquire. Illustrated with Cuts. The Ninth Edition, revised and
corrected. In Two Volumes.
London : Printed for J. and F. Rivington, W. Strahan, T. Longman, S. Crowder, R. Horsfield, T.
Lownds, T. Caslon, T. Becket, T. Davies, and T. Cadell. 1769.
2 vols. 12mo.
CG(BL); EC 218:2; ESTC t089887.
1st edn, 1742. Edns listed in 1751 [84].
BL CUNY YU
* N

1311.
FIELDING Henry
+THE HISTORY OF THE ADVENTURES OF JOSEPH ANDREWS. And his Friend Mr.
Abraham Adams. Abridged from the Works of H. Fielding, Esq;
London : Printed for F. Newbery, at the corner of St. Paul's Church-yard. 1769.
[149]pp. 1s (tp).
SR J131.   1st edn, 1742. Edns listed, 1751 [84].
HU
N

1312.
[GOLDSMITH Oliver]
+THE CITIZEN OF THE WORLD : Or, Letters from a Chinese Philosopher, Residing in
London, to his Friends in the East.
Dublin : Printed for J. Williams. 1769.
2 vols. 12mo.
EC 204:5; ESTC t107731.
1st edn and edns listed, 1762 [716].
BL CNY CUL CUNY HU NLI TCD UC UF YU
* E/M

1313.
[GOLDSMITH Oliver]
+THE VICAR OF WAKEFIELD : A TALE. Supposed to be Written by Himself. The
Fourth Edition.
London : Printed for F. Newbery, in Pater-Noster-Row. 1769.
2 vols. 12mo.
ESTC t146182; TS p.176.
1st edn and edns listed, 1766 [1007].
BL
* N

1314.
[GRIFFITH Richard and Elizabeth]
TWO NOVELS : IN LETTERS. By the Authors of Frances and Henry. In Four Volumes.
The First and Second, entitled, The Delicate Distress : A Novel in Letters, By Frances, The
Third and Fourth, entitled, The Gordian Knot, or Dignus Vindice Nodus, By Henry.
London : Printed for T. Becket. 1769.
4 vols. 12mo. 10s sewed (MR) 12s (CR). Subn.
CR XXVIII 132-142 (Aug. 1769); MR XLI 232-233 (Sept. 1769).
BB; CG(BB,HU); LO 257,258,259 (HU,UI,UP); McB 381.
HU UI UP
E/C

1315.
[HAYWOOD Mrs Eliza]
+THE FRUITLESS ENQUIRY. Being a Collection of several entertaining Histories and Occurences which fell under the observation of a lady in her search after happiness. By the Author of The Female Spectator.
Dublin : Printed for W. and W. Smith. 1769.
273pp.
1st edn, 1727. Edns listed, 1767 [1103].
UM
N/C

1316.
[HAYWOOD Mrs Eliza]
+THE HISTORY OF JEMMY AND JENNY JESSAMY, By the Author of Miss Betsy Thoughtless.
London : 1769.
2 vols. 8vo.
CG
1st edn and edns listed, 1753 [186].
BMC BU
N

1317.
[HERBERTS Mary]
+THE ADVENTURES OF PROTEUS, &c. A Set of Novels, Never Before Published.
Dublin : Printed by James Hoey. 1769.
12mo.
newSG.
1st edn, 1727. Also, 1731.
UP
C

1318.
'INAYĀT Allāh
[DOW Alexander *trans.*]
+TALES, TRANSLATED FROM THE PERSIAN OF THE INATULLA OF DELHI.
Dublin : 1769.
2 vols in 1. 12mo.
CG(HU).
1st edn, 1768 [1217].
HU
C

1319.
[LANGHORNE John]
LETTERS SUPPOSED TO HAVE PASSED BETWEEN M. DE ST EVREMOND AND MR. WALLER. Collected and published By the Editor of the Letters between Theodosius and Constantia. In Two Volumes.
London : Printed for T. Becket and P. A. De Hondt, in the Strand. 1769.
2 vols. 8vo. 5s sewed (MR).
CR XXVIII 110-115 (Aug. 1769); MR XLI 304-309 (Oct. 1769).
CG; ESTC t123008; FB; LO 267 (FB,MR).
Also, 1770.
CUL
* E/M

1320.
[LAWRENCE Herbert]
THE LIFE AND ADVENTURES OF COMMON SENSE. An Historical Allegory.
London : Printed for Montague Lawrence, Stationer, at the Globe, near Durham-Yard, in the Strand. 1769.
2 vols. 8vo.
MR XL 344 (Apr. 1769) & vol.II, MR XLII 135-142 (Feb. 1770).
CG(HU); ESTC t090307; LO 268 (UI); McB 530.
Vols apparently issued separately. Also, 1771 edn.
BL [imperf] HU UI
* N

1321.
[MACHAY Archibald]
PASQUIN, A NEW ALLEGORICAL ROMANCE ON THE TIMES : With The Fortifivead, a Burlesque Poem [3 more lines]
Published by the Editor, Thomas Rowe, Esq. In Two Volumes.
London : Sold by S. Bladon, in Pater-Noster-Row. 1769.
2 vols. 8vo. 5s (CR).
CR XXVIII 147-149 (Aug. 1769).
CG; EC 238:4; ESTC t057351.
BL
* N/M

1322.
MINIFIE Susannah (now Mrs Gunning)
THE COTTAGE; A NOVEL : In a Series of Letters. By Miss Minifie, Author of Barford-Abbey. In Three Volumes.
London : Printed for T. Durham, Charing-Cross; G. Kearsley, Ludgate-Street; S. Bladon, Paternoster-Row; and F. Blyth, No.87, Cornhill. 1769.
3 vols. 12mo. 7s6d (CR,MR).
CR XXVIII 247-256 (Oct. 1768); MR XL 519 (June 1769).
CG; EC 242:4; ESTC t066946; LO 260 (BL,UI); McB 396.
BL PU UF UI UP YU
* E

1323.
MULSO Thomas
+CALLISTUS; OR, THE MAN OF FASHION. And Sophronius; or, The Country Gentleman. In Three Dialogues. By Thomas Mulso, Esq.
Dublin : Printed by John Exshaw. 1769.
206pp. 8vo.
CG.
1st edn, 1768 [1224].
PU UP
N

1324.
[POTTER John]
THE HISTORY OF THE ADVENTURES OF ARTHUR O'BRADLEY. In Two Volumes.
London : Printed for T. Becket and P. A. de Hondt, in the Strand. 1769.
2 vols. 12mo. 5s sewed (CR,MR).
CR XXVIII 69 (July 1769); MR XL 424-425 (May 1769).
CG(BL); EC 243:4; ESTC t070712; LO 273 (UP actually 1771 edn).
Also, 1771.
BL
* N

1325.
[le PRINCE DE BEAUMONT Jeanne Marie]
+THE NEW CLARISSA.
Dublin : 1769.
2 vols.
1st edn, 1768 [1226].
UP
E

1326.
[RESTIF DE LA BRETONNE Nicolas]
LUCILLA : OR THE PROGRESS OF VIRTUE. Translated from the French.
London : Printed for T. Lowndes and G. Kearsley. 1770 [1769].
241pp. 12mo. 3s (MR).
MR XLII 70-71 (Jan. 1770).
CG(MR); ESTC t124724.
A trans. of *Lucile,* by Restif de la Bretonne.
BL
N

1327.
[RICCOBONI Marie Jeanne]
[BROOKE Mrs Frances Moore *trans.*]
+LETTERS FROM JULIET LADY CATESBY, TO HER FRIEND LADY HENRIETTA CAMPLEY. Translated from the French. The Fifth Edition.
London : Printed for J. Dodsley, in Pall-Mall. 1769.
249pp. 12mo.
CG(BL,HU); ESTC t070727.
1st edn and edns listed, 1759 [502].
BL HU PU YU
* E

1327a.
[RICHARDSON Samuel]
+CLARISSA. Or, The History of a Young Lady. An Abridgment.
London : Newbery. [1769] (SR).
1 vol.
SR J315, citing adv. 9 Dec. 1768.
1st abridgment, 1756 [376a]. 1st edn of full work, 1747-8, and edns listed, 1751 [96].
N

1328.
RICHARDSON Samuel
+THE HISTORY OF PAMELA; OR VIRTUE REWARDED. Abridged from the Works of Samuel Richardson, Esq; Adorned with Copper Plates.
London : Printed for F. Newbery, at the Corner of St. Paul's Church-Yard. 1769.
166pp.
SR J316.
1st edn of original work, 1740. Edns listed, 1754 [250].
PU
E

1329.
[ROGERS Arthur]
THE RECLAIMED LIBERTINE; OR, THE HISTORY OF THE HONOURABLE
CHARLES BELMONT, ESQ, AND MISS MELVILL. In a Series of Letters.
London : Nobles. 1769.
2 vols. 12mo. 6s (CR,MR).
CR XXVIII 373-375 (Nov, 1769); MR XL 259 (Mar. 1769).
CG; FB; LO 275,276 (CR,FB,UI); McB 775.
UI
E

1330.
ROUSSEAU Jean Jacques
[KENRICK William *trans.*]
+ELOISA : OR, A SERIES OF ORIGINAL LETTERS Collected and published By J. J.
Rousseau. Translated from the French. The Fourth Edition.
London : Printed for T. Becket and P. A. De Hondt, at Tully's Head, in the Strand. 1769.
4 vols. 12mo.
ESTC t060905; McB 779.
1st English edn and edns listed, 1761 [666].
BL UI UMin
* E

1331.
ROUSSEAU Jean Jacques
+ELOISA : OR, A SERIES OF ORIGINAL LETTERS Collected and published By J. J.
Rousseau. Translated from the French. A New Edition.
London : Printed for T. Becket and P. A. De Hondt, at Tully's Head, in the Strand. 1769.
4 vols. 12mo.
ESTC t147289.
1st English edn and edns listed, 1761 [666].
BL
* E

1332.
SHEBBEARE John
+LYDIA OR FILIAL PIETY. A Novel. By John Shebbeare. M.D. Reg. Acad. Scient. Paris.
Consoc. The Second Edition, With Corrections and Alterations.
London : Printed for T. Davies, in Russel Street, Covent-Garden. 1769.
2 vols. 8vo. 5s sewed (CR).
CR XXXVII 471 (June 1769).
CG(HU); ESTC t071316.
1st edn and edns listed, 1755 [324].
BL DU HU NLC
* N

1333.
[SMOLLETT Tobias]
+THE ADVENTURES OF PEREGRINE PICKLE. In which are included, Memoirs of a
Lady of Quality. In Four Volumes. The Fourth Edition.
London : Printed for R. Baldwin, No 47, and Robinson and Roberts, No 25, in Pater-noster-Row;
and T. Becket and T. Cadell, in the Strand. 1769.
4 vols. 12mo.
ESTC t055349; MW 142.
1st edn and edns listed, 1751 [99].
AAS BL HU IU LC YU
* N

1334.
[SMOLLETT Tobias]
THE HISTORY AND ADVENTURES OF AN ATOM. In Two Volumes.
London : Printed for J. Almon. 1749 [1769].
2 vols. 12mo.
McB 272.
Also, 1769 [1335] [1336] [1337], 1786, 1795, 1797.
UI
N/M

1335.
[SMOLLETT Tobias]
+THE HISTORY AND ADVENTURES OF AN ATOM. In Two Volumes.
London : Printed for Robinson and Roberts, No. 25, in Pater-noster Row. 1749 [1769].
2 vols. 12mo. 3s sewed (MR).
CR XXVII 362-369 (May 1769); MR XL 441-455 (May 1769).
EC 206:3; LO 279 (RL,UI,UP,YU); McB 856.
1st edn and edns listed, 1769 [1334].
BL CUL UI UP YU
* N/M

1336.
[SMOLLETT Tobias]
+THE HISTORY AND ADVENTURES OF AN ATOM.
London : Printed for Robinson and Roberts. 1769.
2 vols. 12mo.
McB 857; MW 273.
Date on tp corrected.
1st edn and edns listed, 1769 [1334].
UI
N/M

1337.
[SMOLLETT Tobias]
+THE HISTORY AND ADVENTURES OF AN ATOM. In Two Volumes.
Dublin : Printed for P. and W. Wilson, J. Exshaw, S. Powell, H. Saunders, H. Bradley, W. Sleater, B. Grierson, D. Chamberlaine, J. Potts, J. Hoey jun. J. Williams, and C. Ingham, Booksellers. 1769.
2 vols. 12mo.
ESTC t055311; McB 858.
1st edn and edns listed, 1769 [1334].
BL UI
* N/M

1338.
[STERNE Laurence]
+THE LIFE AND OPINIONS OF TRISTRAM SHANDY, GENTLEMAN. The Third Edition.
London : Printed in the Year 1769.
Volumes I-IX.
9 vols in 2. 12mo.
EC 164:1; ESTC t014770.
Vols I-II and edns of all vols listed, 1759 [507].
BL Bn UNC
* N

1339.
[STERNE Laurence]
+THE LIFE AND OPINIONS OF TRISTRAM SHANDY, GENTLEMAN. A New Edition.
London : Printed for J. Dodsley. 1769.
Volumes III,IV-
3 vols. 12mo.
KM p.25 notes Dodsley's reprinting of vols III & IV in 1769.
Vols III-IV 1st published, 1761 [673]. Vols I-II and edns of all vols listed, 1759 [507].
UV
N

1340.
[STERNE Laurence]
[and STEVENSON John Hall]
+A SENTIMENTAL JOURNEY THROUGH FRANCE AND ITALY. By Mr. Yorick.
London : Printed in the Year 1769.
5 vols with continuous pagination. 306pp. 12mo.
Vols I-II, 'Sentimental Journey Through France and Italy. By Mr. Yorick'.
Vol III-IV, [John Hall Stevenson] : 'Yorick's Sentimental Journey, Continued. The Works of
Laurence Sterne A.M continued. To which is Prefixed Some Account of the Life and Writings of
Mr. Sterne.'
Of the *Continuation*, CR XXVII 390 (May 1769); MR XL 428 (May 1769).
EC 206:2; ESTC t014751.
1st edn of Sterne's work, and edns listed, 1768 [1234].
BL DU HU NLC OU UI YU
* N/M

1341.
[STERNE Laurence]
[and STEVENSON John Hall]
+A SENTIMENTAL JOURNEY THROUGH FRANCE AND ITALY. The Third Edition.
4 vols. 12mo.
Vols I-II : Dublin : Printed for G. Faulkner, W. and W. Smith, J. Hoey Sen. P. and W. Wilson,
J. Exshaw, H. Saunders, L. Flin, D. Chamberlaine, W. Sleater, J. Potts, J. Williams, and W.
Colles. 1769.
Vol.III : London : Printed for S. Bladon, in Pater-noster-Row. And Dublin : Re-printed and sold
by the Book-sellers. 1769.
Vol.IV : London : Printed for S. Bladon, in Paternoster-Row. 1769.
Vols III-IV have tp 'Yorick's Sentimental Journey, Continued. To which is prefixed, Some
Account of the Life and Writings of Mr. Sterne'.
ESTC t014754.
Sterne's work and edns listed, 1768 [1234].
BL NLI
* N/M

1342.
[TIMBURY Jane]
THE MALE COQUETTE; Or, The History of the Hon. Edward Anstell. In Two Volumes.
London : Printed for Robinson and Roberts, No 25, Pater-noster-Row. 1770 [1769].
2 vols. 12mo. 5s sewed (MR) 6s (CR).
CR XXVIII 450-452 (Dec. 1769); MR XLII 72 (Jan. 1770).
AB(BL); CG; ESTC t072172 FB; nJT p55.
Also, 1789.
BL
* E

1343.
[TOOKE William]
THE LOVES OF OTHNIEL AND ACHSAH. Translated from the Chaldee.
London : Printed for W. Tooke, For J. Wilkie, in St. Paul's-Church-Yard. 1769.
2 vols. 8vo. 6d (MR).
MR XLI 272-278 (Oct. 1769).
CG; EC 228:5; ESTC t099155; LO 280 (UP).
BL CUL UP
* N

1344.
TREYSSAC DE VERGY Pierre Henri
THE LOVERS : OR THE MEMOIRS OF LADY SARAH B—— AND THE COUNTESS P—— Published by Mr. Treyssac de Vergy, Counsellor in the Parliament of Paris.
London : Printed for the Editor, and sold by J. Roson, No. 54, St. Martin's le Grand; and all the Booksellers in Great Britain. 1769.
227pp. 8vo.
CR XXVIII 353-357 (Nov. 1769).
AB(BL); CG(HU); FB; LO 281 (FB,HU,UP).
A Vol.II, entitled 'The Lovers', published 1772 with a note of the final page [p.247] announcing 'The Third Volume will be published some time next month'. If issued, has not been located.
Dublin edn, 1770.
BL HU UP
* E

1345.
TREYSSAC DE VERGY Pierre Henri
THE MISTAKES OF THE HEART : OR, MEMOIRS OF LADY CAROLINE PELHAM AND LADY VICTORIA NEVIL. In a Series of Letters. Published by M. Treyssac de Vergy, Counsellor in the Parliaments of Paris and Bourdeaux.
London : Printed for J. Murdoch in the Strand. 1769.
3 vols. 12mo. 7s6d sewed (MR).
MR XL 511 (June 1769) of vol.I.
CG(HU); ESTC t131116; FB; LO 282 (FB,HU,UP).
Dublin edn, 1770.
HU UP
* E

1346.
[VICTOR Benjamin]
+THE WIDOW OF THE WOOD. Being an Authentic Narrative of a late remarkable transaction in Staffordshire.
Glasgow : Printed in the Year 1769.
164pp. 12mo.
CG(HU); ESTC t052487; SG 1066.
1st edn and edns listed, 1755 [328].
BL HU UP
* N/M

1347.
[WALPOLE Horace]
+THE CASTLE OF OTRANTO; A GOTHIC STORY. The Third Edition.
London : J. Murray. 1769.
200pp. 12mo.
1st edn and edns listed, 1764 [868].
CUNY IU UNC YU
N

Miscellanies

1348.

The Companion for the Fire-Side : Being A Collection of genuine and instructive Adventures, Tales and Stories. Selected from the best Writers in several Languages, many of which were never before published.
Dublin : Printed by William Sleater in Castle-street, near Fishamble-street. 1769.
274pp. 12mo.
ESTC t076200.
Same title as 1768 edn [1244], but with different contents.
BL
* C/M

1349.

**A Letter From Farmer Trusty to his Landlord Sir William Worthy, Bart. Patron of the Living of ——,
In the County of ——. Founded on real Matters of Fact. To which is Annexed, An Evening Conversation
Between Four very good Old Ladies over a Game of Quadrille.**
London : Printed by J. and W. Oliver in Bartholomew-Close : Sold by G. Keith, in Gracechurch-street; E. and
C. Dilly, in the Poultry; M. Folinsby [sic] near Temple-Bar; and Mr. Fletcher, at Oxford. 1769.
32pp. 8vo.
CG(HU); ESTC t087206; LO 269 (HU).
BL HU
* M

1350.

**Memoirs of the Amours, Intrigues, and Adventures of Charles Augustus Fitz-Roy, Duke of Grafton, with
Miss Parsons.** [3 more lines]
London : Printed for J. Meares, in the Old Bailey; W. Bingley, in the Strand; T. Peate, in Fleet Street, and G.
Richards, in Bell Savage Yard, Ludgate Hill. 1769.
202pp. 8vo. 2s6d sewed (tp).
CG(BL); ESTC t004958.
BL CUL
* M

1351.

**Novellas Espanolas : Seven Moral and Entertaining Novels. Translated from the original Spanish by a
Lady. Never before published in England and France.**
London : Newbery. 1769.
1 vol. 2s6d (SR).
CG; SR A387.
C

1352.

**Real Characters, and Genuine Anecdotes, Political, Polite, Gallant, Theatrical, Intriguing, Prudish,
Coquettish, Whimsical, Amorous, Ridiculous, Literary, &c. &c.** [4 more lines]
London : Printed for W. Bingley, opposite Durham-Yard, in the Strand. 1769.
107pp. 12mo.
CG(BL); ESTC t055576.
BL LC YU
* M/C

1353.

The Renowned History of Valentine and Orson Newly Corrected.
Glasgow : R. Duncan. 1769.
108pp. 12mo.
CG(derived from chapbook, BL).
BL [missing]
M

1354.
The Shaver Shaved; A Macaronic Dialogue Between B. and S. By a Matriculated Barber.
London : Printed for J. Fletcher and Co. St. Paul's Church-yard, W. Owen, at Temple-Bar; G. Woodfall, at Charing-Cross; J. Fletcher, at Oxford; and T. Merrill, at Cambridge. 1769.
24pp. 8vo. 6d (tp).
CR XXVII 398 (May 1769).
ESTC t048017.
BL
* M (sat).

1355.
[Amory Thomas]
+Memoirs Containing the Lives of Several Ladies of Great Britain.
[13 more lines]
London : Printed for Johnson and Payne. 1769.
2 vols. 12mo.
ESTC t074408.
Vol II tp misdated 1766.
1st edn, 1755 [336].
BL
M

1356.
[Crisp Mrs.]
The Female Captive : A Narrative of Facts, Which happened in Barbary, In the Year 1756. Written by Herself. In Two Volumes.
London : Printed for C. Bathurst, opposite St. Dunstan's Church, Fleet-Street. 1769.
2 vols. 8vo. 5s (CR). Subn.
CR XXVIII 212-217 (Sept. 1769).
CG(BL); ESTC t106577.
BL
* M/N

1357.
Hughes John *trans.*
+The Letters of Abelard and Heloise. To which is prefixed, a particular Account of their Lives, Amours and Misfortunes. By the late John Hughes Esq. Together with the poem of Eloisa to Abelard. By Mr. Pope. The Tenth Edition, ornamented with Cuts.
Dublin : Printed for J. Williams. 1769.
230pp. 8vo.
CG(BL); ESTC t038497.
1st English edn, 1718. Edns listed, 1751 [112].
BL [missing since 1984]
M/E

1358.
[Jenner Charles]
Letters from Lothario to Penelope. To which is added Lucinda, a Dramatic Entertainment of Three Acts.
London : Printed for T. Becket. 1769.
2 vols.
CG; FB; LO 266 (FB,HU,UP).
HU UP
M

1359.
Langhorne John
Frederic and Pharamond, with Consolations of Human Life. By John Langhorne, D.D.
London : Printed for T. Becket, and P. A. De Hondt, in the Strand. 1769.
157pp. 8vo.
CR XVII 146-149 (Feb. 1769).
ESTC t134207.
BL CUL
* E/M

1360.
[Paterson Samuel]
+Another Traveller! Or Cursory Remarks and Tritical Observations made upon a Journey through part of the Netherlands, In the latter End of the year 1766. By Coriat Junior. In Two Volumes. The Second Edition, corrected.
London : Printed for Johnson and Payne, in Pater-Noster-Row; T. Cadell in the Strand; and J. Robson in New Bond-street. 1769.
3 (?4) vols (2 parts to vol.I and poss BL copy of vol.II imperf). 12mo.
CG(BL); ESTC t056852.
1st edn of each vol, 1768 [1165] and 1768 [1254].
BL
* M

1361.
[Post Peregrine pseud]
A Four Day's Tour; or Cursed and Pitiful Observations made on a Journey through part of the land of Dumplings.
London : Bladon. 1769.
8vo. 1s6d.
BB; CG(BB).
M

1362.
[Povey Charles]
The Fair Wanderer; or, the Triumphs of Virtue.
London : Browne. 1769.
8vo. 1s6d (CR).
CR XXVII 152 (Feb. 1769).
CG.
A re-issue of 1767 [1166]. 'An old edition of *The Virgin in Eden*, republished with the above new title page', CR.
N

1363.
Wagstaffe Jeoffrey pseud.
The Batchelor; or, Speculations of Jeoffrey Wagstaffe.
Dublin : J. Hoey jr. 1769
2 vols.
CG(HU).
Also, 1772 version.
HU
M

Index of Titles

References are to entry numbers. Punctuation and capitalization has been modified. Abridgments and slight title variants are included under one heading, with cross references only for major retitling between editions. Much fuller cross-referencing is provided within individual entries.